The Food of
ASIA

Featuring authentic recipes from master chefs in Burma, China, India, Indonesia, Japan, Korea, Malaysia, The Philippines, Singapore, Sri Lanka, Thailand, and Vietnam

Forewords by Ming Tsai and Cheong Liew

Introductory essays by Kong Foong Ling

PERIPLUS

Published by Periplus Editions (HK) Ltd.,
with editorial offices at
130 Joo Seng Road #06-01/03
Singapore 368357

Copyright © 2002
Periplus Editions (HK) Ltd.
ISBN: 0-7946-0146-4
Library of Congress Control Number: 2002102296

Printed in Singapore

Photo credits:
Food photography by Luca Invernizzi Tettoni,
except as noted below:
Masano Kawana: 112–115
Heinz von Holzen: 72–87, 94–107, 176–187

Location photography by:
Doan Duc Minh: 170; Jean Léo Dugast/ Photobank:
22; Michael Freeman/ Photobank: 89; Jill Gocher: 9
[fishing boys], 66, 68, 117; Tim Hall: 171, 173;
Heinz von Holzen: 9 [Balinese procession], 69, 90,
91, 93, 174; Catherine Karnow: 172; Masano
Kawana: 108, 109, 111; Leong Ka Tai: 34;
Shin Kimura: 18; Kal Muller: 67; Eric Oey: 88;
Photobank: 6, 8 [Japanese girl], 32, 92 [tea ceremony],
137, 139, 153, 154; Dominic Sansoni: 144, 145,
147; Luca Invernizzi Tettoni: 8 [tea house], 9
[banana leaf restaurant], 23, 25, 30, 31, 33, 48,
49, 50, 51, 52, 53, 116, 118, 120, 152, 155, 156;
Sonny Yabao: 136.

08 07 06 05 04 03
8 7 6 5 4 3 2

Distributors

USA, Latin America & Europe	Tuttle Publishing 364 Innovation Drive North Clarendon, VT 05759-9436 Tel: (802) 773-8930 Fax: (802) 773-6993 Email: info@tuttlepublishing.com
Asia Pacific	Berkeley Books Pte. Ltd. 130 Joo Seng Road, #06-01/03, Singapore 368357 Tel: (65) 6280-3320 Fax: (65) 6280-6290 Email: inquiries@periplus.com.sg
Japan	Tuttle Publishing Yaekari Building, 3rd Floor 5-4-12 Osaki, Shinagawa-ku Tokyo 141 0032, Japan Tel: (81-3) 5437-0171 Fax: (81-3) 5437-0755 Email: tuttle-sales@gol.com
Indonesia	PT Java Books Indonesia Jl. Kelapa Gading Kirana Blok A-14/17, Jakarta 14240 Tel: (62-21) 451-5351 Fax: (62-21) 453-4987 Email: cs@javabooks.co.id

Cont

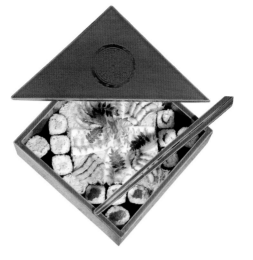

ents

Authenticity and tradition

Whether you're sweating out a spicy curry from India or Sri Lanka, delighting in flavorful grilled meats from Korea or Vietnam, or marveling at the intricate delicacy of a Japanese or Thai meal, Asian food—with its delightfully heady mix of flavors, smells and colors—has plenty to offer the dedicated foodie.

Asian cuisine is so much more than just food—steeped as it is in social and cultural lore. The region's recipes and cooking methods have developed over many centuries and now, thanks to globalization and migration, Asia's time-honored cooking traditions and fabled dishes have made their way to all corners of the globe. Asian ingredients that were once hard to come by are readily available in supermarkets worldwide as well as from Asian grocers and online merchants, and more people than ever before are eating Asian food on a regular basis.

At my restaurant, Blue Ginger, and in my cookbook, I strive to properly blend the flavors of the East with those of the West. My feeling is that in order to successfully combine the two cuisines, one must first learn the proper and traditional methods of preparation for each region. *The Food of Asia* thoroughly and expertly presents the entire spectrum of the Asian culinary landscape, from Burma to Vietnam. For those who lack the time or resources to travel to Asia, this book brings the region to you, all without leaving your own kitchen.

Peace and Good Eating!

Ming Tsai

Inspiration from Asia

I recall sitting in a vine-covered courtyard in Adelaide, South Australia, some 30 years ago and meditating on what Australian cuisine would be like in the future. I remember thinking of the vast resources of food knowledge which abound to the north of us on the Asian continent, and the relative accessibility of it all to young Australian chefs who travel there to gain firsthand information about the best ways of preparing Asian dishes.

The Asian knowledge of fish and seafood preparations, for example, is endless—from knife skills to stir-frying, oil poaching, steaming and multi-step boiling, deep-frying, and steaming—which is another way of braising. Asian methods of grilling after marinating in spices and yogurt, and the appreciation for spice mixtures and the subtle fragrances of a particular spice in combination with various foods—the knowledge and learning of all this is truly without end!

Foods and recipes from Asia have today become an integral part of the Australian diet and it is hard to imagine a restaurant menu or meal without some Asian influences. Herb and spice combinations from Thailand and Indochina add fragrance and excitement to our salads. The dry spice cooking of India provides a wealth of flavors and subtle aromas. The wet spice cooking of Southeast Asia provides aromatic bouquets mingled with the sweetness of creamy coconut. The aquaculture cuisine of Japan teaches us to respect the quality of fresh fish and appreciate raw fish, revealing its true taste. And the classical food science and philosophy of China provides the basis for many of our cooking skills and a better appreciation of food generally.

To know how to cook, one must first learn how to eat! From many Asian traditions, we learn that eating is not only the basis of good living but also of good health, and that certain foods act as preventative medicines. I am so glad that after 30 years, the food traditions of Asia have so profoundly influenced the modern international cuisines of today. And I welcome the publication of *The Food of Asia* which presents a wealth of authentic recipes and dishes as they are prepared and served today in Asia. At the Grange Restaurant at Hilton Adelaide, I am continually striving to perfect the fusion of traditional Asian food cultures represented in this book with our contemporary dining world in Australia, .

Cheong Liew

Left, main picture: Friends and family enjoying a traditional steamboat dinner. The steamboat, a meal which is not only eaten but cooked by all those at the table, demonstrates one of the fundamental roles that food plays in Asia: that of bringing people together.

The Flavors of Asia

From roadside hawker stalls in the large cities to the food courts in shopping malls, the five-star restaurants and the joys of home cooking, food is an all-consuming passion in Asia.

There is so much good food in Asia that the first-time traveler cannot help but be enchanted. It often comes as a surprise to people unfamiliar with Asian cultures how much the joy of living of most Asian peoples centers around the preparation, sharing, and discussion of food. As a chef once said, food in Asia is an exercise in tradition, in aesthetics, mutual caring, and moral lessons.

Even out of Asia, it is hard to find a place on earth with food that has not been touched by some aspect of Asian cooking, be it in the form of ingredients, cooking methods or presentation. From elegant New York brasseries to stylish Sydney restaurants, Asian food has come a long way since the American take on Chinese food, *chop suey*, or soupy, flavorless curries made with lots of curry powder and nothing else. These days, modern cooks around the world use fresh cilantro (coriander) with the same confidence as rosemary; add lemongrass and kaffir limes to their tomato broths; and, with their family and friends, want to eat their food spicier and spicier. Chopsticks are

placed alongside the trinity of spoon–fork–knife in Western-style restaurants—if indeed such a category still holds—that now serve roast lamb and tandoori chicken on the same menu. And just as kids in some Asian countries are demanding cornflakes and milk for breakfast, some people in the West are trading in their breakfast cereals for steaming bowls of noodles or plain rice with *miso* soup and pickles. The popularity and pervasiveness of Asian food, particularly in the West, has never been higher.

But in order to cook Asian food—any food—properly, you need to understand the origins of the particular cuisine. You also need to know the best way of getting the most out of your ingredients. As many good cooks will tell you, if you do the basics properly, the rest will follow. Once you understand why a certain ingredient is tempered with another or used in conjunction with something else, you can then play and let your imagination (and taste-buds) take you to new taste sensations.

Let *The Food of Asia* be your guide through a diverse selection of cuisine from China, India,

Burma (Myanmar), Sri Lanka, Japan, Korea, Indonesia, Malaysia, Singapore, Philippines, Thailand, and Vietnam. Because the countries covered here encompass a diverse geography and climate, from the temperate to the tropical, all the cuisines are quite distinct, despite the similarity in cooking techniques and some ingredients. All, however, emphasize freshness and flavor; in Asia, they believe that good eating is essential to good living.

Many of the popular favorites from each country are represented here: the gorgeous red and green curries of Thailand, invigorating Vietnamese *pho*, fluffy Indian breads, cleansing *sushi* and *sashimi* from Japan, and incendiary *laksa* and noodle soups from Malaysia and Singapore. There are simple dishes that require just a little cooking and no complicated techniques, making them ideal for day-to-day use in the home. For the confident cook, there are more complex dishes that are guaranteed to impress family and friends at your next dinner party or Sunday lunch, and taste delicious too! Most of the dishes are readily adapted to a Western-style table, and hints and tips have been included as to how best to serve them.

Common to the tables of all these countries is grain, which holds pride of place during a meal, as distinct from the Western table where the meat component or main course is the height of the meal. In most tropical countries located on or near the equator such as Malaysia, Singapore, Philippines, and Indonesia, plain steamed rice is the staple. However, be warned: there is rice and there is rice, and they are not always interchangeable. The Chinese prefer the fragrant long-grain jasmine rice, the Japanese a starchier short-grain variety. The Thais and Indonesians often serve glutinous rice to mop up their curries. The Indians favor the basmati. As you venture above the equator, preference is frequently given to wheat, which may be served in the form of noodles, buns, or pancakes.

Another characteristic of Asian food is its dependence on the humble soybean and its by-products. Bean curd (tofu), soy sauce, bean curd wrappers and bean paste sauces are used in dishes from China to Indonesia, with a little tweaking to local tastes.

And then there is the noodle... whether it be flat, round, dried, fresh, or is made of egg, buckwheat, mung bean, potato starch, wheat or ground rice, the Chinese love affair with noodles has left its mark on other Asian cuisines. The machines and factories have taken over from the hand-pulled noodles that the Chinese were particularly famous for, but there is no denying the versatility of the end product. In Asia they are stir-fried or pan-fried, or used in soups, salads, and spring rolls, or eaten with a sauce. They can be eaten as part of a meal or be a meal in a bowl, eaten at all times of the day, from breakfast to supper.

Asian cooks demand—and receive—the very best there is on offer from their local markets and suppliers, a hangover from their agricultural heritage perhaps, or because supermarkets were few and far between until recently. The ingredients have to be of the freshest quality: the vegetables just picked, the fish just out of the water, the chicken just caught. This ingredient is then quickly cooked, usually in a simple manner that would allow the essence of the produce to shine through.

Please do not be wary of the foreignness of some of the ingredients used in this book; remember that the now-ubiquitous ginger and scallions (spring onions) had to start somewhere too! Most of the ingredients called for in *The Food of Asia* are readily available from your local Asian grocery store, and it is worth your while searching out a good one and befriending the people who run it—they will be a rich source of advice and hints on how best to prepare your purchases. Many Asian food stores these days have an extensive range of fresh greens and vegetables, and they do not have to be used only in the Asian way.

Try to use the best of what's in season and don't be afraid to experiment. For instance, there is no reason why you can't serve Chinese broccoli in place of conventional broccoli with your next leg of lamb, or use coconut milk instead of milk to make a crème caramel, or serve steamed baby *bok choy* instead of green beans with a traditional roast chicken. You may also like to try smearing tandoori paste over a rack of lamb for a change of pace, or baste the next chicken you roast with green curry paste, and serve it with roast potatoes and a crisp green salad. The recipes are meant to be a guide and not a constraint! Frequently, ingredients may be substituted for each other without compromising on authenticity—just make sure you do try the recipe as it is set out at least once though. If you are attempting a recipe for the first time, it is very important that you read the recipe all the way through to the end to make sure you have the right equipment and ingredients to hand. With much Asian cooking, the time-consuming work is in the preparation. After the

Below: The men in this Chinese teahouse have gathered to gossip as much as to drink tea. *Right*: Like modern Japanese culture, Japanese food is a striking blend of the old and the new.

ingredients have been cleaned, chopped and sliced, the cooking process itself is usually fairly simple and straightforward.

A comprehensive, illustrated glossary (see pages 10–17) has been included to help you demystify and use some of the knobbly tubers and jars of brown stuff you may find in food stores. There is also a chapter on cooking implements and a few simple techniques to help you prepare Asian food. Despite the advent of modern methods and gizmos in Asian kitchens, some traditional implements are still regarded as irreplaceable. Not all kitchens, for instance, have cookers complete with an oven, as most cooking is done on the top of a stove. Many Asian kitchens are functional rather than aesthetic, with meals cooked over an open fire. In urban areas, gas rings fuelled by LPG are increasingly used.

Measurements in this book are given in volume as far as possible.

Top, main picture: This Balinese ritual should help ensure a plentiful crop of rice. *Above:* In Indonesia, you're never too young to contribute to the family dinner table. *Right:* An array of succulent offerings at a Singaporean banana-leaf restaurant.

Of course you may like to serve a series of Asian dishes for a Western-style dinner, where the dishes come out sequentially (as opposed to all at once). The recipes in this book have been structured with this in mind, into categories such as appetizers, soups, salads, main courses, and desserts for ease of use. You may need to increase the quantities of the main dishes slightly if you are not planning to serve rice or bread with the meal. A number of suggested menus—for family meals, dinner parties etc—are included in each chapter to help you plan your meals.

Most diners in Asian countries drink tea throughout a meal. Spirits are also popular, especially at formal dinners and banquets. But there's no reason why you can't drink your favorite red or white wine if you are eating Asian food—with some judicious tasting you will soon find out which goes best with what.

We hope *The Food of Asia* will inspire you, with its pictures, words and delicious recipes, to prepare these luscious dishes at home. It will also let you gain a better understanding of the wonderful cuisines of the region and give you many years of happy eating. And don't forget to have fun in the kitchen!

A conversion guide has been included on page 188 for your convenience. Unless otherwise stated, these recipes will serve four to six people as part of a shared meal of two to three dishes with rice.

The Asian table is a communal table. All dishes, with the exception of dessert, are usually presented at once and served with rice. Diners help themselves to whatever they want and to as much as they desire. There will usually be a soup, followed by or accompanied with one or two meat dishes and a vegetable dish. Dessert, especially in a domestic situation, is almost always sliced fresh seasonal fruit.

Asafoetida   Bamboo Shoots   Banana Blossom   Horapa Basil

Ingredients

Most of the ingredients called for in this book are readily found at Chinese or Asian grocery stores or some supermarkets.

Benitade   Bonito   Nigella   Candlenuts

AGAR-AGAR A setting agent derived from seaweed which hardens without refrigeration, used for cakes and desserts. It comes in long strands or in powder form; 1 teaspoon of powder sets 1–1$^{1}/_{2}$ cups liquid. To use, sprinkle powdered agar-agar over liquid and bring it gently to a boil, stirring until dissolved.

ANCHOVIES, DRIED Most are usually less than 1 in (2$^{1}/_{2}$ cm) long, and used to season many Malaysian and Indonesian dishes. Discard the heads and any black intestinal tract before using. Sometimes sold as "silver fish".

ANNATTO SEEDS The dark reddish-brown seed of the "lipstick plant," commonly used as a coloring agent. The seeds are fried in oil to extract an orange color and discarded. The oil is used for cooking.

ASAFOETIDA A strong-smelling gum derived from a Persian plant believed to aid digestion. Use sparingly.

ASAM GELUGUR, DRIED Slices of a sour fruit (*Garcinia atnoviridis*) used in place of tamarind pulp in some Malay and Nonya dishes; the latter can be used as a substitute.

EGGPLANT Known also as aubergine or brinjal, this vegetable is much smaller and thinner throughout Asia than its Western counterpart. Japanese eggplants are often no more than about 4–8 in (10–20 cm) long. The Thais also use a rather bitter pea-sized eggplant and the apple variety. Use slender Asian or Japanese eggplants for all recipes in this book—they are less bitter and have a better texture. They do not need salting before use.

BAMBOO SHOOTS Used fresh, vinegared or dried in Asian cookery.

Fresh shoots are sweet and crunchy. Peel, slice and boil for about 30 minutes before adding to dishes. Soak and boil dried shoots before use. If using canned bamboo shoots, drain and boil in fresh water for 5 minutes to remove the metallic taste.

BANANA BLOSSOM The flower bud of the banana plant. Slice finely and use as garnish for noodle soups or in salads.

BANANA LEAVES Used primarily for wrapping sweetmeats, sausages, and pâtés before cooking. The leaves preserve moisture, and impart a mild fragrance to the food.

BASIL Three varieties are used in Thailand. The most common variety, *horapa*, is fairly similar to European and American sweet basil, and used liberally as a seasoning. "Lemon basil" or *manglak* is added to soups and salads. *Kaprow*, sometimes known as "holy basil", is stronger in flavor and has purplish markings. Basil is known as d*aun selasih* or *kemangi* in Indonesia.

BEAN CURD Widely used in Thai, Chinese, Malaysian, and Japanese cuisines. The most common variety is called **"cotton"** or *momen* tofu. Use this unless otherwise specified. "Cotton" bean curd is generally sold packed in water in containers and is firmer and easier to handle than fine-textured **"silken" bean curd**, which is often available in plastic trays or rolls (cut with a sharp knife while still in the plastic so it keeps its shape).

Deep-fried bean curd or *aburage* is available in plastic bags and should be rinsed in boiling water to remove excess oil before using. A **grilled beancurd** (*yakidofu*), which has a speckled brown surface, is also sold in plastic bags. Small cubes of dried

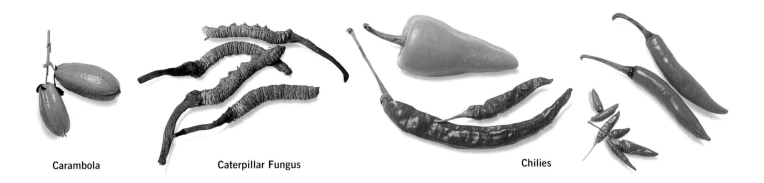

Carambola   Caterpillar Fungus   Chilies

deep-fried bean curd are added to slow-cooked dishes and some soups. Fermented bean curd (*nam yee*), sold in jars and either red or white in color, is used in small amounts as a seasoning in Chinese dishes.

BEAN CURD SKIN The skin that forms on top of soybean milk when it is brought to a simmer, skimmed off and dried. Reconstitute the sheets in warm water before using as a wrapper or in braises. The stuffed skins can be deep-fried, simmered or sautéed.

BEANSPROUTS Sprouted green mung peas are eaten blanched in some salads and soups, or quickly stir-fried as a vegetable. Pinch off the straggly tails just before use if desired.

BELIMBING See CARAMBOLA

BENITADE Decorative maroon-colored sprouts with a slight peppery taste. A popular Japanese garnish. Substitute with alfalfa sprouts or very finely shredded red cabbage.

BESAN Flour made from Bengal gram or *channa dal*, sometimes referred to as gram flour. Used to make a batter for vegetables or fish, or to thicken and add flavor to Indian dishes.

BITTER GOURD A firm gourd that looks like a fat, knobbly, green cucumber. It has a crisp texture and a strong, bitter flavor. Remove the seeds and inner membrane before cooking. Slice thinly if using in salads, or cut into thick chunks for stuffing.

BLACK BEANS, SALTED Fermented salted black soy beans, a common seasoning for fish and beef. Sold in packets or tins, they can be kept for several months if stored in a covered jar in the fridge. Rinse before use to remove excess salt.

BLACK MOSS FUNGUS A fine, hair-like fungus valued in Chinese cooking. Soak in warm water until pliable before using.

BLACK SAUCE, SWEET A thick, treacle-like sauce used in fresh spring rolls (*popiah*).

BONITO, DRIED With dried kelp, an essential component of Japanese stock or *dashi*. Shaved *bonito* flakes (*katsuo-bushi*) are now available in plastic packs.

BOXTHORN BERRIES Oval red berries sometimes known as wolf berries, prized by the Chinese for their medicinal properties. Used in soups.

BURDOCK The root of the burdock plant, popular in Japanese cuisine. Scrape off the skin and place into water to stop it discoloring until ready to slice or shred. Fresh and tinned burdock are available from Japanese stores.

CANDLENUT A waxy, cream-colored nut similar in size and shape to a macadamia, which can be used as a substitute (although less expensive almonds or cashews will also do). It is ground and used to add texture and a faint flavor to Malay and Nonya dishes. Do not eat raw. Store in the fridge.

CARAMBOLA A pale-green acidic fruit about 2–3 in (5–8 cm) long that grows in clusters. A relative of the starfruit, carambola is used whole or sliced to give a sour tang to soups, curries, fish

dishes and *sambals*. Sour grapefruit juice or tamarind juice are good substitutes.

CARDAMOM About 15–20 intensely fragrant brown-black seeds are enclosed in a straw-colored pod. Try to buy the whole pod rather than seeds or powder for maximum flavor. Bruise lightly with the back of a cleaver to break the pod. More common are small, greenish or straw-colored pods containing a dozen or so tiny, intensely aromatic black seeds. Large black cardamom pods, which are at least six times the size of the green, are used in some northern Indian dishes.

CAROM *Carum ajowan* comes from the same family as cumin and parsley. Known as carom or bishop's weed in the West, it is called *ajwain* in India. The flavor is similar to caraway with overtones of thyme.

CATERPILLAR FUNGUS Neither a caterpillar nor a fungus, these dried pods (*Cordyceps sinensis*) are used in Chinese dishes for their medicinal value.

CELERY The celery used in Asia is much smaller than the Western variety, with slender stems and particularly pungent leaves. Often known as "Chinese celery" and used as a herb rather than vegetable, it is added to soups, rice dishes and stir-fries. Substitute with regular celery leaves.

CENTURY EGGS Duck eggs coated with a mixture of powdered lime, rice husks and salt and left to cure for several months. To use, peel off the shell and quarter or chop the eggs, which have a translucent black albumen and greenish-grey yolk.

CHILI Many different varieties of chilies are used in Asia. The flavor of fresh and dried chilies is different, so be sure to use the type specified in the recipes. Large, finger-length **green** (unripe) and **red** (ripe) **chilies** are usually moderately hot.

In India chilies are used fresh only in their unripe green state. The majority of ripe red chilies are dried and a large percentage ground to make **chili powder**. Cut or break dried chilies into pieces and soak in hot water for about 10 minutes to soften before grinding or blending. If you want to reduce the heat without losing flavor, discard some or all of the seeds.

The main types of chili used in Thailand, Malaysia and Indonesia include the normal finger-length **red** or **green chili**; tiny but fiery-hot **bird's-eye chilies** (which may be red, green or yellow-orange) and **dried red chilies**. Be careful to wash your hands thoroughly after handling chilies—use rubber gloves if possible.

CHILI OIL Dried chilies or chili powder steeped in oil, used to enliven some Sichuan dishes.

CHILI PASTE Pounded chilies, sometimes mixed with vinegar, sold in jars. The heat varies from brand to brand. Sichuan chili paste is made from dried chilies, soaked and ground with a touch of oil.

CHILI POWDER Made from finely ground dried chilies. Do not confuse with American chili powder, which is a blend of a variety of seasonings.

CHILI SAUCE Chilies mixed with water and seasoned with salt, garlic, sugar, and vinegar, sold in bottles and jars. Some sauces are sweeter than others, and others may have added flavorings like garlic or ginger.

CHINESE CABBAGE The three most common types are **white cabbage** (*bai cai* or in Cantonese, *bok choy*), which has white stems and bright green leaves and is often sold in immature form; long white or "**celery**" **cabbage**, which has long pale green leaves and white celery-like stems; and **round cabbage**.

CHINESE RICE WINE Wine made from fermented rice used in cooking. Wine from Shaoxing, generally considered the best, is available from Chinese food stores. Dry sherry is a substitute.

CHINESE SAUSAGES Thin, sweet Chinese pork sausages that are delicately perfumed with rice wine. Used as a seasoning rather than eaten on their own. They will keep almost indefinitely without refrigeration.

CHIRONJI NUTS Small brownish nuts that look a little like large sunflower seeds, sometimes ground with other nuts, such as cashews or almonds, or with white poppy seeds to enrich some dishes. The flavor is similar to that of hazelnuts. Substitute with a mixture of hazelnuts and almonds.

CHIVES "Chinese", "coarse" or "garlic" chives have dark green flat leaves about 12 in (30 cm) long. They are used as a vegetable and as a herb. The flavor is stronger than normal chives.

CHOKO An oval-shaped squash that looks like a light green cucumber, with a small white seed inside. Peel before using as a vegetable. Zucchini is a substitute.

CHRYSANTHEMUM LEAVES Enjoyed as a vegetable for their distinctive flavor and bright green color. Spinach leaves can be used as a substitute.

CILANTRO See CORIANDER.

CINNAMON True cinnamon comes from the fragrant bark of a tree native to Sri Lanka, and is lighter in color, thinner and more expensive than cassia bark, which is often sold as cinnamon. Powdered cinnamon is not a substitute.

CLOUD EAR FUNGUS Sometimes known as wood fungus, this crinkly greyish-brown dried fungus swells to many times its original size after soaking in warm water for a few minutes. They have little flavor but are prized for their texture.

CLOVES A small, brown, nail-shaped spice that emits a floral, spicy fragrance. Used in spice blends.

COCONUT Widely used in Malaysia, Singapore, Sri Lanka, Philippines, and Indonesia, not just for cooking but also for palm sugar, alcohol, housing, utensils, and charcoal. The grated flesh is often added to food; it is also squeezed with water to make coconut milk. To make fresh coconut milk, put the flesh of a grated coconut into a bowl and add ¹/2 cup lukewarm water. Squeeze and knead for 1 minute, then squeeze handful by handful, straining into a bowl to obtain thick milk. Repeat the process

with another 2¹/2 cups of water to obtain thin milk. Combine both lots of milk for the coconut milk called for in this book, unless thick milk is specified. Coconut milk can be frozen; thaw and stir thoroughly before use.

The best substitute for fresh coconut milk is instant coconut powder, sometimes sold under the name "santan". Follow the instructions on the packet. Use tinned coconut cream for desserts and cakes.

CORIANDER Widely used in Asian cooking. Thais use the whole coriander plant: leaves, seeds, and roots. The roots are pounded together with garlic and black pepper to make a common basic seasoning. The seeds are roasted and ground for spice blends, and the leaves, known as cilantro or Chinese parsley, are eaten as a vegetable or used as a herb.

CORNFLOUR Known also as cornstarch, this fine white powder is widely used to thicken sauces. Mix cornflour with water, stir and add to the pan. Cook, stirring constantly for a few seconds, until the sauce thickens.

CUCUMBER Japanese cucumbers are short, roughly 1 in (2¹/2 cm) in diameter, and have a sweeter flavor and better texture than large cucumbers. Lebanese cucumbers are an ideal substitute.

CUMIN Pale brown to black fragrant seeds that look similar to caraway. Frequently partnered with coriander in spice mixtures and curry pastes.

CURRY LEAF Sprigs of these small, dark green leaves with a distinctive fragrance are often used in Indian curries. A sprig is about 8–12 individual leaves. Dried curry leaves are milder, but a more satisfactory substitute than *daun salam* or bay leaves.

CURRY POWDER Various spices are ground together to form curry powders. Certain spice combinations are appropriate to different basic foods, and curry powders labelled "fish", "chicken" and other more specific dishes such as "*korma*" or "*rendang*" should be used for that particular purpose only. Curry powders are often blended with water to a stiff paste before being fried. For maximum freshness, store in a jar in the freezer.

DAIKON: see RADISH, GIANT WHITE

DAL Also "*dhal*". Refers to dried legumes, usually husked and split. Varieties include **channa dal** or Bengal gram, which resembles a small yellow pea and is often sold split; **moong dal**, a small green pea; **urad dal** or **blackgram dal**, which is sold either with its black skin still on or husked; **masoor dal** (salmon-pink lentils); **toor**, **tuvar** or **arhar dal**, a pale yellow lentil which is smaller than the Bengal gram; and **kabuli channa** or chickpeas, also known as *garbanzos*.

DASHI A stock made from dried kelp and dried *bonito* flakes, the basis of Japanese soups and sauces. Instant *dashi* granules (*dashi-no-moto*) are sold in glass jars in Japanese stores.

DAUN KESUM This pungent herb (*Polygonum hydropiper*) has long, pointed green leaves tinged with purple. Used in Vietnamese table salads and other Asian dishes.

DEVIL'S TONGUE A greyish-brown mass made from a starchy root

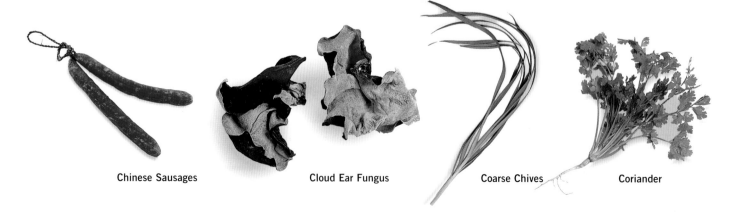

Chinese Sausages   Cloud Ear Fungus   Coarse Chives   Coriander

known as devil's tongue (*konnyaku*). It is sold in plastic packets and used in Japanese soups, one-pot cookery and to make noodles called *shirataki konnyaku*. Keep refrigerated.

DRIED MANGO POWDER Dried and ground unripe mangoes, used to give a sour tang to some Indian dishes. If unavailable, use a squeeze of lemon juice.

FENNEL Only the seeds are used in Asian cooking. The spice smells of aniseed, and looks like a larger, paler version of cumin. Used to add a sweet fragrance to Malay and Indian dishes.

FENUGREEK These almost square, hard yellowish-brown seeds are strongly flavored and generally used whole in southern Indian dishes and frequently in pickles and fish curries. Fenugreek leaves are eaten as a vegetable and because of their rather bitter taste, are combined with other greens or potatoes. Substitute with spinach if fenugreek leaves are not available. The dried leaves (*methi*) are sometimes used as a seasoning.

FISH SAUCE The distinctive *nam pla*, made from salted, fermented fish or prawns, is used in Thai and Vietnamese marinades, dressings and dipping sauces. Good quality *nam pla* is golden-brown in color and has a salty, pungent flavor.

FIVE-SPICE POWDER A Chinese spice combination of star anise, Sichuan peppercorns, fennel, cloves and cinnamon. A very strong seasoning, so use in small amounts.

GALANGAL A member of the ginger family, used in Thai, Malay and Nonya dishes. Peel off the tough skin before pounding or slicing. The young, pinkish galangal is the most tender and imparts the best flavor. Slices of dried galangal (sometimes sold under the Indonesian name, *laos*) must be soaked in boiling water for about 30 minutes until soft before use. Jars of tender, sliced galangal packed in water from Thailand make an adequate substitute for the fresh root. As a last resort, use the powdered form (1 teaspoon = 2.5 cm/1 in).

GALANGAL, LESSER A white, ginger-like rhizome believed to have medicinal properties. Do not confuse with the fragrant greater galangal used in Southeast Asia. Omit if unavailable.

GARAM MASALA An Indian blend of several strongly aromatic spices designed to add flavor and fragrance to meat dishes. Powdered *garam masala* can be bought from stores specialising in spices. Store in a jar in the freezer.

GARLIC Widely used as a flavoring and for its medicinal qualities. It is often pounded or puréed before use in curries. Garlic cloves are often much smaller in Southeast Asia than in Western countries, so adjust to taste.

GINGELLY OIL A light oil made from unroasted sesame seeds, quite different in flavor from Chinese sesame oil. It adds a distinctive touch to Indian pickles.

GINGER This pale, creamy yellow root is widely used not just to season food but for its medicinal properties. Always scrape the skin off fresh ginger before using, and do not substitute the powdered. Store in a cool, dark place. To make ginger juice, finely grate about 8 cm (3 in) fresh ginger. Squeeze it little by little in a garlic press, or wrap in cheesecloth and squeeze to extract the juice. Depending on the age of the ginger (young ginger is far more juicy), you will obtain 1–2 tablespoons of juice. **Pickled ginger** (*benishoga* or *gari*), sometimes dyed red, is sold in jars and widely used as a garnish. Slender pink young ginger shoots are also pickled and sold in jars.

GINSENG A highly prized medicinal root, sometimes used in cooking. Available from Chinese medicine shops.

GREEN PEPPER, JAPANESE Tiny slender green peppers which have none of the spiciness of green chilies. Eight Japanese peppers are the equivalent of a green capsicum. The latter is closer in taste to Japanese peppers and makes a better substitute than seeded green chilies.

HOISIN SAUCE A sweet sauce made of soya beans, with spicy and garlicky overtones. Used to season meat and served as a dipping sauce. Refrigerate the jar after opening.

HORSERADISH See WASABI

IKAN BILIS See ANCHOVIES, DRIED

JACKFRUIT A large, green fruit with a tough, knobbly skin. The segmented flesh is sweet and perfumed when ripe. In Vietnam, young jackfruit, which is whitish in color, is used as a vegetable.

JAGGERY A crude sugar popular in Sri Lankan cookery most commonly made from cane sugar and the sap of coconut or palmyrah palms. Southeast Asian palm sugar makes an acceptable substitute, or use soft brown sugar.

JASMINE ESSENCE The heady perfume of fresh jasmine flowers, soaked overnight in water, adds a unique fragrance to many Thai desserts and cakes. Substitute bottled jasmine essence.

KAFFIR LIME Also known as fragrant lime, this citrus fruit has intensely fragrant skin but virtually no juice. The grated skin or rind is added to food, while the fragrant leaves are used whole in soups and curries, or shredded finely and added to salads. Round yellow-skinned limes slightly larger than a golf ball (*jeruk nipis*) and small, dark green limes (*jeruk limau*) are used in Indonesia and Malaysia for their juice. Use lemons if limes are unavailable.

KALE Known also as *gai lan*, this vegetable is enjoyed for its firm texture and emphatic flavor. Only the leaves and tender portions of the stems are eaten. Peel and halve lengthwise if they are thick. Broccoli stems are a good substitute.

KANGKONG See WATER CONVOLVULUS.

KELP See SEAWEED

KENARI A soft, oily nut found in Maluku; the almond is the closest substitute.

KENCUR *Kaemferia galanga* is sometimes incorrectly known as lesser galangal; the correct English name is zedoary. *Kencur* has a unique, camphor-like flavor, so use sparingly. Wash and scrape off the skin before using. Dried sliced *kencur* (sometimes spelled *kentjoer*) or *kencur* powder are substitutes. Soak dried slices in boiling water for 30 minutes; use 1/2–1 teaspoon of powder for 2.5 cm (1 in) fresh root.

KINOME Their refreshing, minty taste makes the leaves of the

Curry Leaf

Galangal

Kaffir Lime

Kinome

Lime

Shiitake Mushrooms

Golden (enokitaki) Mushrooms

Dried Mushrooms

prickly ash a popular garnish. Available in Japanese stores, they will keep refrigerated for about 1 week, or use watercress.

KRACHAI This rhizome, sometimes referred to as "lesser ginger", looks like a bunch of yellowish-brown fingers. Enjoyed for its mild flavor and crunchy texture. Dried *krachai* is a poor substitute; omit if the fresh is unavailable.

KRUPUK Also known as prawn crackers, these dried wafers made from tapioca flour, prawns or fish are a popular snack and garnish. Dry thoroughly and deep-fry in oil until they puff up and become crisp.

LADIES' FINGERS See OKRA.

LAKSA LEAF See DAUN KESUM

LEMONGRASS A lemon-scented plant that grows in clumps. Use only the bottom 2–4 in (5–10 cm) portion. If it is to be pounded or blended to a paste, discard the outer leaves and use only the pale, tender part. Or bruise the stem before adding to stews. Also available in fresh, frozen, dried and powdered form. About 1 teaspoon powdered equals one stalk.

LILY BUDS, DRIED The Chinese call these "golden needles" because they are thin and golden in color. They are usually knotted for a neater appearance and added to Chinese and Burmese soups or vegetable dishes. No substitute.

LIME Various types are used. Large limes are about the size of a small egg with a greenish-yellow skin, and have a tart flavor similar to lemons. Small green limes, frequently known as *kalamansi*, are about the size of a walnut and have a less acidic, more fragrant juice. These are preferred for squeezing over noodle dishes and into *sambals*. See also KAFFIR LIME.

LOOFAH A gourd with an earthy flavor, often used in Vietnamese soups. Any type of gourd can be substituted.

LOTUS The tumescent root has a delicious crunchy texture and decorative appearance when sliced, making it a popular vegetable and garnish in Japanese and Chinese cooking. Its seeds are used fresh for sweets or dried in stews. Soak dried lotus nuts in boiling water for 1 hour, peel, and poke out the central core with a thin skewer or toothpick. (Canned lotus nuts normally have this core already removed.)

MACE The lacy orange-red covering or aril of the nutmeg seed. Used in spice mixes and *garam masala* for flavoring sweet and savory dishes. For maximum flavor, grind as required.

MINT Peppermint and spearmint are often used in salads and as flavor accents. See also DAUN KESUM.

MIOGA BUD This pretty pale pink bud with green tips, a member of the ginger family, is used for its spicy flavor and appearance in some Japanese dishes. No substitute.

MIRIN A bottled sweet rice wine used in Japanese cooking. If mirin is not available, use 1 teaspoon sugar as a substitute for 1 tablespoon mirin.

MISO A protein-rich salty paste of fermented soya beans, the mainstay of Japanese soups. Many different types are available, varying in taste, texture, color and fragrance. The most common are

red *miso*, which has a reddish-brown color and an emphatic flavor, and white *miso*, which is actually golden-yellow in color, has a lighter flavor and is less salty than the red variety, making it ideal for soups and dressings. Plastic bags or tubs of *miso* are generally sold in Japanese or health-food stores.

MITSUBA Both the stems and leaves of this decorative herb, a member of the parsley family, are used in Japanese cuisine. Parsley makes an acceptable substitute, although the flavor of *mitsuba* is more like celery.

MONOSODIUM GLUTAMATE (MSG) Some cooks in Asia make use of this taste enhancer. If you use only top quality ingredients, there should be no need for MSG.

MORNING GLORY See WATER CONVOLVULUS

MUNG BEANS Husked, dried green mung beans are known as yellow mung beans. Sprouted beans have a subtle flavor and a slight crunchiness. In Vietnam, yellow beans are used to make yellow bean sauce or other sauces. The starch from the beans is processed into cellophane noodles.

MUSHROOMS DRIED Black (*shiitake*) mushrooms are prized in Japanese and Chinese cooking for their flavor and texture. Soak in warm water for 15–20 minutes before use and discard the fibrous stems. Do not substitute with European dried mushrooms. Fresh *shiitake* are increasingly available outside Asia.

Fresh and delicate sheathed **straw mushrooms** are excellent in soups and vegetable dishes. **Button mushrooms** and the large, bland **oyster** variety are good for stir-frying. **Golden mushrooms** (*enokitaki*), clusters of slender cream-colored stalks with tiny caps, are available fresh and tinned – discard the tough ends before use.

Reddish-brown *nameko* **mushrooms** have a slippery texture and attractive reddish-brown cap; they are more commonly found in jars or tins. See also CLOUD EAR FUNGUS.

MUSTARD OIL Oil made from ground mustard seeds is used as a cooking medium in some parts of India, particularly in Bengal. The oil gives a distinctive flavor to the food and is worth looking for in Indian grocery stores. Substitute any refined, flavorless vegetable oil.

MUSTARD SEEDS Both yellow and brownish-black mustard seeds are used in Indian cuisine. They are not interchangeable.

NIGELLA Often referred to as onion seeds, these small, black seeds are known as *kalonji* in India. Omit if not available. If specified for Indian breads, substitute with black sesame seeds.

NOODLES Both fresh and dried noodles made from either wheat flour, rice flour or mung bean flour are used in Asian cooking. The most popular types are **fresh yellow** or "Hokkien" noodles, spaghetti-like noodles made from flour and egg; **dried wheat-flour noodles**, plunged into boiling water to soften; fresh flat **rice-flour noodles**, ribbon-like noodles about 1 cm ($^1/_2$ in) wide, used in soups or fried; fresh *laksa* **noodles**, which look like white spaghetti; dried rice-flour **vermicelli**, sometimes known as rice-stick noodles; and **dried mung bean noodles**,

| Palm Sugar | Pandan Leaf | *Sato-imo* Potato | Giant White Radish |

generally used in soups and sometimes referred to as "glass", "jelly" or "transparent" noodles.

In Japan the wheat noodle, **udon**, comes in various widths and is either flat or round. Packets of dried *udon*, whitish-beige in color, are readily available in Japanese stores. **Somen** are also made from wheat, but are very fine and white in color. **Soba** are made from buckwheat, and are sometimes flavored with green tea. Devil's tongue is used to make *shirataki konnyaku*—soak in hot water until they swell and become transparent.

NORI See SEAWEED

NUTMEG A native of the Moluccan islands, the nutmeg is actually the seed of a fleshy fruit. Try to purchase whole if possible and grate as required.

OIL, COOKING Blended vegetable oils (never olive oil) are used by Chinese cooks for frying. Peanut oil is sometimes specified for its distinctive flavor.

OKRA A green, ridged vegetable about 2 1/2–8 in (7–20 cm) long, favoured by Indians and Southeast Asians as a vegetable. Has a mucilaginous quality. Also known as ladies' fingers.

ORANGE PEEL, DRIED Dried orange peel is added to slow-cooked dishes for flavor. Although usually available in Chinese stores, fresh peel can be used as a substitute.

OYSTER SAUCE A thick sauce made from ground oysters, water, salt, cornflour and caramel coloring, used primarily to flavor stir-fried vegetables and meat. It is commonly used in Chinese cooking. Refrigerate after opening. Look for MSG-free brands.

PALM SUGAR Made by boiling down the sap of various palm trees, usually sold in solid cakes or cylinders and varies in color from gold to light brown. If unavailable, substitute with soft brown sugar or a mixture of brown sugar and maple syrup. To make palm sugar syrup, combine equal amounts of chopped palm sugar and water (add a pandan leaf if it is available). Bring to the boil, simmer for 10 minutes, strain and refrigerate.

PANDAN LEAF A fragrant member of the *pandanus* or screwpine family, pandan leaf is used to wrap seasoned morsels of chicken or pork, and added to various cakes and desserts. Bottled pandan essence can be used as a substitute in sweets.

PAPADS Also known as *poppadum*, these wafer-thin discs of seasoned wheat and lentil flour crisp up when fried in hot oil. Dry thoroughly before frying.

PEPPERCORNS Thought to be native to the Malabar coast of India, peppercorns are generally sold black (with their skins intact) and are frequently added whole to dishes. If crushing or grinding, do so just before use for maximum flavor and freshness.

PLUM SAUCE Sold in tins or jars, this piquant reddish-brown condiment is made from salted plums, chilies, vinegar and sugar. Refrigerate after opening. Available from Chinese stores.

POMELO A citrus somewhat similar to grapefruit, the pomelo is drier, sweeter and has a much thicker and tougher peel. It is eaten as a fruit or broken up for salads.

POPPY SEEDS Tiny white poppy seeds are prized for their delicate nutty flavor and used as a thickening agent. Soak in warm water for 10–15 minutes and grind before use. Substitute with cashews or almonds.

POTATO *Yamato-imo*, often referred to as a potato in Japan, is actually a type of mountain yam which is grated and used raw for its gluey texture and bright white color. **Sato-imo** is a type of yam with a much finer texture and slightly different flavor from Western potatoes. New potatoes make an acceptable substitute.

PRAWNS, DRIED see SHRIMPS, DRIED

RADISH, GIANT WHITE A vegetable about 6–10 in (15–25 cm) long, widely used in Japanese cooking. *Daikon* is shredded and used raw as a garnish, sliced for stews and stir-fries, and pickled. Preserved salted radish keeps almost indefinitely on the shelf, and is often added to rice porridge (*congee*) and other dishes.

RED BEANS Dried red azuki beans are used in Chinese and Japanese sweets, or cooked with sugar to make red-bean paste, a popular filling for buns and pancakes. The paste is also sold in tins.

RED DATES Valued for their medicinal properties as well as their prune-like flavor, these are added to soups. Soak in boiling water for 1 hour to soften before use.

RICE Many types of rice are eaten throughout Asia, the most popular for daily meals being fragrant long-grain **jasmine** rice. Some Indian recipes call for the nutty-flavored **basmati** rice. White and brownish-black **glutinous** rice are used in sweet and savory dishes. The absorbency of rice is affected by its age – young rice absorbs less water than older rice. When you use a new packet of rice, be conservative when adding water until you find out its degree of absorbency.

Wash rice thoroughly in several changes of water before using. To make plain rice, measure a minimum of 1/2 cup of rice per person and wash thoroughly. Put into a heavy-bottomed pan with enough water to cover the rice and come up to the level of the first joint on your forefinger (about 3/4 in or 2 cm). Cover the pan and bring to the boil over high heat. Set the lid slightly to one side, lower heat slightly and simmer until all the water is absorbed and dimples or "craters" appear in the top of the rice. Reduce heat to the absolute minimum, cover the pan and leave the rice to cook for at least another 10 minutes. Remove the lid, fluff up the rice with a fork (do not stir before this), wipe any condensation off the lid and cover the pan. Set aside until required. The rice should keep warm for at least another 15–20 minutes.

Short-grained rice with a somewhat sticky texture is used in Japan. Do not serve fragrant Thai or basmati rice with Japanese food.

RICE PAPER Made from a batter of rice flour, water and salt, then steamed and dried in the sun on bamboo racks. Moisten with a little tepid water before using to make Vietnamese rolls.

RICE WINE See CHINESE RICE WINE

ROCK SUGAR Crystallized cane sugar, sold in chunks in boxes.

Added to Chinese red-braised dishes, desserts and drinks.

ROSE ESSENCE A heady fragrance from the Middle East, used in Malay desserts, drinks and some Indian rice dishes.

SAFFRON The world's most expensive spice, actually the dried stigma of a type of crocus. Infuse saffron strands in warm milk before adding to rice and dessert dishes. Store saffron in the freezer as it loses its fragrance quickly.

SAGO PEARLS The pith of the sago palm that has been ground to a paste and pressed through a sieve. It is very glutinous, with little taste, and used in Asia for desserts.

SAKE Popular as a drink, *sake* or Japanese rice wine is available in many different qualities and is an important cooking ingredient. It is almost always heated to get rid of the alcohol for Japanese cuisine. A bottle of *sake* will keep for about a month after opening. If red *sake* is not available, use regular *sake*.

SALAM LEAF A subtly flavored leaf of a member of the cassia family, infused in curries. If you cannot obtain fresh or dried leaf, omit altogether.

SALTED FISH Salted and sun-dried freshwater fish that do not require soaking before using. Grill whole or cut into fine slices and fry to a crisp, and serve as a condiment. Salted fish is also sometimes pickled.

SALTED CABBAGE Various types of heavily salted cabbage are used in some Chinese and Nonya dishes; the most common is made from mustard cabbage. Soak in fresh water for at least 15 minutes to remove excess salt, repeating if necessary.

SALTED DUCK EGG A popular accompaniment to rice and savory Malay dishes. Wash off the black coating (often added to protect the egg), boil for 10 minutes, then cut egg in half while still in the shell.

SALTED SOYA BEANS Salty and with a distinctive tang, these are often lightly pounded before being used to season fish, noodle or vegetable dishes. Varieties packed in China are sometimes labelled "Yellow Bean Sauce". Mash slightly before using. Sichuan brands contain additional chili. Keeps indefinitely on the shelf.

SANSHO A peppery powder made from the seeds of the prickly ash, available in small glass bottles in Japanese stores. The dried Sichuan pepper is an exact substitute.

SCALLION Also known as spring onion, this popular herb is often used as a garnish and to add flavor to many dishes. It has slender white stalks with dark green strap-like leaves.

SEAWEED Used extensively in Japan. Dark green **dried kelp** or *konbu* is an essential ingredient in basic stock or *dashi*. It is sold in packets. Wipe clean with a damp cloth but do not soak before using. Other varieties include a fine **golden kelp** (*shiraita konbu*), **mozuku**, which are hair-like shreds, small squares of **salted dried kelp** (*shio-kobu*), and **laver** (*nori*), which is dried and sold in very thin, dark green sheets. **Wakame** is sold either dried or in salted form in plastic bags. Reconstitute by soaking in water.

SESAME Both black and white sesame seeds, the latter more common, are used in Japanese cooking. White sesame seeds are toasted and crushed to make a paste; if you don't want to do this yourself, you can buy either a Chinese or Japanese brand of sesame paste. Middle-Eastern *tahina* has a slightly different flavor as the sesame seeds are not toasted.

SESAME OIL Added to some Chinese dishes—usually at the last minute—for its fragrance and flavor, but never used on its own as a frying medium.

SESAME RICE CRACKERS Thin crackers made from rice flour sprinkled with sesame seeds. Grill or lightly bake before serving, and use like a cracker for dipping. Prawn crackers or puffed rice crackers may be used as a substitute.

SEVEN-SPICE POWDER A mixture of different spices and flavors, *shichimi* contains *sansho*, ground chilies, hemp seeds, dried orange peel, *nori* flakes, white sesame seeds and white poppy seeds. *Shichimi togarashi* contains chili. Both are available in bottles in Japanese stores.

SHALLOTS Small, round and pinkish-purple, shallots add a sweet onion flavor to *sambals* and curries. Packets of deep-fried shallots are generally available in Asian supply stores. If they lose their crispness, scatter in a large baking dish and put in a very low oven for a few moments to dry thoroughly. Cool before storing. Indonesian shallots are smaller and milder than those found in many Western countries.

SHARK'S FIN Transparent threads of dried shark's fin (generally sold in packets) are highly valued for their gelatinous texture and added to soups or sometimes cooked with egg. Soak in boiling water for about 30 minutes to soften before use. Shark's fin is also available canned.

SHISO The tangy, attractive green leaves of the *Perilla frutescens* or beefsteak plant, related to the mint family, are a common garnish in Japan. There is no substitute for the flavor of *shiso* leaf. The flower is often used as a garnish, and the tiny seeds for cooking. If the seeds are not available, omit as there is no good substitute.

SHRIMP PASTE Known variously as *kapi*, *trasi*, and *belacan*. A dense mixture of fermented, ground shrimp used extensively in Southeast Asian cooking. There are many different types, ranging in color from pink to blackish-brown. The former is good for curry pastes, the latter for making dipping sauces. Shrimp paste should be cooked before eating; if the recipe you are using does not call for it to be fried together with other ingredients, either grill or dry-fry the shrimp paste before pounding. To grill, wrap a piece of the paste in a piece of foil and toast under a grill or dry-fry in a pan for about 2 minutes on each side.

SHRIMP SAUCE, BLACK A very thick syrupy paste, usually sold in jars or plastic tubs, with a strong shrimp flavor. It is commonly added to *rojak*, a fruit and vegetable salad, and Penang *laksa*.

SHRIMPS, DRIED Small dried shrimps or prawns are a popular seasoning in many Asian dishes, particularly in sauces, condiments (*sambals*), and vegetable dishes. Choose dried shrimps that are bright pink in color, and soak in warm water for about

Seaweed—Kelp (left) and Wakame (right)

Shallots

Shrimp Paste

Star Anise

5 minutes to soften before use.

SICHUAN PEPPER A round, reddish-brown berry with a pronounced fragrance and flavor, used primarily in Sichuan cuisine and as an ingredient in five-spice powder. It is also known as prickly ash or fagara, and often sold powdered under the Japanese name *sansho*.

SOUR PLUMS Salty pickled plums (*umeboshi*) are very popular with plain rice for breakfast in Japan, as they are believed to aid digestion. These dull-red plums are available in jars, and should be refrigerated after opening.

SOY SAUCE Three types are used in Chinese cooking. **Light soy sauce** is thinner, lighter in color and saltier than **black soy sauce**, which is often added to give a dark coloring to a dish. Delicately flavored **red soy sauce** is seldom used and can be substituted with light soy sauce.

For Japanese food, use the Kikkoman brand. **Tamari** is very strong, thick and black and available from Japanese stores; dark soy sauce is a reasonable substitute.

In Indonesia, **thick sweet soy sauce** (*kecap manis*) is most frequently used as a condiment, followed by the thinner, saltier **light soy sauce** (*kecap asin*). If you cannot obtain *kecap manis*, use thick black Chinese soy sauce and sweeten with brown sugar.

SPRING ONION See SCALLION.

STAR ANISE A sweet-smelling star-shaped, eight-pointed pod with a pungent flavor of aniseed or licorice. Frequently used in soups.

STARFRUIT A star-shaped fruit, eaten raw and finely sliced. Young starfruit has a tart taste and is often served on the Vietnamese vegetable platter as a complement to grilled or fried foods.

SUGAR CANE Fresh sugar cane juice—extracted from the stalks by a crushing machine—is a very popular drink in Vietnam. In addition to the familiar uses of sugar cane, the peeled stalks are also used as skewers in cooking.

TAMARIND A large, brown pod with several seeds, tamarind has a tangy, acidic taste, and is a popular sour flavoring. It can be bought fresh, dried or in pulp form, and is most commonly sold in compressed blocks, with the seeds removed. The paste is used in hot and sour soups, and fresh crab dishes. To make tamarind juice, add 1 part pulp to 3 parts hot water for 5 minutes before squeezing to extract the juice. Discard the seeds and fibrous matter before using.

TAPIOCA The root of this plant (also known as cassava) and the tender green leaves are both eaten, though the leaves have to be cooked for at least an hour to remove the mild toxins. The root is grated and mixed with coconut and sugar to make sweetmeats. Fermented tapioca root is added to some desserts, while the dried root is made into small balls and used in the same way as pearl sago. Substitute spinach for tapioca leaves.

TAPIOCA STARCH Used as a thickening agent, and sometimes in the making of fresh rice papers. Combined with rice flour, it adds a translucent sheen and chewiness to pastries. Available in many Asian food markets.

TARO A barrel-shaped oval root, with hairy, brown skin and white flesh with purple-brown fibers, which can be used like a potato in soups. The tubers are best eaten when the fibers are small and barely noticeable.

TEMPEH Cakes of compressed, lightly fermented soy beans with a nutty flavor. Often available in health food stores. No substitute.

TURMERIC A bright yellow-orange tuber from the ginger family, turmeric is often used in curries and as a coloring agent. It is also used for medicinal purposes. Peel before using. Substitute $^1/_2$ teaspoon turmeric powder for $^1/_2$ in (1 cm) fresh.

VIETNAMESE MINT: see DAUN KESUM

VINEGAR Black, red and white Chinese vinegars are all made from rice, and as the flavor differs, be sure to use the type specified. **Red vinegar** has a distinctive tang, while full-bodied **black vinegar**, sometimes known as Tientsin vinegar, has a faint flavor similar to balsamic vinegar. Use sparingly as a seasoning or dip. **Japanese rice vinegar** makes an acceptable substitute for the white. There are no good substitutes for red and black vinegar. Slightly diluted cider vinegar can be used in place of rice vinegar.

WAKAME See SEAWEED

WASABI Indispensable in Japanese cuisine, and widely available in tubes. *Wasabi* powder (available in tiny tins), mixed with a little water 10 minutes before required, gives a much closer approximation of the freshly grated root.

WATER CHESTNUT Although it is troublesome to peel away the dark brown skin of this crunchy tuber, it's well worth using fresh water chestnuts if you can find them. Their crisp texture and sweet flavor make them ideal in salads, stir-fried vegetable dishes and desserts. Fresh yam bean is a better substitute for fresh water chestnuts than the canned variety.

WATER CONVOLVULUS This aquatic plant, a member of the convolvulus or morning glory family, is sometimes known as *kangkong* or water spinach. The arrowhead-shaped leaves and tender tips are usually stir-fried. Discard the tough, hollow stems. Young shoots are often served as part of a mixed platter of raw vegetables for dipping into hot sauces.

WHITE FUNGUS A crinkly golden-colored dried fungus that turns transparent after soaking. Prized for its chewy texture, and used in Chinese soups and desserts.

WILD GINGER BUD The pink waxy flower from a ginger plant, sometimes known as torch ginger (*Etlingera elatior*). Used in some Malay and Nonya dishes. No substitute.

YAM BEAN Known as *jicama* in the Americas, where it originated, this crunchy, mild tuber has a crisp white interior and beige skin, which peels off easily. It taste like a potato and apple cross. Excellent raw with a spicy dip, and can be cooked.

YUNNAN HAM A smoked salted ham used mainly as a seasoning. It is sold in tins.

YUZU ORANGE An orange-colored citrus fruit used for its fragrant rind. Lemon or lime rind could be used as a substitute, or else kaffir lime.

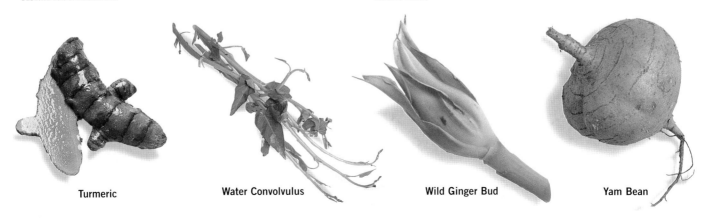

| Turmeric | Water Convolvulus | Wild Ginger Bud | Yam Bean |

The traditional open hearth or *irori* is virtually a museum piece in Japan today

Spoons made of coconut shells or wood are put to countless uses in the Indonesian kitchen.

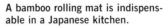

A bamboo rolling mat is indispensable in a Japanese kitchen.

Granite mortar and pestle.

The Asian Kitchen

You do not need a range of exotic implements to cook Asian food. Perhaps that is the most surprising aspect of Asian cooking—that often sophisticated food is prepared with so few utensils! Most of the implements found in the average Western kitchen can be adapted for use in Asian cooking, although several items, such as a wok or rice cooker, will make the preparation and cooking of certain dishes much easier. Far more time is usually spent on the preparation of the ingredients, which have to be peeled, chopped, grated, ground, and blended before the cooking begins. You should be able to obtain most of the implements mentioned here from Asian grocery stores.

Cooking Implements

Perhaps the most essential ingredient in the Asian kitchen is the **wok**—known as a *kuali* in Malaysia and Indonesia—a deep, curved pan traditionally made of cast iron and used for just about everything except cooking rice: stir-frying, deep-frying, braising, making sauces, steaming, and so on. The shape of the wok distributes the heat evenly, while its sloping sides ensure that food falls back into the pan and not over the edge during stir-frying. It's also practical for deep-frying, requiring less oil than a conventional saucepan or skillet. It allows just the right amount of evaporation for many dishes which begin with a large amount of liquid and finish with a thick sauce. When choosing a wok, avoid aluminium or Teflon-coated types; a heavy cast-iron wok that won't tip over easily is preferable, or best of all, a non-stick alloy that will not scratch when metal scoops are used.

A wok should be "seasoned" before its first use so that food will not stick. Wash the inside of the wok with warm soapy water but do not use a scouring pad. Rinse with fresh water and dry thoroughly. Put some oil on a paper towel and wipe the inside of the wok. Repeat until the paper towel comes away clean. Chinese cooks always heat the wok before adding oil to be sure that it is dry and the oil will not splatter. After cooking, never clean your wok with detergent or harsh abrasives; just rinse it with warm water and wipe dry. Remember to buy a lid for your wok—invaluable for when you want to steam food and for finishing off dishes.

In India, the **kadai**, a large wok-like utensil, is used for frying and sautéing. The *kadai* is made of iron, brass or aluminium, and slightly deeper than a wok, but the latter makes an excellent substitute. For rice and curries, a flat-lidded, straight-sided pan known as a **degchi** is used, but a good heavy-based pot will do.

To partner your wok, a **frying spatula**, as well as a **perforated ladle** for lifting out deep-fried food, are useful. Chinese cooks use a round-edged spatula for tossing stir-fried ingredients in the wok. Indonesian cooks use an assortment of wooden or coconut husk spoons for stirring.

Other useful utensils include a **wire mesh basket** on a long handle, good for scooping out deep-fried food or boiled noodles. Chinese cooks also use a pair of long wooden **chopsticks** for turning over food during deep-frying, although this requires a certain dexterity, only acquired with practice. You may be happier with tongs.

The multi-purpose wok

Traditional Indian grinding slab

Chinese claypot for slow cooking

Extremely high heat is needed when stir-frying food in a wok, and many electric cookers cannot achieve the ideal heat. Malaysian cooks—especially Chinese—insist on at least one gas fire, often with a double ring of gas jets. If you are using an old-style electric cooker which cannot reach a very high heat nor be reduced in temperature quickly, you should consider investing in a gas-fired ring to be used with your wok.

Almost any **saucepan** can be used for cooking Asian dishes, but take care to choose one that has a non-reactive lining, since many dishes contain acid such as tamarind or lime juice. Non-stick saucepans are ideal for Asian food as they avoid the problem of spices sticking on the bottom and allow you to use less oil when frying. **Claypots** of various shapes and sizes, with a sandy outside and a glazed interior, are used for slow cooking and for making soups and stocks. These are attractive and inexpensive, but any type of saucepan can be used.

Rice was usually cooked in an aluminium or a stainless steel saucepan, although most homes in the cities now boast an electric **rice cooker**—a great boon if you eat rice fairly often. It's foolproof, produces dry fluffy rice every time, and also keeps rice warm for latecomers. Alternatively, use a heavy saucepan with a firm-fitting lid.

Steaming is a healthy method of cooking in Asia, and a multi-tiered **bamboo steamer** with a plaited cover to absorb any moisture (unlike a metal cover where moisture condenses and falls on the food) is invaluable. If you are using a multi-tiered metal steamer, put a tea towel under the lid to prevent moisture from dripping back onto the food. The steaming basket is placed inside a wok on a trivet above boiling water. Chinese stores also sell perforated metal disks that sit inside a wok above the water level; these are useful for steaming a single plate of food. Cover the wok with a lid and keep the water level topped up and at a gentle simmer during steaming.

Just as indispensable as a wok is the **cleaver**, which comes with either a heavy rectangular blade about 3–4 in (8–10 cm) deep, ideal for cutting through bones, or a lighter weight blade for chopping, slicing, mincing, bruising garlic cloves and scooping up food on the flat edge to carry to the pan. A cleaver does the work of a whole battery of knives in a Western kitchen. You will also need a strong chopping board.

In addition to the usual knives found in any kitchen, a useful implement used by traditional Asian cooks is a narrow, double-bladed knife for carving vegetables into decorative shapes, and slicing fruit and vegetables thinly for the various rolls and wraps.

If the thump-thump of the stone, granite or porcelain **mortar** and **pestle** is not for you, blenders, food processors, and coffee grinders make light work of the pounding, grinding, and blending of spices and seeds. It's essential that all the ingredients to be made into a paste be finely chopped before blending. Whether using a mortar and pestle, blender or food processor, the principle is to grind or blend the toughest ingredients first, adding softer and wetter ingredients towards the end. First grind any dried spices or nuts until fine, then add hard ingredients such as chopped-up lemon grass and galangal. Pound or process until fine, then add softer rhizomes such as fresh turmeric and ginger, soaked dried chilies and sliced fresh chilies. When these are minced, add the ingredients that are full of moisture, such as chopped shallots and garlic, and soft shrimp paste.

If you are using a food processor or blender, you will probably need to add just a little liquid to keep the blades turning. If the spice blend is to be fried, add a little of the specified amount of cooking oil. If it is to be cooked in coconut milk, add some of this. While processing, you will probably need to stop the machine frequently to scrape down the sides. Continue until you have a fine paste.

Some cooks add water rather than the cooking medium to the blender; this means that the spice mixture will need to be cooked for a longer period of time before adding the other ingredients, to allow the water to evaporate and the mixture to fry rather than stew.

The multi-purpose **banana leaf** is often used in Southeast Asia to wrap food in for grilling, steaming, or placing directly onto hot coals. If you are able to obtain banana leaf, wipe it clean and cut to the required size. Hold it directly over a gas flame or plunge in boiling water until it softens before wrapping the food. Aluminium foil is generally recommended as a substitute, but for a texture that is closer to that obtained by using the leaf, wrap food in greaseproof paper first, then in the foil.

In Japan, **bamboo baskets** are used for draining noodles (a colander or sieve makes an adequate substitute). **Bamboo mats**, available in speciality Asian stores, are useful for rolling rice inside wrappers of seaweed, rolling up Japanese omelets and for squeezing

Old stove with a griddle or *tawa* for cooking *chapati.*

Traditional pottery is still used in Indonesian kitchens

Wooden mortar and pestle

Bamboo steamer

A lined copper *kadai*
for frying and sautéing.

Traditional coconut scrapers

the liquid out of cooked vegetables.

The **Japanese grater**, usually made of porcelain or bamboo, is perfect for grating ginger or horseradish, since it breaks down the fibres beautifully.

Indian and Sri Lankan breads are rolled out with a wooden rolling pin on a flat circular stone slab or wooden board, and cooked on a heavy iron griddle or **tawa**. A heavy cast-iron skillet or griddle makes a good substitute.

Coconut graters are essential in Asian countries. They are sometimes available in Western countries.

Cooking Techniques

The general cooking techniques used in Asian cookery are not too different from those used in the West.

The most common cooking method is probably **stir-frying**, which is fast cooking over a high heat in oil, usually in a wok. Evenly sliced ingredients are tossed about constantly; contact with the heat from the sides as well as the bottom of the wok means that food cooks very rapidly, sealing in the juices and flavor. Timing is absolutely crucial to the success of stir-frying, so chop all ingredients, measure all the seasonings, and have the garnishes and serving dishes at hand before starting.

Deep-frying involves cooking food by immersing it totally in heated oil. For best results, cook the food in small amounts so that the temperature of the oil does not drop too much. The optimum temperature for deep-frying is 375–400°F (190–200°C). Properly deep-fried food is not greasy at all—usually the result is a crisp exterior and a moist, succulent interior. Drain well on paper towels before serving.

Steaming is a cooking technique much prized by the Chinese and Japanese. The gentle cooking is an excellent method for showcasing the freshness of the produce, since all the natural flavors are retained. Make sure the water level in your steamer or wok is always topped up when you're steaming.

Grilling is another popular cooking technique, and it is hard to imagine Indonesia, Malaysia, and Singapore without their variations on satay, or Vietnam without its sugar-cane prawns. The meat to be grilled is placed on skewers (remember to soak the skewers in water

beforehand to prevent them from burning). Most of the dishes in this book can be cooked under a domestic grill or over a barbecue. Baste with some of the marinade as you cook. In Korea, where grilled marinated beef is a national dish, many families have their own table-top grill on which to cook *bulgogi* and *galbi* ribs.

Braising involves cooking food over a low heat in flavored liquid for a long time, and is ideal for tougher cuts of meat and some vegetables. To **red braise** meat is to cook it in dark and light soy sauces, star anise or five-spice powder, Chinese cooking wine, and sugar.

Poaching is carried out in water or stock that is barely simmering. The liquid should only just cover the meat which must be fished out as soon as it is ready.

To **blanch**, bring a pot of water to a rolling boil and immerse the food—usually vegetables—in small batches. Cook until they are tender but still crisp.

Many Indian, Sri Lankan, Indonesian, Malaysian, and Thai dishes involve the use of spices, and as each spice takes a different amount of time to release its flavor and aroma, it is important to follow the correct order given when adding spices to the pan. Many spices need to be **dry-roasted** before use. It is best to do this in a heavy cast-iron pan without oil. Watch the heat carefully, shaking frequently so that the spices do not catch. For maximum flavor and aroma, buy whole spices and grind them just before cooking.

When cooking with coconut milk, it is important to prevent it from curdling or breaking apart. Stir the milk frequently, lifting it up with a large spoon or ladle and pouring it back into the saucepan or wok while it is coming to the boil. Once the coconut milk is simmering, be sure never to cover the pan. Thick coconut milk is sometimes added at the final stages of cooking to thicken and enrich the flavor of the dish. Stir constantly while heating but do not allow to boil.

Cooking rice is a subject that often arouses controversy, and if you have a reliable method, stick with it. Whatever method is used, first wash the rice thoroughly to remove any impurities and excess starch until the water runs clear. The absorbency of rice depends on the variety of rice and its age, with older rice absorbing more liquid. Cooking times depend on the type and weight of your saucepan, and the heat of your cooker. See page 15 for a recipe for plain rice.

Thai woven storage baskets are as attractive as they are practical.

Traditional Indonesian rice steamer   Long-handled scoops

"Full of flavor, healthful, sometimes hauntigly Similar to neigh-boring cuisines, at other times dramatically different, the food of Burma is not complex to prepare at home."

BURMA

The undiscovered treasures of this land of gold and gems are its culinary delicacies.

Left: A farmer winnows paddy in the Shan Plateau. Rice is the staple crop in Burma.

Right: The weekly floating market at Ywama village, Inle Lake, is a colorful affair.

Burma, "The Land of Gold" of ancient Indian and Chinese manuscripts, has one of the Asia's least known cuisines. This is more a result of the country's long period of self-imposed isolation than the intrinsic quality of the food itself. However, as Burma—or Myanmar as it is now officially called—opens its doors to visitors and international business, more people are discovering its intriguingly different cuisine.

The Land and its People

Burma's beginning dates back some 2,500 years, when Tibeto-Burman-speaking people moved from Tibet and Yunnan into the northern part of the country. Kingdoms rose and fell over the centuries, many different tribes arrived and established themselves. The British gained control over the country little by little, annexing it to British India in stages, until the last king was dethroned in 1886. Burma regained its independence in 1946, becoming a socialist republic in 1974. In 1979, the ruling authorities changed the name to Myanmar.

Although religion and tribal customs influence the cuisine of the people of this polyglot land—in which today's specialists have identified 67 separate indigenous groups—it is perhaps the terrain and climate, which have had the greatest effect on regional cuisines. These factors determine the basic produce and therefore influence the dishes prepared by the people living in each area. The Burmese tend to classify their country into three broad areas: what used to be referred to as "Lower Burma," the humid Ayeyarwady delta around Yangon, and the land stretching far south into the Isthmus of Kra; "Middle Burma," the central zone around Mandalay, ringed by mountain ranges and thus the driest area in all of Southeast Asia, and "Upcountry," the mountainous regions which include the Shan Plateau and Shan Hills to the east, the Chin Hills to the west and the ranges frequented by the Kachin tribe to the far north.

The long southern coastal strip of "Lower Burma," Tanintharyi, is washed by the waters of the Andaman Sea and shares a border with

Thailand. This region is rich in all kinds of seafood, which is understandably preferred to meat or poultry. While people in other areas of Myanmar eat freshwater fish caught in the rivers, lakes and irrigation canals, this coastal region offers a cornucopia of marine fish, crabs, squid, shrimps, lobsters, oysters, and shellfish.

Flowing in a general north-south direction for some 1,349 miles, the life-giving Ayeyarwady rises in the mountains of the far north, then branches into a maze of rivers and creeks that make up the delta—about 168 miles at its widest. This is the rice granary of the nation. Rice is the staple crop in Myanmar and is consumed not only for the main meals of the day but for snacks as well. It is eaten boiled, steamed and parched; in the form of dough or noodles; drunk as wine or distilled as spirits. A combined coastal length of about 1,492 miles and a network of rivers, irrigation channels and estuaries, particularly in the Ayeyarwady delta region, yields a dazzling array of fresh- and saltwater fish, lobsters, shrimps, shrimp, and crabs. The Ayeyarwady delta supplies the bulk of freshwater fish, sold fresh, dried, fermented or made into the all-important *ngapi*, a dried fish or shrimp paste (similar to Thai *kapi*, Malaysian *belacan* and Indonesian *trassi*).

Mandalay, where the last king of Burma ruled, is the cultural heart of the fiercely hot, dry plains of central Myanmar. Irrigation has made it possible to expand agriculture from dry rice (which depended on seasonal rain for its growth) to include crops such as peanut, sorghum, sesame, corn and many types of bean and lentil. Various fermented bean or lentil sauces and pastes are used as seasonings in this region, rather than the fermented fish and shrimp products typical of the south. Not having access to fresh seafood, the people of the central plains generally eat freshwater fish, with the occasional dish of pork or beef.

The most populated "upcountry" area of Myanmar is the Shan Plateau, a region of mountain ranges and wide fertile valleys with a mean altitude of 3,443 feet above sea level, adjoining China, Laos and Thailand. A wide variety of food is grown here: rice, wheat, soya beans, sugar cane, niger seed, sunflowers, maize, and peanuts; and vegetables including potatoes, cabbage, cucumber, cauliflower, celery, eggplant, hops, kale, kholrabi, lettuce, mustard, rape, roselle, tomatoes, and chayote. Soups from this region are more likely to be based on beef or pork stock than made with fish or dried shrimps. The soups are not as clear as those found elsewhere in Myanmar, as they are often thickened with powdered soya bean. One example of this is the Shan version of Burmese noodles (*kyaukswe*), which is based on pork in a soup thickened with powdered soya bean, rather than made with chicken and coconut milk as in the rest of the country.

A Unique Cuisine Evolves

Poised between two culinary giants, India and China, and inspired by the ingredients and styles of Southeast Asia, the cuisine of Myanmar has developed a unique personality of its own. China has had a marked impact on the food of Southeast Asia, including that of Myanmar. Noodles made from wheat, rice and mung peas are perhaps the most noticeable legacy of China. In Myanmar, these are found in noodle soups like *mohinga*, a spicy, fish-based dish with sliced banana heart that is virtually the national dish. Another widely available dish is chicken in spicy coconut gravy, *ohn-no kyaukswe*, which includes either wheat, rice or mung pea ("transparent") noodles.

The Indian influence on Myanmar food is seen in the widespread use of ingredients such as chickpeas, coriander seeds, cumin, and turmeric. But whereas Indian cuisine relies on a complex blending of spices, Burmese food uses only a few dried spices, adding extra flavor with many fresh seasonings and condiments.

The food of Myanmar has, perhaps, more in common with its Southeast Asian neighbors, Laos and Thailand, than with India. The use of fermented shrimp and fish products such as dried paste, fermented fish in liquid, and clear fish sauce has parallels in both Laos and Thailand, where these ingredients largely replace salt and give a characteristic flavor to many dishes. The sour fruit of the tamarind tree, most commonly used in the form of a dried pulp, is often preferred to vinegar or lime juice in many Burmese dishes.

Coconut milk, so prevalent in the cuisine of Southeast Asia, is also used in many Burmese dishes and for sweetmeats, while agar agar—a setting agent from seaweed—is also popular in Burmese desserts and drinks.

At the Burmese Table

Breakfast in Myanmar is traditionally a light repast of fried rice, or yesterday's rice warmed up, served with boiled garden peas and green tea. Many delicious alternatives are now becoming popular though. Breakfast today could take the form of steamed glutinous rice topped with roasted sesame seeds and fish or vegetable fritters; smoked dried fish; *mohinga*, thin rice noodles in fish soup; or *ohn-no kyaukswe*, wheat flour noodles in chicken and coconut gravy. Rice gruel garnished with chunks of fried Chinese dough sticks might be gulped down, as might *naan*, flat bread fresh from the *tandoor* oven, with either boiled garden pea salad or lamb bone soup. Alternatively, a steaming chickpea broth or a chicken curry might provide the morning's sustenance.

The main meal is not served in courses as in the West. All the dishes, soups, condiments and vegetable dips are arranged in the middle, with a large bowl of rice for second helpings placed on the side. Meat and fish dishes are usually prepared in the form of curries, with fish dishes being much more popular in the lands bordering the lower reaches of the Ayeyarwady River and the delta region, while upcountry palates are partial to beans and pulses and their various by-products. Most curries are prepared with a thin gravy, which is then drizzled over the rice, mixed in and eaten with the fish or vegetables and fish preserve.

Soup is almost always served during the course of a meal and helps wash down the rice. It may be a *hingga*, meaning hot peppery soup, or a *hincho*, a slightly milder concoction. The soup is usually a clear broth with leaves, buds or slices of fruit. On more formal occasions, a thicker broth of fish and vegetables is served with rice noodles. Vegetable and fruit salads are very popular. Some of the heavier salads, such as a rice-based "salad," can be eaten either as snacks between meals or as meals in themselves.

No meal would be considered complete without the condiment *ngapi*, or to use its full name, *ngapi-seinsa*: fish, or sometimes shrimp, boiled and garnished with crushed garlic, toasted dried chilies and chili powder.

After a meal, fruits such as banana, mango, pomelo, and durian are usually eaten in lieu of cooked desserts, which tend to be eaten as snacks throughout the day. As a special treat, *lephet*, or fermented tea leaf salad, might be served. The main ingredient of this unusual salad is fermented tea leaves; these are then mixed with, or accompanied by, peanuts, roasted sesame seeds, fried garlic, coconut, and ginger slices, and so on. Though it may seem unusual to serve a savory dish after the main meal, this is when *lephet* is often eaten; though you may find it served as a first course in Burmese restaurants in the West.

SUGGESTED MENUS

Family meals

For a simple yet satisfying family meal, try serving with steamed white rice and a Fish Sauce Dip (page 29):
• Rice Noodles in Fish Soup (page 27);
• Hand-tossed Salad (page 26);
• Catfish in Tamarind Sauce (page 28);
• Fresh fruits such as mango or papaya,

Dinner parties

For a fun Burmese-style dinner party, serve:
• Pumpkin Soup with Basil (page 26);
• Grilled Eggplant Salad (page 26);
• Burmese Crab Curry (page 28);
• Pork and Mango Curry (page 28).
• Sesame-topped Semolina Cake with Coconut (page 29).

Finger food

The following snacks and appetizers may be eaten throughout the day, even as desserts:
• Fermented Tea Leaf Salad (page 26), which is also served after a meal in Burma;
• Transparent Savory Rice Pancakes (page 29).

A melting pot menu

Enjoy a culinary tour of Asia at your dining table with:
• Shrimp Mousse on Sugar Cane (page 177) from Vietnam as an appetizer;
• Pork and Mango Curry (page 28) from Burma and Shrimps with Sweet and Sour Sauce (page 159) from Thailand with plain rice;
• Mango Jellies (page 134) from Malaysia for dessert.

THE ESSENTIAL FLAVORS OF BURMESE COOKING

Indispensable to the Myanmar pantry are **garlic**, **ginger**, and **cilantro (coriander) leaves**. A good supply of **fresh jasmine rice** is a must and **glutinous rice** would be useful for some dishes. Flavorings you'll need include **fish sauce**, **soy sauce**, and **sesame oil**. **Fresh chilies** and **dried chili flakes** are a common addition to dishes as are **dried shrimps** and **shrimp paste**. **Fermented tea leaves** are easily found at all Burmese foodstores and come ready packed with all the extras making for a great, instant Burmese snack.

While Burma has long been renowned for its natural beauty, its culinary treasures have remained a well-kept secret until recently. The country has absorbed the culinary influences of its neighbors to make its food even more unique.

Lephet Thoke
Fermented Tea Leaf Salad

Lephet is an everyday part of Burmese social culture. *Lephet* is served to welcome guests to a house, as a peace offering after an argument, as a snack in front of the television, as a palate cleanser after a meal, and even as a stimulant to ward off sleep during all-night Burmese opera. Instant, packaged *Lephet Thoke* is now readily available from Burmese shops.

- 4 tablespoons *lephet* (fermented tea leaves)
- 3 cloves garlic, sliced and deep-fried till crisp
- 1 bird's-eye chili, finely chopped
- 2 tablespoons dried shrimps, soaked and blended to powdery fluff
- 2 tablespoons roasted peanuts
- 1 tablespoon toasted sesame seeds
- 2 teaspoons lime juice
- 2 teaspoons fish sauce
- 1 tablespoon peanut oil

Traditionally, *lephet* is served in a lacquer container with different compartments for each ingredient. Diners then choose their ingredients and, using only the thumb and first two fingers of the right hand, delicately serve themselves. Finger bowls would be provided.

Today, most Burmese combine all the ingredients in a bowl and mix them thoroughly as with a conventional salad.

Shwepayon Hincho
Pumpkin Soup with Basil

- 1 tablespoon oil
- 3 cloves garlic, coarsely chopped
- 1 lb 6 oz (700 g) peeled, seeded and cubed pumpkin
- 4 cups (1 liter) chicken stock
- Salt and pepper to taste
- 1/2 cup chopped Thai basil (*horapa*) leaves (substitute with European basil)

Heat oil in pan and lightly sauté garlic for 5 minutes till fragrant. Add pumpkin and chicken stock to the pan and bring to a boil. Cover and simmer for 20 minutes till pumpkin is tender. Transfer to a blender and process till smooth. Return the soup to the pan and add salt and pepper to taste. Add chopped fresh basil just before serving.

Khayanthee Thoke
Grilled Eggplant Salad

- 2 large eggplants (aubergines)
- 2 tablespoons finely sliced onion, soaked in water
- 6 cloves garlic, sliced
- 2 tablespoons peanut oil

Pumpkin Soup with Basil

- 2 tablespoons chopped roasted peanuts
- 1 tablespoon toasted sesame seeds
- 2 bird's-eye chilies, finely sliced
- 2 teaspoons fish sauce
- 2 tablespoons chopped cilantro (coriander) leaves

Grill eggplants over charcoal flame till skin lightly charred; alternatively, bake or cook under grill (broil) till soft. Cool, discard skin and mash the flesh. Heat oil in wok, add garlic and deep-fry till crisp. Remove with slotted spoon and retain oil.

Place the eggplant, onion, garlic, peanuts, sesame, chili, and fish sauce in a salad bowl. Add 1 teaspoon of the garlic-infused oil and mix well. Garnish with cilantro.

Let Thoke Sone
Hand-tossed Salad

Main Ingredients
- 4 small potatoes, peeled and cubed
- 2 pressed (firm) beancurd cakes (about 10 oz/300 g), soaked
- 1/4 cup (60 ml) oil for deep-frying
- 1/2 cup (75 g) cooked rice
- 1 large red chili, finely chopped
- 1 cup (200 g) fresh egg noodles, blanched
- 1 cup (80 g) transparent vermicelli, soaked 2 minutes and boiled 3 minutes
- 1 cup (20 g) shredded cabbage
- 1 cup (80 g) beansprouts, blanched
- 1 cup (150 g) shredded green papaya
- 1 medium tomato, peeled and chopped
- 1 cup (160 g) peeled and shredded cucumber

Garnishes
- 2 tablespoons peanut oil
- 1 medium onion, finely sliced
- 12 cloves garlic, finely sliced
- 2 tablespoons chili flakes
- 2 tablespoons tamarind pulp soaked in 1/2 cup (125 ml) water
- 3 bird's-eye chilies, finely sliced
- 1 teaspoon sugar syrup
- 4 tablespoons dried shrimps, soaked and blended to powdery fluff
- 4 tablespoons roasted pea flour
- 4 tablespoons fish sauce
- 1/2 cup chopped cilantro (coriander) leaves

Grilled Eggplant Salad

For main ingredients, boil potatoes till done. Drain beancurd cakes and dry with paper towel. Slice each one in half then cut each half into 9 pieces to yield 36 cubes. Heat oil, add beancurd and deep-fry over medium-high heat for 5 minutes till golden on all sides. Remove with slotted spoon and set aside. Knead chilies into cooked rice to color it.

For garnishes, heat oil in pan and fry onion and garlic till crisp. Remove and set aside, retain the oil. Sauté chili flakes by spooning the retained hot oil onto the chili flakes in a separate bowl and set aside (if chili flakes are placed directly into very hot oil, they will burn immediately). Stir and strain tamarind water, discard solids. Add bird's-eye chili and sugar syrup to tamarind water and set aside.

To serve, arrange all main ingredients on a large plate. Place each of the garnishes in individual bowls. Take a small handful of each item from the main ingredients. Then sprinkle on a little of each of the garnishes and mix thoroughly by hand.

Monlar Oo Thoke
Daikon Salad

This easy-to-prepare and refreshing salad can be eaten as a starter or as an accompaniment to curries and rice.

- 3 tablespoons rice vinegar
- 1 teaspoon salt
- 1 tablespoon sugar
- 1 large daikon radish (long white Oriental radish) (about 1 lb, or 450 g), peeled and finely sliced

1 small onion, sliced
9 cloves garlic, finely chopped
3 tablespoons peanut oil
2 tablespoons peanuts
1 tablespoon toasted sesame seeds
1 teaspoon fish sauce
2 tablespoons chopped cilantro
(coriander) leaves

Mix rice vinegar, salt, and sugar in a salad bowl and whisk till salt and sugar are dissolved. Add the radish, toss and chill for 15 minutes. Soak the sliced onion in cold water for 5 minutes and drain. Fry the chopped garlic in oil over high heat till golden, remove with a slotted spoon and drain on paper towel. (Discard oil or retain for use in another dish). Dry-roast the peanuts in a pan, cool and grind finely. When ready to serve, remove the radish mixture from the refrigerator and drain excess liquid. Add remaining ingredients and toss well.

Mohinga
Rice Noodles in Fish Soup

Stock
2 lb (1 kg) whole catfish
5 stalks lemongrass, bruised
1 teaspoon turmeric powder
4 tablespoons fish sauce
8 cups (2 liters) water

Soup
3/4 cup (150 g) raw rice, dry-roasted
    till light brown and ground to a
    powder
12 cups (3 liters) water
4 medium dried chilies
1 medium onion, roughly chopped
3 cloves garlic, minced
1 teaspoon ground ginger
2 tablespoons coarsely ground
    lemongrass
1/2 cup (125 ml) peanut oil
1/2 teaspoon turmeric powder
1 1/2 teaspoons salt
1 teaspoon ground black pepper
3 tablespoons fish sauce
12 whole shallots, peeled
7 oz (200 g) banana stem, sliced
    1 in (2 1/2 cm) thick (optional)

Garnish
10 oz (300 g) rice vermicelli noodles,
    soaked for 2 minutes and boiled
    for 2 1/2 minutes, drained and
    tossed with a little peanut oil
4 hard-boiled eggs, peeled and
    quartered

1 small onion, finely sliced and
    fried with a pinch of turmeric
    till crisp
Split-pea Crackers (see below),
    crumbled
Fried Fish Cakes (see below)
3 scallions (spring onions), sliced
1/2 cup chopped cilantro (coriander)
    leaves
4 limes, quartered
Fish sauce
Chili flakes

To make stock, place all ingredients in large pan and boil. Reduce heat, cover and cook for 20 minutes. Remove fish, flake flesh and set aside. Strain stock and discard solids.

To make the soup, add rice powder to water, stir and set aside. Blend chilies, onion, garlic, ginger and lemongrass to a paste. Heat oil in a pan and sauté chili paste with turmeric till fragrant. Stir in fish, then add salt, pepper, fish sauce, and whole shallots and continue to cook for 5 minutes. Add banana stem, stock, and rice powder water. Bring to a boil, stirring to prevent lumps forming. Boil for 15 minutes, reduce heat and simmer for 20 minutes.

Arrange all garnishes on the table, add a little of each to a bowl then add. Add a drop or two of the fish sauce and chili flakes to taste.

Pe Chan Gyaw
Split-pea Crackers

5 tablespoons rice flour
2 cups (500 ml) water
1/2 cup (100 g) dried yellow
    split-peas, soaked overnight
1/4 teaspoon salt
1 cup (250 ml) oil
    for deep-frying

Add rice flour to water and stir well. Stir in split-peas and salt.

Heat oil for deep-frying. Spoon 1 tablespoon of the mixture into the oil and deep-fry till crisp. Deep-fry several crackers at the same time. Drain on paper towel and cool. Crumble by hand if required.

Ngephe Gyaw
Fried Fish Cakes

1 lb (500 g) featherback fish
    (substitute with cod, kingfish
    or flounder)
1 clove garlic
1 teaspoon ground ginger
1/4 teaspoon turmeric powder
1/4 teaspoon salt
1/2 teaspoon chilli flakes
Water to moisten fingers
1 cup (250 ml) oil for deep-frying

Fillet the fish, flake the flesh and transfer to a mortar. Add garlic and ginger and pound to a paste. Add turmeric, salt and chili flakes and continue to pound for 10–15 minutes.

Roll the mixture into 3-in (7-cm) long "sausages", moistening fingers to help shape the mixture. Heat oil in pan, add several of the "fish sausages" at one time (not too many as they expand). Deep-fry for 5 minutes till golden brown. Remove and drain on paper towel.

Rice Noodles in Fish Soup

Ohn-no Kyaukswe
Coconut Noodles

1 lb (500 g) boneless chicken,
    cubed
6 tablespoons fish sauce
1/4 cup (60 ml) oil
3 tablespoons ground onion
1 tablespoon ground garlic
1/2 tablespoon ground ginger
1/2 teaspoon turmeric powder
1 tablespoon chili flakes
1/2 cup (50 g) chickpea flour
1 cup (250 ml) water
7 cups (1 3/4 liters) chicken stock
1 1/3 cups (330 ml) coconut milk

Garnish
4 hard-boiled eggs, peeled and sliced
1 medium onion, soaked and
    finely sliced
1/2 cup chopped cilantro (coriander)
    leaves
2 limes, quartered
1 lb (2 kg) fresh egg noodles,
    blanched in boiling water
12 oz (350 g) fresh egg noodles,
    deep-fried in 1 cup (250 ml) oil
    till crisp, drained on paper
    towel, cooled and crumbled by
    hand into bite-sized pieces
7 tablespoons chili flakes
Fish sauce

Marinate chicken with fish sauce for at least 15 minutes. Heat oil in large pan, sauté onion, garlic, ginger, and turmeric for 5 minutes. Stir in chicken and chili flakes. Cover and cook over medium-low heat for 10 minutes. Stir occasionally to prevent chicken sticking to pan. Meanwhile, add chickpea flour to water and whisk to remove lumps.

Add chicken stock to the pan and bring to a boil. Reduce heat, add chickpea flour paste, cover and simmer for a further 10 minutes. Add coconut milk and continue to simmer for 30–40 minutes, stirring occasionally, till the sauce thickens slightly.

Arrange each garnishing item on a separate plate on the table around a central bowl of chicken and coconut soup. To serve, take a portion of fresh noodles, add a little of each garnishing (a dash of fish sauce if desired) and a generous helping of soup.

Pazunhtok Sebyan
Shrimp in Tomato Curry

Use the freshest large shrimp for this curry. Serve this spicy dish with plain rice and stir-fried vegetables.

- 1 lb (500 g) tiger prawns, shelled and cleaned
- 1 tablespoon fish sauce
- 1/3 cup (80 ml) oil

- 2 tablespoons minced onion
- 3 cloves garlic, minced
- 1/4 teaspoon turmeric powder
- 1 tablespoon chili flakes
- 2 small tomatoes, cut in wedges
- 1 large green chili, halved length wise
- 1/2 teaspoon salt
- 2 tablespoons chopped cilantro (coriander) leaves

Marinate prawns in fish sauce for at least 15 minutes. Heat oil in pan and sauté onion and garlic for 5 minutes till fragrant. Stir in turmeric. Lower heat and add chili flakes, tomato, green chili and salt. Cook for 6–8 minutes stirring to a paste. Add shrimps and cilantro and cook for 3–4 minutes, stirring frequently, till shrimps are done.

Ngakhu Chet
Catfish in Tamarind Sauce

- 4 catfish, about 1 lb (500 g) (substitute with red snapper), gutted and heads removed
- 1/2 teaspoon salt
- 1 cup (250 ml) water
- 2 tablespoons fish sauce
- 2 tablespoons tamarind pulp soaked in 1/2 cup (125 ml) water
- 3 tablespoons oil
- 1 tablespoon sugar
- 2 tablespoons minced onion
- 1 clove garlic, ground
- 1 teaspoon chili flakes
- 1/2 cup chopped cilantro (coriander) leaves

Burmese Crab Curry

Pork and Mango Curry

Score the fish diagonally and marinate in salt for 10 minutes. Transfer fish to pan, add water and fish sauce, cover and simmer for 6–8 minutes. Squeeze soaking tamarind pulp, stir, strain and discard solids. Heat oil in separate pan and sauté onion and garlic till fragrant. Stir in sugar and chili. Add fish and mix well. Add tamarind water, cover and cook for 10 minutes. Garnish with cilantro.

Ganan Hin
Burmese Crab Curry

The natural sweetness of the crab and onion is complemented by the sour tang of tamarind and the aroma of *garam masala*.

- 4 whole live crabs, about 2 lb (1 kg)
- 4 cups (1 liter) water for boiling crab
- 4 medium dried red chilies, soaked
- 3 tablespoons chopped onion
- 2 whole cloves garlic
- 2 tablespoons oil
- 1/4 teaspoon turmeric powder
- 1 tablespoon fish sauce
- 2 teaspoons tamarind pulp soaked in 2 tablespoons water
- 1 teaspoon *garam masala*
- 1 cup (250 ml) water

Plunge live crabs into about 4 cups (1 liter) boiling water for 3 minutes and drain. Clean crab and discard spongy grey matter. Use a cleaver to chop crab into

large pieces; smash the claws lightly with the side of a cleaver to allow the flavors to penetrate.

Drain chilies and transfer to a blender, add onion and garlic and blend to a paste. Heat oil in pan, sauté chili paste for 4 minutes till fragrant. Stir in turmeric and fry for a further 1 minute. Add crab and fish sauce and mix thoroughly. Cover and cook over a medium heat for 5 minutes, stirring occasionally. Stir and strain the tamarind water and discard the solids. Add tamarind juice, *garam masala*, and water to the crab, bring to the boil and simmer for 10 minutes.

Wether Ahchin Chet
Pork and Mango Curry

The sourness of this pork curry depends on the mango used. Serve with plain rice, a vegetable dish and salad.

- 1 lb (500 g) pork loin, cubed
- 1 tablespoon fish sauce
- 2 tablespoons oil
- 3 tablespoons minced onion
- 2 cloves garlic, minced
- 1 teaspoon ground ginger
- 3 medium dried red chilies, soaked and ground
- 11/2 tablespoons peeled and shredded young (unripe) mango
- 1 teaspoon salt
- 11/4 cups (300 ml) water

Chicken Curry with Tomato

Marinate pork in fish sauce for at least 10 minutes. Heat oil in pan and sauté onion and garlic 5 minutes till fragrant. Add ginger and chili and continue to fry for 2 minutes. Stir in pork, mango and salt and mix well. Cover and cook over low heat for 20 minutes, stirring occasionally. Add water and simmer over low heat for 20–25 minutes.

Kyethar Ngapichet
Chicken Curry with Tomato

- 1 chicken, cut into 8 pieces
- 3 medium dried red chillies, soaked and ground
- 3 tablespoons finely sliced onion
- 1 small tomato, seeded and chopped
- 1 tablespoon finely sliced large green chili
- 1/4 cup (60 ml) peanut oil
- 1 teaspoon shrimp paste
- 250 ml (1 cup) water
- 1/4 cup (60 ml) chopped saw-leaf herb, substitute with cilantro (coriander) leaves

Marinade
- 1 tablespoon fish sauce
- 1 teaspoon salt
- 1/4 teaspoon turmeric powder
- 1 teaspoon ground ginger
- 3 cloves garlic, minced

Mix the marinade, combine with the chicken and set aside. Heat oil and sauté chili paste and onions for 5 minutes till fragrant. Stir in shrimp paste. Add tomato, green chili, and chicken, cover and cook for 5 minutes.

Stir occasionally to prevent chicken from sticking. Add water, cover and cook over moderately low heat for 30 minutes till chicken is done. Garnish with saw-leaf herb or cilantro.

Ye Mon
Transparent Savory Rice Pancakes

These deliciously light crêpes can be filled with a variety of different ingredients.

- 2 cups (300 g) rice flour
- 2 1/2 cups (625 ml) cold water
- 1 teaspoon salt
- 1/4 teaspoon baking soda
- 1 teaspoon finely chopped ginger

Transparent Savory Rice Pancakes

- 2 tablespoons peanut oil
- 1/2 cup (100 g) cowpeas (garden peas may be substituted)
- 3 scallions (spring onions), sliced

Mix rice flour, water, salt, baking soda and ginger in a bowl. Place a 12-in (30-cm) frying pan over medium heat and pour 4–5 tablespoons of rice paste into the pan. Lightly brush the pancake with a little oil and sprinkle on cowpeas and scallion. Cook for 3–4 minutes till underside is crisp. Fold in half and cook for 1 minute on each side.

Shwekyi Senyinmakin
Sesame-topped Semolina Cake with Coconut

- 2 1/4 cups (240 g) semolina
- 2 1/2 cups (625 ml) coconut milk
- 2 1/2 cups (625 ml) water
- 2 1/2 cups (550 g) sugar
- 2 teaspoons salt
- 2 eggs, beaten
- 1/2 cup (125 ml) oil, heated
- 2 tablespoons white poppy seeds
- 1/2 cup (75 g) raisins

Preheat oven to 400°F (200°C, gas mark 6). Dry-roast semolina in a frying pan over low heat for 10 minutes till reddishbrown, then cool. In a saucepan, add roasted semolina, coconut milk, water, sugar, salt, beaten eggs, and hot oil. Bring to a boil and cook over medium low heat for 20 minutes till the mixture comes away from the sides of the pan. Stir continuously with a wooden spatula throughout cooking process. If the mixture begins to stick to the pan, add a teaspoon or two of oil. Several minutes before the end of cooking, add raisins and mix well.

Transfer the mixture to a lightly oiled round baking tray 12 in (30 cm) in diameter and 3 in (7 1/2 cm) deep. Smooth the surface with a metal spoon or cake knife and sprinkle poppy seeds on surface. Bake on medium shelf for 15 minutes. Remove from oven and set aside for several hours at room temperature. Cut the cake in the baking tray and arrange slices on a serving plate.

Ngapiyaycho
Fish Sauce Dip

- 1 cup (250ml) water
- 1 tablespoon preserved fish paste
- 1/4 teaspoon turmeric powder
- 2 dried red chilies, soaked
- 2 bird's-eye chilies
- 1 tablespoon dried shrimps, soaked
- 2 cloves garlic

Bring water, fish paste and turmeric to the boil, simmer and reduce by half. Strain and discard solids. Pound remaining ingredients in a mortar and mix with fish stock. Serve with raw vegetables.

"An ancient Chinese proverb says, 'To the ruler, people are heaven; to the people, food is heaven.' "

CHINA

An ancient and inventive cuisine, known and loved all over the world.

Left: Three generations sit down to a meal in the courtyard of an old house in Fujian province, in Southern China.

Right: Steamed dumplings are popular in most regions of China and connoisseurs can recognize their provincial origin by their stuffing and accompanying sauces.

From a country whose usual greeting is *"Chi fan le mei you?"*—Have you eaten?—you can expect nothing less than a passionate devotion to food. Chinese food is known the world over, thanks to the peripatetic nature of its people, but the success of its food hinges on much the same things: fresh ingredients and the balance of flavors. The next time you go to an Asian market, observe: the Chinese shoppers are likely to be the ones who prod the fish, inspect entire bunches of vegetables, and accept and reject a batch of shrimp based on the kick in their legs.

While the array of seasonings and sauces used by Chinese cooks is not vast, every dish must meet three major criteria: appearance, fragrance, and flavor. The Chinese also prize texture and the health-giving properties of food.

An old Chinese proverb says, "To the ruler, people are heaven; to the people, food is heaven." This is no truer than in China, where gastronomy is a part of everyday life.

The Making of a Cuisine

So large is China, and the geographic and climatic variations so diverse, that you can travel through the country and never have the same dish served in exactly the same way twice. The paradox of Chinese food is that it is one borne of hardship and frequent poverty: this is, after all, a country that houses 22 percent of the world's population and has only seven percent of the world's arable land.

There is much debate and confusion about how many regional cuisines there are, but most gourmets agree that at least four major Chinese regional styles exist: Cantonese, centered on southern Guangdong province and Hong Kong; Sichuan, based on the cooking of this western province's two largest cities, Chengdu and Chongqing; Hunan, the cooking of eastern China—Jiangsu, Zhejiang, and Shanghai; and Beijing or 'Northern' food, with its major inspiration from the coastal province of Shandong. Some would add a fifth cuisine from the southeastern coastal province of Fujian.

All regions use various forms of ginger, garlic, scallions, soy sauce, vinegar, sugar, sesame oil, and bean paste, but combine them in highly distinctive ways. What distinguishes these regional styles is not only their cooking methods but also the particular types and combinations of basic ingredients.

The southern school of cooking was the cuisine taken to the West by Chinese migrants—egg rolls, *dim sum*, *chow mein*, sweet and sour pork, *chop suey*, and fortune cookies. With the exception of the last two, which were American inventions, the other dishes are orthodox Cantonese creations.

Cantonese food is characterized by its extraordinary range and the freshness of its ingredients, a light touch with sauces, and the readiness of its cooks to incorporate "exotic" imported flavorings

Smiling Shanghai children enjoying a snack. Each region has its own special array of morsels for when the next meal is just too far away.

such as lemon, curry, and Worcestershire sauce. Cantonese chefs excel in preparing roasted and barbecued meats (duck, goose, chicken, and pork), and *dim sum*, snacks taken with tea for either breakfast or lunch. *Dim sum* can be sweet, salty, steamed, fried, baked, boiled or stewed, each served in their own individual bamboo steamer or plate. To eat *dim sum* is to "*yum cha*" or drink tea. In traditional *yum cha* establishments, restaurant staff walk around the room pushing a cart or carrying a tray offering their tasty morsels. *Dim sum* restaurants are important institutions where the locals go to discuss business, read newspapers and socialize.

The home of spicy food, Sichuan, is a landlocked province with remarkably fertile soil and a population of over 100 million. The taste for piquant food is sometimes explained by Sichuan's climate. The fertile agricultural basin is covered with clouds much of the year and there is enough rain to permit two crops of rice in many places.

Strong spices provide a pick-me-up in cold and humid weather, and make a useful preservative. The most popular spices are chilies and Sichuan peppercorns (prickly ash), tempered with sugar, salt, and vinegar. Despite the province's incendiary reputation, many of the famous dishes are not spicy at all, for example, the famous camphor- and tea-smoked duck, made by smoking a steamed duck over a mixture of tea and camphor leaves. But it is the mouth burners that have made Sichuan's name known all over the world, dishes like *ma po dou fu*—stewed bean curd and ground meat in a hot sauce; *hui guo rou*—twice-cooked (boiled and stir-fried) pork with cabbage in a piquant bean sauce; *yu xiang qiezi*, eggplant in "fish flavor" sauce; and *dou ban yu*—fish in hot bean sauce.

When the Grand Canal was built in the Sui dynasty AD 581–618, it gave rise to several great commercial cities at its southern terminus, including Huaian and Yangzhou, after which this regional cuisine (Hunan) is named. Its location on the lower reaches of the Yangtze River in China's "land of fish and rice" gave it an advantage in terms of agricultural products, and it was renowned for seafood such as fish, shrimp, eel, and crab, which were shipped up the canal to the imperial court in Beijing. Hunan cuisine is not well known outside of China, perhaps because it rejects all extremes and strives for the "Middle Way". Freshness (*xian*) is a very important concept in the food of this region, but *xian* means more than just fresh. For a dish of steamed fish to be described as *xian*, the fish must have been swimming in the tank one hour ago, it must exude its own natural flavor, and must be tender yet slightly chewy. *Xian* also implies that the natural flavor of the original ingredients should always take precedence over the sauce. Some of the best known dishes from this region are steamed or stewed and require less heat and a longer cooking time, for instance chicken with chestnuts, the glorious pork steamed in lotus leaves, duck with a stuffing made from eight ingredients, and the evocatively named "lion head" meatballs.

The cuisine of Beijing has perhaps been subjected to more outside influences than any other major cuisine in China. First came the once-nomadic Mongols, who made Beijing their capital during the Yuan dynasty (1279–1368). They brought with them mutton, the chief ingredient in Mongolian hot pot, one of Beijing's most popular dishes in the autumn and winter. The Manchus, as the rulers of the Qing dynasty (1644–1911), introduced numerous ways of cooking pork. As the capital of China for the last eight centuries, Beijing became the home of government officials who brought their chefs with them when they came from the wealthy southern provinces. But the most important influence comes from nearby Shandong province, which has a pedigree that goes back to the days of Confucius C. 550 BC. Shandong cuisine features the seafood found along China's eastern seaboard: scallops and squid, both dry and fresh, sea cucumber, conch, crabs, and shark's fins, often teamed with the flavors of raw leek and garlic.

Beijing's most famous dish, Peking duck, owes as much to the culinary traditions of other parts of China as to the capital itself. The method of roasting the duck is drawn from Hunan cuisine, while the pancakes, raw leek, and salty sauce that accompany the meat are typical of Shandong.

Beijing is also famous for its steamed and boiled dumplings (*jiaozi*), which are filled with a mixture of pork and cabbage or leeks, or a combination of eggs and vegetables.

The Food of the People

The proliferation of refrigerators in China today is making inroads on an institution that for centuries has been an essential part of daily life: shopping in the local food market. Many housewives and househusbands go to the market two or three times a day. In some state-run offices in Beijing, half-hour rest periods are allotted to enable its employees to shop for fresh produce.

In addition to fresh food markets, there are shops selling a huge variety of prepared and packaged food. Along with food markets, most cities have areas where snack foods are sold in stand-up or sit-down stalls. Breakfast may be a fried egg wrapped in a pancake; an "elephant ear" plate-sized piece of fried bread; noodles; congee (rice gruel) or bean curd jelly accompanied by a deep-fried cruller (*you tiao*); or a slice of cake and a jar of milk. Lunch or dinner could be noodles from a food stall or careful preparation of the just-bought produce from the market.

Esoteric and often extremely expensive ingredients such as shark's fin, dried scallops and dried oysters go into some of China's prized dishes.

Every region has its own particular snacks, very often sold on the street. Snack food is very inexpensive and includes such regional specialties as Beijing's boiled tripe with fresh cilantro, fried starch sausage with garlic, sour bean soup, and boiled pork and leek dumplings (*jiaozi*). Shanghai is known for its steamed *baozi* dumplings, sweet glutinous rice with eight sweetmeats (*babaofan*) and yeasty sweetened wine lees (the sediment of the wine left after fermentation). Sichuan is noted for spicy *dan dan* noodles, dumplings in hot sauce, and bean curd jelly (*dou hua*), while Cantonese *dim sum* is a cuisine unto itself.

The average urban family eats its main meal of the day in the evening. This meal usually consists of a staple such as rice or noodles, one or two fried dishes, at least one of which contains meat or fish, and a soup. Northerners eat more wheat than rice, in the form of steamed buns or noodles, which are fried or simmered in stock.

Beer regularly accompanies meals at home; stronger spirits are reserved for special occasions. The whole family gets involved in the business of shopping and cooking, and friends or relatives may be invited to join in the feast.

Western foods have made tentative inroads into the 6000-year-old bastion of Chinese cuisine, but fast-food outlets succeed mainly because of their novelty and location in Chinese tourist cities.

China's Gourmet Culture

As the Son of Heaven, the emperor of China enjoyed a status so elevated above the common mortal that it is difficult to conceive of the awe in which he was held and the power that he enjoyed. There are no dining rooms in the Forbidden City; tables would be set up before

the emperor wherever he decided to eat. Every meal was a banquet of approximately 100 dishes. These included 60 or 70 dishes from the imperial kitchens, and a few dozen more served by the chief concubines from their own kitchens. Many of the dishes served to the emperor were made purely for their visual appeal, and were placed far away from the reach of the imperial chopsticks. These leftovers were spirited out of the palace to be sold to gourmets eager to "dine with the emperor."

From the palace, this gourmet culture filtered down to the private homes of the rich and powerful and to the restaurants where the privileged entertained. Banquets are important social and commercial events in China today and many high officials attend banquets five or six nights a week. Almost any event can supply the reason for a banquet: the completion (or non-completion) of a business deal, wedding, graduation, trip abroad, return from a trip abroad, promotion, moving house and so on. One can also give a banquet to save or give "face" in the case of some unpleasant situation or mishap.

Some of the best restaurants in China today are the pre–1949 enterprises that have managed to survive by virtue of the quality of their cooking and by their location. One example is Fangshan Restaurant in Beihai Park in Beijing, set in a former imperial palace on the shores of an artificial lake, where many of the recipes are taken from the late-Qing dynasty Forbidden City. Fangshan is renowned for its Manchu-Chinese Banquet, a three-day dining extravaganza that consists of over 100 different dishes, a souvenir of Qing dynasty court banquets. At another famous restaurant, Listening to the Orioles Pavilion, in the gardens of the famed Summer Palace (known to the Chinese as *Yi He Yuan*), dinners for 10 at around $1000 per table are reputedly not uncommon.

The Chinese Kitchen and Table

Rice is essential to a Chinese meal. This is particularly true in South China, although this division is not hard and fast. One reason the Grand Canal was built in the sixth century was to transport rice from the fertile Yangtze delta region to the imperial granaries in the rela-

This child seems to be eating with more gusto than finesse. You may need some practice before becoming adept with chopsticks.

tively dry North. And since the Ming dynasty (1368–1644), an annual crop of short-grain rice has been grown in the suburbs of Beijing, originally for the palace and today for the military leadership. Numerous varieties of rice are produced in China, supplemented by the more expensive Thai rice which is available at urban markets throughout the country. Southerners seem to prefer long-grain rice, which is less sticky than other varieties and has strong "wood" overtones when steaming hot.

The basic Chinese diet and means of food preparation were in place about 6000 years ago, although many imported ingredients entered the Chinese larder and new cooking methods were adopted. From the earliest times, the Chinese have divided their foodstuffs into two general categories: *fan* (cooked rice and staple grain dishes) and *cai* (cooked meat and vegetable dishes). A balanced mixture of grain and cooked dishes has been the ideal of a Chinese meal since time immemorial. Further balances were sought between the *yin* (cooling) and *yang* (heating) qualities of the foods served. The notion of food as both preventative and curative medicine is deeply embedded in the Chinese psyche.

The specific proportion of grain and cooked dishes on a menu depends on the economic status of the diners and the status of the occasion. The grander the occasion, the more cooked dishes and less grain. Even today, this tradition is maintained at banquets, where a small symbolic bowl of plain steamed rice is served after an extensive selection of dishes.

Rice is served steamed, fried (after boiling) or made into noodles by grinding raw rice into rice flour. It is also cooked with a lot of water to produce congee or *zhou* (rice gruel), a popular breakfast food and late-night snack eaten with savory side dishes. Rice is eaten by raising the bowl to the mouth and shoveling the grains in with the chopsticks in a rapid fanning motion.

The Chinese table is a shared table. The average meal would comprise three to four *cai*, *fan*, and a soup, served at once, to be shared between the diners who help themselves. The *cai* dishes should each have a different main ingredient, perhaps one meat, one fish, and one vegetable. Each dish should complement the other in terms of taste, texture and flavor, and the total effect appeal to both the eye and the tongue.

When cooking Chinese food, prepare all the ingredients and have them ready before you start cooking as trying to juggle a hot wok and chop a chicken at the same time inevitably leads to catastrophe!

Tea is drunk before and after a meal, but rarely during a meal. The most famous of clear-spirits drunk "straight up" in small handle-less cups or glasses during a meal is Maotai, made in the south-west province of Guizhou.

Chinese meals are socially important events, and special menus are presented for weddings and birthdays; important festivals also have their traditional dishes and snacks.

Finally, some tips on etiquette. Don't point with your chopsticks and don't stick them into your rice bowl and leave them standing up or crossed. Don't use your chopsticks to explore the contents of a dish—locate the morsel you want with your eyes and go for it with your chopsticks without touching any other pieces.

If you wish to take a drink of wine at a formal dinner, you must first toast another diner, regardless of whether he or she responds by drinking. If you are toasted and don't wish to drink, simply touch your lips to the edge of the wine glass to acknowledge the courtesy.

It is incumbent upon the host to urge the guests to eat and drink to their fill. This means ordering more food than necessary and keeping an eye out for idle chopsticks. It is polite to serve the guest of honor the best morsels, such as the cheek of the fish, using a pair of serving or "public" chopsticks or with the back end of one's chopsticks. And remember, all food is communal and to be shared.

SUGGESTED MENUS

Family meals

For simple family meals, try serving with steamed jasmine rice:
• Winter Melon Soup (page 38);
• Bamboo Shoots with Mushrooms (page 42);
• Sliced fresh fruit.

Alternatively, you could offer:
• Pork-Stuffed Steamed Beancurd (page 36);
• Beef with Black Pepper (page 41);
• Red Bean Soup (page 46).

Dinner parties

For a dinner party that is guaranteed to impress, present a selection of appetizers and two main dishes served with noodles instead of rice, such as.
• Marinated Sliced Beef (page 36), Carrot and Radish Rolls (page 38) and Seafood in Beancurd Skin (page 36);
• Teochew Steamed Pomfret (page 42) or the classy Shrimp-stuffed Lychees (page 43) and Chicken with Dried Chilies (page 45);
• Fried Noodles Xiamen Style (page 39);
•White Fungus with Melon Balls (page 46).

One-pot meals

Many of the noodle soup dishes here are meals-in-a-bowl, and make an ideal lunch or supper. In China, dishes such as the following are often eaten for breakfast and in-between meals:
• Hot and Spicy Hawker Noodles (page 38);
• Cold Chengdu Noodles (page 39).

A melting pot menu

For a festive culinary tour around Asia:
• Shark's Fin Soup (page 38) from China;
• the ubiquitous but always delicious Chicken Rice from Malaysia/Singapore (page 128);
• Kale with Crispy Pork (page 164) from Thailand served with rice;
• Almond Jelly (from Malaysia/Singapore) in individual servings (page 134).

THE ESSENTIAL FLAVORS OF CHINESE COOKING

Indispensable to the Chinese pantry are **garlic**, **ginger**, and **scallions**. A good supply of **fresh jasmine rice** and **dried egg noodles** is also a must. Flavorings you'll need include **soy sauce**, **rice wine**, **sesame oil**, and **chili sauce**. **Bamboo shoots** and **bean curd** are a common addition to everything from stir-fries to one-pot braises. **Rock sugar** is frequently used in red-braised dishes. **Sesame paste** is mixed into dipping sauces, and **Sichuan peppercorns** add a subtle heat to dishes.

Some of these appetizers would make very good starters to a formal dinner. Some, like the Seafood in Beancurd Skin and Pork-stuffed Steamed Beancurd, can be served as part of a main meal—just adjust the quantities of the ingredients accordingly.

Nu Er Hong Niu Rou
Marinated Sliced Beef

Red rice is available from Chinese medicine or specialty food shops.

- 1 x 13 oz (400 g) piece beef topside
- Water as required
- 2 teaspoons red rice (optional)
- 2 tablespoons Chinese rice wine
- 2 teaspoons salt
- 4 bay leaves

Put the beef in a pan with sufficient water to cover. Add all other ingredients and simmer, covered, until the beef is tender. Turn the meat from time to time and add a little more water if it threatens to dry up. Allow to cool. To serve, slice the beef thinly and arrange on a plate. Serve with a dipping sauce.

Pork-stuffed Steamed Beancurd

Chao Lian Xia Xie Jiao
Seafood in Beancurd Skin

- 7 oz (200 g) peeled shrimp
- 3 1/2 oz (100 g) crabmeat, fresh or canned
- 2 water chestnuts, roughly chopped
- 1 tablespoon chopped cilantro (coriander) leaves
- 1 teaspoon salt
- 3–4 large sheets of dried beancurd skin

- 1 teaspoon cornstarch blended with water
- Oil for deep-frying

Blend the shrimp and crabmeat in a food processor until coarsely chopped. Add water chestnuts, cilantro, and salt and process for a few more seconds.

Wipe the beancurd skin with a damp cloth to make it pliable, cut into 5-in (13-cm) squares. Put in a heaped spoonful of filling and spread across. Smear the far end of the beancurd skin with cornstarch paste, then fold over the sides of the skin and roll up to seal the filling in firmly.

Deep-fry in hot oil until crisp and golden. Cut rolls into bite-sized pieces before serving.

Dou Fu Rou Jiang Zha
Pork-stuffed Steamed Beancurd

- 1 lb (500 g) beancurd
- 3 teaspoons cornstarch
- 3 1/2 oz (100 g) finely minced lean pork
- 3 dried black mushrooms, soaked and finely chopped
- 2 teaspoons chicken stock powder
- 1/2 teaspoon salt
- 1 teaspoon sugar
- 1 teaspoon Chinese rice wine
- 1 1/2 cups leafy greens (spinach, Napa cabbage or *bok choy*), blanched
- 1/2 cup (125 ml) chicken stock

Cut the beancurd into squares about 3 x 1 1/2 in (8 x 4 cm) thick squares. Use a teaspoon to scoop out some of the bean curd from the center to make a hole for the pork filling. Combine 1 teaspoon cornstarch with all other ingredients, except leafy greens and stock, mixing well. Stuff this into the beancurd and steam over high heat for 4 minutes.

While the beancurd is steaming, cook the greens in chicken stock. Drain, keeping the stock. Arrange greens on a plate. Blend remaining 2 teaspoons cornstarch with water and thicken the stock. Pour over vegetables, arrange the cooked beancurd on top and serve.

Ma La Lian Ou
Lotus Root Salad

The lotus has special associations for Buddhists, for it is said that Gautama Buddha likened man striving to achieve goodness to an exquisite lotus bloom rising unsullied from the muddy bottom of a lake!

- 6–8 in (15-20 cm) lotus root
- 1 tablespoon white rice vinegar
- 2 tablespoons sugar
- Salt to taste

Peel the lotus root and cut crosswise into 1/4-in-(1/2-cm-) thick slices. Heat a pan of water until boiling, then drop in the lotus root slices and blanch for about 5 seconds. Drain and rinse in cold water.

Toss the lotus root slices in a bowl with the vinegar, then arrange on a plate. Sprinkle with sugar and salt to taste and serve immediately.

Carrot and Radish Rolls

- 2 1/2 oz (75 g) carrot, shredded
- 2 1/2 oz (75 g) giant white radish, peeled and sliced
- 3 teaspoons sugar
- 2 teaspoons white rice vinegar
- 2 teaspoons sesame oil
- 1/2 teaspoon salt

Blanch the carrot and radish separately in a little boiling water. Drain well and pat dry with paper towel. Place the slices of radish flat on a board and put some shredded carrot crosswise in the center of each. Roll up to enclose the carrot, then cut each roll on the diagonal into 1/2-in (1-cm) pieces.

Arrange on a plate. Combine all remaining ingredients, mixing until the sugar dissolves. Pour over the rolls and serve.

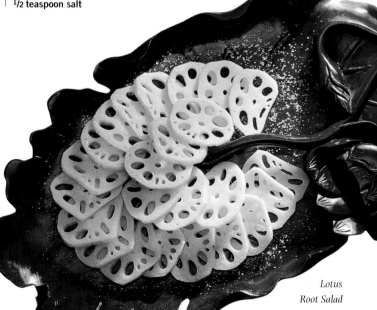

Lotus Root Salad

Boiled Dumplings in Hot Sauce

Sesame Squid

- 5 oz (150 g) squid, skinned and cleaned
- 1 cup (250 ml) water
- 1 teaspoon salt
- 1 tablespoon sesame paste
- 2 teaspoons sesame oil

Cut the squid in pieces about 2 x 3/4 in (5 x 2 cm). Score crosswise in a diamond pattern with a sharp knife, cutting about halfway into the squid meat so that it will curl during cooking. Bring water and salt to a boil and drop in squid. Simmer just until the squid turns white and curls (about 1 minute), then drain.

Combine sesame paste and oil in a mixing bowl and add squid. Toss and serve at room temperature or chilled, if preferred.

Gong Cai Xian Shen Pian
Duck Giblets

Duck or chicken giblets, often discarded by Western cooks or relegated to the stockpot, are favored for their firm texture and flavor in China. The word *gong* in the name of this dish means gratuity to the emperor.

- 10 oz (300 g) duck or chicken giblets
- 2 teaspoons salt
- 4 whole star anise
- 4 bay leaves
- 1 cup (100 g) salted mustard cabbage, soaked, squeezed and sliced
- 1 teaspoon sesame oil

Clean the giblets and drain. Put in a pan with salt, star anise, and bay leaves. Cover with water, bring to a boil and simmer for about 30 minutes until tender. Remove giblets, drain and keep refrigerated until required.

To serve, slice the giblets thinly, then mix with salted cab-bage and sesame oil. If desired, garnish with a little sliced red chili. Serve cold.

Chuan Wei Hun Tun
Boiled Dumplings in Hot Sauce

Steamed or boiled dumplings are a favorite snack in most of China, from Beijing in the north to Shanghai on the east coast, from the southern province of Guangdong to Sichuan in the far west. The filling differs from one area to another, as well as according to the season. In summer time in Beijing, the basic pork stuffing might be seasoned with fresh dill. The dumplings may be steamed, fried, boiled, served in soup (like the famous Cantonese *wonton* soup) or, as in this Sichuan version, bathed in a tangy sauce.

- 50 fresh *wonton* wrappers
- 7 oz (200 g) lean pork, finely minced
- 1 egg, lightly beaten
- 1 1/2 teaspoons very finely chopped ginger
- 2 tablespoons Chinese rice wine
- 1 teaspoon salt
- 1/4 teaspoon ground white pepper

Sauce
- 1 teaspoon finely chopped garlic
- 4 tablespoons black soy sauce
- 1/2 teaspoon sugar
- 1/2 teaspoon ground cinnamon
- 4 tablespoons chili oil
- 1 tablespoon finely sliced scallion (spring onion)

Most *wonton* wrappers are 3–4 in (8–10 cm) square. Turn a small Chinese soup bowl or a glass upside down on the wrappers and cut around the bowl or rim of the glass with a sharp knife to form circles.

Combine pork, egg, ginger, rice wine, salt, and pepper. Put a heaped teaspoonful of this in the center of a wrapper. Use your fingertip to smear a little water around the edge of the circle, then fold across to make a semicircle, pressing firmly to enclose the filling. When all the dumplings are ready, drop in rapidly boiling water and simmer for 2–3 minutes. Drain.

Take 4 bowls and prepare the sauce separately for each portion. Put 1/4 teaspoon garlic, 1 tablespoon black soy sauce, a pinch of sugar and a pinch of cinnamon in the bottom of each bowl. Divide the boiled dumplings among the 4 bowls and pour 1 tablespoon chili oil over each serving. Garnish with a little scallion. Stir before eating.

Duck Giblets (below right) and Marinated Sliced Beef (below left)

Restorative and satisfying, Chinese soups are usually drunk throughout a meal. Don't despair at the "exoticism" of some of the ingredients; most can be found in Asian food shops.

Dong Gua Tang
Winter Melon Soup

- 1 large winter melon
- 1 teaspoon salt
- 6 cups (1 1/2 liters) gourmet or chicken stock (page 47)
- 4 oz (125 g) straw mushrooms, halved
- 1/3 cup (50 g) shredded cooked chicken breast
- 1/3 cup (50 g) shredded cooked duck (or double the amount of chicken)
- 1/3 cup (50 g) shredded cooked liver (duck, chicken or pork)
- 1/4 cup (25 g) cooked or canned crabmeat
- 1/4 cup (50 g) canned asparagus tips, drained
- 6 dried lotus nuts, soaked, peeled and hard core removed
- Salt to taste

Choose a winter melon that will hold at least 6 cups liquid. Cut off the top or, if the melon is very large, slice it in half. Carve the skin decoratively. Remove central fiber and seeds. Scrape out some of the flesh, leaving about 3/4 in (2 cm) flesh still clinging to the skin. Sprinkle the inside with salt and put winter melon in a large deep pan with boiling water to cover. Simmer for 30 minutes, drain and then put in a large steamer and steam for another 30 minutes.

Bring the stock to a boil and pour into the melon. Cover and steam for 25 minutes. Add all other ingredients and serve. Add some of the winter melon flesh, scraped out with a spoon, when serving the soup in individual bowls.

Yu Chi Tang
Shark's Fin Soup

Shark's fin is a real gourmet item, enjoyed for its texture and its ability to absorb the flavors of other ingredients.

- 1 oz (30 g) shredded dried shark's fin
- 3 cups (750 ml) gourmet or chicken stock (page 47)
- 3 teaspoons black soy sauce
- 1/2 teaspoon salt
- 1/4 teaspoon ground white pepper
- 1 1/4 in (3 cm) ginger, very finely shredded
- 1/3 cup (50 g) finely shredded cooked chicken
- 2 tablespoons cornstarch, blended with water
- 1 teaspoon shallot oil (see Note)
- 1/3 oz (10 g) dried scallops (optional)

Shark's Fin Soup

- 1/3 oz (10 g) dried fish maw (optional)
- 1 1/2 cups (375 ml) chicken stock (optional)
- 1 teaspoon dry sherry (optional)
- 1/2 in (1 cm) ginger, sliced (optional)
- 1 scallion (spring onion) (optional)
- 1 heaped tablespoon finely shredded Yunnan ham

Soak dried shark's fin in hot water for about 30 minutes until swollen and transparent. Drain.

Heat stock with soy sauce, shallot oil, salt, and pepper, then add shark's fin, scallops, fish maw, ginger, and chicken. Thicken with cornstarch and serve. Garnish with shredded Yunnan ham. In southern China, a few drops of black rice vinegar are generally added to the soup at the table.

The scallops and fish maw depicted in the photograph opposite are optional, and may be ready-bought in dried form. To prepare the scallops, place them in a bowl containing chicken stock, dry sherry, ginger, and scallion. Steam in a steamer until the scallops are soft.

To prepare the fish maw, place them in a bowl, pour enough hot water over to soak them, cover with a lid, and set aside until soft.

Note: To make shallot oil, peel and slice about 8 shallots.

Heat 1 cup of oil, add the shallots and simmer in the oil until the shallots are golden. Do not allow the shallots to burn or the flavor will be bitter. Drain and store the oil in a jar with a tight-fitting lid.

Hong Tang Dan Dan Mian
Hot and Spicy Hawker Noodles

It's hard to think of any time of day when noodles are not popular in China; they're eaten for breakfast, as a mid-morning snack, for lunch, as something to keep you going until dinner and as a late-night restorative. This spicy favorite, often sold by mobile vendors or at streetside stalls, originates in Sichuan.

- 1 lb (500g) fresh wheat-flour noodles, or 3/4 lb (375 g) narrow flat dried noodles
- 1 teaspoon cooking oil
- 8 oz (250 g) lean pork, very finely minced
- 1/2 cup (100 g) preserved salted radish, finely chopped
- 2 cups (500 ml) chicken stock
- 4 tablespoons black soy sauce
- 1 1/2 tablespoons black rice vinegar
- 1 tablespoon very finely chopped garlic
- 2 teaspoons Sichuan pepper oil (page 47)

Winter Melon Soup

- 2 teaspoons sesame oil
- 1 teaspoon chili oil (page 47)
- 1 teaspoon ground
  white pepper
- 1 heaped tablespoon finely sliced
  scallion (spring onion)

Set the noodles aside for blanching later. Heat cooking oil and stir fry the pork over very high heat for 2–3 minutes, until cooked. Mix well with the preserved radish and set aside.

Heat chicken stock and add all other ingredients except noodles and scallion. Keep stock warm while blanching noodles in rapidly boiling water for 1 minute.

Drain noodles and divide among 4 small bowls. Pour over hot stock, top with the pork mixture, garnish with scallion and serve.

HELPFUL HINT
Preserved salted radish is available from Asian stores. If unavailable use Tientsin preserved vegetables (*tung choy*) instead if you like.

Chao Mian Xian
Fried Noodles Xiamen Style

Very fine fresh wheat-flour noodles, like angel-hair pasta, are used for this dish. Try to get fresh ones as the texture is superior to dried noodles.

- 10 oz (300 g) small shrimp
- 1 lb (500 g) fresh wheat-flour
  noodles
- Oil for deep-frying
- 2 tablespoons very finely chopped
  garlic
- 7 oz (200 g) bamboo shoots, in
  matchstick shreds
- 4 oz (125 g) lean pork, finely
  shredded
- 1 small carrot, in matchstick shreds
- 3–4 dried black mushrooms,
  soaked and finely shredded
- 1/4 cup chopped Chinese coarse
  chives
- 2 tablespoons Chinese rice wine
- 1 teaspoon salt
- 1/2 teaspoon ground white pepper
- 4 shallots, sliced and deep-fried
  until golden brown

*Hot and Spicy
Hawker Noodles*

Peel shrimp, remove heads and devein. Keep shrimp aside and put heads and shells in a pan with 1 cup (250 ml) water. Bring to a boil, then simmer 10 minutes. Strain through a sieve, pressing on heads and shells to extract the maximum stock. Set aside.

Shake the noodles to separate if using fresh noodles, then deep fry in very hot oil for a few seconds until golden brown. Drain well and set aside, discarding oil. If using dried noodles, blanch in boiling water until just softened.

Put 1 tablespoon of fresh oil into the wok, stir fry the garlic for a few seconds, then add the shrimp, bamboo shoots, pork, carrot, mushrooms, and chives. Stir- fry until the pork and shrimp change color. Pour in 1/2 (125 ml) cup of the reserved shrimp stock, add wine, salt and pepper and simmer, uncovered, for 5 minutes, stirring from time to time. Add the noodles and continue stir-frying, mixing well, for another 5 minutes. Serve garnished with fried shallots.

Chengdu Leng Mian
Cold Chengdu Noodles

- 1 lb (500 g) fresh wheat-flour
  noodles, boiled, drained and
  chilled
- 3/4 cup beansprouts, blanched for
  a few seconds and chilled
- 1 scallion (spring onion), finely
  sliced

Sauce
- 2 tablespoons very finely chopped
  ginger
- 1 tablespoon very finely chopped
  garlic
- 1 tablespoon sesame paste
- 1 tablespoon peanut butter
- 1 teaspoon peanut oil or
  cooking oil
- 3 tablespoons black soy sauce
- 2 teaspoons sugar
- 2 teaspoons black rice vinegar
- 1 teaspoon sesame oil
- 1 teaspoon chili oil

Combine all sauce ingredients in a bowl, mixing well. Add the noodles and stir to coat the noodles with the sauce, then add bean sprouts and mix carefully with chopsticks or a fork, taking care not to break the sprouts. Divide among 4 bowls and sprinkle each portion with a little scallion.

Cold Chengdu Noodles

Yu Xiang Qie Zi
Fragrant Eggplant with Pork

8 oz (250g) eggplant (aubergine), peeled and cut in 3 x 1/2-in (8 x 1-cm) pieces
Oil for deep-frying
1/4 cup (50 g) ground lean pork
2 tablespoons dried shrimp, soaked and very finely chopped
2 teaspoons chili paste
1 teaspoon salted soy beans, mashed
2 teaspoons very finely sliced scallion (spring onion)
1 teaspoon very finely chopped soaked dried black mushroom
1 cup (250 ml) chicken stock
1 teaspoon Chinese rice wine
1 teaspoon sesame oil
2 teaspoons commercial sweet and sour sauce
1/2 teaspoon dark soy sauce
1/4 teaspoon salt
1 teaspoon cornflour, mixed with water
Cilantro (coriander) leaves to garnish

Deep-fry the eggplant pieces in very hot oil for 1 minute. Drain and set aside.

Pour out all but 2 teaspoons of the oil and stir-fry pork over high heat for 2 minutes. Add dried shrimp, chili paste, salted soy beans, 1 teaspoon of the scallion and the mushrooms. Stir-fry for 30 seconds, then add all remaining ingredients, except remaining scallion, cornflour, and cilantro. Heat, then put in eggplant and cook another 30 seconds. Thicken with cornflour and serve garnished with the cilantro leaves and remaining scallion.

Ma Po Dou Fu
Spicy Beancurd with Minced Beef

The dominant ingredient is meltingly soft beancurd laced with pungent Sichuan seasonings.

3 tablespoons oil (or chili oil)
4 oz (125 g) minced lean beef
1 tablespoon chopped, salted black beans
1 tablespoon chopped, salted soy beans
1 tablespoon very finely chopped garlic
1 tablespoon very finely chopped ginger
2 tablespoons chili paste
2–3 scallions (spring onions), finely sliced
1 cup (250 ml) chicken or beef stock
1 lb (500 g) soft beancurd, diced
1 tablespoon black soy sauce
Salt to taste
2 teaspoons cornflour, blended with water
1 teaspoon powdered Sichuan peppercorns

Heat oil and stir-fry beef and black beans for 3–4 minutes. Add salted soy beans, ginger, garlic, chili paste, and half the scallion. Stir-fry for another 2 minutes, then add the stock and beancurd.

Simmer for 5 minutes, season with soy sauce and salt, then thicken with cornflour. Sprinkle with Sichuan pepper and scallion, then serve.

Fragrant Eggplant with Pork (top) and Stir-fried Mixed Vegetables (bottom)

Jiang Cong Chao Zhu Gan
Stir-fried Pork Liver

10 oz (300 g) pork liver, thinly sliced
2 tablespoons Chinese rice wine
2 teaspoons oil
2 teaspoons finely chopped garlic
1 1/4 in (3 cm) ginger, finely sliced
1 scallion (spring onion), cut in 1 1/4-in (3 cm) lengths
1/2 red chili, deseeded and sliced (optional)
1 teaspoon chicken stock powder
1 teaspoon light soy sauce
1/2 teaspoon sugar
1 teaspoon cornstarch, blended with water

Marinate liver with wine for about 5 minutes. Heat oil and fry the garlic for a few seconds, then add drained liver, ginger, scallion, and chili (if using). Stir-fry over high heat for a few seconds. Add stock powder, soy sauce, and sugar and continue stir-frying for 1–2 minutes, until the liver is cooked. Thicken with cornstarch and serve immediately.

Chao Qing Cai
Stir-fried Mixed Vegetables

1/2 cup (75 g) snow peas, ends trimmed
2 teaspoons oil
Pinch of salt
1/4 teaspoon sugar
3 oz (90 g) bamboo shoots, quartered lengthwise then cut in 2-in (5-cm) lengths
6–8 dried black mushrooms, soaked
1 cup (250 ml) chicken stock
1 teaspoon oyster sauce
1/4 teaspoon sesame oil
1/4 teaspoon salt
1/4 teaspoon dark soy sauce
dash of ground white pepper
1 teaspoon cornflour, blended with water

Blanch snow peas in boiling water for 5 seconds, then drain. Heat oil and stir-fry blanched snow peas with salt and sugar for 30 seconds. Remove from wok. Add bamboo shoots, mushrooms, chicken stock and all seasonings and bring to a boil. Simmer 1 minute, add the snow peas, then thicken with cornstarch. Serve immediately.

Stir-fried Pork Liver

Shuan Yang Rou
Mongolian Lamb Hotpot

Mongolian Hotpot is popular in winter and as a reunion dinner, with everyone sitting around in a cozy warm circle, cooking their own portions of food in the bubbling hotpot

1 lb (500 g) boneless lamb leg
1–2 cakes beancurd, sliced
3 cups (200 g) Napa cabbage, coarsely chopped
4 oz (125 g) dried rice vermicelli, soaked in hot water to soften

Stock
1 1/4 in (3 cm) ginger, finely sliced
1 scallion (spring onion), coarsely chopped
2 teaspoons dark soy sauce
6 cups (1 1/2 liters) stock made from lamb leg bone boiled with water

Dips and Garnishes
1/2 cup (125 ml) sesame paste
2 tablespoons fermented beancurd, mashed
1/2 cup (125 ml) light soy sauce
1/2 cup (125 ml) red rice vinegar
1/2 cup (125 ml) Chinese rice wine
1/4 cup (60 ml) chili oil (page 47)
4 tablespoons pickled garlic
Bunch of cilantro (coriander) leaves, chopped

Slice the lamb paper thin, leaving on a little of the fat (this is typical in Beijing, but can be omitted if preferred). Roll up the slices and arrange on a plate. Put the beancurd and cabbage on separate plates, and divide the soaked vermicelli among 6 individual soup bowls.

Arrange all dips and garnishes in small bowls and place on the table for diners to use according to taste.

Heat all stock ingredients in a pan, then carefully transfer to a hotpot. Bring back to a boil. Each diner cooks his own portions of meat, beancurd, and cabbage, seasoning them afterwards with the dip of his choice, accompanied by pieces of pickled garlic and cilantro. When all the ingredients are used, the rich stock is poured into the soup bowls over the noodles and eaten as a final course.

Mongolian Lamb Hotpot

Hei Jiao Niu Rou
Beef with Black Pepper

Simple and quick to prepare, this Sichuan dish tastes like a flavor-enhanced version of Western black pepper steak, with Sichuan peppercorns adding a distinctive difference.

8 oz (250 g) beef fillet, trimmed and cut in 1-in (2 1/2-cm) cubes
2 tablespoons Chinese rice wine
1 tablespoon water
1/2 teaspoon salt
1/4 teaspoon ground white pepper
Oil for deep-frying
1 tablespoon finely chopped garlic
2 teaspoons coarsely crushed black peppercorns
1 teaspoon crushed Sichuan peppercorns
2 teaspoons oyster sauce
2 teaspoons light soy sauce
1 teaspoon sesame oil
Sliced lettuce for garnish

Put beef in a bowl and sprinkle with wine, water, salt and white pepper. Massage well for about 30 seconds until all the liquid is absorbed by the beef.

Heat oil and deep-fry the beef over very high heat for 30 seconds. Drain and set aside. Tip out all but 1 teaspoon of oil and stir fry the garlic for a few seconds, then add the beef and all other ingredients, except for the lettuce. Stir-fry for a few seconds until well mixed and serve immediately on a bed of shredded lettuce.

HELPFUL HINT
If using a charcoal hotpot for the Mongolian Hotpot recipe, light charcoal over a gas flame and then use tongs to insert it down the central chimney of the hotpot and into the bottom.

Beef with Black Pepper

Stuffed Vegetables and Beancurd

Guang Dong Niang San Bao

Stuffed Vegetables and Beancurd

This Cantonese and Hakka favorite uses a selection of vegetables and beancurd stuffed with a shrimp filling. The sauce, flavored with salted black beans, gives an emphatic salty tang to the delicate stuffed vegetables.

1 large green bell pepper (capsicum)
1 long thin eggplant (aubergine)
1 hard beancurd
1 teaspoon cornflour
Oil for deep-frying

Stuffing
1 cup (200 g) peeled shrimp, chopped
1/4 cup (50 g) lard (pork fat), chopped
1 tablespoon black moss fungus, soaked to soften
1/2 teaspoon salt
Dash of ground white pepper

Sauce
1 teaspoon salted black beans, mashed slightly with the back of a spoon
1 teaspoon finely chopped red chili
1 teaspoon very finely chopped garlic
1 teaspoon very finely chopped ginger
1 cup (250 ml) chicken stock
1/2 teaspoon black soy sauce
2 teaspoons cornflour, blended with water

Prepare the stuffing first by blending together all ingredients. Set aside.

Cut the green pepper into four and discard seeds. Cut the eggplant across into 1 1/2-in (4- cm) lengths and make a lengthwise slit down one side to form a pocket for the stuffing. Cut beancurd into four and slit a pocket in each. Sprinkle the inside of the vegetables and beancurd with cornflour to help make the stuffing adhere, then fill with the stuffing.

Heat oil in a wok and deep-fry the stuffed items, a few at a time, until golden and cooked. Remove and set aside, leaving 1 teaspoon of oil in the wok for preparing the sauce.

To make the sauce, stir-fry the black beans, chili, garlic, and ginger for a few seconds until fragrant, then add the stock and soy sauce. Heat, then add the fried vegetables and beancurd and simmer for 1 minute. Thicken with cornflour and serve immediately.

HELPFUL HINT
Stuffed Vegetables and Beancurd: Other vegetables which can be stuffed include bitter gourd and seeded green or red chilies. The stuffing can be prepared in advance.

Xiang Gu Chao Jiao Bai

Bamboo Shoots with Mushrooms

The special type of bamboo shoot used for this dish in southern China has an excellent texture and flavor. If fresh *jiao bai* is available, substitute canned bamboo shoots.

12 oz (375 g) *jiao bai* or bamboo shoots
2 teaspoons oil
1 heaped teaspoon very finely chopped garlic
10 dried black mushrooms, soaked
1 teaspoon Chinese rice wine
1 teaspoon chicken stock powder
1 teaspoon sugar
1/2 teaspoon salt

If using fresh *jiao bai*, peel off the outer layer, then slice coarsely. If using canned bamboo shoots, simmer in boiling water for 5 minutes, drain and slice coarsely.

Heat oil in a wok and stir-fry the garlic and mushrooms until fragrant. Add the jiao bai or bamboo shoots and all seasonings and stir-fry for 1–2 minutes. Serve immediately.

Chao Zhou Zheng Chang Yu

Teochew Steamed Pomfret

1 fresh pomfret, pompano, butter fish or plaice, about 1 1/2 lb (750 g)
1/2 cup (100 g) salted mustard cabbage, soaked and finely sliced
1 tomato, deseeded and cut in strips
2 sour salted plums (available in jars)
1 red chili, deseeded and finely shredded
3 in (8 cm) celery stalk, finely shredded
1 scallion (spring onion), chopped in 1 1/2-in (4-cm) lengths
3 in (8 cm) ginger, finely shredded
1 cake beancurd, shredded
1 dried black mushroom, soaked and finely shredded
2 teaspoons chicken stock powder
1/2 teaspoon sugar
1/4 teaspoon salt
Cilantro (coriander) leaf to garnish peas

Clean the fish inside and out and wipe dry. Place fish on an oval plate and arrange over all the ingredients, except chicken stock powder, sugar and salt. Sprinkle with the stock powder, sugar and salt and put inside a large steamer. Steam over high heat for about 8 minutes, until the fish is cooked. Take care not to overcook for optimum texture and flavor. Garnish with cilantro leaf.

Teochew Steamed Pomfret

Yu Xiang Cui Pi Gui Yu
Crispy Fried Mandarin Fish

The Chinese believe that fresh-water fish from lakes, rivers and fish ponds are more delicate in flavor and texture than fish from the sea. Although this recipe calls for freshwater Mandarin fish, fine-textured ocean fish such as perch, grouper, bream or snapper could be substituted.

1 fresh fish (see above), 1¹/₂–2 lb (³/₄–1 kg), cleaned and scaled
3 in (8 cm) ginger, finely sliced
1 scallion (spring onion), chopped coarsely
1 teaspoon ground white pepper
¹/₂ cup (125 ml) Chinese rice wine
2 tablespoons cornstarch
Oil for deep-frying
1 scallion (spring onion), finely sliced for garnish

Sauce
1–2 tablespoons chili paste
1¹/₂ teaspoons finely chopped garlic
1¹/₂ teaspoons finely chopped ginger
1¹/₂ teaspoons white rice vinegar
1 teaspoon sugar
¹/₂ teaspoon salt
³/₄ cup (185 ml) chicken stock
1 scallion (spring onion), finely sliced
2 teaspoons cornstarch, blended with water

Cut 4 or 5 deep diagonal slashes on each side of the fish to help it cook more quickly. Marinate the fish for 15 minutes with ginger, chopped scallion, pepper, and rice wine. Drain fish and scrape off any pieces of the marinade. Dry thoroughly.

Heat a wok and add oil. When the oil is hot, sprinkle the fish on both sides with corn-starch, shaking it to remove any excess. Carefully lower the fish into the oil and cook, over moderate heat, for about 5–8 minutes until golden brown and cooked through. Drain and keep warm on a serving dish.

Discard all but 1 teaspoon of the frying oil. To prepare the sauce, stir-fry the chili paste, garlic and ginger for a few seconds until fragrant, then add all other ingredients, except cornstarch. Simmer for 2 minutes, then thicken with cornstarch. Pour the sauce over the fish and garnish with scallion. Serve immediately.

Shrimp-stuffed Lychees

Zeng Cheng Bai Hua Niang Xian Guo
Shrimp-stuffed Lychees

A fine example of the creativity and delicacy of Cantonese food. If you cannot obtain fresh lychees, use canned fruit, but rinse well to remove any sugar syrup.

8 oz (250 g) peeled shrimp, finely chopped or blended
1 teaspoon salt
1 teaspoon cornstarch
¹/₄ teaspoon ground white pepper
10 fresh or canned lychees, peeled and stones removed
Few lettuce leaves for garnish
Cilantro (coriander) leaf to garnish
Chili flakes to garnish (optional)

Sauce
1 cup (250 ml) chicken stock
1 teaspoon cooking oil
¹/₂ teaspoon salt
1 teaspoon cornstarch, mixed with water
2 egg whites

Mix together the shrimp, salt, cornstarch and pepper. Divide mixture in 10 portions. Sprinkle the inside of each lychee with a dusting of additional corn-starch and stuff with the shrimp paste, pushing it in well. Put the lychees on a plate and steam over high heat for 6–8 minutes,

until the shrimp filling is firm and cooked.

Arrange lettuce leaves in a shallow bowl and put the lychees on top. Prepare sauce by bringing stock, oil and salt to a boil. Lower heat and thicken with cornstarch, then stir in the egg white and remove from the heat. Pour over the lychees and serve immediately.

Suan Rong Zheng Dan Cai
Steamed Mussels with Minced Garlic

This way of cooking mussels can be used also for oysters or clams. The shellfish can be boiled in advance, and refrigerated until just before you are ready to steam them.

12 fresh mussels or oysters, or 24 clams
6–8 cloves garlic
1 teaspoon oil
1 teaspoon chicken stock powder
1 teaspoon sugar
¹/₂ teaspoon light soy sauce
1 red chili, finely chopped
1 scallion (spring onion), finely sliced
Cilantro (coriander) leaf (optional)

Bring a wok full of water to a boil. Put in mussels or other shellfish and cook until the shells open. Remove, drain, and discard one side of the shell. Put the half-shell with the mussel attached on a plate.

Slice half the garlic and fry gently in oil until crisp and golden. Drain and set aside. Chop the remaining garlic very finely and scatter a little over each mussel. Sprinkle with chicken stock powder, sugar and soy sauce. Put inside a steamer and cook over high heat for 3 minutes.

Garnish with the fried garlic, chili, scallion, and cilantro and serve immediately.

Steamed Mussels with Minced Garlic (outside of plate)

You Bao You Yu Juan
Squid with Bamboo Shoots

As is common in Asia, Chinese cooks often score the squid so that it has an attractive "pine cone" appearance after cooking.

- 1 lb (500 g) fresh squid, peeled and cleaned
- 1 cup (100 g) bamboo shoots
- 1/4 cucumber
- 1 carrot
- Oil for deep-frying
- 1 teaspoon finely chopped garlic
- 1 scallion (spring onion), sliced
- 2 tablespoons Chinese rice wine
- 1 teaspoon salt
- 1 teaspoon cornstarch, blended with water

Cut the cleaned squid in half lengthwise and score each piece with a sharp knife in a diamond pattern, taking care not to cut right through the flesh. Cut the scored squid into pieces about 2 1/2 x 3/4 in (6 x 2 cm). Dry thoroughly.

Thinly slice bamboo shoots, cucumber, and carrot lengthwise, then cut into 2-in (5-cm) pieces.

Heat oil and, when very hot, deep-fry the squid for 5 seconds only. Drain and set aside. Pour out all but 1 teaspoon of the oil and reheat it. Stir-fry the garlic for a few seconds until fragrant, then add the squid and stir-fry for 1 minute. Add the bamboo shoots, cucumber, carrot, and scallion and stir-fry for 1 minute. Season with rice wine and salt, then thicken with cornstarch. Serve immediately.

Beggar's Chicken

Qi Gai Ji
Beggar's Chicken

According to legend, this dish was created by a poor man who stole a chicken. He was about to cook it on a fire when the landowner passed by. To conceal it, he hastily wrapped the chicken in mud and tossed it on the fire. Later, when the danger had passed, he broke open the mud casing to find a succulent cooked bird inside. This version encases the chicken in an edible bread dough instead of mud!

- 1 fresh chicken, about 3 lb (1 1/2 kg), cleaned
- 2 dried lotus leaves or parchment pepper

Stuffing
- 5 oz (150 g) pork, finely shredded
- 3 oz (90 g) preserved dried vegetable (*mei cai*), finely chopped
- 5 dried black mushrooms, soaked and shredded
- 3 in (8 cm) ginger, finely shredded
- 1–2 scallions (spring onions), finely sliced
- 2 teaspoons chicken stock powder
- 2 teaspoons sugar
- 2 teaspoons light soy sauce
- 3 tablespoons rice wine
- Pinch of powdered ginger

Dough
- 8 cups (1 kg) all-purpose (plain) flour
- 4 teaspoons dried yeast
- 2 tablespoons sugar
- 1 tablespoon salt
- 2 eggs, beaten
- 2 cups (500 ml) warm water

Make the dough wrapping first. Sift flour into a bowl, add all other ingredients and mix well to make a pliable dough. Add a little more water or flour if necessary to achieve the right consistency. Cover and leave to rise while preparing chicken.

Combine all ingredients for the stuffing, mixing well. Stuff the chicken and close each end with a strong toothpick. Wrap in the lotus leaves, overlapping to enclose the chicken. Put on a plate and steam over high heat for 30 minutes.

Knead the dough and roll out into a rectangle large enough to enclose the chicken. Put steamed chicken in the dough and close, pinching well to seal. Bake at 375°F (190°C, gas mark 5) until the dough is golden brown (about 15 minutes). Cut open at the table and serve the chicken and stuffing. The dough can also be eaten.

Squid with Bamboo Shoots

Cui Pi San Dong Ji
Deep-fried Shandong Chicken

Like many Chinese recipes, this dish from the northeastern province of Shandong involves two methods of cooking: the chicken is first simmered very gently, then deep-fried. It is served with a clear, non-thickened sauce with a slightly hot and sour edge to it. This is a dish that can be partially prepared in advance; simmer and dry the chicken and keep for several hours before the final frying.

1 fresh chicken, about 2^1/2 lb (1^1/4 kg)
^{1}/2 teaspoon salt
Oil for deep-frying
1 scallion (spring onion), white part only, shredded
4 cloves garlic, finely chopped and deep-fried

Sauce
1 red chili, deseeded and sliced
4 cloves garlic, sliced
1 teaspoon chili paste
1 cup (250 ml) chicken stock
1 tablespoon light soy sauce
^{1}/4 cup (60 ml) white rice vinegar
2 tablespoons sugar or honey
Salt to taste

Rub the chicken inside and out with salt and set aside for 30 minutes. Bring a large pot of water to a boil and put in the chicken. Lower heat to the minimum and simmer the chicken for 30 minutes. Drain the chicken, pat dry and hang in an airy place to dry thoroughly.

Just before the dish is required, heat oil for deep frying in a wok. To ensure a crisp texture, make sure the chicken is thoroughly dry (a brief session with a hair dryer sometimes helps). Lower the whole chicken, breast side down, into the oil and fry for about 5 minutes until golden brown. Turn and fry the other side for another 5 minutes. Remove chicken from oil, drain, chop into bite-sized pieces and arrange on a serving dish deep enough to contain 1^1/2 cups (375 ml) sauce.

Tip out all the oil from the wok but do not wipe. Add the sauce ingredients and simmer for 2 minutes. Pour over the chicken and garnish with scallion and fried garlic.

HELPFUL HINT
Dried chilies give this dish a smoky finish, so do try to get them. If using fresh chilies, don't dry-fry but add with the garlic and ginger so that they cook through.

Gong Bao Ji Ding
Chicken with Dried Chilies

1 lb (500 g) chicken breast
^{1}/2 teaspoon salt
1 egg white
2 tablespoons Chinese rice wine
2 teaspoons cornstarch
Oil for deep-frying
1 teaspoon finely chopped garlic
1 teaspoon finely chopped ginger
1 tablespoon black soy sauce
1 tablespoon white rice vinegar
1 teaspoon sugar
2–3 dried chilies, cut in ^{1}/2-in (1-cm) pieces, dry-fried until crisp and lightly browned
1 tablespoon finely sliced scallion (spring onion)
2 tablespoons fried peanuts, skinned

Cut the chicken breast into pieces about ^{1}/4 in x ^{3}/4 in (^{1}/2 x 2 cm). Mix the chicken pieces well with salt, egg white, wine and cornstarch. Set aside for 2–3 minutes while heating oil for deep-frying. Deep-fry the chicken over very high heat for about 30 seconds, drain and set aside.

Tip out all but 1 teaspoon of oil from the wok. stir-fry the garlic and ginger for a few seconds, then add soy sauce, vinegar, and sugar. Stir well and put in the chicken, dried chilies and scallion and and stir-fry for 3–4 minutes. Stir in the fried peanuts and serve immediately.

Chicken with Dried Chilies

Pi Pa Xia
Pi Pa Shrimp

This dish is fancifully named after the *pi pa*, a classical Chinese stringed instrument, which the shrimp are thought to resemble. Whole shrimp are dipped into a blended shrimp paste and steamed. They can be set aside for a few hours and deep-fried just before serving.

12 large shrimp
Oil for deep-frying
1 egg white, lightly beaten
2 tablespoons cornstarch
12 small Chinese wine cups or egg cups

Shrimp Paste
10 oz (300 g) shrimp
6 tablespoons lard, diced
1 dried black mushroom, soaked and finely chopped
1 tablespoon finely chopped bamboo shoot or water chestnut
1 teaspoon salt
2 egg whites
2 tablespoons cornstarch

Sauce
1 cup (250 ml) chicken stock
1 teaspoon rice wine
Salt to taste
2 teaspoons cornstarch, blended with water

Prepare the shrimp paste first. Peel the shrimp, discarding heads, tails, and shells. Devein. Process shrimp in a blender for a few seconds with the diced lard.

Add all other shrimp paste ingredients and process just until well blended. Grease tiny Chinese wine or egg cups with a little oil, then divide the shrimp paste among these, packing it in firmly.

Peel the medium shrimp, discarding heads and shells but leaving on the tail for a more decorative appearance. Push the head end of each shrimp into a paste-filled cup, leaving the tail end protruding. Repeat until all the shrimp are used up, then steam for 20 minutes. Allow to cool, then remove from the cups with the tip of a knife.

Just before the dish is required, prepare the sauce by bringing stock, wine and salt to a boil. Thicken with cornstarch and keep warm.

Heat oil for deep-frying in a wok. Dust each steamed shrimp with a little cornstarch, dip into the egg white and deep-fry until golden brown. Put on a serving dish and pour the sauce over the top.

Deep-fried Shandong Chicken

The most popular Chinese dessert is a platter of sliced, fresh fruits. For more formal banquets one of the desserts in this section may be served; however, these are more commonly eaten as snacks or as a late-night supper.

Bing Tang Yin Er
White Fungus with Melon Balls

White fungus is virtually tasteless, but is prized for its texture as well as its health-giving properties. Serve warm or chilled.

1¹/2 oz (50 g) dried white fungus
¹/2 cup (90 g) rock sugar
3 cups (750 ml) water
3 oz (90 g) Hami melon, rock melon or honeydew

Wash the fungus well, then soak in warm water for 1 hour. Remove the stems and any tough portions and cut into bite-sized pieces. Set aside.

Heat rock sugar and water in a pan, stirring until sugar dissolves. Pour into a bowl and add the white fungus. Cover the bowl and put in a steamer. Steam for 1¹/2 hours until the fungus is soft. Leave to cool, then chill.

Just before serving, make small balls of the melon. Add to the chilled fungus and serve in small individual bowls.

Lian Zi Hong Dou Sha
Red Bean Soup

¹/2 cup (50 g) dried or canned lotus nuts
1 cup (250 g) dried red azuki beans
1 strip dried or fresh orange peel
4 cups (1 liter) water
¹/2–³/4 cup sugar

Red Bean Pancakes

White Fungus with Melon Balls

If using dried lotus nuts, soak in hot water for 1¹/2 hours, drain, peel and use a toothpick to push out the bitter central core. If using canned nuts, drain and discard liquid.

Soak the red beans in warm water to cover for 30 minutes. Drain and combine with orange peel and water and simmer gently, covered, for 1 hour. Add the lotus nuts and cook for 1 more hour. Add sugar to taste and stir until dissolved. Serve warm.

Dou Sha Wo Bing
Red Bean Pancakes

If canned red bean paste is not available, soak ¹/2 cup red beans for 2 hours. Steam until soft with a strip of dried orange peel. Mash, adding sugar to taste.

1¹/4 cups (150 g) all-purpose (plain) flour
¹/4 teaspoon custard powder
1 egg
Water to mix
4 oz (125 g) red bean paste
Oil for shallow-frying

Combine flour, custard powder, egg, and sufficient water to make a batter the consistency of thin cream. Heat wok and grease with 1 teaspoon oil, swirling the wok around so that the oil covers all sides. Pour in about ¹/4 cup of the batter and swirl the wok around to make a thin pancake. Cook until the top of the pancake has set and the underside is golden. Remove, set aside and repeat until the batter is used up.

Place the pancakes, browned side up, on a flat surface. Spread the center of each pancake with bean paste and fold in the edges to enclose the paste. Heat a little oil in a wok and fry the stuffed pancake until golden. Cut into bite-sized pieces and serve.

Ba Si Ping Guo
Candied Apples

Make sure you have everything laid out before you start cooking.

4 large green apples, peeled, cored and cut into 8 slices
Oil for deep-frying

Batter
1 cup (125 g) all-purpose (plain) flour
2 tablespoons cornstarch
1 teaspoon baking soda
¹/2 beaten egg
Water as required

Syrup
¹/2 cup sugar
2 tablespoons water

Prepare the batter by combining all ingredients, adding enough water to achieve the consistency of a thick cream.

Heat the sugar and water over moderate heat, stirring, until the syrup turns golden brown. Keep warm.

Ready a bowl of iced water and a greased serving dish. Heat the oil until very hot. Dip slices of apple, a few at a time, into the batter and fry until golden brown. Remove from oil, drain, and dip into the syrup, turning to coat thoroughly. Plunge apple slices into the iced water to set the syrup into a toffee-like coating, then put on the serving dish. Serve immediately.

Chili Oil

3/4 cup (175 ml) peanut oil
1 tablespoon Sichuan peppercorns
2 dried chilies, sliced

Heat wok and add oil, peppercorns and chilies. Cook over low heat for 10 minutes. Allow to cool, then store in a covered jar for 2–3 days. Strain and discard peppercorns and chilies. Store oil in a tightly sealed jar and keep in a cool place for up to 6 months.

Sichuan Pepper Oil

2 tablespoons Sichuan peppercorns
3/4 cup (175 ml) peanut oil

Stir-fry peppercorns in dry wok until fragrant. Add the oil and cook over low heat for 10 minutes. Allow to cool, then store in a covered jar for 2–3 days. Strain and discard peppercorns. Store oil in a tightly sealed jar and keep in a cool place for up to 6 months.

Gourmet Stock

1 lb (500 g) pork ribs, blanched
12 oz (375 g) chicken pieces, blanched
12 oz (375 g) duck pieces, blanched
12 oz (375 g) smoked ham hock
2 spring onions, coarsely chopped
2 in (5 cm) ginger, sliced
1/4 cup (60 ml) Chinese rice wine
20 cups (5 liters) water

Combine all ingredients and simmer, uncovered, for 2 hours. Strain stock through cheesecloth.

Chicken Stock

1 old hen or 3 lb (1 1/2 kg) chicken pieces
1 celery stalk, with leaves still attached, chopped
2 in (5 cm) ginger, bruised
10 cups (2 1/2 liters) water

Plunge the hen or chicken pieces into a large pan of boiling water and simmer for 1 minute. Discard water and refill pan with water and all other ingredients. Bring to a boil and simmer gently,

uncovered, for 2 hours. Keep removing any scum or impurities as they rise to the top of the pan. Strain stock through cheesecloth. This can be made in large quantities and frozen in smaller portions for future use.

Pickled Garlic

30 green chilies, sliced
4 cups (1 liter) white rice vinegar
1 teaspoon salt

Bring water to a boil in a pan, add the garlic and remove from the heat. Add remaining ingredients and leave to cool. Put garlic in a covered jar, top with liquid and marinate for 3 days before using. Drain and serve as an accompaniment or appetizer.

Ginger Garlic Sauce

1 oz (30 g) young ginger
6 cloves garlic
1 teaspoon salt
1 teaspoon sugar
1 teaspoon sesame oil
1 tablespoon cooking oil

Blend ginger and garlic. Combine with all other ingredients. Put in a covered jar and shake just before serving. Good with boiled meats.

Chili Garlic Sauce

5 red chilies, chopped
3 cloves garlic, chopped
3 tablespoons white rice vinegar
1 teaspoon sugar
1/2 teaspoon sal

Process all ingredients in a blender until fine. Keep refrigerated in a covered jar. Serve with steamed poultry or with rice and other cooked dishes

Soy and Ginger Dip

2 teaspoons light soy sauce
2 tablespoons very finely chopped ginger
1 tablespoon finely sliced scallion (spring onion)
1/2 teaspoon sugar
2 tablespoons peanut oil
1 tablespoon sesame oil

Combine soy sauce, ginger, scallion, and sugar. Heat both oils together until they smoke, then pour over the ginger mixture and stir. Serve immediately with steamed chicken or fish.

Ginger and Black Vinegar Dip

3 in (8 cm) young ginger, scraped and very finely shredded
3 tablespoons black rice vinegar

Combine ginger and vinegar. Serve with Peking dumplings and other *dim sum* dishes.

Sesame Sauce

4 tablespoons sesame paste
4 tablespoons cold chicken stock
1 teaspoon sesame oil
1/2 teaspoon salt
1/2 teaspoon sugar

Mix all ingredients well and serve with any seafood dish.

Ginger Garlic Sauce (top),
Chili Garlic Sauce (above
left) and sliced chilies in
soy sauce (no recipe)

"Cooking and eating Indian cuisine is a discovery of the culture, the richly varied history and the spicy treasures of this fascinating land."

INDIA

Three thousand years of tradition and change are reflected in the cuisine of the subcontinent.

Left: The ultimate in Indian dining, an elegantly laid antique table set with thalis of Rajasthani food, while attentive retainers hover nearby.

Right: One of the peaceful canals that criss-cross the southern state of Kerala.

India is a vast and ancient land, with a recorded history that dates back over three thousand years. It is divided into many provinces that stretch from the snowy mountains of Kashmir to the southern tip of verdant Kerala, from the harsh arid deserts of Rajasthan in the west across to the remote tribal region of Assam along the Burmese border. Thus India has it all—from palm-fringed beaches to desert, and bustling cities to small one-ox towns.

This is also the land that gave rise to two of the world's major religions, Buddhism and Hinduism, and produced Jainism and Sikhism. Caste, too, plays its role in influencing the food of the people.

With all these differences Indian cuisine may seem undefinable, but there are enough common strands that combine to form a thrilling and exciting tapestry.

The Land and its People

Located in southern Asia, India ranges from the Himalayas in the north to the great Gangetic plain with its immense and sacred waters, to the lush tropical splendor of Kerala in the south. With its considerable land area—it is the seventh largest country in the world—India naturally encompasses four defined seasons.

In the cooler north and in the Gangetic plain of the middle and eastern part of India, rice and wheat are the main staples; while in the deserts of Rajasthan and Gujarat, it is millet and corn. Rice is also a basic food in the eastern belt of India, where its large and fertile alluvial lands make it an ideal rice-growing region. Along the coastal area of Kerala, fish and meat are the basic foods in the people's diet.

Spices, the foundation of Indian cooking, are widely cultivated according to region. Cardamom, cloves and peppers are harvested mainly in the south, while Rajasthan, Kashmir, and Gujarat are known for their chilies and turmeric. One of the

Above: **Nutmegs being weighed in the wholesale spice market of Cochin.**
Right: **A southern Indian thali with an array of vegetables, pickle, soup, rice, bread, banana, and dessert.**

glorious sights of Kashmir is the fields of purple-blue crocuses, source of the world's most expensive spice, saffron.

Islam has been in India since the 8th century, but it was not until the 16th century that the Muslims gained control over large parts of India. The Mughal dynasties, which ruled various independent states of pre–Independence India, upstaged the mainstream Hindu culture and cuisine significantly.

Besides the Muslims and Hindus, Jewish settlers also came to Kerala in AD 7, bringing with them the notion of kosher meat. The Christians settled here during the fourth century AD. Zoroastrians came and settled in large numbers when they were hounded out of Persia as far back as AD 850. Parsis, as they are now known, settled largely in Gujarat.

Besides the British, other Europeans who established themselves in India were the Portuguese, who remained largely in Goa, north of Kerala, from the 16th century until after Indian independence from the British.

The Making of a Cuisine

The Vedas, ancient historical and religious texts dating from 1700–1500 BC, set the framework for what is broadly known as Hindu culture. They record the civilization of the Aryans or nomadic tribes from the upper Urals, who traveled as far east as India on one side and as far west as Ireland on the other. Most Hindu food practices were influenced by the Aryans, beginning in the north and the northwest of India and gradually spreading all over the country.

The Aryans did not treat food simply as a means to physical sustenance but saw it as part of a cosmic circle, their dictum being that "food that man eats and his universe must be in harmony." Food, they believed, can be grouped into three types: those which needed expulsion, those which

were absorbed into the flesh, and those which were transformed into thought or mind. The last were the finest and rarest of foods and referred to as *manas*. The term *prasad* was used for food left over from offerings to the gods, food which was considered nectar, left no trace, and which maintained man's spirituality.

Food was classified into different categories: cereals, legumes, vegetables, fruit, spices, milk products, animal meats, and alcoholic beverages. This was the time when ghee or clarified butter emerged as a popular cooking medium because of its associations with purity, as it was used in religious sacrifices and offerings. Most traditional Indian cooking in the north still uses cholesterol-high ghee, although modern Indians have switched to cooking oil.

Ancient food habits were altered by religion and trade, through occupation and invasion, with Indian cuisines becoming more varied and vibrant. Religion was a major influence in changing food habits, with Buddhism and Jainism starting the first indigenous movements which challenged Hindu practices. Abstinence, austerity and simplicity were the tenets of changes which questioned, among other things, the eating of meat. Jainism underlined the importance of innocent foods and vegetarianism was born. Sikhism followed to reaffirm simplicity, with tobacco and alcohol becoming inscribed targets.

Geography also plays a role in what is served. In Gujarat, *nasto* is made from Bengal gram flour (*besan*) mixed with an assortment of spices and fried. *Chevda* or beaten rice is fried and mixed with salt, spices, almonds, raisins, and peanuts. The Parsis brought with them a strong meat-eating tradition and a love of egg dishes, raisins, nuts, butter and cream. They inevitably absorbed Gujarati influences and a hybrid cuisine developed. One of the most famous of these dishes is the Parsi fish steamed in banana-leaf packets. Another is *dhansak*, a one-pot meal that combines several types of *dal* with spices, meat, and vegetables.

New flavors, rich relishes, meats with cream and butter sauces, dates, nuts, and delectable sweets were the hallmarks of Mughal cuisine, which is widely known and famed for its exotic non-vegetarian food.

Finally, the period of British colonial rule in India—the Raj—has left an indelible mark on both the food and eating practices of this country. In middle-class homes, the dining table replaced the kitchen floor and porcelain, the banana leaf. Cutlery was introduced.

The blending of eastern spices into "western" food began at this time, and some of these "crossings" have endured to this day: kedgeree (a rice and lentil mixture, known as *kichidee* in India), mulligatawny soup (literally, pepper water or *mooloogoo thani*), and the ubiquitous curry. Curry is a catch-all term used initially by the Raj to refer to any sauced dish of spicy meat, fish or vegetables and is probably a corruption of the Tamil word for sauce "*kari.*"

The Food of the People

In temperate Kashmir, tucked into the Himalayas, the food is characterized by a subtle blend of fragrant spices, richness and pungency. Some of the most popular dishes include lamb marinated in yogurt; mutton simmered in milk and scented with nutmeg; and rich meat curries.

In the Ganges, plain rice is usually accompanied by vegetables sautéed with spices, *dal,* unleavened bread, plain yogurt, and a sweet. Chutneys and pickles are commonplace.

Bengali cuisine is considered elaborate and refined: Bengal being the only place in India where food is served in individual courses, the sequence of which is based on ancient beliefs relating to the aiding of the digestive process. Fish plays a large part in this cuisine, as do rice, *dal,* and chutney.

In the south, where rice is the staple, it appears in many guises: steamed, puffed, made into paper-thin crêpes known as *dosay* (page 55) or steamed to form *idli,* which are served with a variety of chutneys, vegetables and light *dal* broths known as *sambar.*

In Karnataka, the central southern state, the basic meal consists of vegetables which accompany *dosay, idli* or steamed rice. Popular southern vegetables include eggplants and bitter gourd, and lots of relishes are served to punctuate a meal.

Goans are known for their use of vinegar and kokum fruit (other Indians add sourness with tamarind, lime juice or dried mango powder), and, of course, for their love of fiery chilies. Classic examples of Goan dishes include the pork curry *vindaloo,* which gets its name from the Portuguese words for vinegar and garlic, and *sorpotel,* a sour hot curry of pork, liver, and pig's blood.

We can't leave the food of the people without making mention of the food of the Raj. The culinary fusion has yielded piquant dishes that pay homage to their roots; the spiced chutneys and curries of today have their humble beginnings in the Indian kitchen.

The Indian Table and Kitchen

At the heart of Indian cuisine is spice—carefully overlaid, one on the other, into dishes, with care. The use of spices in India was recorded in Sanskrit texts three thousand years ago.

Walk into an Indian home at meal time or into a good Indian restaurant and you will be engulfed by a wave of heavenly aromas. So great was the importance of spices for seasoning, as preservatives and as medicine that the search for their source pushed the Europeans into the Age of Exploration in the 15th century.

The Indian kitchen's range of spices is hard to beat in terms of

Offerings of coconut, bananas, flowers and incense on display at a market stall in a typical southern Indian village.

variety, color and aroma—from the sweetness of cumin and coriander to the pungency of *asafoetida* and turmeric. In a culinary sense, "spices" as used in India embraces dried seeds, berries, bark, rhizomes, flowers, leaves, and chilies. These may be used dried or fresh, come in the form of pods or seeds, be roasted, ground or put into hot oil to expel their flavors. Certain spices are used whole, others always ground; some are used only with meat, since they would overpower more delicate seafood and vegetable dishes. Some, such as cardamom, saffron, and cinnamon, are also used for desserts.

Any combination of spices is referred to as a *masala.* The most widely used is *garam masala,* a fragrant combination of cinnamon, cloves, black pepper, and cardamom, with the optional addition of nutmeg, mace, and saffron in northern regions. The spices are then combined with fresh rhizomes and leaves such as ginger, garlic, turmeric, garlic, mint, and chilies.

The medicinal properties of spices are always taken into account when food is prepared, as well as the interaction of each spice with the natural properties of a particular vegetable or *dal.*

The Indian kitchen is a place of surprising simplicity: it has a stove, often heated by charcoal, and a few implements such as the *kadai* (a wok-like utensil), straight-sided pots, and pans.

The house guest is looked on as a visiting god in India, and treated with attendant respect. By and large, home food is influenced by such factors as climate, nutritional balance and religion, and is usually simple fare, where rice, bread, and *dal* constitute the core of the meal. Each region and household then adds its distinctive touch with the vegetables, meat and fish, and the palate teasers: the pickles, *pappadums, raita,* or chutneys.

All Indian food is served with either rice or bread, or both. In the cooler north, breads are commonplace; in the south, rice is the

The richness of Mughal cuisine—the food of emperors—has seen its popularity spread throughout India and the rest of the world.

staple. Food is generally served on a banana leaf or a stainless steel *thali*. Washing the hands before meals is an important ritual, since Indians generally use their fingers to eat and the meal is eaten squatting down, usually on the kitchen floor. A small straw mat is placed for sitting and the *thali* or banana leaf is laid in front of the mat, either on the floor or on a low stool.

Families eat together, except for the mother or wife who serves the meal. In middle-class homes, this role is taken over by the household help. The family usually sits in a straight line and the women of the household serve and refill the *thali* repeatedly.

The *thali* contains all the courses of the meal, but there is usually an order in which the food is eaten. The first mouthfuls of rice are eaten with ghee or chutney and spicy additives. *Dal* is served with a variety of dry-cooked vegetables seasoned with different spices and garnishes. Pappadums and relishes are replenished, as are the *dal* and rice. The best portions of fish and meat are always offered to the guest. *Roti* or unleavened bread, *puri* and *paratha* are common in the north and eaten with *dal* and vegetables.

The sweet, which is milk-based, completes the meal, although in the south it is followed by rice with curds or buttermilk which are believed to soothe the stomach after a spicy meal.

A very Indian end to a meal is the betel leaf and its seasonings or *paan*. The leaf is chewed along with a slice of areca nut, a dab of slaked lime and a smear of *katha* paste (another wood extract). The betel quid can mean many things: hospitality, moral and legal commitment, a digestive, and a fitting end to the remarkable hospitality displayed during a meal.

Many of the curries in this chapter store very well—indeed many people believe that curries taste better the day after they are made, since the flavors are allowed to mature. You may wish to double the quantities of whatever you're making and freeze a batch in an airtight container—very convenient for quick meals and if unexpected guests turn up!

If properly stored, many of the condiments will keep for up to a month in the refrigerator. Just make sure you use a clean, dry spoon when taking any from the jar and seal the top with a thin film of vegetable oil before refrigerating. However, it is worthwhile roasting and grinding spices for the *garam masala* as you need it, as ground spices lose their aroma very quickly.

SUGGESTED MENUS

A family meal

What's so good about this menu, apart from how delicious everything is, is that most of it can be cooked ahead and served at room temperature if you like.
• Samosa (page 54) and some Pakora (page 54);
• Spiced Chickpeas (page 57) and Chicken Tikka (page 59) with a fresh green salad and a selection of breads (or just one type);
• fresh fruit with Kulfi (page 63).

A dinner party

For a dinner party that mixes the familiar with the more exotic, serve the following foods:
• Plantain and Potato Balls (page 55);
• Skewered Homemade Cheese (page 57) and skewered pieces of Tandoori Chicken (page 58); with these you should serve a selection of raitas and chutneys (page 64) (you may wish to buy the latter if you do not want to make your own);
• Gulab Jamun (page 63) that have been gently dusted with edible gold or silver foil.

A regional menu

For a gastronomic tour around the country, offer curries from the different regions in India:
• Lemon Rice (page 56) and some bread (the Puris [page 54] are particularly elegant);
• Spiced Potatoes in Yogurt (page 57), Mild Chicken Curry (page 58), some Goan Pork Curry (page 61), and Creamy Shrimp Curry (page 60);
• Cream Cheese Balls in Syrup (page 63).

A melting pot menu

An all-Asian menu:
• from Indonesia, Karedok, the Indonesian raw vegetable salad (page 74), accompanied by Crisp Peanut Wafers (page 73);
• Indian Crab Curry (page 60) served with lots of plain rice or, for a change, *dosay* (page 55);
• Thai Rice Balls in Coconut Milk (page 168).

THE ESSENTIAL FLAVORS OF INDIAN COOKING

Spices are the backbone of Indian cooking, so buy the freshest you can to roast and grind—**cardamom**, **cumin**, **nutmeg**, **cinnamon**, **fennel seeds**, and **fenugreek**—as you need. **Chilies**, dried and fresh, are pounded and sliced into cooking pastes with **garlic**, **onions**, and **ginger**. **Lentils** and **beans**, **breads** and **basmati rice** are eaten with curries. **Saffron** and **turmeric** are used to add flavor and color to dishes. **Yogurt** is not only used in both sweet and savory dishes but is also the main ingredient in *lassi*, a popular drink.

Here are the recipes for all those tasty morsels you see at the local Indian corner store or take-away. The fried items such as *samosas* and *pakoras* are ideal for parties, and the breads are ideal for mopping up all those curry juices. And don't think that all fried foods are fatty and greasy—as long as you keep the oil hot and drain the items well, they are truly delicious and will not leave you feeling heavy.

Chapati
Unleavened Bread

For the best result, *chapati* should be properly kneaded; using slow speed and a plastic blade in a food processor is an acceptable alternative to 10 to 15 minutes of hand-kneading.

- 2 cups (250 g) very fine whole wheat (wholemeal) flour (*atta*), or all-purpose (plain) flour
- About 1/2 cup (125 ml) warm water
- 2 teaspoons softened ghee or butter

Mix the flour and water in a bowl to make a dough that is pliable yet not too sticky. Add *ghee* or butter and turn the mixture out onto a floured board or put in a food processor. Knead by hand for 10 to 15 minutes or process at low speed for 5 minutes. Roll into a ball, cover with a damp cloth and set aside for at least 1 hour.

Knead the dough again for 3 to 4 minutes, then break into pieces the size of a golf ball. Flatten into a circle with your hands, then roll out into circles about 8 in (20 cm) in diameter.

Heat a heavy griddle (*tawa*) or frying pan until very hot. Put on a *chapati* and cook until brown spots appear underneath. Turn over and cook the other side, pressing on the top of the *chapati* with a clean cloth to help make air bubbles form and keep the *chapati* light. As each *chapati* is cooked, wrap in a clean cloth to keep warm. Serve with curries, *dal* or vegetables.

Puri
Deep-fried Bread

Puri are a delicious alternative to *chapati* and use exactly the same dough. To ensure they puff up when cooking, keep flicking the oil over the top while the puri are frying.

- 1 quantity *chapati* dough
- Oil for deep-frying

Roll out the dough as for *chapati*, make into 8-in (20-cm) circles and cover with a cloth. Heat plenty of oil in a wok until very hot. Put in a puri and immediately start flicking hot oil over the top of it with a spatula so that it will swell up like a ball. This should take only a few seconds. Flip the *puri* over and cook on the other side until golden brown. Serve immediately with curries, *dal* or vegetables.

Samosa
Vegetable-stuffed Pastries

- 7 tablespoons (100 g) *ghee* or butter
- 2 cups (250 g) all-purpose (plain) flour
- 1/2 teaspoon carom seeds (*ajwain*)
- 1/2 teaspoon salt
- Water to make a firm dough
- Oil for deep-frying

Filling
- 3 tablespoons oil
- 1/2 teaspoon cumin seeds
- 8 oz (250 g) potato, boiled in salted water and very finely diced
- 1/3 cup (50 g) green peas, cooked
- 1/2 teaspoon salt
- 1 teaspoon coriander powder
- 1/2 teaspoon turmeric powder
- 1/2 –1 teaspoon chili powder
- 1 green chili, deseeded and finely chopped
- 1 teaspoon dried mango powder

Rub *ghee* or butter into the flour until the mixture is crumbly. Mix in the carom seeds and salt, then add sufficient water to make a firm but pliable dough. Leave for 30 minutes, covered with a damp cloth.

Prepare the filling. Sauté the cumin seeds in the oil until they crackle, add remaining ingredients and sauté for 1 minute. Leave to cool. Roll out the pastry thinly, then cut into 3-in (7 1/2-cm) circles. Cut each circle in half. Put a spoonful of filling on one semi-circle of pastry and roll over the top, pressing the edges firmly to seal. Heat oil and deep-fry the *samosas* until golden brown. Drain and serve with a chutney or chili sauce.

Pakora
Batter-coated Vegetables

- 1 potato, peeled
- 1 small eggplant (aubergine)
- 1 large onion
- 2 cups (250 g) Bengal gram or chickpea flour (*besan*)
- 1 teaspoon salt
- 1 teaspoon chili powder
- 1/2 teaspoon baking soda (bicarbonate of soda)
- Water as required

Cut the potato in half lengthwise, then cut in slices about 1/4 in (1/2 cm) thick. Do not peel the eggplant but cut in slices the same size as the potato. Peel the onion and slice the same thickness. Set the vegetables aside.

Combine the flour, salt, chili, and baking soda, mixing well. Add enough cold water to make a very thick batter of coating consistency.

Heat oil and dip the vegetables, one at a time, into the batter, coating thoroughly. Deep-fry until half-cooked (about 2 to 3 minutes), then drain and set aside. Just before the *pakora* are needed, reheat the oil and deep-fry until golden brown and cooked through. Serve hot.

Deep-fried Bread

Plantain and Potato Balls

Naan
Tandoor-baked Bread

This bread gets its characteristic tear-drop shape from the way the dough droops as it cooks on the wall of a *tandoor*.

- 4 cups (500 g) all-purpose (plain) flour
- 1/2 teaspoon baking powder
- 1 teaspoon salt
- 1/2 cup (125 ml) milk
- 1 tablespoon sugar
- 1 egg
- 4 tablespoons oil
- 1 teaspoon nigella seeds

Sift the flour, baking powder, and salt together into a bowl and make a well in the middle. Mix the milk, sugar, egg, and 2 tablespoons of the oil in a bowl. Pour this into the center of the flour and knead, adding more water if necessary to form a soft dough. Add the remaining oil, knead again, then cover with a damp cloth and allow the dough to stand for 15 minutes.

Knead the dough again, cover and leave for 2 to 3 hours. About half an hour before the *naan* are required, turn on the oven to the maximum heat. Divide the dough into 8 balls and let them rest for 3 to 5 minutes. Sprinkle a baking sheet with nigella seeds; place in oven to heat up while dough is resting. Shape each ball of dough with the palms to make an oval shape. Bake until puffed up and golden brown. Serve hot.

Kele Ka Tikka
Plantain and Potato Balls

- 3/4 lb (350 g) plantains, steamed until soft (see Note)
- 5 oz (150 g) boiled potatoes, mashed
- 1 teaspoon *chaat masala* (page 64)
- 1 teaspoon coriander seeds, toasted and ground
- 1/4 teaspoon *garam masala* (page 64)
- 1/2 teaspoon salt
- 3/4 in (2 cm) ginger, finely chopped
- 1 heaped tablespoon chopped cilantro (coriander) leaves
- 2 green chilies, deseeded and finely chopped
- 1 heaped tablespoon cornstarch
- 4 oz (100 g) fine wheat vermicelli, broken into small pieces
- Oil for deep-frying

Grate the steamed plantains, then combine with the potato and all other ingredients, except vermicelli and oil. Mix well, then shape into balls and roll in the vermicelli, pressing to make sure the vermicelli adheres. Heat oil and deep-fry the balls until golden brown. Drain and serve with mint and coriander chutney (page 64).

Note: If plantains are not available, use 1 lb (500 g) potatoes.

Dosay
Southern Indian Rice-flour Pancakes

A southern Indian breakfast favorite, these tangy pancakes are often served with fresh Coconut Chutney and Tomato Chutney, with *dal* as a dip. Alternatively, they can be stuffed with spiced potato to make *Masala Dosay*.

- 3 cups (550 g) long-grain rice
- 1 cup (220 g) husked blackgram *dal* (*urad dal*)
- 1 teaspoon salt
- 1 onion, cut in half
- 3 tablespoons oil

Put the rice and *dal* into separate bowls, cover each with water and soak overnight. Grind the rice and *dal* separately in a food processor, adding a little water if necessary to obtain a smooth consistency. Mix the ground rice and *dal* together and leave at room temperature for up to 24 hours to ferment. The dough can now be refrigerated for up to 24 hours until required.

Stir the dough, adding salt and sufficient water to achieve the consistency of a very thick cream. Heat a nonstick pan or heavy griddle and rub with half an onion. Grease lightly with a little of the oil and pour in a ladle (about 1/4 cup, or 60 ml) of the batter, smearing it quickly with the back of the ladle to form a thin pancake about 5 to 6 in (12 to 15 cm) in diameter. Cook for about 2 to 3 minutes until the bottom is golden and the top is starting to set. Turn over and cook on the other side, then serve hot with Coconut Chutney.

Note: If desired, stuff with hot spiced potato or with boneless Chicken Masala.

Vecchu Paratha
Flaky Fried Bread

- 4 cups (500 g) all-purpose (plain) flour, sifted
- 3 eggs, lightly beaten
- 1 teaspoon salt
- 1 cup (250 ml) water
- 3/4 cup (180 ml) oil

Make a very soft dough with flour, eggs, salt and water, kneading well. Divide into balls about 2 in (10 cm) in diameter, cover with a damp cloth and leave to stand for 30 minutes.

Spread out each ball on a well-oiled tabletop, pulling the edge gently with the hands to stretch it out as wide and as thin as possible, as for a strudel. Dust the surface with flour and fold over and over to make a fan. Roll up the pleated dough to make a curled ball and leave to rest for 15 minutes. Use your hands to pat the ball into circles about 6 in in diameter, or use a rolling pin.

Oil a griddle or heavy frying pan and cook the bread, turning so that it is golden brown on each side. Repeat until all the dough is used up. Serve hot with *dal* or curries.

Flaky Fried Bread

Lemon Rice

Undiya
Spiced Mixed Vegetables

This Gujarati dish is served as part of a main meal. It goes well with any type of Indian bread or rice. If yam or plantains are unavailable, increase the amounts of potato, eggplant, and sweet potato slightly.

- $1/3$ cup (75 g) red *dal* (*masoor dal*), soaked 4 hours in warm water
- $1/3$ cup (75 g) coarsely chopped tomatoes
- $1/3$ cup (75 g) peeled and diced potatoes
- $1/3$ cup (75 g) diced eggplant (aubergine)
- $1/3$ cup (75 g) peeled and diced sweet potatoes
- $1/3$ cup (75 g) peeled and diced purple or white yam (optional)
- $1/3$ cup (75 g) peeled and diced plantain (optional)
- 2 tablespoons oil
- 1 teaspoon cumin seeds
- $1/2$ teaspoon carom seeds (*ajwain*)
- Pinch asafoetida powder

Rinse and soak *dal* and beans overnight. Combine *dal* and beans in a pan with ginger, salt, and water to cover. Bring to a boil, cover the pan and simmer until just soft.

Heat the *ghee* or butter, add cumin seeds and chilies and sauté until the cumin seeds crackle. Add to the cooked *dal* together with the tomatoes and half the *garam masala*, and simmer until the tomatoes soften. Keep aside 1 tablespoon of the cream for garnish and add the rest to the pan. Heat through and serve garnished with reserved cream and the remaining *garam masala*. Serve with any of the Indian breads.

- $2^1/2$ tablespoons lemon juice
- 1 teaspoon salt
- 1 tablespoon water
- Cilantro (coriander) leaves to garnish

Boil the rice in plenty of water until the grains are just tender. Drain thoroughly and set aside.

Heat oil in a pan and add the mustard seeds. When they begin to pop, add asafoetida, curry leaves, ginger, green chili, dried chilies, cashews, blackgram dal, Bengal gram, and turmeric powder. Sauté for a few seconds, then add lemon juice, salt, and water. Simmer for 2 to 3 minutes, then toss in the rice and heat through. Serve garnished with cilantro leaves.

Don't forget the rice and breads when you make the recipes here, or you'll miss out on the wonderful flavours of the juices. These dishes are a testament to Indian ingenuity with blending spices: a little more of this and a little less of that, and you'll end up with something else. Enjoy!

Chitrannam
Lemon Rice

- $1^1/2$ cups (280 g) long-grain rice, washed and drained
- 1 tablespoon oil
- 1 teaspoon black mustard seeds
- Pinch asafoetida powder
- 1 sprig curry leaves
- $1/2$ teaspoon finely chopped ginger
- $1/2$ green chili, finely chopped
- 2–3 dried chilies, broken in 1-in ($2^1/2$ -cm) pieces
- 1 tablespoon split raw cashews, lightly toasted
- 1 teaspoon husked blackgram *dal* (*urad dal*)
- 1 teaspoon split Bengal gram (*channa dal*), lightly toasted
- $1/2$ teaspoon turmeric powder

Dal Maharani
Bean and Lentil Stew

- $1/2$ cup (100 g) whole blackgram *dal* (*urad dal*), skin on
- 2 tablespoons (30 g) dried pinto or kidney beans
- 1 in ($2^1/2$ cm) ginger, sliced
- 1 teaspoon salt
- 1 tablespoon *ghee* or butter
- 1 teaspoon cumin seeds
- 1–2 green chilies, slit lengthwise
- 2 medium-sized tomatoes, chopped
- 2 teaspoons *garam masala* (page 64)
- $1/2$ cup (125 ml) cream

Spiced Mixed Vegetables

2 tablespoons freshly grated
   or moistened dried coconut,
   to garnish

Masala
2 tablespoons coriander seeds
1 teaspoon cumin seeds
1/2 teaspoon carom seeds
   (*ajwain*)
2 tablespoons raw peanuts
3–4 green chilies, chopped
2 tablespoons chopped cilantro
   (coriander) leaves
1 teaspoon crushed garlic
1 teaspoon crushed ginger
1 tablespoon freshly grated
   coconut or moistened dried
   coconut (desiccated coconut)
1 tablespoon chopped palm sugar
   (jaggery)
1 teaspoon salt
2/3 cup (150 ml) water

Drain the soaked *dal*. Prepare all
the vegetables and set aside.
Prepare the *masala* by toasting
the coriander, cumin, carom
seeds, and peanuts together
until the spices crackle, then
grind to a paste with the water.
Combine with all other *masala*
ingredients and blend or process
until smooth.

   Heat the oil in a pan and sauté
the cumin, carom, and asafoetida
until the spices start to crackle.
Add the ground *masala* and
sauté for about 5 minutes. Put
in the tomatoes and continue
cooking until they soften, then
add the drained *dal* and the
prepared vegetables. Cover the
pan and cook gently until the
vegetables are tender. Sprinkle
with coconut and serve.

Pindi Channa
Spiced Chickpeas

1 cup (200 g) chickpeas
1 tea bag or 1 tablespoon black
   tea leaves tied in cheesecloth
6 cups (1 1/2 liters) water
2 1/2 in (6 cm) ginger, 3/4 in
   (2 cm) of it shredded finely
2–3 tablespoons oil
2 onions, chopped
2 green chilies, sliced
2 teaspoons finely crushed garlic
3 medium-sized tomatoes,
   chopped
2 teaspoons coriander powder
1 1/2 teaspoons cumin powder
1/2 teaspoon turmeric powder

1 teaspoon chili powder
1 teaspoon salt
2 teaspoons chopped cilantro
   (coriander) leaves
1/4 teaspoon *garam masala*

Soak chickpeas 1 hour, drain
and discard liquid. Put chickpeas, 6 cups (1 1/2 liters) fresh
water and tea bag into a pan
and simmer until chickpeas are
tender. Drain, reserving 1 cup
(250 ml) of the cooking liquid.
Finely chop the remaining
ginger. Heat oil and sauté
onions until golden, then add
garlic, chopped ginger and
chilies. Sauté for 5 minutes. Add
tomatoes, coriander, cumin,
turmeric, and chili powders and
sauté over low heat until the oil
separates. Add the chickpeas,
the reserved cooking liquid, salt
and half the cilantro leaves.
Simmer uncovered until the
liquid has been absorbed. Add a
pinch of *garam masala* and serve
sprinkled with the remaining
garam masala, cilantro leaves,
and ginger shreds.

Dum Aloo
Spiced Potatoes in Yogurt

1 lb (500 g) baby new potatoes
3 tablespoons oil
2 onions, sliced and fried
   until brown
1 cup (250 ml) plain yogurt
4 black cardamom pods
1 teaspoon fennel
2 in (5 cm) cinnamon stick
1 1/2 in (4 cm) ginger, finely chopped
4 cloves garlic, finely chopped
1 1/2 teaspoons coriander powder
1 teaspoon cumin powder
1 teaspoon turmeric powder
1/2 teaspoon chili powder
2 tablespoons melon seeds or
   cashews, soaked and ground to
   a paste with water
1 cup (250 ml) water
1 teaspoon salt

Parboil the potatoes, then peel
and sauté in the oil until golden.
Drain and set aside, leaving the
oil in the pan. Purée the onions
and half the yogurt in a blender.
   Toast the cardamom, fennel,
and cinnamon in a dry pan
until the spices start to smell
fragrant, then blend or grind to
a powder. Set aside.

Skewered Homemade Cheese

Sauté the ginger and garlic
in the oil left from frying the
potatoes, then add coriander,
cumin, turmeric, and chili
powders and stir for 1 minute.
Whisk the remaining yogurt
and add together with the nut
paste. Heat, then put in the
potatoes, water, and salt and
simmer, uncovered, until the
potatoes are tender. Stir in the
reserved ground spices and
onion mixture, and serve.

Paneer Shashlik
Skewered Homemade Cheese

1 lb (500 g) *paneer*, cut into
   1/2-in-(1-cm-) thick cubes
2 green or red bell peppers
   (capsicums)
2 onions
2 tomatoes
1 cup (100 g) pineapple wedges
8 button mushrooms
Oil to brush the skewers

Marinade
3 tablespoons plain yogurt
1 tablespoon oil

1 teaspoon tomato paste
1 teaspoon salt
1 teaspoon chili powder
1/2 teaspoon coriander powder
1/2 teaspoon cumin powder

Cut the paneer, peppers, onions,
tomatoes, and pineapple into
squares of about 1 1/4 in (3 cm)
and set aside.
   Combine all marinade
ingredients and mix with the
paneer, vegetables, pineapple
and mushrooms. Leave for 1
hour, then thread onto skewers.
Cook in a tandoor, under a
broiler or over a hot barbecue
until done, brushing with oil
halfway through cooking.

HELPFUL HINT
Other fruits and vegetables can
be used—try making these with
zucchini, baby eggplant, and
cubed mango—not authentic,
but delicious all the same!

Bhindi Bharwan
Stuffed Okra

1 lb (500 g) okra (ladies' fingers),
   washed and dried
3 tablespoons oil
1 teaspoon cumin seeds
1 medium-sized onion, chopped
2 green chilies, deseeded and
   chopped
3/4 in (2 cm) ginger, finely chopped
Pinch of asafoetida powder
1 tomato, chopped

Stuffing
3 teaspoons coriander powder
2 teaspoons turmeric powder
2 teaspoons fennel powder
2 teaspoons dried mango powder
1 teaspoon chili powder
1/2 teaspoon salt

Cut the stalk off each okra and
make a lengthwise slit.

Combine stuffing ingredients,
mixing well, then stuff each
okra with the mixture.

Sauté cumin with a little oil
until it starts to crackle. Add
onion, chilies, and ginger, and
sauté until the onion turns
transparent; then put in the
asafoetida and cook for a few
seconds. Add tomato and cook
until it turns pulpy. Add the
okra and cook for 5 minutes,
or until tender and well coated
with the sauce.

Murgh Korma
Mild Chicken Curry

A *korma* is a Mughal creation,
rich in fragrant spices and
nuts. Chicken *korma* is probably
the best-known *korma* dish,
although vegetable, mutton,
and lamb are frequently used.

1 1/2 lb (750 g) boneless chicken
2 onions, finely chopped
4–6 cloves garlic, finely chopped
1 1/2 in (4 cm) ginger, chopped
1/4 cup (60 ml) water
4 tablespoons (100 g) *ghee* or
   butter
4 green cardamom pods, bruised
1 black cardamom pods, bruised
1 1/2 in (4 cm) cinnamon stick
2 bay leaves
2 cloves
1/2 teaspoon cumin powder
1/2 teaspoon coriander powder
1 cup (250 ml) whipped yogurt
   (page 65)
1/4 teaspoon freshly grated nutmeg
1 1/2 teaspoons ground white pepper
2 tablespoons cream
1 teaspoon salt
1 teaspoon *garam masala*
   (page 64)
1 teaspoon chopped cilantro
   (coriander) leaves to garnish

Nut paste
3 tablespoons white poppy seeds,
   soaked and simmered 30 minutes
3 tablespoons unsalted melon
   seeds, soaked
3 tablespoons *chironji* nuts or
   blanched almonds
3 tablespoons raw cashew
   nuts, soaked

Cut the chicken into bite-sized
pieces and set aside. Sauté the
onions, garlic, and ginger until
transparent and very slightly
browned. Blend together with
the water to obtain a paste and
set aside. Blend the nut paste
ingredients with just enough
water to make a paste and
set aside.

Heat the ghee and sauté the
cardamom, cinnamon, cloves,
and bay leaves for a couple of
minutes, then add the cumin,
coriander, and blended onion
paste. Sauté over very low heat,
stirring constantly, until the oil
separates, taking care that the
mixture does not change color.
Add the yogurt and continue
cooking for 15 minutes, stirring
from time to time. Add the nutmeg, pepper, and chicken and
simmer over low heat, uncovered, for 10 to 15 minutes, until
the chicken is tender. Add the
nut paste and simmer gently for
3 to 5 minutes.

Add 1 tablespoon of the
cream, salt and half of the
garam masala, stirring well.
Remove from the heat and serve
garnished with the remaining
cream, *garam masala,* and the
chopped cilantro.

Murgh Tandoori
Tandoori Chicken

Originally from the northwest of
India, food baked in a *tandoor,* or
clay oven, heated with charcoal
is very popular all over the
country. Marinated chicken
cooked in a tandoor achieves an
unrivaled succulence and flavor;
even using an electric or gas
oven, the result is very good.

2 spring chickens, each weighing
   around 1 1/4 lb (650 g)
1 tablespoon chili paste
2 teaspoons lemon juice
1 teaspoon salt
1 teaspoon *chaat masala* (page 64)
Melted butter to baste

Marinade
2 cups (500 ml) hung yogurt
   (page 65)
1 1/2 tablespoons chili paste
1 tablespoon crushed garlic
1 tablespoon crushed ginger
1 tablespoon oil
2 teaspoons lemon juice
1 teaspoon *garam masala*
   (page 64)
Few drops of red food coloring
   (optional)

Make deep gashes on the breast,
thighs and drumsticks of each
chicken, both inside and outside, to allow the marinade to
penetrate. Combine the chili
paste, lemon juice and salt and
rub all over the chickens.
Refrigerate for 30 minutes.

Prepare the marinade by
combining the hung yogurt
with all other ingredients. Rub
this well into the chickens,
saving some marinade to rub
inside the chest cavity. Marinate
chickens for 3 to 4 hours. Heat
an oven to maximum heat. Put
the chickens on a wire rack in
a baking dish and baste with
a little melted butter. Cook for
about 15 minutes, until the
chickens are brownish-
black and cooked. Sprinkle
with *chaat masala* and serve
with Mint & Cilantro
Chutney (page 64), onion
rings, and lemon wedges.

Note: The chickens can be
marinated as much as 24 hours
in advance. An alternative
method of cooking is to barbecue
the chickens over hot charcoal.

Stuffed Okra (left) and Mild Chicken Curry (right)

Murgh Tikka
Chicken Tikka

1 1/2 cups (375 ml) hung yogurt (page 65)
1 1/2 teaspoons crushed garlic
1 teaspoon crushed ginger
2 teaspoons chili paste
1 1/2 tablespoons oil
2 teaspoons lemon juice
1 teaspoon salt
1 teaspoon *garam masala* (page 64)
Few drops of red food coloring (optional)
1 1/4 lb (600 g) boneless chicken leg, cubed

Combine all the marinade ingredients and mix in with the chicken. Leave in the refrigerator to marinate for 2 to 3 hours.

Thread the chicken on skewers and brush with additional oil. Cook over charcoal or under a very hot grill for 6 to 8 minutes, turning once, until cooked and golden brown. Serve with Mint & Cilantro Chutney (page 64), onion rings, lemon wedges, and Indian bread such as *naan*.

Keema Kofta
Spicy Meatballs

A specialty of Uttar Pradesh, these meatballs are bathed in a sauce enriched with pounded cashews and almonds. In India, the meat would be bought in one piece, mixed with the seasonings and then taken to a shop to be put through a mincer.

Spicy Meatballs

1 lb (500 g) lean lamb, cubed
3 green chilies, sliced
1 tablespoon chopped cilantro (coriander) leaves
1/2 in (1 cm) ginger, finely chopped
1/4 teaspoon powdered cloves
1/4 teaspoon powdered mace
Pinch of *garam masala* (page 64)
1/2 teaspoon salt
1 tablespoon ghee or butter

Sauce
2 tablespoons raw cashews
2 tablespoons blanched almonds
1 heaped tablespoon ghee or butter
3 onions, finely chopped
3/4 teaspoon crushed garlic
3/4 teaspoon crushed ginger
1/4 teaspoon turmeric powder
1/2 teaspoon chili powder
3 tomatoes, finely chopped or blended
1/4 cup (60 ml) whipped yogurt (page 65)
1 tablespoon chopped fresh mint leaves
1 teaspoon salt
Pinch of *garam masala* (page 64)

Mix lamb with the chilies, cilantro, ginger, spices, and salt, keeping the ghee aside. Blend seasoned meat in a food processor until very finely ground. Shape into balls about 3/4 in (2 cm) in diameter and sauté in *ghee* or butter until browned. Set aside.

Make the sauce. Soak the cashews and almonds in hot water to cover for about 10 minutes, then pound or process to make a paste. Heat the *ghee* and sauté the onions until golden. Add the garlic, ginger, turmeric, and chili and sauté until the oil separates. Add the tomatoes and cook until they become pulpy. Add the yogurt and nut paste and simmer over low heat until the oil separates.

Add the meatballs, cover the pan and simmer for 5 to 7 minutes, stirring gently from time to time. Add half the chopped mint and salt to taste, then garnish with the remaining mint and *garam masala*.

HELPFUL HINT

Yogurt is also frequently hung to drain off some of the whey and obtain thicker curds. Although this is done using cheesecloth or muslin fabric in India, cooks elsewhere may find an easier method is to put the yogurt in a paper-lined coffee filter and set the cone-shaped device over a jar. The whey will drip through, leaving the curds in the filter. This is **hung yogurt**, which is preferred for cooking, as it does not change its texture.

Chicken Tikka

Creamy Shrimp Curry

Chingdi Macher
Creamy Shrimp Curry

³/4 in (2 cm) ginger
6 cloves garlic
¹/2 teaspoon cumin seeds
3 tablespoons mustard oil
1 bay leaf
4 cloves
2 in (5 cm) cinnamon stick
4 green cardamom pods, bruised
1 large onion, chopped
4 green chilies, deseeded and
  chopped
Salt to taste
¹/2 cup (125 ml) water
1 lb (500 g) shrimp peeled and
deveined
1 cup (250 ml) thick coconut milk
1 teaspoon sugar
Chopped cilantro (coriander) leaves
  to garnish

Pound the ginger, garlic, and cumin.

Heat oil and sauté the bay leaf, cloves, cinnamon, and cardamom until fragrant. Add onion and sauté gently for 5 minutes.

Add green chilies and ginger-garlic-cumin paste. Sauté for 2 minutes, then add salt and water. Simmer uncovered for 5 minutes, then put in the shrimp and simmer for 3 minutes. Add coconut milk and simmer gently, stirring occasionally, until the shrimp are tender. Add sugar, stir and serve garnished with cilantro leaves.

Nandu Kari
Crab Curry

This dish comes from Mangalore, on the southwest coast, an area renowned for its appreciation of both fish and coconuts. This succulent curry uses coconut milk plus freshly grated coconut for a wonderfully rich sauce.

4 live crabs, each weighing
  about 8–10 oz (250–300 g)
  2 tablespoons oil
1 teaspoon black mustard seeds
3 sprigs curry leaves
2 bay leaves
3 green chilies, halved lengthwise
Pinch of asafoetida powder
3 onions, chopped
¹/4 teaspoon turmeric powder
1 teaspoon chili powder
2 tomatoes, chopped
1 cup (250 ml) coconut milk
Salt to taste
¹/4 cup (20 g) freshly grated or
  moistened dried coconut
  (desiccated coconut)

Plunge crabs in a large pan of boiling water for 2 to 3 minutes, then drain and chop into large pieces, cracking the shell to allow the flavorings to penetrate. Clean and discard the spongy grey matter. Drain the crabs thoroughly.

Heat oil in a wok and fry mustard seeds until they start popping. Add the curry and bay leaves and green chilies and sauté gently for 1 minute, before adding the asafoetida. Add onions and cook until the onion is transparent, then sprinkle in turmeric and chili powders. Sauté for 1 minute, then add the crab pieces and tomatoes. Cover the wok and cook, without adding water, stirring occasionally. When the crab is cooked (about 10 minutes), add the coconut milk and salt. Bring just to a boil, stirring constantly, then add the grated coconut and serve with plain steamed rice.

Aatirachi
Kerala Lamb Curry

2 tablespoons oil
6 green cardamom pods, bruised
¹/2 teaspoon black peppercorns
8–10 shallots, sliced
1¹/4 lb (600 g) boneless lamb,
  cut in 1-in (2¹/2-cm) cubes

¹/2 teaspoon salt
³/4 cup (180 ml) water
Fresh cilantro (coriander) leaves
  to garnish

Masala
3 onions, chopped
³/4 in (2 cm) ginger, chopped
4–6 cloves garlic, chopped
¹/4 in (¹/2 cm) fresh turmeric or
  ¹/2 teaspoon turmeric powder
2 ripe tomatoes, chopped
4–6 dried chilies, broken and
  soaked to soften
2 green chilies, chopped
6 green cardamom pods
1 teaspoon black mustard seeds
¹/2 teaspoon black peppercorns

Process or blend the *masala* ingredients to make a paste. Set aside.

Heat oil and fry the green cardamoms and peppercorns for 2 minutes. Add the shallots and sauté until they turn golden brown. Add the meat and sauté until brown, then add the *masala* and sauté on low heat for 10 to 15 minutes. Add the salt and water, cover the pan and cook gently until the meat is tender. Garnish with cilantro and serve with rice or Flaky Fried Bread (page 55).

Crab Curry

Goan Pork Curry

1 lb (500 g) pork, cut in $^3/4$-in
  (2-cm) cubes
8 cloves garlic
3 teaspoons chili powder
4 green chilies
1 teaspoon black peppercorns
1 in ($2^1/2$ cm) fresh ginger,
  finely chopped
1 teaspoon cumin seeds
1 cup (250 ml) coconut vinegar
2 onions, chopped
$^1/2$ teaspoon salt
1 teaspoon sugar
2 tablespoons *feni* or brandy

Cut about 1 tablespooon of fat
from the pork and set aside.

Grind or blend the garlic,
chili powder, chilies, pepper, ginger, and cumin seeds with the
vinegar. Marinate the pork in
the vinegar and spice mixture
for $^1/2$ hour.

Fry the 1 tablespoon of pork
fat until the lard comes out of it,
then sauté the onions until
golden brown. Add the pork,
marinade, and salt. Simmer
until the pork is tender and the
gravy is thick. Pour off the
excess oil, then add the sugar
and *feni* or brandy. Stir through
and serve with bread or rice.

HELPFUL HINT
If you cannot obtain coconut
vinegar, use rice vinegar, or cider
vinegar diluted with 1 part of
water to 4 parts of vinegar.

Macher Jhol
Bengali Fish Curry

$1^1/2$ lb (750 g) white fish cutlets
  or fillets
2 teaspoons salt
1 teaspoon turmeric
Mustard oil for pan-frying
1 large potato, cut in wedges
1 small eggplant (aubergine),
  sliced
$1^1/2$ cups (375 ml) water
4 green chilies, deseeded and slit
  lengthwise

Masala
$^1/2$ teaspoon cumin seeds
$^1/2$ teaspoon fennel seeds
$^1/2$ teaspoon black mustard seeds
$^1/4$ teaspoon fenugreek seeds
$^1/4$ teaspoon nigella seeds (*kalonji*)

Wipe the fish dry, sprinkle both
sides with salt and turmeric
and set aside to marinate for
5 minutes.

Heat oil in a pan and sauté
the fish until golden brown on
both sides and cooked through.
Set fish aside.

Using the same oil, sauté the
masala spices until they start to
crackle. Add the potato and eggplant and sauté until well coated with the spices. Put in the
water and simmer until the vegetables are tender. Add fish and
chilies and heat through. Serve
with plain rice.

Kesari Murgh
Saffron Chicken

2 lb (1 kg) chicken
1 teaspoon salt
3 tablespoons or butter
3 in (8 cm) cinnamon stick
4 green cardamom pods, bruised
3 whole cloves
$^1/2$ lb (250 g) onions, peeled,
  boiled whole then puréed
1 teaspoon crushed garlic
2 teaspoons crushed ginger
1 cup (250 ml) whipped yogurt
  (page 65)
Pinch of saffron, soaked in
  1 tablespoon warm milk
$^3/4$ cup (100 g) cashew nuts,
  soaked and ground to a paste
$^1/2$ cup (125 ml) cream
Cilantro (coriander) leaves to
  garnish

Debone the chicken and
sprinkle with salt. Set aside.

Heat ghee and sauté
cinnamon, cardamom, and
cloves for a minute, then add
puréed onions, garlic, and ginger and continue to sauté until
they begin to take color. Add
the yogurt and saffron and
cook for 15 minutes, stirring
occasionally. Add the chicken,
simmer for 5 minutes, then
add the cashew nut paste and
blend well. Simmer until the
chicken is tender. Add the

cream, heat through and serve
garnished with cilantro leaves.

Vindaloo
Goan Pork Curry

Vindaloo can be very pungent,
although this recipe should
cause just a gentle sweat.
Choose pork that has some
fat on it.

Saffron Chicken

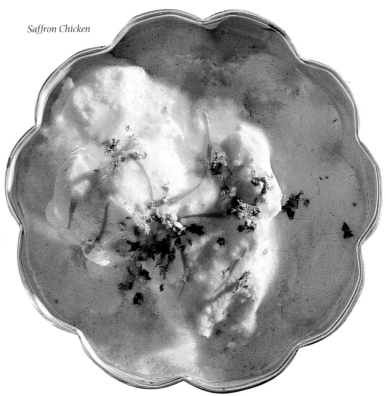

Once again, nothing quenches the heat of a fiery curry quicker than a plate of sliced fresh fruit. That is not to say that desserts and sweetmeats are not eaten—they are, with much relish, especially among the Bengalis. Here are some of the more popular Indian treats.

Kheer
Rich Rice Pudding

^{1}/2 cup (100 g) long-grain rice, washed and drained
3 cups (750 ml) milk
2–3 green cardamom pods, bruised
2 tablespoons blanched slivered almonds
Pinch of saffron threads, soaked in a little hot milk
1 tablespoon skinned pistachio nuts, chopped
1 tablespoon raisins (optional)
2–3 tablespoons sugar

Put the rice, milk, and cardamom into a pan, bring to a boil and simmer gently until the rice is soft and the grains are starting to break up. Add the almonds, saffron, pistachios, and raisins (if using) and simmer for 3 to 4 minutes. Add the sugar and stir until completely dissolved. Remove from heat and serve either warm or chilled.

Sweet Yogurt with Saffron

Shrikand
Sweet Yogurt with Saffron

In India, this Gujarati favorite is always served with deep-fried bread (*puri*) As it is so rich and substantial, you may prefer it simply on its own. If desired, the saffron can be omitted and about ^{1}/2 cup (125 ml) concentrated mango pulp added for a different flavor.

Rich Rice Pudding

6 cups (1^1/2 liters) plain yogurt
^{1}/2 cup (125 g) superfine (castor) or confectioners' (icing) sugar
1 tablespoon skinned pistacho nuts, chopped
2 teaspoons *chironji* nuts, hazel nuts or almonds, chopped
^{1}/4 teaspoon cardamom powder
Pinch of saffron threads, soaked in a little hot milk

Put the yogurt into a large sieve or colander lined with wet cheesecloth and allow to drain for 6 to 8 hours, until it is relatively firm.

Sprinkle the drained yogurt with sugar, stirring to dissolve it, then push the mixture through a fine sieve to obtain a silken smooth texture. Add half of the pistachos, the *chironji* nuts, cardamom, and saffron (or mango pulp, if preferred). Mix and chill before serving garnished with the remaining pistachios. Additional saffron can be used for garnishing if desired.

HELPFUL HINT

If the Sweet Yogurt with Saffron is made a day in advance and refrigerated, the flavor of the saffron and cardamom will be much stronger.

Channa Dal Payasam
Southern Indian Dessert

Payasam is made of sweetened milk with a variety of nuts, *dal*, pearl sago or even wheat-flour vermicelli added. This version is enriched with coconut milk.

2 tablespoons split Bengal gram
2 cups (500 ml) milk
^{1}/2 cup (125 ml) thick coconut milk
3 tablespoons (50 g) palm sugar (jaggery)
1 tablespoon *ghee*
1–2 green cardamom pods, bruised
1 tablespoon raw cashew nuts, coarsely chopped
1 tablespoon raisins or sultanas

Wash the Bengal gram and simmer together with 1 cup (250 ml) of water until half cooked. Add the milk and simmer until the gram is very soft, then add the coconut milk and palm sugar. Cook, stirring frequently, until the mixture thickens. Heat the ghee and sauté the cardamom pods, cashew nuts, and raisins until golden brown, then add to the cooked mixture. Although Payasam is normally served warm or at room temperature, it can be chilled if preferred.

Rasgulla
Cream Cheese Balls in Syrup

Soft homemade cream cheese or *chenna* is shaped into balls and simmered in syrup to make a simple but richly satisfying dessert. Silver leaf is sometimes used for decoration.

8 oz (250 g) *chenna* (page 65)
1 teaspoon flour

Syrup
2 lb (1 kg) sugar
3 cups (750 ml) water

Make the syrup by bringing the sugar and water to a boil. Turn off the heat and set aside.

Combine the *chenna* and flour and shape into balls. Reheat the syrup and when it is boiling, add the balls and simmer for about 20 minutes. Add another 2 tablespoons of water to the syrup every 5 minutes to replace water lost by evaporation; this is essential to avoid having the syrup become too thick. When the balls are cooked, remove from the syrup, drain and keep covered in water until required. Serve with a spoonful or two of the syrup poured over the top.

Kulfi
Indian Ice Cream

8 cups (2 liters) whole (full-fat) milk
1/2 cup (125 g) sugar
1–2 tablespoons skinned pistacho nuts, chopped
2 tablespoons almond, finely ground (optional)

Falooda
1 1/2 cups (200 g) cornstarch
4 cups (1 liter) water

To make the ice cream, put the milk into a wide, heavy pan and cook over very low heat. Stir constantly until the milk has thickened and is reduced to about 2 cups (500 ml), or until the milk is the color of the *kulfi* in the photo. Stir the sides of the pan constantly to prevent the milk from burning. Add the sugar and nuts, and allow to cool. Freeze in individual metal containers such as jelly molds.

To make the *falooda*, dissolve the cornstarch in 1 cup (250 ml) of water. Heat the remaining water in a pan, add the blended cornstarch and cook to make a thick gel.

While the mixture is still hot, put into a press capable of making fine threads the size of vermicelli.

Fill a bowl full of cold water right up to the brim and set the press over the water so that when the *falooda* is pushed through the press, it touches the water immediately. Push all of the gel through the press. Store the *falooda* in water until required. To serve, unmold the ice cream and garnish with drained *falooda*.

*Cream Cheese
Balls in Syrup*

Gulab Jamun
Fried Milk Balls in Syrup

2 lb (1 kg) *khoa*
7 oz (200 g) *chenna*
2 tablespoons all-purpose (plain) flour
Pinch of baking soda (bicarbonate of soda) 2 tablespoons skinned pistachio nuts, chopped
Oil for deep-frying

Syrup
6 cups (1 1/2 liters) water
5 1/2 lb (2 1/2 kg) sugar

Make the syrup by boiling the water and sugar together, stirring from time to time, for about 10 minutes until thickened slightly. Set aside.

Crumble the *khoa* and mix with *chenna*, flour, baking soda, and pistachios to make a soft dough. Make one very small ball for testing the consistency. Heat oil until moderately hot and fry the ball; if it breaks apart, the mixture is too moist and a little more flour should be mixed into the dough. When the mixture is the correct consistency, shape it into balls about 2 1/2 in (6 cm) in diameter and deep-fry, a few at a time, until golden brown. Drain the fried balls and put into the warm syrup. Serve warm or at room temperature.

Indian Ice Cream (left) & Fried Milk Balls in Syrup (right)

Saunth Ki Chatni
Tamarind and Ginger Chutney

- 5 tablespoons (100 g) dried tamarind pulp
- 5 dates, stones removed (optional)
- 1 teaspoon chili powder
- 3/4 teaspoon ginger powder
- 1/4 teaspoon nigella seeds, toasted and ground
- 3/4 teaspoon fennel seeds, toasted and ground
- 1 teaspoon cumin seeds, toasted and ground
- 1/4 cup (60 g) palm sugar (jaggery)
- 1 teaspoon white sugar or more to taste
- Salt to taste

Soak the tamarind pulp with 2 cups (500 ml) water for a minimum of 4 hours. Put pulp and liquid together with dates (if using) into a nonreactive pan, cover and simmer for 30 minutes. Push through a sieve, discarding the seeds and fibrous matter.

Return the sieved pulp to the pan and add chili, ginger, nigella, fennel, and cumin. Cook over low heat for 10 minutes, then add palm sugar and stir until dissolved. Add white sugar and salt to taste. Serve with any appetizers such as Pakora or Samosa, or serve with simple vegetable dishes for extra tang. Will keep refrigerated for about 1 week.

Hussaini Tamatar Qoot
Tomato Chutney

- 1 tablespoon oil
- 3/4 teaspoon black mustard seeds
- 1/2 teaspoon nigella seeds
- 1 sprig curry leaves
- Pinch of asafoetida powder
- 4 green chilies, slit lengthwise and deseeded
- 1 teaspoon crushed garlic
- 3/4 teaspoon crushed ginger
- 4 medium-sized ripe tomatoes, chopped coarsely
- 1/2 teaspoon turmeric powder
- 1 teaspoon chili powder
- 2 teaspoons sugar
- Salt to taste

Heat oil and fry mustard seeds, nigella seeds, curry leaves, and asafoetida until the spices start to crackle. Add the garlic and ginger and sauté gently for a couple of minutes, then put in the chilies and tomatoes and cook for about 10 minutes, until the tomatoes turn pulpy. Add the turmeric, chili powder, and sugar and stir until the sugar dissolves. Add salt to taste and serve hot. This chutney keeps for 3 to 4 days if refrigerated in a covered jar.

Pudina Ki Chatni
Mint and Cilantro Chutney

- 1 cup cilantro (coriander) leaves
- 1/2 cup mint leaves
- 2 green chilies, chopped
- 1/2 in (1 cm) ginger, chopped
- 3 cloves garlic, chopped
- 2 tablespoons plain yogurt
- 1 teaspoon sugar
- 1/2 teaspoon chili powder
- Salt to taste
- 1 teaspoon *chaat masala*
- Lemon juice to taste

Put all ingredients in a blender and process until very fine. Serve with snacks or *tandoori* dishes.

Mangga Thuvial
Green Mango Chutney

- 3 unripe green mangoes, weighing a total of about 1 lb (500 g)
- 1/2 teaspoon sesame seeds
- 3–4 dried chilies, cut in 1-in (2 1/2-cm) lengths
- 2 medium-sized onions, chopped
- 2 tablespoons freshly grated or dried coconut
- 1 sprig curry leaves
- 1 tablespoon chopped cilantro (coriander) leaves
- 1 teaspoon oil
- 1 teaspoon black mustard seeds
- 1 1/2 teaspoons split Bengal gram (*channa dal*)
- Salt to taste

Peel the mangoes, discard the seeds and chop the flesh coarsely. Gently toast the sesame seeds and chilies until crisp. Combine the mango flesh, sesame seeds, chilies, onion, coconut, curry leaves, and cilantro leaves and grind or blend coarsely. Heat the oil and fry mustard seeds and *dal* until the mustard seeds start to pop. Pour into the other ingredients, mix and add salt to taste; serve.

Garam Masala

- 1/2 cup (75 g) cumin seeds
- 2 tablespoons coriander seeds
- 4 2-in (5-cm) cinnamon sticks
- 10–12 green cardamom pods, bruised
- 4–5 black cardamom pods, bruised
- 10 cloves
- 1/2 nutmeg, broken
- 3–4 blades of mace
- 1 tablespoon black peppercorns
- 4 whole star anise
- 5 bay leaves

Put all the spices in a dry pan (preferably nonstick) and heat over a very low fire, shaking the pan from time to time. When the spices give off a fragrance, allow to cool slightly, then grind finely in a coffee mill or electric blender. Store in an airtight bottle. (If stored in the freezer portion of the refrigerator, spices keep fresh almost indefinitely.)

Rasam Masala

- 2 teaspoons coriander seeds
- 1/2 teaspoon cumin seeds
- 1 teaspoon fenugreek seeds
- 1 teaspoon black peppercorns
- 1 teaspoon black mustard seeds
- 6 dried chilies, broken into several pieces
- 1 sprig curry leaves
- 1/2 teaspoon husked blackgram *dal* (*urad dal*)
- 1/2 teaspoon split Bengal gram (*channa dal*)
- Pinch of asafoetida powder

Put all ingredients except asafoetida in a pan over low heat and cook until the chilies become crisp and the spices smell fragrant, taking care not to burn them. Cool slightly, then grind all ingredients together, then mix with the asafoetida powder. This is used to flavor the southern Indian soup, Rasam.

Kadai Masala

- 6 dried chilies, broken into several pieces
- 2 tablespoons coriander seeds
- 1/4 teaspoon *garam masala*

Heat chilies and coriander in a pan, shaking from time to time, until they smell fragrant. Grind and add *garam masala*.

Chaat Masala

- 1 tablespoon cumin seeds
- 1 tablespoon black peppercorns
- 5 cloves
- 3 cubeb or long pepper (optional)
- 1/2 tablespoon dried mint leaves
- 1/4 teaspoon carom seeds (*ajwain*)
- 1/4 teaspoon asafoetida powder
- 1 tablespoon rock salt
- 2 1/2 tablespoons dried mango powder
- 1 teaspoon ground ginger
- 1 teaspoon chili powder
- 1/4 teaspoon cream of tartar (tartaric acid)
- 2 teaspoons table (refined salt)

Put first seven ingredients in a dry pan and heat gently, shaking the pan from time to time, until the spices begin to smell fragrant. Remove from heat, add the rock salt and grind while still warm. Mix in all other ingredients, cool and store tightly bottled. This salty, sour *chaat masala* (the approximate translation of the name is "finger licking"!) is sprinkled over cooked food for additional flavor.

Khoa
Condensed Milk

- 4 cups (1 liter) fresh milk

Bring the milk to a boil in a wide, heavy-bottomed pan, stirring constantly. Continue stirring over high heat until the milk changes to a dough-like consistency, about 25 minutes. Yields about 3 oz (90 g) *khoa*.

Dahi
Plain Yogurt

- 4 cups (1 liter) fresh milk
- 2 tablespoons powdered full-cream milk
- 1 tablespoon plain yogurt

Combine the fresh and powdered milks, stirring to dissolve, then put over moderate heat and bring almost to a boil, stirring from time to time. Remove from the heat and allow to cool to about 100°F (40°C). You should be able to hold your finger in the milk up to the count of 10 without it stinging. Put the plain yogurt starter in a clean container and stir in the hot milk. Cover with a cloth and leave in a warm place until set. In cooler temperatures, a wide-mouth insulated jar or thermos flask should ensure that the temperature stays warm enough for the yogurt to set. Refrigerate the yogurt as soon as it has set and use some of this as a starter for your next batch.

Before it is used in Indian cuisine, yogurt is often vigorously stirred to ensure the whey is reincorporated with the curds; this is referred to as whipped yogurt. Yogurt that is drained for several hours to remove the whey is called hung yogurt.

To make, put yogurt in a cheesecloth or muslin over a jar. The whey will drip through, leaving the curds.

Chenna/Paneer
Homemade Cream Cheese

- 4 cups (1 liter) fresh milk
- 1 tablespoon of lemon juice or 1 tablespoon vinegar mixed with 1 tablespoon water

Put the milk into a heavy-bottomed pan and bring slowly to a boil, stirring occasionally. Remove from heat and add the lemon (or vinegar and water) while the milk is still hot, stirring vigorously until the milk starts to curdle. Strain through a muslin or cheese-cloth-lined sieve until all the whey has drained off. The curds left are known as *chenna* and should be kneaded lightly to make a smooth mixture, then

refrigerated until needed for various desserts. To obtain *paneer*, wrap the cheese in the same cheese-cloth and shape into an oblong or square. Wrap tightly and place it under a heavy weight for about 2 hours to compress it. Remove the weight and cut into desired shapes.

Pyaz Ka Achar
Onion Mustard Pickle

- 1 cup (250 ml) mustard oil
- 4 tablespoons black mustard seeds
- 2 teaspoons chili powder
- 1 teaspoon turmeric powder
- 3 tablespoons vinegar
- 2 1/2 tablespoons sugar
- 1/2 tablespoon salt
- 3 tablespoons dried mango powder
- 15–18 green chilies
- 30 cloves garlic, peeled and left whole
- 1 1/2 tablespoons crushed ginger root
- 1 1/2 tablespoons crushed garlic
- 2 lb (1 kg) onions, sliced
- 1/2 teaspoon ascorbic acid crystals

Heat oil to smoking point, then set aside to cool. Grind or blend the mustard seeds, chili, turmeric, vinegar, sugar, salt, and mango powder to make a paste. Add this to the oil, together with all other ingredients. Stir to mix well and store in sterilized jars, with the pickle covered by oil. Keeps 3 to 4 weeks.

Clockwise, from the top left: chili pickle (no recipe), Lemon Mango Pickle, Mixed Vegetable Pickle, green chili pickle (no recipe) and Onion Mustard Pickle

Nimbu Aur Aam Ka Achar
Lemon Mango Pickle

- 2 lb (1 kg) lemons, quartered
- 10–15 green chilies, halved lengthwise
- 3–4 unripe green mangoes, peeled and diced
- 1 cup (250 ml) lemon juice
- 1 1/2 tablespoons cumin powder
- 1 tablespoon turmeric powder
- 1 1/2 teaspoons chili powder
- 4 1/2 tablespoons salt
- 2 1/2 tablespoons sugar
- 1 1/2 cups (375 ml) mustard oil

Combine the lemons, chilies, mangoes, and lemon juice in a bowl and sprinkle with the spices, salt, and sugar. Put into a large glass jar covered loosely with a cloth and leave in the sun for 6 days. Heat the oil to smoking point, allow to cool and then stir into the lemon mixture. Leave in the sun for another 4 days, then cover the jar with a lid and store in a cool, dry place away from the light. Keeps for several months.

Sabzi Achar
Mixed Vegetable Pickle

- 8 oz (250 g) each of carrots, unripe green mangoes, green chilies and lotus root
- 1 cup (250 ml) mustard oil
- 2 teaspoons fennel seeds
- 1 teaspoon nigella seeds
- 1 teaspoon black mustard seeds
- 2 1/2 teaspoons chili powder
- 2 1/2 teaspoons turmeric powder
- 2 teaspoons *garam masala*
- 1 onion, chopped and puréed
- 1 1/2 tablepoons crushed ginger
- 1 1/2 tablepoons crushed garlic
- 4 lemons, quartered
- 1/2 teaspoon ascorbic acid crystals
- 4 1/2 tablespoons salt

Peel and cut the carrots and mango into small wedges. Peel and slice the lotus root. Leave the chilies whole. Heat the mustard oil to smoking point, then add the fennel, nigella, and mustard seeds and sauté until the spices crackle. Add the chili, turmeric, *garam masala*, onion, ginger, and garlic and stir, then add the vegetables and lemons. Remove from the heat and add the ascorbic acid and salt. Stir to mix well. Put the pickle in sterilized jars, making sure it is covered with oil. If necessary, add more oil which has first been heated to smoking point, then cooled. Keeps 3 to 4 months.

"Silakan makan", or "please eat", are two of the most welcome words you will hear in Indonesia.

INDONESIA

As the languages, religions, and cultures of the archipelago are many and varied, so too are its cuisines.

Left: Chilies, whether sold whole or ground into a paste, are an indispensable part of Indonesian cuisine.

Right: A Javanese man on his way to the market, his bike loaded with terra cotta cooking wares.

Indonesia is the world's largest archipelago, consisting of literally thousands of islands. With terrain that ranges from snow-capped mountains and lush rainforests to arid savannah, swamps and irrigated rice fields, it's hard to imagine a more appropriate national motto than "*Bhinneka Tunggal Ika*"—Unity in Diversity.

Over the past two thousand years, Buddhist, Hindu, and Muslim kingdoms rose and fell in Sumatra, Java, and Borneo, attracting merchants from China, the Middle East, and India, as well as Siam and Malacca. Their quest was spice—not surprising, since some of the archipelago's eastern isles were the original Spice Islands.

With its geographic and cultural diversity, it is to be expected that the cuisines of Indonesia are so varied. Indigenous styles have been influenced degrees over the centuries by the introduction of ingredients and cooking styles from China, India, the Middle East, and Europe.

Tanah Air: Land and Water

Stretching some 5,000 miles, Indonesia's 17,000 or so islands (home to some 220 million people) range from roughly six degrees north of the equator to 11 degrees south. Indonesia is within the so-called "Ring of Fire," the meeting point of two of the earth's tectonic plates, which gives rise to frequent seismic activity. Smoldering volcanoes periodically shower fertile ash on the land.

To a large extent, the western islands of Indonesia are lush and evergreen. While Borneo has rainforests and swampy coastlines, Java and Sumatra abound with fertile gardens, coconut groves, and paddy fields.

All of Indonesia enjoys tropical warmth and relatively high humidity, although the temperature drops significantly on the mountains. Most parts of the archipelago experience a definite dry season followed by life-giving monsoon rains. However, the eastern islands of the archipelago, especially

Nusa Tenggara, the chain of islands in between Lombok east to Timor, are often rocky and semi-arid. The dry seasons there are longer and harsher than elsewhere in Indonesia, and the land often degraded by tree felling and subsequent erosion.

Different parts of Indonesia receive their monsoon rain at different times of the year. The Maluku islands conform to the image of the lush tropics, while Irian Jaya, the western portion of the island of New Guinea, has everything from swamps to rainforest to the highest mountain east of the Himalayas, the almost 16,000-foot Mount Jaya.

The preferred staple throughout Indonesia is rice, which is grown both in irrigated paddies—where up to three crops a year can be achieved by using special strains of rice and fertilizers—and in non-irrigated fields, which depend on the monsoon rains. In areas where insufficient rainfall or unsuitable terrain make rice-growing impossible, crops such as sweet potato, tapioca (cassava or manioc), corn, and sago are the staple.

The most popular accompaniment to rice is fish, which is often simply fried with a seasoning of sour tamarind, turmeric, and salt, or simmered in seasoned water or coconut milk. Although vegetables are grown throughout Indonesia, they do not always figure prominently in the diet. Some wild leaves and plants, as well as the young leaves of plants grown for their fruit or tubers, such as starfruit, papaya, sweet potatoes, and tapioca, are cooked as a vegetable. These are supplemented with water convilvulus (*kangkung*), long beans, eggplants, pumpkins, and cucumbers. Elevated areas, especially in islands with rich volcanic soil, have proved perfect for temperate-climate vegetables introduced by the Dutch.

A Culinary Tour of the Islands

Over the centuries Indonesia's cuisines, especially in the major islands, have borrowed ingredients and cooking styles from many sources. Arab and Indian traders brought their spices and sweet rose water. The Spanish were responsible for the introduction of chilies. The Chinese introduced the now-ubiquitous noodles (*mie*); soy sauce, which the Indonesians modified to suit their taste by adding sugar (*kecap manis*); mung peas; bean curd and soybeans, which the Indonesians fermented to make *tempeh*.

Despite their long period as colonial rulers, the Dutch did not really have an enormous impact on the local cuisine, apart from,

Special Indonesian *es* (ice) drinks, both refreshing and delicious, are sold at stalls and mobile carts throughout Indonesia.

A sambal served in *daun mangkokan*, a decorative leaf used as a herb in Sumatra.

perhaps, the *rijstaffel*. This colonial invention is a larger-than-life adaptation of the Indonesian style of serving rice with several savory side dishes and condiments—only the Dutch modified it to a "rice table" where as many as 18 to 20 dishes might be served.

The Javanese of the sultanates of Yogyakarta and nearby Surakarta have a very refined culture. Theirs is a highly structured society where harmony depends upon consideration for others, the group being more important than the individual. Ritual events are marked by a communal feast (*selamatan*). Centerpiece of the *selamatan* may be a cone-shaped mound of yellow rice, with at least a dozen dishes accompanying, including *gudeg* (young jackfruit cooked in coconut milk); fried chicken, which had first been simmered in spiced coconut milk; fermented soybean cakes (*tempeh*) fried with shrimp and sweetened with palm sugar; red chili *sambal* and crisp shrimp wafers (*krupuk*).

Less subtle is the food of the west Sumatran region of Padang—ideal, however, if you like it hot and spicy! Most of the food in restaurants are served as a smorgasbord: portions are taken from ten to as many as twenty different dishes and carried from their display counter to the restaurant table. You help yourself to whatever you desire and pay only for what you consume. Vital to Padang food are the herbs, rhizomes and other seasonings that include chilies, ginger, garlic, shallots, galangal, turmeric, lemongrass, basil, fragrant lime and *salam* leaves, and pungent dried shrimp paste. Coconut flesh is squeezed to make the rich, creamy milk that soothes (if only slightly) the impact of much Padang food. Steaming white rice is served to counterbalance the emphatic flavors.

Sulawesi (Celebes) is renowned for its fish. *Ikan bakar*, fish roasted over charcoal and served with a variety of dipping sauces, is a regional favorite.

Feasts are commonplace in Bali, and, as the island did not turn to Islam when the rest of the nation did, pork is a popular meat.

Game from the interior highlands of the so-called wilds of Borneo include wild boar, used to make the famous roast pig *babi guling*. Many leafy greens are gathered wild, such as the young shoots of trees found in the family compound (starfruit is a favorite), or young fern tips and other edible greens found along the lanes or edges of paddy fields. Immature fruits like the jackfruit and papaya are also used as vegetables. Mature coconut is used almost daily: grated to add to vegetables, fried with seasonings to make a condiment, or the grated flesh squeezed with water to make coconut milk.

The Food of the People

To properly savor the diversity of Indonesian cuisine, take a walk along local streets and do as the locals do—frequent the *warung* (simple food stall). The social center of most villages and small towns, the *warung* is usually made of either woven bamboo or wood, open-fronted with dirt or cement floors, and offers everything you might need for the home—mosquito coils, laundry powder or the ubiquitous clove-scented cigarettes.

Warungs also sell a colorful array of packaged snacks, cakes, biscuits, bottles of drink and whatever fresh fruit is available that day: fresh bananas, avocados, papayas or guavas gathered from a nearby garden.

Eating out for many Indonesians is usually a necessity rather than a luxury, and basic food stalls selling cooked food at very reasonable prices are found in any large village as well as in towns and cities. Stalls are often a good source of regional favorites. You can find *soto Makassar* (a rich beef soup) and grilled fish (*ikan bakar*) along Ujung Pandang's waterfront in Southern Sulawesi. Lombok's favourite chicken, which is grilled over coals and served with a spicy sauce (*ayam taliwang*) is found at many foodstalls in the capital, Mataram, and almost any market in Bali will feature the famous roast pig (*babi guling*).

Market foodstalls often sell *nasi campur* (literally "mixed rice") with small portions of several "dishes of the day," the various vegetables, meat, poultry or fish dishes are often cooked in the regional style.

Hawkers on rumbling pushcarts, makeshift wooden contraptions resting on a couple of bicycle wheels, are also a popular sight, offering

Indonesia is blessed with an abundance of luscious fruit: the giant jackfruit, notorious durian, and spiky rambutan are only a few.

mie bakso (noodle and meatball soup), or bowls of shaved ice with the syrups, jellies and fruits of your choice added. Another hawker with a charcoal fire will grill satay on request.

What Westerners may consider desserts are eaten as snacks throughout the day, and may include treats such as fermented rice or cassava (*tape*), slivers of young coconut, chunks or strips of colorful jelly, sweet corn kernels or vivid green "noodles" of transparent mung pea flour.

Coffee is more popular than tea in many areas of Indonesia. Finely ground coffee is put straight into the serving glass and mixed with boiling water. The trick of drinking the coffee (known as *kopi tobruk*) without getting a mouthful of grounds is to stir it a little so that the grounds settle. Indonesians love sugar and coffee is served sweet unless one asks for it *pahit* (literally "bitter").

Stronger drinks can be found, except in conservative Islamic areas (Muslims are forbidden to drink alcohol). Two popular local brands of beer, Bintang and Anker, are made to Dutch specifications and are similar to any European lager. In many non-Muslim areas, a local brew is made from either rice or the sap of the coconut or lontar palm. Bali is noted for its *brem*, a sweetish type of rice beer. Palm wine (toddy) is made by tapping the sap that flows from the inflorescence of the coconut or lontar palm. It is enjoyed fresh the day it is gathered, or left to mature for a few days; leftovers are distilled to made a fierce *arrack*.

The Indonesian Table and Kitchen

"*Silakan makan*" is the Indonesian invitation that precedes any meal served to guests, and a phrase foreigners should wait for before beginning even as much as a snack served by their Indonesian hosts. But in countless homes throughout the archipelago, meals are usually an informal affair and often eaten alone.

The most popular staple food is rice, and Indonesians eat large quantities of it with savory side dishes and condiments. Only small amounts of savory dishes—which may include fish, poultry, meat, eggs, vegetables, beancurd or *tempeh*—are eaten. Variety is preferred over quantity; a little of four or five side dishes rather than large helpings of only one or two.

Condiments are as important as savory dishes and will usually include a chili *sambal* and something to provide a crunchy contrast. This could be deep-fried *tempeh*, peanuts, deep-fried tiny anchovies (*ikan teri*), *krupuk* (wafers made of tapioca flour seasoned with anything from shrimp to melinjo nuts), a seasoned fried coconut concoction such as *serundeng* or fried peanut wafers (*rempeyek*).

The rice and accompanying dishes are normally cooked early in the day, immediately after a trip to the market. The prepared food is left in the kitchen, and members of the family help themselves to whatever they want whenever hungry, or take a container of food to the fields. Evening meals, taken at the end of the day when family members return from the fields, school or their work in the towns and cities, are often based on food left over from the main midday meal, with one or two extra dishes cooked if necessary.

As food is often served some time after it has been prepared, it is usually eaten at room temperature. Where meals are communal, the rice and all the accompanying dishes are placed in the middle of the table or on a mat on the floor for everyone to help themselves. It is considered impolite to pile one's plate with food at the first serving; there's plenty of opportunity to take more food as the meal progresses.

Indonesians traditionally eat with the right hand (the left is considered unclean by Muslims), although serving spoons are used to transfer the food to individual plates or bowls from the serving dishes. Many modern homes and almost all restaurants provide a spoon and fork, while chopsticks can be expected in Chinese restaurants.

In more affluent homes, the choice of dishes to accompany the rice is made with a view to achieving a blend of flavors and textures. If one of the savory dishes has a rich, creamy coconut-milk sauce, this will be offset by a dry dish with perhaps a sharper flavor. There may well be a pungent *sambal goreng* (food fried with a spicy chili seasoning), but this will be balanced with other mild or even sweet dishes using *kecap manis* (sweet black soy sauce) or palm sugar.

For a family celebration, food is prepared by the family involved. Larger feasts involve the whole *banjar*, or local community, the work supervised by a ritual cooking specialist, invariably a man. There is a strict division of labor along gender lines, with men being responsible for butchering the pig or turtle, grating coconuts and grinding spices. The women of the community perform the more fiddly tasks of peeling and chopping the fresh seasonings, cooking the rice and preparing the vegetables.

The Indonesian kitchen is a combination of simplicity and practicality. The gleaming modern designer kitchen is unknown to the majority of Indonesians; meals are usually cooked over a wood fire or a *kompor*, a kerosene burner.

A little known fact: despite the Moluccas's reputation as the Spice Islands—islands literally responsible for starting the Age of Exploration and for the discovery of the Americas by Christopher Columbus—cloves and nutmeg are rarely used in cooking in the Moluccas. A little grated nutmeg may be added to a rich beef soup at a pinch, but in the main, nutmeg and cloves are regarded more as medicinal plants. Nutmeg fruit, the fleshy covering of the hard nut which is used as a spice, is usually pickled and eaten as a snack.

The most widely used spice is coriander, a small round beige seed with a faintly orange flavor, commonly partnered with peppercorns and garlic to flavor food, especially in Java.

SUGGESTED MENUS

Family meals

For an easy but elegant family meal, serve the following selection of small dishes with Yellow Rice (page 78):
• Marinated Sour Shrimps (page 72);
• Grilled Fish in Banana Leaf (page 72);
• Fern Tips in Coconut Milk (page 79);
• Coconut Pancakes (page 85) as a sweet.

Or, you may like to consider:
• Spicy Sparerib Soup (page 76);
• Vegetables with Spicy Coconut (page 78) and Simmered River Fish (page 81) with steamed rice;
• Sago Flour Rolls (page 84) for a good make-ahead dessert.

Dinner party (1)

Many of the dishes in this chapter make very good dinner-party nibbles:
• Grilled Fish in Banana Leaf (page 72), Dry Spiced Beef (page 80) and Spicy Fried Sardines (page 81);
• Buginese Chicken (page 82) or Yogya Fried Chicken (page 83) and Hot Spicy Fried Tempeh (page 79) served with rice to follow the appetizers;
• Black Rice Pudding (page 85) makes a dramatic ending.

Dinner party (2)

Other great dinner party suggestions are:
• Beef or Seafood Satays (page 73);
• Yogya Fried Chicken (page 83) and Padang-style Eggs in Coconut Milk (page 78) with Gado Gado (page 74);
• Rice Flour Cake with Palm Sugar (page 84) completes the meal.

Salad meals

The salads in this chapter (pages 74-75) are a vegetable lover's delight, and easy to assemble once you've prepared all the ingredients. They make an ideal lunch, served with bread or rice.

A melting pot menu

For a mixed dinner menu serve:
• Green Papaya Soup (page 76) from Indonesia;
• Spicy River Shrimp (page 182) from Vietnam and Chinese Stuffed Vegetables and Beancurd (page 42);
• Sago with Honeydew from Malaysia/Singapore (page 134) makes an excellent finale.

THE ESSENTIAL FLAVORS OF INDONESIAN COOKING

For making the Indonesian *rempah*, **garlic**, **ginger**, **galangal**, **chilies,** and **shrimp paste** are a must. You'll also need freshly squeezed **lime juice** and *salam* **leaf**. Unique to Indonesian cuisine is the use of *tempeh*. **Coconuts**—the milk and flesh—are an integral part of Indonesian cooking, and are used in salads, curries, and desserts. **Palm sugar** is used in sweet and savoury dishes. **Noodles** and **rice** are the main staples.

Marinated Sour Shrimp (upper left) and Tuna Sambal (lower right)

In Indonesia these dishes would be used as side dishes to accompany rice. If you like you can increase the quantities slightly and serve as part of a shared main meal with rice.

Asam Udang
Marinated Sour Shrimp

Belimbing *wuluh*, small sour carambola fruits, grow abundantly in many kitchen gardens throughout Indonesia, as well as in other areas of Southeast Asia. They add a delicious tang to this North Sumatran salad, although sour grapefruit or sour oranges can be used as a substitute.

- 2 lb (1 kg) large shrimp (with shells)
- 6 shallots, peeled and finely chopped
- 3 red chilies, deseeded and finely sliced
- 4 sour carambola (*belimbing wuluh*), sliced, or 1 sour grapefruit, peeled and chopped

Put shrimp in a pan with 8 cups (2 liters) water and bring to a boil. Simmer for 4 minutes, drain and plunge shrimp in iced water for 30 seconds. Drain, then peel shrimp.

Grind or blend shallots, chilies, and carambola or grapefruit to a fine paste. Taste and add a little lime or lemon juice if not sour enough. Combine with shrimp and serve.

Sambal Tappa
Tuna Sambal

This recipe comes from Ambon, in Maluku, where tuna is abundant. Although the flavor is not as good, drained canned tuna can be used as a substitute, if fresh tuna is not available.

- 5 sour green mangoes, peeled and coarsely shredded
- 2 teaspoons salt
- 1 1/4 lb (600 g) fresh tuna, grilled and flaked
- 3 shallots, peeled and sliced
- 1 teaspoon white peppercorns, ground
- 1/4 cup (60 ml) thick coconut milk

Mix mangoes with salt and set aside for 10 minutes. Squeeze to remove sour liquid. Mix with the tuna, shallots, pepper, and coconut milk and serve.

Otak-otak
Grilled Fish in Banana Leaf

This Kalimantan recipe calls for steamed bundles of minced, seasoned fish to be cooked directly on hot charcoal, giving an inimitable flavor.

- 1 1/4 lb (600 g) boneless white fish fillets (such as snapper), skinned and chopped
- 15 shallots, peeled and sliced
- 3 garlic cloves, peeled and sliced
- 3 scallions (spring onions), chopped
- 1 teaspoon white peppercorns, crushed
- 1/2 cup (125 ml) thick coconut milk
- 1 tablespoon lime juice
- 1 teaspoon salt
- 3 eggs
- Pieces of banana leaf or aluminum foil, 5 in (12 cm) square, for wrapping

Put fish in a blender and process for a few seconds. Add all other ingredients, except for banana leaf, and process until well blended.

Put 3 heaped tablespoons of fish in the center of each square of banana leaf, roll firmly and secure with toothpicks. Steam the parcels for 15 minutes, then place directly onto charcoal or under a broiler (grill) for 5 minutes, turning from time to time, until the leaves are charred.

Serve still wrapped in banana leaf.

Grilled Fish in Banana Leaf

Sate Sapi
Beef Satay

1¼ lb (600 g) top round beef, in
   ½-in (1-cm) cubes
3–5 bird's-eye chilies
2 tablespoons brown sugar

Spice Paste
10 shallots, peeled and sliced
6 cloves garlic, peeled and sliced
4 in (10 cm) galangal (*laos*),
   peeled and sliced
2 in (5 cm) ginger peeled and sliced
6 red chilies, sliced
7 bird's-eye chilies, sliced
10 candlenuts
1 tablespoon black peppercorns
1 tablespoon coriander seeds
4 tablespoons chopped palm sugar
2 *salam* leaves
4 tablespoons oil

Prepare spice paste by blending all ingredients, except *salam* leaves and oil. Sauté blended mixture in oil with *salam* leaves for 5 minutes until golden brown. Cool, then combine with meat, chilies, and sugar. Marinate in the refrigerator for 24 hours (can be kept up to 4 days).

Thread meat onto satay skewers and grill over high heat until cooked. Serve with peanut sauce.

Raw Vegetables (left) and Cooked Vegetables in Peanut Sauce (right), recipes on page 74

Sate Lilit Bebek
Minced Duck Satay

1¼ lb (600 g) duck or chicken
   meat, minced
2 cups (200 g) freshly grated
   coconut
5 kaffir lime leaves, very finely
   shredded
1 teaspoon black peppercorns,
   crushed
1 teaspoon salt
3–5 bird's-eye chilies, very finely
   chopped
2 tablespoons chopped palm
   sugar
Lemongrass or satay skewers

Spice Paste
12 shallots, peeled and sliced
6 cloves garlic, peeled and
   sliced
3 red chilies, sliced
1 in (2½ cm) galangal (*laos*),
   peeled and sliced
1 in (2½ cm) *kencur*, peeled and
   sliced
2 in (5 cm) fresh turmeric, peeled
   and sliced
2 teaspoons coriander seeds
½ teaspoon black peppercorns
3 candlenuts
1 teaspoon dried shrimp paste (*trasi*)
Pinch of freshly grated nutmeg
2 cloves
2 tablespoons oil

Grind or blend all spice paste ingredients, except oil. Heat oil and sauté spice paste for about 5 minutes. Cool, then combine with duck and all other ingredients except lemongrass skewers. Mold about 2 tablespoonfuls on lemongrass or skewers and grill over hot charcoal until cooked and golden brown.

HELPFUL HINT
Soak skewers for at least 30 minutes before use.

Rempeyek Kacang
Crisp Peanut Wafers

1¼ cups (200 g) raw peanuts
14 tablespoons (150 g) rice flour
¾ cup (100 g) all-purpose (plain)
   flour
1 cup (250 ml) coconut milk
Oil for deep-frying

Spice Paste
1 teaspoon coriander seeds
2 candlenuts
2 cloves garlic
½ in (1 cm) fresh turmeric,
   peeled and sliced (or
   ½ teaspoon powder)
5 kaffir lime leaves, shredded
   (optional)
1 teaspoon salt

Dry fry the peanuts in a wok over low heat for 5 minutes. Rub to remove the skin and set aside. Grind or blend the spice paste ingredients, then add to flours. Mix well, stirring in the coconut milk to blend well. Add the peanuts. Heat plenty of oil in a wok and drop in a tablespoonful of batter at a time, cooking until golden brown. Drain and cool thoroughly before storing.

Beef Satay

Vegetable Salad with Peanut Sauce

The Indonesian salad differs completely from Western-style salads. Be prepared for the sweet, sour, hot, salty, and spicy assailing your senses all at once!

Karedok
Raw Vegetables

1/4 medium-sized round green
    cabbage, shredded
1 small cucumber, peeled, halved
    lengthwise and sliced
2 cups (200 g) beansprouts,
    cleaned
4 tiny round eggplants (aubergines),
    or 1 small long eggplant, finely
    sliced
1 cup (100 g) diced young long
    beans
4 sprigs basil
Fried shallots and prawn wafers
    (*krupuk*) to garnish

Spice Paste
4 cloves garlic, peeled and sliced
8 red chilies, seeded and sliced
2 in (5 cm) *kencur*, peeled and
    sliced
1 teaspoon dried shrimp paste
    (*trasi*), toasted
1 tablespoon tamarind juice
4 tablespoons chopped palm sugar
2 teaspoons salt

Arrange vegetables in a bowl. Grind or blend the spice paste ingredients together, adding a little water if necessary. Pour sauce over vegetables. Mix well and garnish with fried shallots and *krupuk*.

Lotek
Cooked Vegetables in Peanut Sauce

8 oz (250 g) water convolvulus
    (*kangkung*) or spinach, steamed
    (about 5 cups)
8 oz (250 g) pumpkin or chayote,
    cut in chunks and steamed
    (about 2 cups)
8 oz (250 g) long beans, cut in
    1 1/2-in (4-cm) lengths and
    steamed (about 2 cups)
8 oz (250 g) young jackfruit,
    cubed and simmered in water
    until tender (about 2 cups)
1 cup (100 g) beansprouts,
    blanched
1 large potato, boiled, peeled
    and diced
5 bird's-eye chilies, sliced
3/4 in (2 cm) *kencur*, sliced
1/2 teaspoon dried shrimp paste
    (*trasi*), toasted
1 teaspoon chopped palm sugar
1/4 teaspoon salt
1/2 cup (80 g) fried peanuts,
    ground

Prepare the vegetables and set aside. Grind or blend the chilies, *kencur*, shrimp paste, palm sugar, and salt. Mix well to make a sauce. Adjust seasonings to taste. Serve vegetables with sauce poured over and sprinkle with the ground fried peanuts.

Gado Gado
Vegetable Salad with Peanut Sauce

1 cup (100 g) long beans, cut
    and blanched
1 cup (100 g) beansprouts,
    blanched
2 cups (100 g) spinach,
    blanched
1/4 small cabbage, chopped and
    blanched
1 medium-sized carrot, thinly sliced
    and blanched
4 squares hard beancurd,
    deep-fried and sliced
4 hard-boiled eggs,
    cut in wedges
2 tablespoons fried
    shallots

Peanut Sauce
3 cups (500 g) deep-
    fried peanuts
4 cloves garlic, peeled
10 bird's-eye chilies, sliced
3 in (8 cm) *kencur*, peeled
    and chopped
3 kaffir lime leaves
1/2 cup (125 ml) sweet soy sauce
2 teaspoons salt

6 cups (1 1/2 liters) water
3 tablespoons fried shallots
    (page 87)
1 tablespoon lime juice

To make the peanut sauce, blend the first four ingredients until coarse. Put in a pan with all other sauce ingredients, except fried shallots and lime juice. Simmer over very low heat for 1 hour, stirring to prevent sticking. Stir in shallots and lime juice just before use. Arrange all vegetables on a dish and pour over the sauce. Garnish with beancurd and eggs, sprinkle with shallots and serve.

Timun Mesanten
Cucumber with Coconut Sauce

The bland flavor of cucumbers can be enhanced when prepared with coconut milk and spicy seasonings.

- 2 tablespoons oil
- 3 shallots, peeled and sliced
- 2 cloves garlic, peeled and sliced
- 2 large red chilies, seeded and sliced
- 1/2 teaspoon dried shrimp paste
- 2 cups (500 ml) coconut milk
- 2 medium-sized cucumbers, peeled, seeded and sliced
- 1 teaspoon salt
- 1/4 teaspoon black peppercorns, crushed
- Fried shallots to garnish (page 87)

Heat oil in heavy saucepan. Add shallots, garlic, and chilies and sauté for 2 minutes over low heat. Mix in shrimp paste and sauté for another minute. Pour in coconut milk and bring to a boil. Reduce heat and simmer for 5 minutes.

Add cucumbers and bring to a boil. Reduce heat and simmer until cucumbers are cooked and sauce thickens. Season to taste with salt and pepper.

Garnish with fried shallots.

HELPFUL HINT

If possible, use Japanese cucumbers which have a better flavor and texture.

Green Bean Salad with Chicken

Lawar
Green Bean Salad with Chicken

No big religious or private celebration would be held without serving this ritual dish. Only the eldest and most experienced men are allowed to mix the many ingredients.

- 3 cups blanched long beans cut in 1/4 -in (1/2 -cm) slices
- 1/2 cup (50 g) grated coconut, roasted
- 6 cloves garlic, peeled, sliced and fried
- 6–8 shallots, peeled, sliced and fried
- 2 large red chilies, seeded and cut in fine strips
- 4–6 bird's-eye chilies, finely sliced
- 3 teaspoons fried bird's-eye chilies (page 87)
- 2 tablespoons spice paste for chicken (page 86)
- Fried shallots to garnish (page 87)

Dressing
- 1/2 lb (250 g) boneless chicken, minced
- 2 tablespoons spice paste for chicken (page 86)
- 12 in (30 cm) square of banana leaf
- 1 teaspoon freshly squeezed lime juice
- 1 teaspoon salt
- 1/2 teaspoon black peppercorns, crushed

Combine beans, coconut, garlic, shallots, all the chilies, and chicken spice paste in a large bowl and mix well.

To prepare the dressing, combine chicken mince with 2 tablespoons of chicken spice paste and mix well. Place minced chicken lengthwise in center of banana leaf and roll up very tightly. Place banana leaf roll on aluminum foil and roll up again very tightly. Turn sides simultaneously in opposite directions to tighten the roll. Steam the roll for 20 minutes. Remove aluminum foil and banana leaf, break up meat with a fork to its original minced form.

Combine minced chicken with bean mixture, season to taste with salt, pepper, and lime juice. Garnish with crispy fried shallots.

Shredded Chicken with Chilies and Lime

Ayam Pelalah
Shredded Chicken with Chilies and Lime

Use any type of leftover chicken (roast, steamed or fried) for this delightfully tangy chicken salad.

- 1 whole chicken, weighing about 2 1/2 lb (1 1/4 kg)
- 1 cup (250 ml) spice paste for chicken (page 86)
- 1/2 cup (125 ml) Tomato Sambal (page 86)
- 3 tablespoons freshly squeezed lime juice

Preheat oven to 350°F (180°C, gas mark 4). Rub the chicken outside and in with the spice paste. Place on wire rack in oven and roast until done. When cool, remove and discard the skin. Remove meat from bones and shred by hand into fine strips. Combine the chicken strips with the remaining ingredients. Mix well and season to taste.

Serve at room temperature with steamed rice.

HELPFUL HINT

Should there be any leftover chicken, it can be mixed with mashed potato and made into patties; just fry them in a little hot oil until golden. The use of potato is not strictly Balinese, but the result is very good.

Rujak
Vegetable and Fruit Salad with Palm Sugar Sauce

- 1 small pineapple, peeled and sliced evenly
- 1 sour mango, peeled and sliced
- 1 pomelo or grapefruit, peeled and cut in segments
- 1 small cucumber, peeled, seeded and sliced
- 3 water apples (*jambu*), quartered (optional)
- 1 medium-sized starfruit, sliced
- 1/2 small papaya, peeled, cut in half, seeded and sliced in even segments
- 1 green apple, peeled and sliced

Sauce
- 6 tablespoons tamarind pulp
- 1 cup (250 ml) palm sugar syrup (page 87)
- 1 teaspoon dried shrimp paste (*trasi*), roasted
- 6 bird's-eye chilies, left whole
- 1/2 teaspoon salt
- 1/2 cup (125 ml) water

To make the sauce, combine all ingredients in a heavy pan and bring slowly to the boil. Stir well and simmer for 10 minutes. When cool, squeeze to extract all the juice from the tamarind and strain through a sieve.

Combine all ingredients in salad bowl and mix well. Serve at room temperature.

Spicy Spare Rib Soup

Daging Belacang
Beef Soup with Chilies and Tamarind

An excellent way of dealing with tough cuts of beef, this soup from Timor in eastern Indonesia has a sweet-sour edge to it.

2 lb (1 kg) top round beef, in 1 piece
8 cups (2 liters) water
3 tablespoons oil
5 shallots, peeled and sliced
1 clove garlic, peeled and sliced
1/2 teaspoon dried shrimp paste (*trasi*), toasted
3/4 tablespoon chopped palm sugar
1 teaspoon sweet soy sauce
1 tablespoon tamarind juice
Salt to taste
2 red chilies, deseeded and sliced in fine strips
2 scallions (spring onions), cut in 1-in (2 1/2-cm) lengths

Simmer the meat in the water until half cooked, then cut in 3/4-in (2-cm) cubes, reserving the stock. Sauté beef in 2 tablespoons oil, then set aside.

Grind or blend the shallots, garlic, shrimp paste, and palm sugar, then sauté in 1 tablespoon oil until fragrant. Add fried meat and sweet soy sauce and sauté for a couple of minutes. Add reserved beef stock, tamarind juice, and salt then simmer until the beef is tender. Garnish with chilies and scallions.

Konro Makasar
Spicy Sparerib Soup

2 lb (1 kg) beef spareribs, cut in 2-in (5-cm) lengths
4 quarts (4 liters) water
4 shallots, peeled and sliced
2 cloves garlic, peeled and sliced
3 candlenuts
3 cups (300 g) freshly grated or dessicated coconut, fried until golden, then pounded
5 stalks lemongrass, bruised and tied
1 in (2 1/2 cm) galangal (*laos*), peeled and sliced
3 kaffir lime leaves
1/2 teaspoon white peppercorns, crushed
1 teaspoon salt
1 tablespoon fried shallots (page 87)
2 tablespoons sliced Chinese celery leaves

Put the beef ribs and water in a large pan and simmer, uncovered, until beef is tender.

Grind or blend the shallots, garlic, candlenuts, and add to the pounded coconut. Put into the stock together with all remaining ingredients, except fried shallots and celery leaves. Simmer until the meat is very tender, but not falling from the bones. Serve garnished with fried shallots and celery.

Sop Kepala Ikan
Fish-head Soup

This dish can be made with either one large fish head or a couple of smaller heads. There is not much flesh on the head, which is used to flavor the soup rather than to provide a substantial meal in itself.

4 cups (1 liter) water
1 teaspoon salt
3 stalks lemongrass, bruised
5 kaffir lime leaves
1 lb (500 g) snapper heads, cleaned and well rinsed
1 tablespoon fried shallots (page 87)

Spice Paste
7 red chilies, deseeded and sliced
6 shallots, peeled and chopped
3 cloves garlic, peeled and chopped
2 in (5 cm) ginger, peeled and chopped
1 1/2 in (4 cm) fresh turmeric, peeled and sliced (or 1 1/2 teaspoons powder)
1 tablespoon oil

Prepare the spice paste by grinding or blending all ingredients except oil, then sauté in oil for 2 to 3 minutes. Add water, salt, lemongrass, and lime leaves and bring to a boil. Put in the fish heads, return to a boil and then simmer, uncovered, until the fish heads are cooked. Serve garnished with fried shallots.

Gedang Mekuah
Green Papaya Soup

If you prefer to eat your papayas ripe and golden, you could try making this soup with any summer squash or Chinese winter melon instead.

1 unripe papaya, weighing roughly 1 1/2 lb (750 g)
4 cups (1 liter) chicken stock (page 87)
1 cup (250 ml) spice paste for vegetables (page 86)
2 *salam* leaves
1 stalk lemongrass, bruised
1/4 teaspoon ground white pepper
1 teaspoon salt
Fried shallots to garnish (page 87)

Peel the papaya, cut in half lengthwise and remove the seeds. Slice the papaya lengthwise into 4 or 6 slices, then slice crosswise in slices about 1/4 in (1/2 cm) thick. Heat stock, add spice paste and bring to a boil. Simmer 2 minutes, then add the *salam* leaves, lemongrass, and papaya and simmer gently until the papaya is tender. If the stock reduces too much, add more. Season to taste with pepper and salt and garnish with fried shallots.

HELPFUL HINT
To save time, you can use canned chicken broth in place of homemade chicken stock, although the taste will not be as good.

Fish-head Soup

Gulai Tempeh
Tempeh Stew

Any leafy green vegetable, such as spinach or water convolvulus (*kangkung*), can be substituted for tapioca (*cassava*) leaves.

- 2 cups (500 ml) coconut milk
- 2 whole cloves
- 4 fermented soy bean cakes (*tempeh*), cut in cubes
- 1 bunch (about 8 oz/250 g) tapioca leaves or substitute
- Salt to taste
- Fried shallots to garnish (page 87)

Spice Paste
- 4 cloves garlic, peeled and sliced
- 1 teaspoon white peppercorns, crushed
- 1 in (2 1/2 cm) ginger, peeled and sliced
- 1 1/2 in (4 cm) fresh turmeric, peeled and sliced (or 1 1/2 teaspoons powder)
- 1 tablespoon chopped palm sugar

Prepare the spice paste by grinding or blending all ingredients. Bring coconut milk to a boil, then add the spice paste, cloves, tempeh and tapioca leaves.

Simmer, uncovered, until tender and the sauce has thickened. Season to taste with salt and garnish with fried shallots.

Cram Cam
Clear Chicken Soup with Shallots

- 4 cups (1 liter) chicken stock (page 87)
- 1/2 cup (125 ml) spice paste for chicken (page 86)
- 1 teaspoon crushed black pepper
- 1 *salam* leaf
- 1 stalk lemongrass, bruised
- 13 oz (400 g) boneless chicken, skin removed and minced
- Salt and pepper to taste
- 2 tablespoons fried shallots (page 87)

Bring chicken stock to the boil in stockpot or large saucepan. Wrap spice paste and black pepper into a piece of cotton cloth and tie with string. Add the spice paste bundle, the *salam* leaf, and lemon grass to the soup and simmer for 10 minutes.

Add minced chicken and simmer for 15 minutes. Remove spice paste bundle from the soup and discard. Season soup to taste with salt and pepper.
Garnish with fried shallots.

Clear Chicken Soup with Shallots

Soto Babat
Clear Tripe Soup

The sugar cane is used to help soften the tripe rather than to add any sweetness to the soup; if this is not available, the cooking time will be slightly longer.

- 1 1/4 lb (600 g) beef tripe, cleaned and washed well
- 12 cups (3 liters) water
- 4 cups (1 liter) beef stock
- 2 in (5 cm) sugar cane stem, split lengthwise (optional)
- 1 in (2 1/2 cm) ginger, peeled and sliced lengthwise
- 4 cloves garlic, peeled and sliced
- 1 tablespoon distilled white vinegar
- 6 1/2 oz (200 g) giant white radish (*daikon*), peeled and diced in 1/2-in (1-cm) cubes
- 5 sprigs celery leaf, chopped
- 1 tablespoon fried shallots (page 87)

Rinse tripe well under running water until very clean. Bring water to a boil in a large pan, add tripe and simmer until soft (approximately 1 hour).

Strain water and cool tripe in iced water. Cut in pieces approximately 1 x 1/2 in (2 1/2 x 1 cm).

Bring beef stock, sugar cane, ginger, garlic, and vinegar to a boil. Add tripe and radish. Simmer until vegetables are soft. Garnish with celery leaf and fried shallots.

HELPFUL HINT
Any type of summer squash or Chinese winter melon can be used instead of giant white radish (Japanese *daikon*). This soup reheets well.

Tempeh Stew

To take the grind out of making the spice pastes, make enough for several meals and store, covered with a film of oil, in a jar in the refrigerator. Make sure you use a clean spoon each time you take some out, and it should keep for at least 2 weeks.

Nasi Kuning
Yellow Rice

Rice colored with turmeric and shaped into a cone is often present on festive occasions. The shape echoes that of the mythical Hindu mountain, Meru, while yellow is the color of royalty and one of the four sacred colors for Balinese Hindus.

- 1^1/2 cups (300 g) uncooked long-grain rice, washed thoroughly
- 2 in (5 cm) fresh turmeric, peeled and scraped
- 1^1/2 cups (375 ml) coconut milk
- ^{1}/2 cup (125 ml) chicken stock
- 1 *salam* leaf
- 1 pandan leaf, tied in a knot
- 1 stalk lemongrass, bruised
- ^{3}/4 in (2 cm) galangal (laos), peeled and sliced
- 2 teaspoons salt

Drain the rice in a sieve or colander. Put the fresh turmeric in a blender with ^{1}/4 cup (60 ml) water and process until fine. Strain through a sieve, pushing to extract all the juice. Measure 2 tablespoons and discard the rest. If fresh turmeric is not available, mix 2 teaspoons turmeric powder with 2 tablespoons water.

Put rice, turmeric water and all other ingredients in a heavy

Padang-style Eggs in Coconut Milk

Yellow Rice

saucepan. Cover and bring to a boil over moderate heat. Stir, lower heat to the minimum and cook until the rice is done. Remove all leaves and galangal before serving, pressed into a cone shape, if desired.

HELPFUL HINT
If the rice seems to be too dry before the grains are soft and swollen, sprinkle with a little more hot chicken stock and continue cooking.

Gulai Telur
Padang-style Eggs in Coconut Milk

A full-bodied dish often served at a typical West Sumatran or Padang-style meal.

- 2 cups (500 ml) coconut milk
- ^{1}/2 turmeric leaf, shredded (optional)
- 8 hard-boiled eggs, peeled
- 1 tablespoon tamarind juice
- Salt to taste
- Fried shallots to garnish (page 87)

Spice Paste
- 5 shallots, peeled and sliced
- 3 cloves garlic
- 4 bird's-eye chilies, chopped
- 1 in (2^1/2 cm) ginger, peeled and chopped
- ^{1}/2 in (1 cm) fresh turmeric, peeled and sliced
- 1 in (2^1/2 cm) galangal (laos), peeled and chopped

Grind or blend spice paste ingredients until coarse. Bring coconut milk gradually to a boil and add the spice paste, turmeric leaf and eggs. Simmer until the sauce thickens, then add tamarind juice and salt and simmer for another minute. Serve garnished with fried shallots.

Jangan Olah
Vegetables with Spicy Coconut

- 2 cups (100 g) chopped long beans
- 2 cups (100 g) young fern tips (fiddleheads) or chopped spinach
- 1 cup (100 g) beansprouts, blanched
- Fried shallots to garnish (page 87)

Sauce
- 7 bird's-eye chilies, sliced
- 8 red chilies, deseeded and sliced
- 1 tablespoon dried shrimp paste (*trasi*), toasted
- 4 cloves garlic, peeled and sliced
- 4 shallots, peeled and sliced
- 1 in (2^1/2 cm) fresh turmeric, peeled and sliced (or 1 teaspoon powder)
- 1 tablespoon chopped palm sugar
- 3 cups (300 g) freshly grated or desiccated coconut
- 4 cups (1 liter) water
- 3 *salam* leaves
- Salt to taste

Prepare sauce first by grinding or blending first 7 ingredients. Simmer with remaining ingredients until the sauce thickens. Cool to room temperature.

Lightly boil or steam the long beans and fern tips or spinach. Drain thoroughly and arrange on a plate. Add blanched beansprouts. Serve vegetables with sauce poured over and garnished with fried shallots.

Pork in Sweet Soy Sauce

Sambal Goreng Tempeh
Hot Spicy Fried Tempeh

Sweet with palm sugar and tangy with chilies, this is a Javanese favorite, which is served with rice and other dishes.

- 2 fermented soy bean cakes (*tempeh*), cut in long narrow strips and deep-fried
- 1 tablespoon oil
- 2 shallots, peeled and sliced
- 3 cloves garlic, sliced
- 2 red chilies, sliced
- 1 in (2 1/2 cm) galangal (*laos*), peeled and sliced
- 1/2 teaspoon dried shrimp paste (*trasi*)
- 5 tablespoons chopped palm sugar
- 3 tablespoons water
- 1 tablespoon tamarind juice
- Salt to taste
- 8 bird's-eye chilies, chopped

Deep-fry *tempeh* and set aside. Heat the oil and sauté the shallots, garlic, chilies, galangal, and shrimp paste for 2 to 3 minutes. Add the palm sugar, water, and tamarind juice and stir until the sugar has dissolved. Put in the *tempeh* and cook, stirring frequently, until the sauce has reduced and caramelized. Season to taste with salt. Add the bird's-eye chilies just before serving.

Fern Tips in Coconut Milk

Gulai Daun Pakis
Fern Tips in Coconut Milk

The young tips of several varieties of wild fern are enjoyed in many parts of Southeast Asia and have an excellent flavor.

- 3 cups (750 ml) coconut milk
- 1 lb (500 g) fern tips, cleaned
- 2 turmeric leaves (optional)
- 1 tablespoon tamarind juice
- Salt to taste

Spice Paste
- 3 shallots, peeled and sliced
- 2 cloves garlic, peeled and sliced
- 10 red chilies, seeded and sliced
- 1 in (2 1/2 cm) galangal (*laos*), peeled and sliced
- 1 in (2 1/2 cm) fresh turmeric, peeled and sliced
- 1 in (2 1/2 cm) ginger, peeled and sliced

To make the spice paste, grind or blend all ingredients together. Put spice paste in a saucepan with the coconut milk and bring to a boil, stirring. Simmer for one minute, then add the fern tips, turmeric leaves, and tamarind juice. Simmer, stirring frequently, until the fern tips are tender. Season to taste with salt.

HELPFUL HINT
If you are unable to find fern tips, spinach or asparagus is an acceptable substitute.

Be Celeng Base Manis
Pork in Sweet Soy Sauce

This delicious sweet pork dish with a hint of ginger and plenty of chilies to spice it up often appears on festive occasions.

- 2 tablespoons oil
- 5 shallots, peeled and sliced
- 5 cloves garlic, peeled and sliced
- 1 1/4 lb (600 g) boneless pork shoulder or leg, cut in 3/4-in (2-cm) cubes
- 3 in (8 cm) ginger, peeled and sliced lengthwise
- 4 tablespoons sweet soy sauce
- 2 tablespoons thin soy sauce
- 1 teaspoon black peppercorns, crushed
- 2 cups (500 ml) chicken stock (page 87)
- 6–10 bird's-eye chilies, left whole

Heat oil in a wok or heavy saucepan. Add shallots and garlic and sauté for 2 minutes over medium heat or until lightly colored. Add pork and ginger and continue to sauté for 2 more minutes over high heat. Add both types of soy sauce and black pepper and continue sautéing for 1 minute.

Pour in chicken stock and chilies and simmer over medium heat for approximately 1 hour. When done, there should be very little sauce left and the meat should be shiny and dark brown. If the meat becomes too dry during cooking, add a little chicken stock.

HELPFUL HINT
For a thicker sauce, pound the shallots, garlic, and ginger together and fry them before adding the pork.

Babi Masak Tomat
Pork Cooked with Tomatoes

A simple recipe from Kalimantan, where pork (particularly wild boar from the jungle) is popular among the Dyaks.

- 1 lb (500 g) pork, cut in 3/4-in (2-cm) cubes
- 4 tomatoes, sliced
- 4–6 coarse chives (*kucai*), or scallions (spring onions)
- 1 stalk lemongrass, bruised
- 1 cup (250 ml) water
- Spice Paste
- 4 shallots, peeled and sliced
- 4 red chilies, sliced
- 1 in (2 1/2 cm) ginger, peeled and sliced
- 1 teaspoon salt

Prepare spice paste by grinding or blending all ingredients together. Combine in a saucepan with all other ingredients and simmer until the pork is tender. If the gravy threatens to dry out before the pork is cooked, add a little more warm water.

Be Sampi Mesitsit
Dry Spiced Beef

This dish is so wonderfully flavored, that it's worth making a large amount. It is excellent as a finger food with cocktails, and also makes a tasty accompaniment to rice-based meals.

2 lb (1 kg) beef top round, cut in
    4 steaks of 8 oz (250 g) each
8 cloves garlic, peeled
2 teaspoons coriander seeds,
    crushed
1 tablespoon chopped palm sugar
2 large red chilies, seeded
2 tablespoons galangal (*laos*),
    peeled and sliced
2 teaspoons dried shrimp paste
    (*trasi*)
2 cloves, ground
1 teaspoon salt
1 teaspoon black peppercorns,
    coarsely ground
2 tablespoons oil
2 teaspoons freshly squeezed
    lime juice

Bring 5 quarts (5 liters) of lightly salted water to a boil in stockpot. Add beef and boil for approximately 1 hour until very tender. Remove from stock. Meat must be so tender that its fibers separate very easily. Reserve stock. Pound meat until flat and shred by hand into fine fibers.

Place garlic, coriander, palm sugar, red chilies, *laos*, dried shrimp paste, cloves, salt, and pepper in a food processor and purée coarsely, or grind in a stone mortar. Heat oil in heavy saucepan and sauté the marinade for 2 minutes over medium heat. Add shredded beef, mix well and sauté until dry. Season with lime juice.

Remove from heat and allow to cool. Serve at room temperature with steamed rice.

HELPFUL HINT
Do not be tempted to use a food processor to shred the meat; you will obtain the correct texture only by shredding the meat with your fingers or a fork.

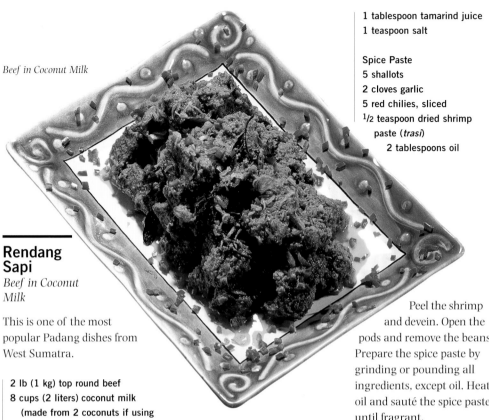
Beef in Coconut Milk

Rendang Sapi
Beef in Coconut Milk

This is one of the most popular Padang dishes from West Sumatra.

2 lb (1 kg) top round beef
8 cups (2 liters) coconut milk
    (made from 2 coconuts if using
    freshly grated coconut)
3 *salam* leaves
3 kaffir limes
3 fresh turmeric leaves (optional)
3 in (8 cm) cinnamon stick
5 whole star anise
5 cardamom pods, bruised
1 teaspoon salt

Spice Paste
8 red chilies, sliced
12 shallots, peeled and sliced
10 cloves garlic, peeled and sliced
2 in (5 cm) ginger, peeled and
    sliced
2 in (5 cm) galangal (*laos*), peeled
    and sliced
1 teaspoon black peppercorns,
    crushed

Prepare the spice paste by grinding or blending all ingredients finely.

Cut the beef into 1/4-in (1/2-cm) thick slices about 1-in (2 1/2-cm) square. Put the beef, spice paste and all other ingredients into a wok and bring slowly to a boil, stirring constantly to prevent the coconut milk from separating. Cook over low heat, stirring from time to time, until the meat is very tender and all the sauce has evaporated. Continue cooking the beef, which will fry in the oil that has come out of the coconut milk, until rich brown.

Sambal Udang
Shrimp in Hot Sauce

Even if stinkbeans (*petai*) are not available, the shrimp partnered with potatoes and a rich sauce are excellent.

1 lb (500 g) shrimp
5 pods (about 20 beans) stinkbeans
    (*petai*), optional
2 cups (500 ml) coconut milk
4 potatoes, peeled and cut in wedges

1 tablespoon tamarind juice
1 teaspoon salt

Spice Paste
5 shallots
2 cloves garlic
5 red chilies, sliced
1/2 teaspoon dried shrimp
    paste (*trasi*)
2 tablespoons oil

Peel the shrimp and devein. Open the pods and remove the beans. Prepare the spice paste by grinding or pounding all ingredients, except oil. Heat oil and sauté the spice paste until fragrant.

Add the shrimp and sauté until they change color. Put in the stinkbeans and coconut milk and bring to a boil, stirring. Add the potatoes and tamarind juice and simmer, uncovered, until potatoes and shrimp are cooked and the sauce has thickened. Season with salt and serve.

Shrimp in Hot Sauce

Udang Pantung Kuning
Lobster in Yellow Sauce

A real gourmet treat from Bali, this could also be made with huge shrimp.

4 small lobsters, weighing about
    1 lb (500 g) each, or 2 lb (1 kg)
    large shrimp
5 cups (1¼ liters) water
2 stalks lemongrass, bruised
2 fragrant lime leaves
Few drops white vinegar
4 cups (1 liter) coconut milk
Fried shallots to garnish (page 87)

Spice Paste
5 red chilies, deseeded and chopped
3 cloves garlic, peeled and chopped
7 shallots, peeled and chopped
2 in (5 cm) fresh turmeric, peeled
    and chopped (or 2 teaspoons
    powder)
2 in (5 cm) ginger, peeled
    and chopped
5 candlenuts
1½ teaspoons coriander seeds
½ teaspoon dried shrimp paste
    (*trasi*), toasted
1 small tomato, peeled and seeded
2 tablespoons oil
1½ tablespoons tamarind pulp
1 *salam* leaf
1 stalk lemongrass, bruised

Prepare spice paste by grinding or blending all ingredients except oil, tamarind, *salam* leaf, and lemongrass. Heat oil, add spice paste and all other ingredients. Cook over moderate heat for about 5 minutes, then cool.

Wash lobsters and leave whole. Bring water to a boil, add lobsters and simmer for 15 minutes. Remove lobsters, plunge in iced water for 1 minute, then drain and remove meat. Return shells to the pot of water, keeping lobster meat aside.

Add spice paste, lemongrass, lime leaves, and vinegar to the water with the shells and simmer until 4 cups (1 liter) of stock remain. Add coconut milk and simmer for 10 minutes. Strain stock and return to pan. Add lobster and simmer for 1 minute. Serve garnished with fried shallots and accompanied by white rice.

Arsin Ikan Mas
Simmered River Fish

1½ lb (750 g) freshwater fish,
    either 1 large fish or 2–4 smaller
    fish, cleaned and gutted
½ teaspoon salt
Liberal sprinkle of ground white
    pepper
2 cups (500 ml) water
2 stalks lemongrass, bruised
2 tablespoons tamarind juice

Spice Paste
8 shallots, peeled and chopped
3 cloves garlic, peeled and
    chopped
½ teaspoon salt
6 candlenuts
1 in (2½ cm) ginger, peeled and
    sliced
1 in (2½ cm) fresh turmeric,
    peeled and sliced (or 1 teaspoon
    powder)
1 in (2½ cm) galangal (*laos*),
    peeled and sliced
15 red chilies, deseeded and
    sliced

Garnish
3 scallions (spring onions),
    chopped
½ small pineapple, peeled and
    sliced
2 fresh limes or lemons, cut in
    wedges

Season fish inside and out with salt and pepper. Prepare spice paste by grinding or blending all ingredients finely. Put in a pan with water and other ingredients, except fish. Bring to a boil, reduce heat and simmer, uncovered, for 10 minutes. Add a little more water if the stock evaporates too much.

Spicy Fried Sardines

Add fish and continue to simmer until cooked, turning fish over gently from time to time. Remove fish carefully from stock, arrange on platter and pour stock over. Garnish with scallions, pineapple, and lime.

Ikan Bumbu Acar
Spicy Fried Sardines

1¼ lb (600 g) sardines or other
    small fish, cleaned
2 teaspoons salt
6 tablespoons oil
2 red chilies, deseeded and sliced
13 green bird's-eye chilies, sliced
2 cloves garlic, peeled and sliced
7 shallots, peeled and sliced
½ in (1 cm) ginger, peeled
    and sliced

½ in (1 cm) galangal (*laos*),
    peeled and sliced
1 large tomato, cut in wedges
2 tablespoons tamarind juice
1 *salam* leaf
½ teaspoon brown sugar
3 tablespoons water
Basil sprigs to garnish (optional)

Spice Paste
1 in (2½ cm) fresh turmeric,
    peeled and chopped (or
    1 teaspoon powder)
½ in (1 cm) ginger, peeled and
    chopped
2 candlenuts
2 shallots, peeled and sliced
2 cloves garlic, peeled and
    chopped
1 teaspoon white peppercorns,
    crushed
½ teaspoon coriander seeds,
    crushed
2 tablespoons vegetable oil

Prepare spice paste by grinding or blending all ingredients, except oil. Heat oil and gently sauté the spice paste for 3 to 5 minutes until fragrant, then set aside.

Wash the sardines, drain and sprinkle with salt. Heat 3 tablespoons of the oil in a wok and sauté the chilies, garlic, shallots, ginger, galangal, tomato, tamarind juice, and *salam* leaf over high heat for 1 minute, stirring constantly. Add sugar, then the spice paste and fry for another 2 minutes, stirring frequently.

*Lobster in
Yellow Sauce*

In another pan, heat remaining oil and fry the fish until golden brown. Drain, then combine with the spicy sauce in the wok and add water. Cook for another minute, stirring to mix well, then serve garnished with basil.

Pesan Be Pasih
Grilled Fish in Banana Leaf

- 1 lb (500 g) skinned boneless snapper fillet, cut in 4
- 1 teaspoon salt
- 1 cup (250 ml) spice paste for seafood (page 86)
- 4 banana leaves, cut in 6 in (15 cm) squares
- 8 sprigs lemon basil
- 4 *salam* leaves

Season fish fillet with salt and cover evenly with seafood spice paste. Cover and leave to marinate in cool place for 6 hours. Place each fillet in center of each banana leaf, top each with 2 sprigs of lemon basil and 1 *salam* leaf. Fold banana leaves around fillets in shape of a small parcel and fasten with a toothpick. Steam parcels for 15 minutes, then place on charcoal grill or under a broiler and cook for 5 minutes until banana leaves are evenly browned.

> **HELPFUL HINT**
> You can steam the packets several hours before barbecuing.

Kenus Mebase Bali
Balinese Squid

If squid is unavailable, replace with large cuttlefish or any other firm fish fillets, such as snapper or sea bass.

- 1 1/4 lb (600 g) baby squid
- 1 tablespoon freshly squeezed lime juice
- 1/4–1/2 teaspoon ground white pepper
- 1/2 teaspoon salt
- 3 tablespoons oil
- 5 shallots, peeled and sliced
- 2 large red chilies, seeded and sliced
- 1/2 cup (125 ml) spice paste for seafood (page 86)
- 1 cup (250 ml) chicken stock (page 87)
- 5 sprigs lemon basil, sliced
- Fried shallots (page 87)
- Sprigs of lemon basil to garnish

Remove skin of squid and pull out the tentacles and head. Cut off and discard the head and beaky portion, but reserve the tentacles, if desired. Clean the squid thoroughly inside and out. Marinate squid with lime juice, pepper and salt.

Heat oil in wok, add shallots, chilies and squid and sauté for 2 minutes over high heat. Add seafood spice paste and continue to sauté for 1 more minute. Pour in chicken stock, add the sliced basil and bring to a boil. Reduce heat and simmer for 1 minute.

Buginese Chicken

Season to taste and garnish with lemon basil and fried shallots

Ayam Masak Bugis
Buginese Chicken

- 1 whole chicken (2–3 lb/1–1 1/2 kg)
- 4 cups (1 liter) chicken stock
- 2 cloves garlic, peeled and sliced
- 12 shallots, peeled and sliced
- 1 tablespoon dried shrimp paste (*trasi*), toasted
- 2 tablespoons tamarind juice
- 2 teaspoons white peppercorns, crushed

Balinese Squid

- 2 *salam* leaves
- 3 in (8 cm) cinnamon stick
- 4 cloves
- 1/4 teaspoon freshly grated nutmeg
- 1 teaspoon salt
- 1 teaspoon chopped palm sugar
- 1 tablespoon white vinegar
- 4 cups (1 liter) coconut milk
- Fried shallots to garnish (page 87)

Bring chicken stock to a boil in a heavy saucepan, then add all other ingredients, except chicken, coconut milk and fried shallots. Bring back to a boil, lower heat and simmer, uncovered, for 5 minutes. Add whole chicken and coconut milk. Bring back to a boil, stirring frequently, then lower heat. Simmer uncovered, turning chicken from time to time, until it is tender. Remove chicken and continue simmering the stock until reduced by half. Serve garnished with fried shallots.

> **HELPFUL HINT**
> Balinese Squid: If you are using frozen squid, plunge in boiling water for 30 seconds to seal the squid, thus ensuring that it sautés rather than stews.

Ayam Goreng Yogya
Yogya Fried Chicken

- 1 fresh chicken (2 lb/1 kg), cut in
  8 pieces
- 2 cups (500 ml) water
- Oil for deep-frying

Spice Paste
- 1 tablespoon coriander seeds
- 3 cloves garlic, peeled and sliced
- 3/4 in (2 cm) fresh turmeric,
  peeled and sliced
- 3/4 in (2 cm) ginger, peeled and
  sliced
- 1/2 in (1 cm) galangal (*laos*),
  peeled and sliced
- 1 tablespoon chopped palm sugar
- 2 tablespoons oil
- 2 *salam* leaves

Prepare the spice paste by grinding or blending all ingredients, except oil and *salam* leaves, until fine. Heat oil in a wok and sauté the spice paste and *salam* leaves for 3 minutes. Add chicken and cook, stirring, until well coated. Add water and simmer, uncovered, until chicken is almost cooked and sauce is dry. Leave to cool.

Just before chicken is required, heat oil and deep-fry chicken until crisp and golden brown. Serve with the *sambal* of your choice.

Bebek Menyatnyat
Duck Curry

Ducks waddling along the banks of the rice fields or following the flag held by their owner (or his children) are a common sight in Bali. On festive occasions, duck is a great favorite. Chicken could be used as a substitute for duck, if preferred.

- 1 whole duck, weighing about
  4 lb (2 kg)
- 8 cups (2 liters) coconut milk
- 2 stalks lemongrass, bruised
- 2 *salam* leaves
- 1 tablespoon salt
- 1 teaspoon black peppercorns,
  crushed
- Fried shallots to garnish (page 87)

Spice Paste
- 12 shallots, peeled and sliced
- 6 cloves garlic, peeled and sliced
- 4 red chilies, sliced
- 1 in (2 1/2 cm) galangal (*laos*),
  peeled and sliced
- 1 in (2 1/2 cm) *kencur*, peeled and
  sliced
- 2 in (5 cm) fresh turmeric, peeled
  and sliced
- 2 teaspoons coriander seeds, crushed
- 3 candlenuts
- 1 teaspoon dried shrimp paste (*trasi*)
- 1/4 teaspoon black peppercorns,
  crushed
- Pinch of freshly grated nutmeg
  2 cloves
    3 tablespoons oil

Cut the duck into 12 pieces and pat dry. Prepare the spice paste by grinding or blending all ingredients, except oil. Heat the oil and sauté the spice paste for 2 minutes. Add the duck, increase heat and sauté for 3 minutes, stirring frequently. Add the coconut milk and all other ingredients, except fried shallots, and simmer, uncovered, until the duck is tender and the sauce has thickened. Garnish with fried shallots and serve with white rice.

Duck Curry

Chicken with Green Tomatoes

Ayam Cincane
Chicken with Green Tomatoes

This recipe comes from West and South Kalimantan, where it is usually made with a free-range or *kampung* chicken. As this is often as tough as it is flavorful, the meat is simmered in water first. If you are using a normal tender chicken, this preliminary step is very brief.

- 1 fresh chicken (2–3 lb/1–1 1/2 kg),
  cut in 8–12 pieces
- 1 teaspoon salt
- 1 tablespoon lime or lemon juice
- 10 red chilies, deseeded and sliced
- 12 shallots, peeled and sliced
- 4 green tomatoes, sliced
- 1 sprig basil
- 3 kaffir lime leaves
- 2 scallions (spring onions), sliced
- 1/2 in (1 cm) ginger, peeled and
  sliced
- 5 bird's-eye chilies, sliced

Season the chicken with salt and lime juice and set aside for 20 minutes. Put the chicken in a wok, add 2 cups (500 ml) water and simmer, uncovered, until the chicken is just tender. Add all remaining ingredients, except bird's-eye chilies, and continue cooking for another 5 minutes.

Sprinkle with bird's-eye chilies and serve.

Indonesian desserts are usually very colorful, and you'll notice that coconut, palm sugar, and pandan (screwpine) leaves are indispensable.

Es Campur
Mixed Ice

1 1/4 ripe papaya, peeled and diced

1/2 avocado, peeled and diced

1 tomato, diced

1/4 ripe pineapple, peeled and diced

8 tablespoons agar-agar jelly cubes or flavored gelatin cubes

8 tablespoons diced fermented tapioca (*tape*), (optional)

8 tablespoons diced *kolang kaling* (palm fruit, available in cans)

1 young coconut, flesh removed with spoon (optional)

1 cup (250 ml) coconut water from young coconut

1/2 cup (125 ml) condensed milk

1/2 cup (125 ml) palm sugar syrup (page 87)

4 cups crushed ice

Cut all fruits into 1/4 in (1/2 cm) dice. Combine with all other ingredients, except ice, and mix well. Add crushed ice and serve immediately.

Ongol-ongol
Sago Flour Roll

1 cup (160 g) sago flour

1 cup (150 g) chopped palm sugar

2 pandan leaves

3 1/2 cups (875 ml) water

Large square of banana leaf or parchment paper

Freshly grated coconut or moistened dried unsweetened coconut

1/2 teaspoon salt

Palm sugar syrup (page 87)

Combine flour, sugar, pandan leaves, and water in a heavy pan and bring to a boil. Simmer over low heat for 30 minutes until thickened, then leave until cool enough to handle.

Place the mixture on a large square of banana leaf and roll up in a cylinder. Fasten the ends with toothpicks and allow to cool. Serve the *ongol-ongol* sliced, sprinkled with a little coconut mixed with salt, and pour over palm sugar syrup.

Sago Flour Roll

Kue Nagasari
Steamed Banana Cakes

Bananas are the most common fruit in Indonesia, so it's not surprising they appear in so many desserts and cakes.

1 1/2 cups (240 g) mung pea flour (*tepong hoen kwe*) or rice flour

1/3 cup (80 g) white sugar

2 1/4 cups (550 ml) coconut milk

Pinch of salt

6 in (15 cm) squares of banana leaf

6 small or 2 large bananas, cut in 1/2-in (1-cm) thick slices about 2 1/2-in (6-cm) in length

Combine the flour and sugar in a bowl and stir in coconut milk, mixing well. Add salt and slowly bring the mixture to a boil in a heavy pan (preferably nonstick). Simmer until the mixture is very thick, then leave to cool.

Put 1 heaped tablespoon of the mixture onto a square of banana leaf. Top with a piece of banana and cover with another tablespoonful of mixture. Wrap up the banana leaf, tucking in the sides first and then rolling it over envelope style. Steam for about 20 minutes, cool and serve at room temperature.

HELPFUL HINT

Tepong hoen kwe is sold in paper-wrapped cylinders; sometimes, the flour is colored pink or green and the paper wrapper is correspondingly colored. This flour gives a more delicate texture than rice flour, although the latter is an acceptable substitute often used in Indonesia.

Wajik
Rice Flour Cake with Palm Sugar

There are a couple of variations on this popular cake, which can be stored in the refrigerator for several days. It is normally served at room temperature, but can also be served warm topped with coconut milk. Another variation is to add ripe diced jackfruit (or substitute with sultanas) after the rice is partially cooked.

1 cup (200 g) uncooked glutinous (or sticky) white rice

1 cup (250 ml) water

1 pandan leaf

1/2 cup (125 ml) palm sugar syrup (page 87)

1/4 cup (60 ml) thick coconut milk

Pinch of salt

Rinse the rice very well under running water for 2 minutes and soak for 4 hours. Rinse again until water becomes clear. Place rice, 1 cup (250 ml) water and *pandan* leaf in rice cooker or steamer and cook for approximately 20 minutes, or until liquid has evaporated.

Add the palm sugar syrup, coconut milk and salt, and steam for 15 minutes. Spread the rice evenly 1 in (2 1/2 cm) thick on tray and allow to cool to room temperature. Wet a sharp knife with warm water and cut into even squares to serve.

HELPFUL HINT

To speed up the soaking process, pour boiling water over the rice and let stand for 1 hour. Drain, then add another lot of boiling water and soak for another 30 minutes. If you are using a steamer to cook the rice, line the bottom with a wet cloth to prevent the rice grains from falling through.

Dadar
Coconut Pancake

Both the pancakes and the filling can be made in advance and refrigerated; allow both to come to room temperature before filling.

Pancakes
3 1/2 oz (100 g) rice flour
2 tablespoons sugar
1/4 teaspoon salt
3 eggs
1 cup (250 ml) fresh coconut milk
2 tablespoons coconut oil

Filling
1/2 cup (125 ml) palm sugar syrup (page 87)
1 cup (100 g) freshly grated coconut
1 pandan leaf

To make the pancakes, combine rice flour, sugar, salt, eggs, coconut milk, and coconut oil in a deep mixing bowl. Stir well with whisk until all lumps dissolve. Strain through a sieve. Batter should be very liquid in consistency. Heat non-stick pan over low heat. For each pancake, pour in 4 tablespoons of the batter and cook for about 2 minutes, until the top is just set. Turn the pancake over and cook a further minute. Repeat until all the batter is used up. Cool pancakes down to room temperature.

To make the filling, combine sugar syrup and grated coconut and mix well. Add pandan leaf and fry over low heat in frying pan for 2 minutes, stirring continuously. Cool and use at room temperature.

Place 1 tablespoon of coconut filling in center of each pancake, fold at edge and roll tightly into tube shape.

Pisang Goreng
Fried Banana Cakes

Whole bananas dipped in batter and deep fried are very popular; if the bananas become over-ripe, they are often mashed and prepared by the following method.

6 medium-sized ripe bananas, peeled
1 tablespoon white sugar
1 tablespoon all-purpose (plain) flour
Oil for deep-frying

Mash bananas finely and mix with sugar and white flour. Heat oil in a wok and drop in a large spoonful of batter. Cook several at one time, but do not over of crowd the wok or the temperature the oil will be lowered. When cakes are crisp and golden brown, drain on paper towel and serve while still warm.

Black Rice Pudding

HELPFUL HINT
As fresh coconut milk turns rancid fairly quickly, a pinch of salt is usually added to the milk to help preserve it for a few hours.

Bubuh Injin
Black Rice Pudding

1 cup (200 g) black glutinous rice
3/4 cup (150 g) white glutinous rice
2 pandan leaves
5 cups (1 1/4 liters) water
1/2 cup (125 ml) palm sugar syrup (page 87)
Pinch of salt
1 1/2 cups (375 ml) freshly squeezed thick coconut milk

Rinse both types of rice thoroughly for 2 minutes under running water. Drain. Put 5 cups (1 1/4 liters) water, both types of rice and pandan leaf into heavy pan. Simmer over medium heat for approximately 40 minutes.

Add palm sugar syrup and cook until most of the liquid has evaporated. Season with a pinch of salt. Remove from heat, allow to cool. Serve at room temperature, topped with freshly squeezed coconut milk.

Coconut Pancake

Base be Siap
Spice Paste for Chicken

14 shallots, peeled
26 cloves garlic, peeled
1 in (2^{1}/$_{2}$ cm) *kencur*, peeled
   and chopped
1^{1}/$_{2}$ in (4 cm) galangal (*laos*),
   peeled and chopped
10 candlenuts
5 in (12 cm) fresh turmeric,
   peeled and chopped (or
   5 teaspoons powder)
4 tablespoons chopped palm sugar
4 tablespoons vegetable oil
2 stalks lemongrass, bruised
2 *salam* leaves
10 bird's-eye chilies, finely sliced

Put shallots, garlic, *kencur*, *laos*, candlenuts, turmeric, and palm sugar into a food processor and grind coarsely. Heat oil and fry all ingredients until very hot, stirring frequently, until the marinade changes to a golden color. Cool before using.

Spice Paste for Beef

Base be Sampi
Spice Paste for Beef

10 shallots, peeled and chopped
6 cloves garlic, peeled and
   chopped
2 in (5 cm) ginger, peeled and
   chopped
4 in (10 cm) galangal (*laos*),
   peeled and chopped
6 large red chilies, seeded and
   chopped
7 bird's-eye chilies
10 candlenuts
1 tablespoon coriander seeds
1 tablespoon black peppercorns
4 tablespoons chopped palm sugar
4 tablespoons oil
2 *salam* leaves

Combine all ingredients, except oil and *salam* leaves, place in food processor and grind coarsely. Heat vegetable oil in heavy saucepan or wok until very hot. Add ground ingredients together with *salam* leaves and cook over medium heat for 5 minutes, stirring frequently, until marinade changes to a golden color. Set aside and cool before using.

Base be Pasih
Spice Paste for Seafood

10 large red chilies, seeded and
   chopped
6 cloves garlic, peeled and chopped
15 shallots, peeled and chopped
4 in (10 cm) ginger, peeled
   and chopped
4 in (10 cm) fresh turmeric, peeled
   and chopped (or 4 teaspoons
   powder)
1 medium-sized tomato, skinned
   and seeded
1 tablespoon coriander seeds
10 candlenuts
1 teaspoon dried shrimp paste
   (*trasi*)
4 tablespoons oil
2 *salam* leaves
2 stalks lemongrass, bruised
3 tablespoons tamarind pulp

Process all ingredients, except oil, tamarind pulp, *salam* leaves, and lemongrass, until coarsely ground. Heat oil, add ingredients, except tamarind. Stir frequently over moderate heat until fragrant and golden, 5 minutes. Finish with tamarind. Let cool.

Base Jukut
Spice Paste for Vegetables

8 shallots, peeled and chopped
10 cloves garlic, peeled and chopped
12 in (30 cm) galangal (*laos*),
   peeled and thinly sliced
1 teaspoon coriander seeds
4 in (10 cm) fresh turmeric,
   peeled and sliced
6 large red chilies, seeded and
   chopped
3–5 bird's-eye chilies
2 in (5 cm) *kencur*, peeled
   and chopped
1 teaspoon dried shrimp paste
   (*trasi*)
2 tablespoons oil
1 teaspoon salt
^{1}/$_{4}$ teaspoon ground white pepper
1 *salam* leaf, whole
1 stalk lemongrass, bruised

Place shallots, garlic, *laos*, coriander seeds, turmeric, chilies, *kencur*, and dried shrimp paste in food processor and purée lightly, or grind coarsely in mortar. Heat oil in wok or heavy saucepan. Add the ground paste and remaining ingredients, and sauté for 2 minutes or until marinade changes color. Cool before using.

Sambal Tomat
Tomato Sambal

4 tablespoons oil
15 shallots, peeled and sliced
10 cloves garlic, peeled and
   sliced
14 large red chilies, seeds removed,
   sliced
2 medium-sized tomatoes cut in
   wedges
2 teaspoons roasted dried shrimp
   paste (*trasi*)
2 teaspoons freshly squeezed lime
   juice
Salt to taste

Heat oil in a heavy saucepan or wok. Add shallots and garlic and sauté 5 minutes over low heat. Add chilies and sauté another 5 minutes, then add tomatoes and shrimp paste and simmer for another 10 minutes.

Add lime juice. Put all ingredients in a food processor and purée coarsely. Season to taste with salt. Cool before using. This sambal can be frozen. An ideal accompaniment to grilled fish.

Tomato Sambal

Sambal Sere Tabia
Fried Bird's-eye Chilies

25 bird's-eye chilies
1/4 cup (60 ml) oil
1 1/2 teaspoons dried shrimp paste (*trasi*)
1/4 teaspoon salt

Clean and discard the stems of the chilies. Heat oil in a wok or saucepan until smoking. Crumble dried shrimp paste and combine with salt.

Add chilies, shrimp paste, and salt to the oil, stir over heat for 1 minute and then remove from heat and allow to cool. Store chilies and cooking oil in an airtight container for up to 1 week in a refrigerator.

Base Kacang
Peanut Sauce

3 cups (500 g) raw peanuts, deep fried for 2 minutes
4 cloves garlic, peeled
10–15 bird's-eye chilies, sliced
3 fragrant lime leaves
1/2 cup (125 ml) sweet soy sauce

2 tablespoons fried shallots (page 87)
3 in (8 cm) *kencur*, peeled and coarsely chopped
1 tablespoon freshly squeezed lime juice
2 teaspoons salt
6 cups (1 1/2 liters) water

Combine peanuts, garlic, *kencur* and chilies and process or grind until coarse. Put in a heavy pan with all other ingredients, except lime juice and shallots, and simmer over very low heat for 1 hour, stirring constantly to prevent the sauce from burning. Stir in lime juice and sprinkle with shallots just before serving.

Kuah Siap
Chicken Stock

1 lb (500 g) chicken bones, chopped in 1-in (2 1/2-cm) pieces
1 1/2 cups (375 ml) spice paste for chicken (page 86)
1 stalk lemongrass, lightly bruised
3 fragrant lime leaves
2 *salam* leaves
1 teaspoon black peppercorns, coarsely crushed
1 teaspoon salt

Rinse bones until water is clear, put in large saucepan with cold water to cover and bring to a boil. Drain water, wash bones under running water. Return bones to the pan, cover with fresh water and boil. Reduce heat and remove scum with a ladle.

Add all seasoning ingredients and simmer stock gently uncovered for 3 to 3 1/2 hours, removing scum. Strain stock, cool and store in small containers in the freezer.

Sambal Matah
Shallot & Lemongrass Sambal

15 shallots
4 cloves garlic, sliced finely
10–15 bird's-eye chilies, sliced
5 fragrant lime leaves, cut in fine shreds
1 teaspoon roasted dried shrimp paste (*trasi*)
4 stalks lemongrass, tender part only, very finely sliced
1 teaspoon salt
1/4 teaspoon black peppercorns, finely crushed
2 tablespoons freshly squeezed lime juice
1/3 cup (90 ml) oil

Peel shallots and slice in half lengthwise, then cut in fine crosswise slices. Combine with all other ingredients and mix thoroughly for a couple of minutes before serving with fish or chicken.

Bawang Goreng
Fried Shallots

1/4 cup (60 ml) oil
10–15 shallots, peeled and thinly sliced

Heat oil until moderately hot. Add shallots and fry until golden brown. Remove and drain thoroughly before storing in an airtight jar.

Palm Sugar Syrup

Combine 2 cups of chopped palm sugar and 1 cup of water, adding 2 pandan leaves if available. Bring to boil, simmer for 10 minutes, strain and store in the refrigerator.

"Japanese cuisine today is a symbiosis of culinary influences imported from the outside world, refined and adapted to reflect local preferences in taste and presentation."

JAPAN

From the land of endless ingenuity has come a cuisine designed for the eyes as well as the palate.

Left: Everyone enjoys a box lunch, from school children and salary men to Buddhist monks.

Right: The serene beauty of Kyoto's Golden Pavilion temple is emblematic of traditional Japanese culture.

More than any other cuisine in the world, Japanese food is a complete aesthetic experience for the eyes, the nose and the palate. The presentation of food is as important as the food itself, with great care given to detail, color, form, and balance. In Japan, cuisine is culture, and culture cuisine; food is meant to create order out of chaos, complement nature from whence it came and still be presentational. It is a cuisine developed out of austerity and a sense of restraint.

The Land and its People

Japan's position north-east on the Southeast Asian monsoonal belt means the islands generally experience a temperate oceanic climate. Surrounded by sea, the Japanese have made its bounty—seaweed, fish and shellfish—a vital part of their diet. There is a Japanese saying that a meal should always include "something from the mountain and something from the sea," hence vegetables and rice.

Poultry and meat are also eaten, although they are less important than the humble soybean, which appears as nutritionally rich bean curd (*tofu*); as *miso*, fermented soybean paste used for soups and seasoning; and as soy sauce.

Over 43 percent of the nation's 124 million people is crammed into the three major coastal metropolises of Tokyo, Osaka, and Nagoya. Fully two-thirds of the land is mountainous or forested; just over 14 percent is agricultural, and a little over four percent is used for housing.

Japan is composed of four main islands—Hokkaido, Honshu, Shikoku, and Kyushu—and several thousand smaller islands stretching 1900 miles from Hokkaido.

Hokkaido is a land of wide expanses, dairy farms, ranches, and meadows, reminiscent of the American Midwest, and home to the Ainu, the indigenous people of Japan, a small Caucasoid minority. They were once hunters and fishermen who are thought to have roamed large areas of northern Honshu.

Each season has its special foods. Restaurants and private homes change their serving dishes to suit the season, as in this autumnal spread.

Central Japan encompasses the Sea of Japan coastal areas, where fishing villages can still be found, and the Japan Alps region centred in Nagano Prefecture, sometimes called the Roof of Japan. Three major mountain ranges traverse Nagano, and from the Koumi train line that runs through central Nagano, it is possible to enjoy views of the Japan Alps, the still-active volcano Mount Asama, and Mount Fuji, at 12,300 feet, Japan's highest mountain and a sacred symbol of the nation.

Kyushu, the third largest of Japan's islands, is renowned for its Imari and Arita pottery, hot springs resorts and active volcanoes. Nagasaki in western Kyushu was traditionally the center of trade with China and Holland and Japan's door to the outside world. Shikoku is Japan's fourth largest island.

The Ryukyu archipelago includes the southernmost province of Okinawa, comprising 160 islands, and stretches towards Taiwan.

The Making of a Cuisine

Japan's distinctive style of cuisine began to develop during the Heian Period (794–1185). The capital was moved from Nara to Kyoto, and the thriving aristocracy indulged its interests in art, literature, poetry, fine cuisine, and elaborate games and pastimes. Elegant dining became an important part of the lifestyle and the aristocracy were not only gourmets, but gourmands who supplemented their regular two meals a day with numerous between-meal snacks. Today, *Kyo ryori*, the cuisine of Kyoto, represents the ultimate in Japanese dining and features an assortment of carefully prepared and exquisitely presented delicacies.

In 1185, the government moved to Kamakura, where the more austere samurai lifestyle and Zen Buddhism fostered a more simple cuisine. *Shojin ryori* (vegetarian Buddhist temple fare), heavily influenced by Chinese Buddhist temple cooking, features small portions of a wide variety of vegetarian foods prepared in one of five standard cooking methods. *Shojin ryori* guidelines place emphasis on food of five colors (green, red, yellow, white, and black-purple) and six flavors (bitter, sour, sweet, hot, salty, and delicate). It was an extremely important culinary influence and the tradition lives on today. *Shojin ryori* also led to the development of *cha kaiseki*, food served before the tea ceremony, in the mid–16th century.

Japan's trade with the outside world from the 14th to 16th centuries brought many new influences. Kabocha, the green-skinned winter squash, was introduced by the Portuguese in the 16th century. The Portuguese are also credited with introducing *tempura* (batter-fried foods) as well as the popular cake *kasutera* (*castilla*). A century later, the Dutch brought corn, potatoes, and sweet potatoes. European cooking created some interest and developed into what came to be known in Japan as "the cooking of the Southern Barbarians" or *Nanban ryori*.

During the Edo Period (1603–1857), Japan underwent almost three centuries of self-imposed seclusion from the outside world, which led to the development of a highly refined and distinctive Japanese culture. The Meiji Period (1868–1912) marked the return of contact and trade, and the early 20th century renewed interest in things foreign.

Japanese cuisine today is a symbiosis of culinary influences imported from the outside world, refined and adapted to reflect local preferences in taste and presentation. The desire to adapt outside influences to local tastes has produced unique blendings of East and West, including green-tea ice cream and seaweed-flavored potato chips, even cod-roe spaghetti!

The Chinese influence is discernible: it was from China that Japan learned the art of making bean curd and how to use chopsticks. China was also the origin of soy sauce, although today's Japanese-style soy sauce is a product of the 15th century. Tea was first introduced from China in the 9th century, but gradually faded from use only to be reintroduced by a Zen priest in the late 12th century. Rice cultivation began in Japan around 300 BC and is still the cornerstone of a Japanese meal.

The Food of the People

The drastic extremes in Japan's climate—from the very cold northern island of Hokkaido to the subtropical southern islands of Okinawa—have led to the creation of regional cuisines.

In Hokkaido, which is not conducive to rice cultivation, the people have acquired a taste for potatoes, corn, dairy products, barbecued meats, and salmon. Their version of Chinese noodles, called *Sapporo ramen*, is often served with a dab of butter. Seafood *o-nabe* (one-pot stew) featuring crab, scallops, and salmon is also a specialty of the region.

There are differences in the food preferences of the residents of the Kanto region (centered around Tokyo and Yokohama) and the Kansai region (Kyoto, Osaka and environs). In the Kansai area, fermented *miso* is almost white compared with the darker brown and red *miso* favored in the Kanto region. Eastern and Western Japan are also divided by differing tastes in *sushi*, sweets, and pickles. The Kyoto area is identified with the light, delicately flavored cuisine of the ancient court, true *haute cuisine*.

Located halfway between Tokyo and Kyoto is Nagoya, known for its flat *udon* noodles and *uiro*, a sweet rice jelly. The island's famous Sanuki *udon* noodles, fresh sardines, and mandarins are popular with pilgrims visiting the Buddhist temples on Shikoku. Kyushu is known for its tea, fruits, and seafood, and for the Chinese and Western culinary influences that developed because of Nagasaki's role as a center of trade with the outside world.

On the islands of Okinawa, dishes featuring pork are favored. Sweets made with raw sugar, pineapple, and papaya are also popular, as are several powerful local drinks: *awamori*, made from sweet potatoes, and *habu* sake, complete with a deadly *habu* snake coiled inside the bottle.

The *o-bento* or box lunch is a microcosm of Japanese cuisine, consisting of white rice and an assortment of tiny helpings of meat, fish, vegetables, egg, fruit, and a sour plum (*umeboshi*), all arranged in a small rectangular box. Since only small portions of each dish are included and a well-balanced variety of foods is necessary, preparing a proper *o-bento* can be a time-consuming ritual. As with almost all Japanese dishes, attention to detail and attractive presentation are paramount. The most famous of the commercially made *o-bento* are the *ekiben*, the box lunches available at most of the nation's train stations. These vary greatly from one area of the country to another and are considered to be an important way of promoting regional delicacies, customs, and crafts.

The Four Seasons

One of the most striking aspects of Japanese cuisine is the emphasis on seasonal cuisine. Every food has its appropriate season, which not only ensures that Japanese tastes are in harmony with nature but that the cooks use the freshest possible ingredients.

By far the most important of seasonal dining specialties is *osechi ryori*, the special foods that are served during the first week of the new year. Dozens of items are decoratively arranged in tiered lacquer boxes which are brought out again and again over the first few days of the new year. Customs vary from home to home and region to region, but the typical New Year foods usually include *kamaboko* fish sausages bearing auspicious bamboo, plum, and pine designs; *konbu* seaweed rolls tied into bows with dried gourd strips; chestnuts in a sticky sweet-potato paste; herring roe, shredded carrot and white radish in a sweet vinegared dressing; and pickled lotus root. Vegetables such as *shiitake* mushrooms, radishes, lotus root, carrots, and burdock are boiled in a soy sauce and *dashi* broth. The savory steamed egg custard *chawan-mushi* is also often eaten.

The staple accompaniment for these dishes is *o-mochi*, rice cakes that can be grilled or boiled in a soup called *o-zoni*. *Mochi-gome*, a special type of glutinous rice, is prepared and molded into a ball while still hot and placed in a large round wooden mortar where it is pounded rhythmically. The final product is rolled out flat and cut into rectangular cakes.

Cherry blossom-viewing parties are a seasonal must for the majority of Japanese to signal the coming of spring. Top restaurants may serve a cup of cherry blossom tea with several delicate blossoms floating in the clear, slightly salty beverage to signal the auspicious event. Other spring delicacies include bamboo sprouts, bonito, and rape blossoms.

Summer is the time for grilled eel, which is believed to supply the energy needed to survive the sticky, humid weather. It is also the time for octopus, abalone, and fresh fruits and vegetables, especially the summer favorite, *edamame*—fresh soybeans boiled in the pod and dusted with salt—the perfect accompaniment for beer on a hot summer's night. Another summer treat is cold noodles served with a *dashi* and soy sauce dip.

Strings of persimmons drying can be seen dangling from the eaves of many a farmhouse in the countryside in autumn. This is also the season for roasted chestnuts, *soba* noodles, and mushrooms. *Matsutake*, highly prized mushrooms savored for their distinctive fragrance, appear now and are used in soups and rice dishes. Late autumn is the time for preserving the year's vegetable harvest for winter. A large variety of pickling methods are popular in Japan, the most common using *miso*, salt, vinegar or rice bran as preservatives.

Winter brings *fugu sashimi*, strips of raw blowfish which can be a deadly delicacy if the fish is not handled properly by a licensed chef. Mandarins and *o-nabe*, warming one-pot stews, are also enjoyed. On the final day of the year, it is customary to eat *soba* to guarantee health and longevity in the new year.

Few things are as quintessentially Japanese as the ritual tea ceremony which encapsulates all the refinement, discipline and mystique of Japanese culture. Cha-noyu, the Way of Tea, began in the 15th century, and in its early form placed much emphasis on displaying and admiring imported Chinese art objects. The Way of Tea gave rise to two of the more interesting aspects of Japanese cuisine: cha kaiseki, Japanese haute cuisine designed to be served as a light meal before a tea ceremony, and wagashi, traditional Japanese sweets which became an important accessory to the tea ceremony from the mid–16th century.

The Japanese Kitchen and Table

Don't be misled into thinking that because the individual portions of food that make a Japanese meal are small, you'll finish a Japanese meal hungry. With the variety of tastes, textures and flavors, you're certain to feel satisfied—physically and mentally—at the end of a meal.

A Japanese meal can be divided into a beginning, a middle and an end. The beginning includes appetizers, clear soups and raw fish (*sashimi*). The middle of the meal is made up of a number of seafood, meat, poultry and vegetable dishes prepared by either grilling, steaming, simmering, deep-frying or serving as a vinegared "salad." To ensure variety, each style of preparation would be used only once for the foods making up the middle of the meal. For example, if the fish was deep-fried, the vegetables might be simmered in seasoned stock, the meat grilled and a mixture of egg and savory tidbits steamed. Alternatively, this variety of "middle" dishes might be replaced by a hot-pot (*nabe*), a one-dish combination of vegetables, seafood, meat, bean curd, and noodles. The meal concludes with rice, *miso* soup and pickles, green tea and fresh fruit—the basis of every main meal in Japan.

Accompanying dishes are varied according to availability, season, how much time you have for preparation of the meal and so on. The Japanese do not categorize their food by the basic ingredient (for example, vegetables, beef or fish), but by the method with which it is prepared. Food is thus classified as grilled, steamed, simmered, deep-fried or vinegared.

The two extremes of Japanese cuisine are a full *kaiseki ryori*, an array of a dozen or more tiny portions of food, and the basic meal consisting of boiled rice, miso soup, and pickles. If you are new to Japanese cuisine, keep the menu simple. You might like to prepare an appetizer and a couple of other dishes using fish, meat, poultry or vegetables around the basic rice, soup, and pickles. You might even limit the meal to one simple appetizer and a one-pot dish such as *sukiyaki*, followed by

This beautifully presented meal shows the imaginative use of ceramics, lacquer-ware, porcelain and basketware that is typically Japanese.

the rice, soup, and pickles. It is better to serve three carefully cooked, beautifully presented dishes than six less-than-perfect ones.

In private homes and many restaurants, all the dishes making up the meal are presented at the same time. At a formal meal, the appetizers arrive first, followed by the "middle" dishes, each served in the order dictated by their method of preparation.

The presentation of Japanese food is an art that encourages the cook's imagination and creativity. Even the choice of tableware is influenced by the season and the type of food being served. Generally speaking, foods which are round, such as pieces of rolled meat or slices of lotus root, are presented on rectangular or square plates, while square-shaped foods are likely to be served on round plates for contrast. Such imagination is shown in Japan, however, that plates and bowls are not just square, rectangular or round; they might be hexagonal, semicircular, fan-shaped or resemble a leaf or shell. And, it has been said in Japan that "a person cannot go out naked in public, neither can food." In most cases, garnishes are edible.

The secret to preparing Japanese cuisine at home is an understanding of the basic ingredients and of how a meal is composed; the culinary methods used are actually very simple. But the most important requirement of all is simply a love of good food, prepared and presented with a sense of harmony.

The formal tea ceremony, with its bitter powdered green tea, led to the creation of delicate *wagashi* sweets during the 16th century.

SUGGESTED MENUS

A family meal (1)

With Japanese meals many small dishes are served, and often there is no "main" attraction—they all are! But you do not necessarily have to follow this practice.

For a family meal, you may like to serve the following:
• Rolled Sushi (page 98);
• Miso-Topped Bean Curd (page 100) and a small side dish of Green Beans with Sesame (page 100) with rice;
• Jellied Plums (page 106) are a simple dessert to make but look dramatic.

A family meal (2)

Another great menu for a family dinner.
• Begin with individual bowls of Savory Custard (page 95);
• Miso Soup with Mushrooms (page 96) and Shrimp with Sake (page 102);
• Green Tea Ice Cream is always a favorite with which to finish (page 106).

A dinner party

For a dinner party that will delight your guests, you can't go wrong with dishes such as:
• Shrimp-stuffed Mushrooms (page 94), served with small side dishes of Spinach with Sesame Dressing (page 94) and Tempura Whitebait in Soup (page 96);
• Sukiyaki (page 104) or Shabu-Shabu (page 104) that diners can cook as they eat;
• the beautiful Lily Bulb Dumplings (page 106) for dessert are a refreshing and unusual finish.

A melting pot menu

If you prefer a mix-and-match menu, put together a meal that features the following:
• Salmon Beancurd Balls (page 94) from Japan;
• Saffron Chicken (page 61) with Naan (page 55) from India and a dish of Spicy Kang kung (page 132) from Malaysia/Singapore;
• Round off the meal with some homely but delicious Pineapple Tartlets (page 186) from Vietnam, served with sliced fresh fruit.

THE ESSENTIAL FLAVORS OF JAPANESE COOKING

Dried bonito and **konbu** **seaweed** are essential for making the clear *dashi* that is used in much of Japanese cooking. Flavorful **miso**, with **bean curd** and **wakame** or **nori** **seaweed**, makes a quick and easy soup. Popular flavorings are **ginger**, **sake,** and **soy sauce**. **Mirin** and **rice vinegar** are added to rice for **sushi**. **Sesame paste** is used in dipping sauces.

Spinach with Sesame Dressing

Japanese appetizers are usually served in small portions on patterned lacquer or ceramic ware. Many of the dishes here would make ideal first courses at a formal dinner or as canapés with drinks.

Horenso Goma Ae
Spinach with Sesame Dressing

This is a very elegant dish. Serve at room temperature at the start of a meal.

- 10 oz (300 g) spinach, washed but left whole
- 5 tablespoons (50 g) white sesame seeds
- 5 teaspoons light soy sauce
- 2 teaspoons sugar
- 4 teaspoons basic *dashi* stock (page 107)
- 1 tablespoon very finely shredded toasted laver (*nori*)

Bring a large pan of water to a boil, add the spinach leaves and cook until the leaves soften and darken in color. Pour the spinach into a colander or sieve and cool under running water. Drain, pressing on the spinach with the back of a wooden spoon to extract the water. Put the spinach in a bamboo rolling mat and roll up tightly to squeeze out all the moisture and shape into a roll.

Toast the sesame seeds in a dry pan until golden brown, then crush in a mortar or small blender until coarsely blended. Add the soy sauce, sugar, and *dashi* to form a soft paste. Just before serving, cut the rolled spinach into pieces 1 in (2 1/2 cm) thick and divide among 4 small plates. Top each with a little of the sesame paste and sprinkle with the shredded *nori*.

Urajiro Shiitake
Shrimp-stuffed Mushrooms

- 3/4 lb (400 g) fresh shrimp, peeled
- 16 fresh *shiitake* mushrooms, stems discarded
- 3 tablespoons cornstarch
- Oil for deep-frying
- 4 sprigs of watercress or parsley
- 1/2 cup (125 ml) *tempura* batter (page 107)
- 2 tablespoons daikon (giant white radish), very finely grated and mixed with chili powder to taste

Dipping Sauce
- 1 cup (250 ml) basic *dashi* stock (page 107)
- 4 tablespoons sugar
- 4 tablespoons dark soy sauce

Chop or process the shrimp to make a smooth paste. Press a little of the shrimp paste into each mushroom, dust the top with a little cornstarch. Deep-fry the mushrooms, a few at a time, in hot oil for 2 minutes. Drain and divide among 4 serving plates.

Dip each sprig of watercress or parsley in *tempura* batter and deep-fry until the batter is golden brown. Remove, drain and put beside the mushrooms. Garnish each serving with 1/2 tablespoon of the daikon. To prepare the dipping sauce, combine the *dashi*, sugar, and soy sauce, mixing well, and divide among 4 bowls.

Sake No Tsumire-age
Salmon Beancurd Balls

This combination of delicately seasoned salmon and beancurd makes a light and palate-pleasing dish.

- 1/2 lb (200 g) salmon fillet, coarsely chopped
- 9-oz (280-g) block beancurd
- Handful of *mitsuba* leaves or parsley with stalks attached
- 2 fresh *shiitake* mushrooms, stems discarded and caps very finely shredded
- 1 1/4-in (3-cm) piece carrot, cut in matchsticks
- 1 cloud-ear fungus, soaked until swollen and very finely shredded
- 1 egg, lightly beaten
- 1/2 teaspoon salt
- 2 teaspoons light soy sauce
- 1 teaspoon sugar
- 5 teaspoons cornstarch
- Oil for deep-frying

Accompaniments
- 4 tablespoons light soy sauce
- 2 teaspoons Japanese mustard paste

Put the chopped salmon in a bowl. Soak the beancurd in water for 1 to 2 minutes, drain in a cloth-lined sieve, then squeeze out excess moisture by wrapping the beancurd in the cloth and twisting tightly. Add this to the salmon.

Separate the stalks from the *mitsuba* or parsley and chop finely, keeping the whole leaves aside. Add 1 to 2 teaspoons of the chopped stems to the salmon and beancurd, then add all other ingredients except oil and accompaniments. Mix well and shape into small balls.

Deep-fry in hot oil, turning frequently, until golden brown and cooked. Drain and put in individual serving baskets. Spray the *mitsuba* or parsley leaves with a little water, then dip in additional cornstarch. Deep-fry in hot oil for a few seconds until the coating sets. Garnish the salmon balls with the fried *mitsuba* and accompany with side dishes, each containing 1 tablespoon of soy sauce with 1/2 teaspoon of mustard.

HELPFUL HINT
The effect will be different, but firm-fleshed fish also works well with this dish.

Shrimp-stuffed Mushrooms (left) and Salmon Beancurd Balls (right)

Gyuniku No Tataki
Seared Beef

- 1 lb (500 g) beef sirloin or rump, in one piece
- 1 teaspoon salt
- 2 medium-sized onions, about 6¹/₂ oz (200 g)
- 3 in (8 cm) daikon (giant white radish), shredded
- 4 *ohba* leaves or sprigs of watercress
- 4 teaspoons finely grated daikon mixed with chili powder to taste
- 1 tablespoon finely sliced scallion (spring onion)
- ¹/₄ cup (75 ml) *ponzu* sauce (page 107)

Sprinkle the beef with salt and sear in a very hot pan for a few seconds on each side, just until the color changes. Remove from heat, plunge in iced water for a few second to cool. Dry with a cloth and cut in ¹/₄-in (¹/₂-cm) slices.

Peel the onions, halve lengthwise, then cut in thin crosswise slices. Break up the slices with your fingers and put in iced water. Rinse, drain and dry the onion.

To serve, arrange the daikon in the center of a plate and surround with the beef. Arrange the *ohba* or watercress in the center, top with the onion, garnish with scallion and surround with tiny balls of the grated daikon and chili. Serve with tiny dishes of *ponzu* sauce as a dip.

Tori No Matsukaze
Chicken Loaf

Tiny poppy seeds scattered over the top of this seasoned chicken loaf are supposedly reminiscent of sand on a beach, which is perhaps why the dish is known as "Wind in the Pines."

- ³/₄ lb (400 g) ground chicken
- 2 eggs, lightly beaten
- ³/₄ in (2 cm) ginger, very finely chopped
- 2 tablespoons red *miso*
- 2 teaspoons *sake*
- 2 teaspoons dark soy sauce
- 2 tablespoons sugar
- 2 teaspoons all-purpose (plain) flour
- 1 tablespoon white poppy seeds

Blend the chicken in a food processor to make a paste, or grind a second time. Add all other ingredients except poppy seeds and process until well mixed, or mix with a wooden spoon.

Grease an 8-in-(20-cm) square baking pan and line with baking paper or oiled foil. Put in the chicken mixture, spreading evenly, then sprinkle with the poppy seeds. Set in a pan half-filled with water and bake in a 350°F (180°C, gas mark 4) oven for about 30 minutes, until the center is firm.

Remove from oven and lift out the baking paper or foil with the loaf on it. Cut the loaf into rectangles or fan shapes. Serve at room temperature.

Chicken Loaf

Chawan-mushi
Savory Custard

- 2 oz (60 g) chicken breast, in bite-sized pieces
- 2 teaspoons light soy sauce
- 1¹/₂ oz (50 g) baked eel (sold in vacuum packs), cut in 4 pieces
- ²/₃ oz (20 g) lily root, cleaned and cut in 4 pieces (optional)
- 4 fresh *shiitake* mushrooms, stems discarded
- 4 large shrimp, peeled and intestinal veins removed
- 1 tablespoon *mitsuba* or parsley stalks, cut in 1¹/₄-in (3-cm) lengths
- 8 ginkgo nuts, peeled, blanched and thin skins removed
- 2 large eggs
- ³/₄ cup (180 ml) basic *dashi* stock (page 107)
- 3 teaspoons light soy sauce
- Shredded *yuzu* orange or lemon peel to garnish

Sprinkle the chicken with soy sauce. Assemble the eel, lily root, mushrooms, shrimp, *mitsuba* or parsley stalks, and ginkgo nuts.

Break the eggs in a bowl and mix gently with chopsticks to avoid making bubbles. Add the *dashi* stock and soy sauce. Mix well and strain. Divide all the assembled ingredients among 4 individual china bowls or cups with lids and pour in the egg mixture. Steam for 10 minutes over medium heat. Serve garnished with *yuzu* orange or lemon peel.

Tamago Dofu
Cold Savory Custard

A refreshing summer appetizer.

- 3 eggs
- 14 tablespoons (200 ml) basic *dashi* stock (page 107)
- 2 tablespoons light soy sauce
- 1 teaspoon *mirin*
- 4 medium-sized shrimp weighing about 3 oz (80g), cooked, peeled and tails left on
- ²/₃ cup (150 ml) *soba dashi* (2) (page 107)
- Grated *yuzu* orange or lime or lemon peel
- 4 sprigs of *shiso* flower

Combine the eggs, basic *dashi* stock, soy sauce, and *mirin*. Pour through a strainer into a small dish about 4 in (10 cm) square. Put this into a steamer and steam over boiling water for about 25 minutes, until it sets. Cool, then refrigerate.

Just before serving, cut the savory custard into 4 squares and place each in small glass or china bowl. Place a shrimp on top of each serving, pour in a little of the *soba dashi* and top of each serving with grated peel and a *shiso* flower sprig.

Seared Beef and Cold Savory Custard

Soups in Japan are quite different from Western-style soups, and are usually lighter and clean-tasting—rather like consommé. Use the freshest ingredients you can get your hands on and watch them shine!

Wakatake Sui
Clear Bamboo Shoot Soup

- 4 medium-sized shrimp, about 3 oz (80 g), peeled and halved lengthwise
- 2 teaspoons cornstarch
- 3 cups (750 ml) clear soup (page 107)
- 1 oz (30 g) simmered bamboo shoots, sliced
- 2^1/2 oz (80 g) *wakame* seaweed
- Sprigs of *kinome*, watercress or parsley

Shake the shrimp and cornstarch in a plastic bag, then put shrimp in a sieve and shake to dislodge excess cornstarch. Blanch shrimp in boiling water for about 20 seconds, until the cornstarch sets. Remove immediately, plunge in iced water for a few seconds, then set aside.

Pour the clear soup in a pan, add the bamboo shoots, bring to a boil, then add the shrimp and the *wakame*. Return to a boil and immediately remove from the heat. Divide the bamboo shoots, *wakame*, and shrimp among 4 lacquer bowls and pour over the soup. Garnish with the *kinome*, watercress or parsley and serve at the beginning of a meal.

Shirauo Fubuki Jitate
Tempura Whitebait in Soup

The slight crunch of the *tempura* whitebait gives added contrast to the clear, clean soup.

- 1 egg yolk
- 2 tablespoons *tempura* batter (page 107)
- 1^1/2 oz (50 g) fresh whitebait
- 2 tablespoons all-purpose (plain) flour
- Oil for deep-frying
- 1 lb (500 g) daikon (giant white radish)
- 3 cups (750 ml) clear soup (page 107)
- Salt to taste
- Sprigs of *mitsuba* or parsley
- Grated *yuzu* orange or lime or lemon peel

Mix the egg yolk with the *tempura* batter. Shake the white fish and flour together in a plastic bag, then dip into the batter and fry in hot oil until crisp and golden.

Peel and grate the daikon, place in a towel and squeeze out all the moisture. Bring the clear soup to a boil and add the grated daikon. Season with salt to taste and add the *mitsuba* or parsley. Divide among 4 lacquer soup bowls and add the fried fish just before serving, topped with a little grated peel.

Tempura Whitebait in Soup

Tofu To Nameko No Miso Shiru
Miso Soup with Mushrooms

Nameko mushrooms, attractive reddish-brown little fungi with a slippery texture, are excellent fresh, although the bottled or canned variety could be used in this soup if fresh *nameko* are not available

- 3 cups (750 ml) basic *dashi* stock (page 107)
- 1/4 cup (60 g) *inaka miso*
- 1 oz (30 g) *nameko* mushrooms, rinsed
- 5 oz (150 g) silken beancurd, finely diced
- 4 teaspoons very finely sliced scallion (spring onions)

Put the *dashi* into a saucepan and bring to a boil. Add the *miso*, stirring to dissolve. Put in the mushrooms and beancurd and heat, but do not allow to boil. Pour the soup into 4 lacquer soup bowls and sprinkle each portion with 1 teaspoon of scallion.

Tempura Soba
Buckwheat Noodles with Tempura

- 12 cups (3 liters) water
- 1 teaspoon salt
- 9 oz (280 g) buckwheat (*soba*) noodles
- 4 cups (1 liter) *soba dashi* stock (1) (page 107)
- 4 teaspoons finely sliced scallion (spring onion)
- Seven-spice powder (*shichimi*) to taste

Tempura
- 8 medium-sized shrimp
- 1 heaped tablespoon flour
- 4 fresh *shiitake* mushrooms, stems discarded and caps cross cut
- 4 *shiso* leaves
- 2/3 cup (300 ml) *tempura* batter (page 107)
- Oil for deep-frying

Bring the water and salt to a boil and add the noodles. Boil uncovered for 4 to 5 minutes, until the noodles are cooked. Drain, chill in iced water and drain again.

Put the stock into a saucepan and bring to a boil. Keep warm while preparing the *tempura*.

To prepare the *tempura*, peel the shrimp, discarding the head but leaving on the tail. Split open down the back, remove intestinal tract and press the shrimp open gently with the hand to make a butterfly shape. Dip the shrimp into flour, shake, dip into the batter and deep-fry until golden brown and cooked. Drain. Dip the *shiitake* mushrooms and *shiso* leaves in batter and deep-fry. Drain.

Put the cooked noodles back into the stock and reheat. Divide the noodles among 4 bowls. Taste the stock and season with salt if needed, then pour over the noodles. Top each portion of noodles with 2 shrimp, 1 mushroom, and 1 *shiso* leaf and garnish each with 1 teaspoon of scallion and a little seven-spice powder.

Clear Bamboo Shoot Soup

Cold Buckwheat Noodles with Assorted Toppings

Banshu-mushi

Fish with Noodles

8 oz (250 g) red snapper fillet
1/2 teaspoon salt
4 oz (125 g) dried fine wheat
   noodles (*somen*)
4 oz (100 g) *shimeji* mushrooms
1 heaped tablespoon very finely
   grated daikon, mixed with chili
   powder to taste
1 1/2 in (4 cm) scallion (spring
   onion), very finely shredded
   lengthwise

Stock
1 cup (250 ml) basic *dashi* stock
   (page 107)
2 1/2 tablespoons *mirin*
2 1/2 tablespoons light soy sauce

Sprinkle the fish with salt, cut
in 4 pieces and put on a plate.
Cook in a steamer for 5 to 6
minutes, remove and set aside.

   Heat all the stock ingredients
together in a saucepan and
reserve.

   Divide the noodles in
4 bundles and tie one end of
each bundle with cotton thread
to prevent the noodles from
separating during cooking.
Cook the noodles in plenty of
boiling water until just cooked,
then rinse under cold water and
drain, leaving the thread still
in position.

   Place each bundle of noodles
in a serving bowl, leaving half
of the bundle hanging out.
Top each bundle of noodles
with a piece of red snapper
and fold back the noodles
hanging out of the bowl so
as to enclose the fish. Cut off
the end of the noodles tied with
the thread and discard. Add the
mushrooms to the bowl and
return to the steamer. Cook
over rapidly boiling water
for 5 minutes.

   Remove the fish from the
steamer and pour over the
hot stock. Garnish each
portion with 1/2 tablespoon
of grated daikon shaped
into a ball and sprinkle
a little of the scallion
on top.

HELPFUL HINT

For crispy but not oily *tempura*
make sure your oil is very hot
before adding food, otherwise
it will absorb oil and give a
soggy finish. Drain on paper
towels before serving.

Wanko Soba

*Cold Buckwheat Noodles with
Assorted Toppings*

3/4 lb (400 g) dried buckwheat
   (*soba*) noodles
2 cups (600 ml) *soba dashi*
   stock (2) (page 107)

Toppings
Simmered *shiitake* mushrooms
   (see below)
Tempura fritters (see below)
4 teaspoons Japanese *wasabe* paste
4 heaped tablespoons finely
   shredded dried laver (*nori*)
2 eggs, lightly beaten, fried as an
   omelet, shredded
8 *shiso* leaves, shredded
2 scallions (spring onions), white
   part only, finely shredded
   lengthwise
1 1/4 oz (40 g) salmon or tuna,
   flaked
2 tablespoons Japanese pickles
   (optional)

Simmered *Shiitake* Mushrooms
4 dried *shiitake* mushrooms
2 cups (500 ml) water
1 1/2 teaspoons sugar
1 1/2 teaspoons dark soy sauce

Tempura Fritters
2 oz (50 g) burdock, peeled and
   cut in matchsticks 1 1/4 in
   (3 cm) long
1/3 cup (50 g) sliced onion

1 tablespoon finely chopped
   mitsuba or parsley leaves
1/4 cup (60 ml) *tempura* batter
   (page 107)
Oil for deep-frying

Prepare the simmered *shiitake*
mushrooms first by soaking the
mushrooms in the water until
soft. Drain and put the soaking
water into a saucepan and bring
to a boil. Add the mushrooms and
sugar, return to a boil, skim the
surface and reduce the heat.
Cover and simmer gently for 40
minutes. Add the soy sauce and
simmer for another 40 minutes.
Cool, then shred finely.

   Boil the noodles in plenty of
lightly salted water for 4 to 5
minutes, drain and chill in cold
water. Drain again and refrigerate.

   Prepare the *tempura* fritters
by combining all ingredients
and deep-frying, a spoonful at a
time, in hot oil until golden
brown. Drain and keep aside.

   At serving time, arrange small
handfuls (enough for two mouthfuls) of the noodles in lacquer
bowls. Put the remaining noodles
in a basket or dish and keep on
the table. Pour a little of the stock
over the small bowl of noodles
and add the preferred topping.
When this is finished, add more
noodles and stock to the bowl, add
a different topping and continue
until the noodles are used up.

Buckwheat Noodles with Tempura

Sushi and sashimi, both of which feature the best the seas and oceans have to offer, are now very popular in many countries. For these dishes, it is imperative that you buy the freshest fish possible, nothing less will do.

Hosomaki
Rolled Sushi

Three different fillings are used in these *nori*-wrapped rolls of vinegared rice: tuna, cucumber, and pickled giant white radish, the last available in jars in Japanese stores.

- 4 8 x 7-in (20 x 18-cm) sheets toasted dried laver (*nori*)
- 1 1/2 cups (600 g) vinegared rice (page 107)
- 6 oz (160 g) fresh tuna
- 6 oz (160 g) cucumber
- 6 oz (160 g) pickled daikon (giant white radish) strips
- 1 teaspoon Japanese *wasabi* paste
- 2 tablespoons (20 g) pickled ginger slices

Cut the raw tuna in 4 strips of the same length as the *nori*. Cut the cucumber in quarters lengthwise, remove the seeds and cut into sticks. Cut the *nori* in half. Place the half nori sheet on a bamboo rolling mat, with the shiny side down. Top the *nori* with 1/2 cup (200 g) of the sushi rice, spread evenly on the sheet leaving a border of 1/2 in (1 cm) free on the inside of the sheet.

Take a little *wasabi* paste on your finger and spread it across the rice in the center.

Place the tuna across the center of the *wasabi* and start to roll using the bamboo mat, making sure the *nori* sheet end goes under the rice. Roll the mat up firmly and squeeze gently. Remove the rolled sushi from the mat, cut in half and then into three pieces with a wet knife. Repeat the process with a filling of cucumber and again with a filling of pickled radish. Serve garnished with pickled ginger.

Chirashi-zushi
Sushi Rice with Topping

The tiny dried fish called for are sold in packets; they are actually dried and cooked silver fish.

- 2 1/2 cups (1 kg) cooked vinegared rice (page 107)
- 1 tablespoon tiny dried fish (optional, see below)
- 4 tablespoons finely shredded toasted laver (*nori*)
- 4 eggs, lightly beaten and fried as an omelet and shredded
- 4 medium-sized cooked shrimp, halved and opened butterfly style
- 3 oz (80 g) raw tuna, cut in strips
- 2 oz (60 g) squid, blanched and cut in strips
- 2/3 oz (20 g) grilled eel (available canned or in vacuum packs)
- 1/3 cup (40 g) shrimp flakes
- 4 tablespoons pickled ginger slices
- 4 teaspoons light soy sauce
- 4 teaspoons Japanese *wasabi* paste

Rolled Sushi

Mixed Rolled Sushi

Mix the sushi rice with dried fish (thread-like dried and cooked silver fish sold in packets). Put the mixture in 4 lacquer bowls or wooden boxes and level the surface. Scatter with seaweed and omelet and place all other ingredients decoratively on top.

> ### HELPFUL HINT
> The trick to making sushi rolls is to have all the ingredients cut up and ready to go. These can be prepared ahead of time and refrigerated in airtight containers.

Battera Sushi
Vinegared Rice with Kelp

Shiraita konbu, very fine golden-colored kelp, is used to cover this sushi. The sushi can be pressed into a rectangular container if you like. Place the skin on the bottom and layer it with rice, fish, sesame seeds and golden kelp. Cover and put on a weight to compress the sushi.

Leave to stand for 15 minutes before cutting.

- 10 oz (300 g) mackerel fillets
- 3/4 cup (200 g) salt
- Large sheet or 2 sheets golden kelp (*shiraita konbu*)
- 14 tablespoons (200 ml) rice vinegar
- 3/4 cup (300 g) vinegared rice (page 107)
- 1 teaspoon white sesame seeds
- 4 tablespoons light soy sauce
- 4 tablespoons pickled ginger slices

Sprinkle the mackerel fillets lightly with salt and refrigerate for 1 1/2 hours. Rinse and pat dry. Soak the golden kelp in water to cover until soft and transparent. Remove any small bones from the mackerel. Place vinegar in a glass or ceramic dish, add the mackerel fillets and refrigerate for 40 minutes. Cut the skin from fish.

Wet a cotton cloth, wring it dry, then place it on a bamboo rolling mat. Put the skin across the cloth and spread the rice evenly over the skin. Top with a fillet of fish, sprinkle with sesame seeds and cover the top with the golden kelp. Start to roll up, helping to shape the contents into a smooth, even roll.

Unroll, cut in 3/4-in (2-cm) slices and serve with soy sauce and pickled ginger.

Norimaki
Mixed Rolled Sushi

1 1/4 oz (40 g) grilled eel (available
   canned or in vacuum packs)
2 oz (40 g) cooked shrimp, peeled
2 oz (60 g) cucumber
1/4 cup (30 g) shrimp flakes
   (see below)
2 eggs, beaten and fried as an
   omelet
2 sheets of toasted dried laver
   (*nori*)
1 cup (400 g) vinegared rice
   (page 107)
4 tablespoons pickled ginger slices
4 tablespoons light soy sauce

Shrimp Flakes
5 oz (150 g) small shrimp,
   peeled and deveined
1 egg yolk
2 1/2 tablespoons (30 g) sugar
1/4 teaspoon salt
Red food coloring

Prepare the shrimp flakes first by
rinsing the shrimp in lightly salted
water. Drain and then simmer
in a little salted water until they
change color. Drain, cool and
blend in a food processor to
make a purée. Tie the shrimp in
cheesecloth and leave to soak in
water for 1 to 2 minutes to remove
any smell. Drain the shrimp and
knead the cheesecloth gently to
extract all the moisture.

Put the shrimp in a bowl and
add egg yolk, sugar, and salt,
mixing well. Add just a touch of
food coloring diluted in water to
make the shrimp a pale pink.
Put the shrimp into a non-stick
pan and cook over low heat,
stirring from time to time, for

about 30 minutes or until almost
dry. (This can be kept refrigerated
for up to 1 week.)

Cut the eel, shrimp, cucumber,
and omelet into sticks of the same
length. Place the *nori* on a
bamboo rolling mat and spread
half the sushi rice on the *nori*,
leaving the upper and bottom
border free by 1/2 in (1 cm).
Sprinkle the rice with half the
shrimp flakes. Arrange half the
ingredients side by side in a row
on the rice. Start to roll using the
bamboo mat, making sure the
nori sheet end goes under the
rice. Roll the mat up firmly and
squeeze gently. Remove the rolled
sushi from the mat, cut in half
and then into 3/4-in (2-cm) slices
with a wet knife. Repeat the
process with remaining filling.

Serve garnished with pickled
ginger and soy sauce for
dipping.

> **HELPFUL HINT**
> Packets or jars of prepared
> shrimp flakes are often available
> in Japanese grocery stores.

Tsukuri Moriawase
Assorted Sashimi

A wide variety of seafood is
enjoyed raw as sashimi, cut in
different ways depending upon
the texture of each particular
ingredient. Sashimi is served
with a variety of garnishes,
condiments and dipping sauces,
some sauces being considered
more appropriate to certain
types of seafood than others.

4 large shrimp
1/4 lb (125 g) scallops
1/2 teaspoon oil
5 oz (150 g) halfbeak fillet or tuna
10 oz (300 g) snapper fillet
1/4 cup (30 g) shredded daikon
   (giant white radish)
4 *shiso* leaves
4 teaspoons Japanese *wasabi*
   paste
4 tablespoons *tosa* soy sauce
   (page 107)

Peel the shrimp, remove the
dark intestinal vein but leave
on the head and tail for a more
attractive appearance. Clean
and dry the scallops. Heat the
oil in a non-stick pan until
moderately hot and sear the
scallops for 30 seconds on each
side. Remove and set aside.

Scale the fish and remove any
small bones. Cut the halfbeak
fillet on the diagonal into strips
about 1/2 in (1 cm) wide and
1 1/4 in (2 1/2 cm) long. If using
tuna, cut into 3/4-in (2-cm)
cubes. The snapper can either
be sliced paper thin or cut to
resemble a leaf (see photo).

Serve the shrimp, scallops, and
cut fish arranged decoratively
on a rectangular plate. Garnish
with daikon, *shiso* leaf, and
wasabi, and serve with bowls of
tosa soy sauce for dipping.

> **HELPFUL HINT**
> You may decide to serve just
> one or two types of fish, or a
> range of several, but whatever
> variety you choose, be absolutely
> certain that the fish is spanking
> fresh.

Onigiri
Rice Balls

These hearty triangular rice
balls make ideal snacks or a
light lunch, and the choice of
the filling is up to you. Leave the
nori off until you are ready to
serve. The amounts given here
should make 12–13 rice balls.

5 1/3 cups (1 kg) short-grain rice
Salt to taste
3–4 sheets of toasted laver (*nori*),
   cut in strips about 5 x 2 in
   (12 x 5 cm)

Filling
Sour plums (*umeboshi*), 1/2 teaspoon
   per rice ball

Assorted Sashimi

Cured salmon, 1 teaspoon per rice
   ball
Dried bonito flakes mixed with a
   little light soy sauce, 1 heaped
   teaspoon per rice ball
Strips of salted dried kelp
   (*shiokobu*), 1 heaped teaspoon
   per rice ball

Wash the rice gently under
running water until the water
runs clear. Leave to drain for
1 hour, then put into a saucepan
with the water and bring to a
boil over high heat. Reduce the
heat and simmer gently for
15 to 20 minutes until the
rice is cooked and the water
absorbed. Remove from the
heat, cover the rice with a towel
to absorb any moisture and put
back the lid. Leave to stand for
20 minutes.

To prepare the rice balls,
sprinkle a little salt onto the
palm of one hand and take a
handful (about 1/2 cup of rice).
Flatten it to make a depression
in the center and put in a little
of your chosen filling. Mold
the rice to enclose the filling
and shape into a triangle.
Wrap with a piece of nori
and moisten the end to seal.
Set aside while preparing the
remaining rice balls. Serve at
room temperature.

Vinegared Rice with Kelp

Seared Bonito with Tangy Dressing

Katsuo Tataki
Seared Bonito with Tangy Dressing

Tangy and light, this refreshing chilled dish is perfect for a hot summer's day.

- Oil to grease pan
- 3/4 lb (350 g) bonito fillet, skin left on
- 1/3 cup (30 g) scallion (spring onion), very finely shredded lengthwise
- 1 oz (30 g) ginger, very finely shredded lengthwise
- 1–2 cloves garlic, very finely chopped
- 1/2 lemon, thinly sliced
- 1/3 cup (80 ml) *ponzu* sauce (page 107)
- 1/4 cup (30 g) shredded daikon (giant white radish)
- 1 heaped tablespoon finely grated daikon mixed with seven-spice powder or chili to taste

Heat a lightly greased non-stick frying pan. Put in the bonito fillet, skin side up, and sear just until the outside of the fish turns white. Turn and sear the other side, then soak in iced water for 10 to 15 seconds to chill. Wipe away any moisture and marinate the whole fillet with half of the scallion,

ginger, garlic, lemon, and half of the *ponzu* sauce, patting the fish with the side of a knife to let the sauce penetrate. Chill in the refrigerator for a minimum of 10 minutes. Cut the marinated bonito in 1/2-in (1-cm) slices.

Arrange the bonito on a bed of daikon strips garnished with the remaining sliced scallion, ginger, and garlic on a platter. Arrange the remaining lemon slices and and seasoned grated daikon on the side and served either at room temperature or chilled.

Ingen Goma-ae
Green Beans with Sesame

Green beans marry beautifully with the flavor of sesame, although spinach can be substituted if preferred.

- 2 cups (200 g) green beans
- 1/4 cup (60 g) sesame paste
- 1/4 cup (50 ml) basic *dashi* stock (page 107)
- 4 teaspoons light soy sauce
- 5 teaspoons sugar
- 4 tablespoons finely shredded toasted laver (*nori*)

Boil the beans in lightly salted water until just tender. Drain and cool under cold running water. Cut in 1 1/2-in (4-cm) lengths, on the diagonal if desired.

Mix the sesame paste, *dashi*, light soy sauce, and sugar. Put the beans into 4 serving bowls, top each with a spoonful of the sesame dressing and garnish with 1 tablespoon of shredded *nori*.

Tofu Dengaku
Miso-topped Beancurd

- 2 blocks of beancurd, about 16–18 oz (550 g)
- 3/4 cup (200 g) white *dengaku miso* (page 107)
- 6 tablespoons (100 g) red *dengaku miso* (page 107)
- 1 teaspoon very finely grated *yuzu* orange or lemon peel
- 1/3 cup (10 g) *kinome*, watercress, parsley leaves or spinach leaves

To remove excess moisture from the beancurd, wrap in a clean towel, place between 2 cutting boards and let stand for 20 minutes. Cut the beancurd into pieces 3/4 in (2 cm) thick, 2 in (5 cm) long and 3/4 in (2 cm) wide.

Prepare the three *miso* toppings. For the red topping, put the red *dengaku miso* in a bowl; it needs no further addition. To make the yellow topping, mix 6 tablespoons of the white *dengaku miso* with the grated *yuzu* peel and set aside. To make the green topping, purée the *kinome*, watercress or parsley leaves to obtain a juice and mix with 6 table-spoons white *dengaku miso*.

For a stronger green color, use spinach leaves.

Grill the pieces of beancurd until lightly colored on both sides. Spread each piece of beancurd with one of the three colored toppings and return to the grill until they take color. Carefully insert a skewer into each bean-curd and serve hot.

Butaniku Shoga-Yaki
Pork with Ginger

- 1 lb (500 g) pork loin, sliced
- 4 teaspoons ginger juice (page 107)
- 3 tablespoons light soy sauce
- 3 tablespoons *sake*
- 2 (200 g) medium-sized onions
- 2 teaspoons vegetable oil
- 1/2 lb (200 g) cabbage cut in 1 1/2-in (4-cm) squares
- 1 cup (60 g) cubed green bell pepper (capsicum), in 1 1/2 -in (4-cm) squares

Cut pork slices into 1 1/2-in cubes and set aside. Mix ginger juice, soy sauce, and *sake* and keep aside. Cut onions in half length-wise and then cut crosswise in 1/2 -in (1-cm) slices.

Heat the oil in a skillet or wok and stir-fry the pork until it changes color. Add the cabbage, pepper, and onion and continue stir-frying until the vegetables and pork are cooked. Pour in the prepared seasoning, mix well and serve hot.

Miso-topped beancurd

Katsudon
Pork Cutlets on Rice

This unusual recipe, a Japanese variation of a traditional European dish, incorporates Western ingredients with the essentials of the Japanese kitchen: rice, *dashi,* and soy.

- 6–8 cups (1–1$\frac{1}{3}$ kg) hot cooked rice
- 2 (200 g) medium-sized onions, sliced
- 1 cup (250 ml) basic *dashi* stock (page 107)
- $\frac{1}{3}$ cup (80 ml) *mirin*
- $\frac{1}{3}$ cup (80 ml) thick soy sauce
- 4 teaspoons sugar
- 4 sprigs of *mitsuba* or parsley with long stems
- 4 eggs

Pork Cutlets
- 1 lb (500 g) pork loin
- Sprinkle of salt and pepper
- 2 tablespoons all-purpose (plain) flour
- 1 egg, lightly beaten
- 2 cups (200 g) breadcrumbs
- Oil for deep-frying

Prepare the pork cutlets first by cutting the pork loin into 4 steaks, making incisions along the fatty edge to prevent it from curling during frying. Season the meat lightly with salt and pepper, dust with flour on both sides, dip in beaten egg and then press into breadcrumbs. Deep-fry the crumbed pork until golden brown and cooked. Drain and keep aside.

Divide the rice among 4 large bowls. Put the onion, *dashi, mirin,* soy sauce, and sugar in a pan and simmer until the onion is tender. Put one-quarter of this mixture into a small pan, place one cooked pork cutlet on top, add one-quarter of the *mitsuba* or parsley and pour the beaten egg over the top. Simmer for just a moment, until the eggs are just cooked but still runny; they must not be overcooked so that they become firm and dry. Top one portion of rice with this mixture. Repeat for the remaining three pork cutlets and serve with a side dish of pickles.

Chikuzen-ni
Vegetables Simmered in Soy Sauce

Any combination of vegetables can be used for this recipe, so take advantage of the best of the season. The amount of stock used is sufficient for about 1 pound of vegetables.

- 3 oz (80 g) each of bamboo shoots, carrot, burdock, lotus root, Japanese *sato-imo* or new potatoes, devil's tongue jelly (*konnyaku*)
- 4 fresh *shiitake* mushrooms
- 12 sugar snap or snow peas
- 3 oz (80 g) chicken
- 2 teaspoons oil

Stock
- 3 cups (750 ml) basic *dashi* stock (page 107)
- $\frac{1}{3}$ cup (90 ml) dark soy sauce
- 2 tablespoons sugar
- $\frac{1}{4}$ cup (60 ml) *sake*

Peel and dice all vegetables and chicken. Separate the devil's tongue jelly (*konnyaku*) with a spoon. Boil the vegetables and devil's tongue jelly, one at a time, in lightly salted water for 5 minutes. Blanch the chicken in boiling water for 20 seconds, drain, chill in iced water and drain again.

Heat the oil and stir-fry the vegetables for 2 minutes.

To make the stock, put the *dashi* into a pan and add the stir-fried vegetables. Skim the surface and add all other stock ingredients and chicken. Bring to a boil and simmer gently with the pan covered for 20 to 30 minutes, until the ingredients are cooked.

Arrange the vegetables and chicken in bowls, add a little of the cooking liquid and serve.

Kobocha No Nimono
Simmered Winter Squash

Winter squash or pumpkin is a very popular vegetable, not only because of its sweet taste, but also because of its beautiful color. This simple but delicious recipe also makes an excellent side dish as part of just about any Western meal.

Vegetables Simmered in Soy Sauce

- 1 lb (500 g) winter squash or pumpkin
- 3 cups (750 ml) basic *dashi* stock (page 107)
- 7 tablespoons (80 g) sugar
- $\frac{1}{4}$ cup (60 ml) light soy sauce

Remove the seeds from the squash and scoop out any fibers with a spoon. Cut into 2-in-(5-cm-) square pieces, and peel off the skin on the edges of each piece so that the squash holds its shape during cooking. Cut the squash into decorative shapes as desired.

Put the *dashi* and sugar into a pan and bring to a boil. Add the squash and simmer gently for 7 to 8 minutes. Turn the squash pieces over, add the soy sauce and continue cooking until the squash is tender. Serve warm or at room temperature, with a little of the cooking liquid poured into each bowl

HELPFUL HINT
The best winter squash to use for this recipe is butternut variety, although any other dense-fleshed winter squash may be used.

Simmered Winter Squash (left) and Green Beans with Sesame (right)

Yosenabe

Seafood, Chicken, Vegetable, and Noodle Hotpot

Yosenabe literally means a mixture of anything, so the ingredients included in this hotpot can be adjusted to suit your taste and availability.

    5 oz (150 g) seabream fillet
    5 oz (150 g) salmon fillet
    5 oz (150 g) Spanish mackerel
        fillet
    5 oz (150 g) chicken
    5 oz (150 g) oysters
    7 oz (200 g) daikon (giant white
        radish)
    5 oz (150 g) clams
    5 oz (150 g) shrimp peeled, tails
        left on and intestinal vein
        removed
    1 lb (500 g) long white Chinese
        (Napa) cabbage
    4 fresh *shiitake* mushrooms, stems
        discarded and caps cross cut
    4 oz (100 g) edible chrysanthemum
        leaves, hard stems removed
    4 oz (100 g) golden or enoki
        (*enokitake*) mushrooms, hard
        ends of stems removed
    1 large carrot, peeled and sliced
    1 cup (100 g) scallions (spring
        onions) cut in 1 1/2 -in (4-cm)
        lengths
    1/2 lb (250 g) beancurd, cut in
        large dice
    3 1/2 oz (100 g) cellophane noodles,
        soaked until transparent
    Sprigs of *kinome* or watercress to
        garnish

    Stock
    7 cups (1 3/4 liters) basic *dashi*
        stock (page 107)
    1/2 cup (100 ml) light soy sauce
    2 tablespoons *mirin*

Cut the fish fillets and chicken into 1 1/4-in (3-cm) squares. Blanch each separately in boiling water until they change color, drain and set aside.

Remove the oysters from their shells and place oysters in a colander. Grate half of the daikon and mix gently by hand with the oysters to remove dirt.

Clean by shaking the colander in salted water. Drain and set the oysters aside. Put the clams, still in their shells, and peeled shrimp to one side.

Boil the cabbage for 2 minutes, drain and spread on a bamboo rolling mat. Roll up and squeeze tightly to remove excess moisture. Unroll and cut the cabbage roll into slices 3/4 in (2 cm) thick. Cut the chrysanthemum leaves into 2- to 3-in (5- to 8-in) lengths. Slice the remaining daikon.

Arrange all ingredients attractively on a large platter.

Prepare the stock by putting all ingredients into a large pan and bringing to a boil. Pour the stock into a heatproof casserole and set on a fire in the center of the table, with the platter of raw ingredients nearby. To cook, put the chicken and clams into the stock, followed by the fish, shrimp, oysters, noodles, and vegetables. Wait until the ingredients are cooked before adding the next batch of ingredients.

Ebi-ni
Shrimp with Sake

    12 fresh shrimp, about 8–10 oz
        (250–300 g)
    1 cup (250 ml) basic *dashi* stock
        (page 107)
    1/2 cup (100 ml) *sake*
    2 tablespoons sugar
    2 tablespoons light soy sauce
    3/4 in (2 cm) ginger, sliced
    8 snow peas, blanched in lightly
        salted water and chilled

Trim the whiskers and legs of each shrimp but do not peel. Use a toothpick to remove the intestinal vein at the back of the head. Place the shrimp in a pan with the *dashi*, *sake*, sugar, soy sauce, and ginger.

Prawns with Sake (left) and Prawns with Noodles (right)

Simmer for 3 to 4 minutes over high heat. Add the snow peas at the last moment. Drain the shrimp and peel, leaving on the head and tail. Arrange on a plate with the snow peas and serve at once.

Ebi Amondo-Age
Deep-fried Shrimp with Almonds

A modern Japanese dish that uses almonds rather than the more traditional broken noodles for a crunchy exterior. If desired, 12 ounces of shredded sweet potato, tossed in 2 tablespoons of white flour, can be substituted for the almonds. Dust the shrimp with a little cornstarch, then dip in lightly beaten egg white rather than *tempura* batter before pressing into the sweet potato.

    12 fresh shrimp, about
        8 oz (250 g)
    2 tablespoons all-
        purpose (plain) flour
    1/2 cup (200 ml) *tempu-
        ra* bat-
    ter (page 107)
    2 1/3 cups (200 g) slivered
        almonds
    Oil for deep-frying

Seafood, Chicken, Vegetable and Noodle Hotpot

    4 fresh *shiitake* mushrooms, stalks
        discarded and caps cross cut
    8 small Japanese green peppers,
        or 1 green bell pepper (capsicum),
        cut in strips
    1 cup (200 ml) *tempura dashi*
        (page 107)
    4 tablespoons finely grated white
        daikon (giant white radish)
    Seven-spice powder (*shichimi*),
        to taste

Trim the whiskers and legs of the shrimp with scissors. Peel the body section, but leave on the head and the tail. Remove the dark intestinal vein with a toothpick. Make two or three incisions on the underside of each shrimp to prevent it from curling. Pat dry and dust with flour. Dip each shrimp into the *tempura* batter and then press into the almonds to coat well. Deep-fry the shrimp in hot oil until golden brown. Drain and set aside.

Dust the *shiitake* mushrooms and green peppers in flour, dip in *tempura* batter and deep-fry.

Arrange the fried shrimp, mushrooms, and green peppers on 4 plates. Serve with small bowls of *tempura dashi* for dipping and daikon. Each diner sprinkles his portion with seven-spice powder to taste.

Shirauo Kara-Age
Deep-fried Whitebait

1 lb (500 g) fresh whitebait
4 tablespoons cornstarch
Oil for deep-frying
Salt to taste
1 lemon, cut in wedges

Wash and dry the whitebait. Toss in cornstarch and shake in a colander or sieve to remove excess. Deep-fry a handful at a time in very hot oil until crisp and golden brown. Drain and sprinkle with salt just before serving, garnished with lemon wedges.

Karei Shio-yaki
Flat Fish with Salt

1¹/₃ lb (600 g) flat fish, such as flounder, sole or pomfret
2 tablespoons salt
Lemon wedge to garnish
10 oz (300 g) daikon (giant white radish), very finely grated and squeezed to extract moisture

Lotus Root Garnish
2 oz (60 g) fresh lotus root, peeled and thinly sliced
3 tablespoons (50 ml) sweet vinegar (see below)
1 red chili, seeds discarded
¹/₃ cup (80 ml) *ponzu* sauce (page 107)

Sweet Vinegar
2 cups (500 ml) water
1 cup + 1 tablespoon (275 ml) rice vinegar
5 oz (150 g) sugar
2 teaspoons salt

Prepare lotus root garnish several hours before it is required.

For the sweet vinegar, bring water and vinegar to a boil, then add sugar and salt and stir until dissolved. Remove from heat.

Boil the sliced lotus root in water for 30 seconds, drain and put it in the sweet vinegar. Heat the chili in a dry pan for a few seconds, then add to the vinegar and *ponzu* sauce. Refrigerate.

Clean and scale the fish. Dry with a paper towel and make two deep crosswise incisions on each side. Put a skewer through the tail end of the fish, making it come out in the center and continuing to the head so that the fish has a wave shape. Sprinkle both sides of the fish lightly with salt, then press a liberal amount of salt onto the tail and fins.

Cook the fish over a moderately hot charcoal fire or under a broiler (grill), turning it with the skewer to avoid damaging the skin, until the fish is golden on both sides and cooked through. Serve on a plate garnished with lemon wedge, grated daikon, and the marinated lotus root.

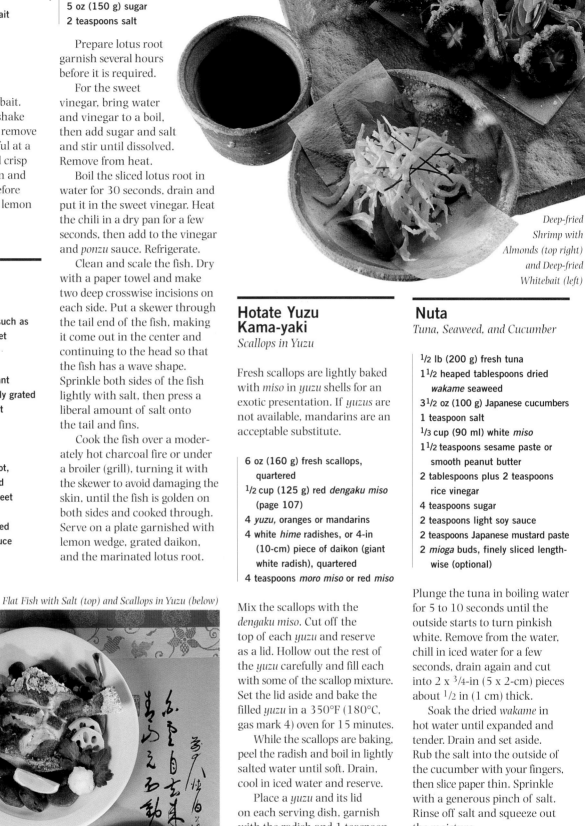

Deep-fried Shrimp with Almonds (top right) and Deep-fried Whitebait (left)

Hotate Yuzu Kama-yaki
Scallops in Yuzu

Fresh scallops are lightly baked with *miso* in *yuzu* shells for an exotic presentation. If *yuzus* are not available, mandarins are an acceptable substitute.

6 oz (160 g) fresh scallops, quartered
¹/₂ cup (125 g) red *dengaku miso* (page 107)
4 *yuzu*, oranges or mandarins
4 white *hime* radishes, or 4-in (10-cm) piece of daikon (giant white radish), quartered
4 teaspoons *moro miso* or red *miso*

Mix the scallops with the *dengaku miso*. Cut off the top of each *yuzu* and reserve as a lid. Hollow out the rest of the *yuzu* carefully and fill each with some of the scallop mixture. Set the lid aside and bake the filled *yuzu* in a 350°F (180°C, gas mark 4) oven for 15 minutes.

While the scallops are baking, peel the radish and boil in lightly salted water until soft. Drain, cool in iced water and reserve.

Place a *yuzu* and its lid on each serving dish, garnish with the radish and 1 teaspoon of *miso*.

HELPFUL HINT
Shelled shrimp can be substituted for scallops.

Nuta
Tuna, Seaweed, and Cucumber

¹/₂ lb (200 g) fresh tuna
1¹/₂ heaped tablespoons dried *wakame* seaweed
3¹/₂ oz (100 g) Japanese cucumbers
1 teaspoon salt
¹/₃ cup (90 ml) white *miso*
1¹/₂ teaspoons sesame paste or smooth peanut butter
2 tablespoons plus 2 teaspoons rice vinegar
4 teaspoons sugar
2 teaspoons light soy sauce
2 teaspoons Japanese mustard paste
2 *mioga* buds, finely sliced lengthwise (optional)

Plunge the tuna in boiling water for 5 to 10 seconds until the outside starts to turn pinkish white. Remove from the water, chill in iced water for a few seconds, drain again and cut into 2 x ³/₄-in (5 x 2-cm) pieces about ¹/₂ in (1 cm) thick.

Soak the dried *wakame* in hot water until expanded and tender. Drain and set aside. Rub the salt into the outside of the cucumber with your fingers, then slice paper thin. Sprinkle with a generous pinch of salt. Rinse off salt and squeeze out the moisture.

Mix the *miso* with the sesame paste, vinegar, sugar, soy sauce and mustard.

Arrange the tuna, *wakame* and cucumber in a bowl. Garnish with a little of the *miso* mixture and top each serving with a little shredded *mioga*.

Flat Fish with Salt (top) and Scallops in Yuzu (below)

Sukiyaki
Beef with Vegetables

Sukiyaki only became known in Japan around the turn of the century, when the Japanese began eating beef (previously proscribed by Buddhist law). There are two styles of cooking this mixture of meat, vegetables, beancurd, and noodles: the Osaka style involves cooking the sauce in the pan at the table with each new addition of ingredients. The Tokyo style requires the sauce to be prepared in advance.

1^1/4 lb (600 g) prime sirloin beef, sliced

3 (300 g) small onions, cut crosswise in ^{1}/4-in (^{1}/2-cm) slices

5 cups (500 g) scallions (spring onions), diagonally sliced in ^{3}/4-in (2-cm) pieces

2 cups (100 g) chrysanthemum leaves, cut in 3-in (8-cm) pieces

2 oz (75 g) fresh *shiitake* mushrooms, stems discarded and caps cross cut

^{1}/4 lb (100 g) golden or enoki (*enokitake*) mushrooms, hard part of stems discarded

^{1}/4 lb (100 g) burdock, shaved thinly (optional)

^{3}/4 lb (400 g) *shirataki konnyaku* or wheat noodles (*udon*), boiled until just cooked and drained

1 piece grilled beancurd (*yakidofu*), cut in small pieces

8 small baked gluten cakes (*fu*) or 1 cake cotton beancurd, cubed

4 tablespoons beef fat (suet)

4 eggs

Sauce
^{3}/4 cup (180 ml) light soy sauce
^{2}/3 cup (150 ml) *mirin*
^{2}/3 cup (150 ml) *sake*
^{1}/2 cup (125 g) sugar

Arrange the beef, vegetables, noodles, and both types of beancurd on a platter. Keep the beef fat on a small dish to use for greasing the cooking pan. Put the eggs into individual bowls for dipping the cooked ingredients later.

Prepare the sauce by putting all ingredients into a pan. Bring to a boil, remove from heat and pour the sauce into a jug.

When it is time to eat the *sukiyaki*, put the beef fat in a heavy deep skillet and heat gently so that is melts and spreads over the whole surface of the pan.

Beef with Vegetables

Discard the fat. Add a little of the sliced beef and vegetables, pour on a little of the prepared sauce and simmer. When the ingredients are cooked, each person helps themselves to whatever they fancy, dipping each morsel in the egg (lightly stirred with the chopsticks) before eating.

Shabu-shabu
Japanese One-Pot

Beef slices, vegetables and cellophane noodles are cooked at the table in a type of fondue generally known as a steamboat.

1^1/4 lb (600 g) prime sirloin beef, cut in paper-thin slices

1 lb (500 g) long white Chinese (Napa) cabbage

10 oz (300 g) edible chrysanthemum leaves, hard part of stems discarded

8 fresh *shiitake* mushrooms, stems discarded and caps cross cut

8 oz (200 g) golden or enoki (*enokitake*) mushrooms, hard end of stems removed

2 cups (200 g) scallions (spring onions), diagonally sliced in ^{3}/4-in (2-cm) pieces

3^1/2 oz (100 g) cellophane noodles, soaked in water until transparent

6 oz (180 g) silken beancurd, cubed

Stock
5 x 3 in (12 x 8 cm) dried kelp (*konbu*)
8 cups (2 liters) water
2 teaspoons salt

Accompaniments
1 cup (250 ml) sesame sauce
1 cup (250 ml) *ponzu* sauce (page 107)

4 tablespoons finely sliced scallion (spring onion)

4 tablespoons finely grated daikon (giant white radish), mixed with chili to taste

8 cups (2 liters) water

2 teaspoons salt

Arrange the beef slices on a plate. Cut the cabbage into 1^1/2-in (4-cm) squares. Cut out the hard part of the stalk and slice into threads. Arrange the cabbage and all other ingredients on a platter.

To prepare accompaniments, put the sesame sauce into 4 separate bowls. Do the same for the *ponzu* sauce. Put 1 tablespoon each of the scallion and grated daikon onto 4 separate dishes. Give each diner a bowl of sesame sauce, a bowl of *ponzu* and a dish of scallion with radish.

To prepare the stock, wipe the kelp lightly with a damp cloth to clean. Slash in a few places with scissors to release the flavor. Put water and kelp into a saucepan and bring to a boil. Remove the kelp immediately when the stock reaches the boiling point. Reduce the heat and simmer for 2 to 3 minutes. Add the salt. Pour the stock into the steamboat and bring to a boil. Each person selects a morsel of food and swishes it in the stock with chopsticks until cooked.

Japanese One-Pot

The food is dipped into one of the sauces, with a little of the scallion added to the sesame sauce, and the onion or chili radish added to the *ponzu*.

Skim the stock of any foam that arises during cooking. When all the ingredients have been finished, serve the remaining stock (which will have become a rich soup) in bowls with a little scallion on top if desired.

Tebasaki To Sato-imo
Braised Chicken Wings

| 1 lb (500 g) chicken wings
| 4 teaspoons *sake*
| 1 tablespoon oil
| 3/4 in (2 cm) ginger, sliced
| 12 (100 g) scallions (spring onions), cut in 2-in (5-cm) lengths
| 3/4 lb (400 g) *sato-imo* or new potatoes, peeled
| 2 teaspoons sugar
| 3 tablespoons plus 1 teaspoon dark soy sauce
| 12 snow peas, blanched in lightly salted water
| 4 strips of orange or lemon peel

Marinate chicken wings in *sake* for 30 minutes. Heat the oil and stir-fry the chicken wings until they change color. Add ginger, scallion and just enough water to just cover the chicken.

Cover the pan and simmer for 10 to 15 minutes, then add the potatoes, sugar, and soy sauce. Simmer for about 30 minutes until the potatoes are soft.

Divide the chicken wings and potatoes among 4 bowls and garnish each portion with 3 snow peas and a strip of orange or lemon peel.

Teriyaki Suteki
Sirloin Steak Teriyaki

Tender cubes of steak are brushed with *teriyaki sauce* and grilled with vegetables.

| 1 1/3 lb (650 g) sirloin steak, cut in 1 1/4 -in (2 1/2-cm) cubes
| 8 small Japanese green peppers, or 1 large green bell pepper (capsicum) cut in 8 strips
| 1 teaspoon oil
| 2 cups (200 g) beansprouts
| 1 cup oyster mushrooms, cut in 1/4-in (1/2-cm) slices

Teriyaki Sauce
| 1 cup (200 ml) dark soy sauce
| 1 cup (200 ml) *sake*
| 1 1/4 cups (300 ml) *mirin*
| 2 1/2 tablespoons sugar

Prepare the *teriyaki* sauce first by combining all ingredients in a saucepan and bringing to a boil over medium heat. Simmer until the sauce is reduced to just over 1 cup (250 ml).

Put the cubes of steak on skewers and grill until about half-cooked. Brush with the *teriyaki* sauce and return to the grill for another 30 seconds or so. Brush again, cook a little longer, then give the steak a final brushing and cook for another 30 seconds or so.

If using Japanese peppers, make a small slit in the side of each. Thread the Japanese peppers or bell pepper strips onto skewers and grill until done.

Heat the oil and stir-fry the bean sprouts and mushrooms until just cooked. Serve the vegetables as a garnish for the steak, which should be removed from the skewers before serving.

Renkon Hasami Age
Lotus Root, Pork, and Eggplant Slices

This is rather like a sandwich with a filling of seasoned ground pork between slices of lotus root or eggplant. The "sandwich" is then dipped in a *tempura* batter and deep-fried. The pork filling can be prepared in advance.

| 10 oz (300 g) lotus root, peeled and cut in 1/2-in (1-cm) slices and kept in water
| 2 tablespoons all-purpose (plain) flour
| 1/2 lb (200 g) eggplant (aubergine), cut in 1/2-in (1-cm) slices
| Oil for deep-frying
| Salt and pepper to taste
| 2 teaspoons Japanese mustard paste

Pork Filling
| 1/2 lb (200 g) ground pork
| 1/4 cup (50 g) finely chopped onion

Lotus Root, Pork, and Eggplant Slices (left) and Sirloin Steak Teriyaki (right)

| 2 teaspoons cornstarch
| 1 egg, lightly beaten
| 1 teaspoon dark soy sauce

Tempura Batter
| 2 egg yolks
| 1 cup (250 ml) water
| 1 3/4 cups (200 g) all-purpose (plain) flour

Prepare pork filling by combining all ingredients and mixing well.

Just before the dish is required, dry the lotus root slices well and dust both sides with a little of the flour. Place some of the pork filling on the lotus root and top with another slice of root. Repeat this process for the slices of eggplant.

Prepare the *tempura* batter by mixing the egg and water, stirring in the flour quickly and leaving any lumps in the batter. Dip the pork-filled vegetable slices in the batter and deep-fry in hot oil until golden brown. Sprinkle with a little salt and pepper and serve on a plate with a dab of Japanese mustard. Sprinkle with a little salt and pepper to taste and serve with Japanese mustard.

HELPFUL HINT

To obtain paper-thin slices of beef, place the beef in the freezer until half-frozen. Remove and slice with a very sharp knife.

Sakura Mochi
Cherry Blossom Dumplings

Wrapped in cherry leaves, these dumplings filled with red-bean jam are inevitably associated with spring time or *sakura*. If you can't find edible cherry leaves packed in brine, the dumplings can be served without them.

- 1 cup (110 g) all-purpose (plain) flour
- 2 teaspoons sugar
- 1/2 cup (125 ml) water
- 1/2 egg white, beaten until fluffy and white
- Pinch of salt
- Oil to grease pan lightly
- 3 1/2 oz (100 g) red-bean jam
- 8 cherry blossom leaves (soaked in water for 2 hours if using brine-soaked leaves)

Sift flour into a bowl and add the sugar. Add water a little at a time. Fold in the egg white and salt. Lightly grease a non-stick frying pan and put over low heat. Spread in some of the batter into an oval shape. Cook until the top of the dumpling becomes dry and turn over. Cook on the second side but do not allow the dumpling to take color. Remove the dumpling, spread with red bean jam. Fold over and wrap with a cherry blossom leaf.

Matcha Aisukuriimu
Green Tea Ice Cream

A popular summertime dessert in Japanese restaurants, this might be termed a "modern classic." Finely powdered green tea gives a uniquely Japanese flavor to this delightfully rich ice cream.

- 1 1/2 oz (50 g) green tea powder
- 1/2 cup (100 ml) cognac or brandy
- 5 cups (1 1/4 liters) fresh milk
- 1 cup (250 ml) fresh cream
- 1 1/3 cups (100 g) instant non-fat (skimmed) dry milk powder
- 1 3/4 cups (350 g) sugar

Put the green tea powder into a bowl, add the cognac and mix well. Put the milk, cream, sugar, and dry milk powder into another bowl and mix well. Transfer to a saucepan and

Lily Bulb Dumplings (left) and Cherry Blossom Dumplings (right)

bring to a boil over moderate heat. Remove from the heat and allow to cool to a lukewarm temperature, then add the green tea paste, mixing well.

Chill immediately in the freezer portion of the refrigerator until ice crystals start to form around the edges of the container. Put the mixture into a blender or food processor and blend for a few seconds to break up the crystals. Return to the freezer and leave until set. Alternatively, freeze in an ice-cream maker according to the manufacturer's instructions.

Chakin-shibori
Lily Bulb Dumplings

The sweet, nutty flavor and floury texture of lily bulbs, which are readily available in Japan during the winter months, go well with a red-bean filling.

- 3/4 lb (400 g) lily bulb or sweet potato
- 1/4 cup (50 g) sugar
- 2 1/2 oz (80 g) red-bean jam, strained
- 2 tablespoons finely grated *yuzu* orange or lemon peel

Separate the lily bulb, which looks somewhat like a head of garlic, into petals. Put the petals onto a plate and steam for about 3 minutes or until soft. Drain.

Alternatively, steam the unpeeled sweet potatoes whole, then drain and peel.

Mash the steamed vegetable, then mix with sugar and knead well. Shape about 2 tablespoons of the purée into a dumpling and fill with a teaspoon of red-bean jam. Shape into a dumpling by putting the ball into a cloth and squeezing gently at the top. Remove from the cloth and sprinkle with grated peel. Repeat until all the purée is used up, then serve.

Kingyoku-Kan
Jellied Plums

A simple but decorative dessert, with large grapes or plums set in jellied plum wine (*umeshu*). If plum wine is not available, substitute any fruit wine such as peach or raspberry.

- 8 large black or white grapes, or small plums
- 1 1/2 cups (400 ml) wine (*umeshu*) or peach or raspberry wine
- 2 1/2 envelopes (25 g) unflavored (powdered) gelatin
- 1/4 cup (60 ml) warm water
- 2 1/2 tablespoons (30 g) sugar
- 1 teaspoon cognac or brandy

Blanch the grapes or plums in hot water for about 10 seconds, drain and put in cold water to chill for a few seconds. Peel and set aside.

Sprinkle the gelatin over the warm water and leave until it softens. Heat the wine in a non-reactive saucepan and add sugar and gelatin. Stir until dissolved, then remove from the heat. Add the cognac and pour into 8 tiny containers (such as ramekins or small porcelain soup bowls). Put 1 grape or plum into each bowl of still-liquid jelly, then chill until the jelly is firm. Unmold and serve chilled.

Green Tea Ice Cream

Katsuo Dashi
Basic Dashi Stock

- 2$\frac{1}{2}$ x 1$\frac{1}{2}$ in (6 x 4 cm) dried kelp (*konbu*)
- 7 cups (1$\frac{3}{4}$ liters) water
- 4 cups (50 g) dried bonito flakes

Wipe the kelp with a damp cloth. Put it in a saucepan with water. Bring to a boil uncovered; just before the water comes to a boil, remove and discard the kelp. Sprinkle in the bonito flakes and remove saucepan from heat. As soon as the bonito flakes sink, strain stock and discard bonito flakes. This stock is the basis of many sauces and soups, and can be refrigerated for up to 3 days.

Soba Dashi (1)
Stock for Hot Soba Noodles

- $\frac{2}{3}$ cup (150 ml) basic *dashi* stock
- 2 teaspoons light soy sauce
- $\frac{1}{2}$ teaspoon *mirin*

Put all ingredients into a saucepan, bring to a boil and remove from the heat immediately. Serve with hot soba noodles. Keeps refrigerated for 2 days.

Soba Dashi (2)
Stock for Cold Soba Noodles

- 2 cups (500 ml) basic *dashi* stock
- 7 tablespoons (100 ml) dark soy sauce
- 7 tablespoons (100 ml) *mirin*

Put all ingredients into a pan, bring to a boil and remove from heat immediately. Skim the surface and allow to cool. Serve with cold soba noodles. Keeps refrigerated for up to 4 days.

Suiji
Clear Soup

A variety of ingredients can be added to this clear soup, such as small cubes of silken beancurd, clams, shrimp, diced fish, sliced scallion, *wakame* seaweed, mushrooms, cooked carrots etc.

- 2$\frac{1}{2}$ cups (600 ml) basic *dashi* stock

- 1 teaspoon light soy sauce
- 1 teaspoon salt
- $\frac{1}{2}$ teaspoon *sake*

Put the stock, soy sauce, and salt into a saucepan and heat until it comes almost to a boil. Remove from the heat immediately and add the *sake*.

Tempura Dashi
Tempura Dipping Sauce

- 14 tablespoons (200 ml) basic *dashi* stock
- 2$\frac{1}{2}$ tablespoons light soy sauce
- 2$\frac{1}{2}$ tablespoons *mirin*

Bring *dashi* stock to a boil in a saucepan and add soy sauce and *mirin*. Remove from heat immediately and serve hot as a dipping sauce for *tempura*.

Tosa Shoyu
Tosa Soy Sauce

If red *sake* is not available, use 3 tablespoons of regular *sake*.

- 1$\frac{1}{2}$ tablespoons red *sake*
- 1$\frac{1}{2}$ tablespoons regular *sake*
- 1$\frac{3}{4}$ cups (450 ml) dark soy sauce
- $\frac{1}{3}$ cup (80 ml) *tamari* soy sauce
- $\frac{1}{2}$ oz (15 g, about 1$\frac{1}{3}$ cups) dried bonito flakes
- 5 x 2 in (12 x 5 cm) dried kelp (*konbu*)

Put both types of *sake* in a small pan and bring to a boil to remove the alcohol. Allow to cool, then combine with all other ingredients and store for 1 week before straining. Can be stored for up to 1 year. Use as a dipping sauce for sashimi.

Dengaku Miso

- 1$\frac{3}{4}$ cups (500 g) red or white *miso*
- $\frac{1}{3}$ cup (100 ml) *sake*
- $\frac{1}{3}$ cup (100 ml) *mirin*
- 3 tablespoons (50 g) sugar

Put all ingredients into a saucepan, preferably non-stick, and heat slowly, stirring from time to time. When it has come to the boil, reduce heat to a minimum and cook, stirring from time to time, for 20 minutes. Cool and refrigerate for up to 1 month.

Hoba Miso

- 2$\frac{1}{2}$ tablespoons (50 ml) *sake*
- $\frac{1}{2}$ cup (150 g) red *dengaku miso*
- 2 tablespoons (30 g) *inaka miso*

Heat *sake* in a saucepan and simmer for a few seconds to remove the alcohol. Add both types of *miso*, mix and refrigerate for up to 1 month. Can be used to brush on scallops or fish before grilling.

Tempura Ko
Tempura Batter

- 2 egg yolks
- 1 cup plus 2 tablespoons (275 ml) iced water
- 1$\frac{3}{4}$ cups (200 g) all-purpose (plain) flour, sifted

Put the egg yolks in a bowl and mix in the water gradually. Add the flour all at once and stir briefly (preferably with a pair of chopsticks), leaving in any lumps. Be sure not to mix the batter to a smooth paste; a tempura batter should contain lumps of dry flour. The mixture can be refrigerated until required, although it is best made immediately before it is needed.

Sushi-Meshi
Vinegared Rice

- 4 cups (1 kg) short-grain rice
- 5 cups (1$\frac{1}{4}$ liters) water
- 2$\frac{1}{4}$ -in (3-cm) square of dried kelp (*konbu*)

Dressing
- $\frac{1}{2}$ cup (125 ml) rice vinegar
- 3 tablespoons sugar
- 5 teaspoons salt

Wash the rice gently under running water, taking care not to crush the grains, until the water runs clear. Leave the rice to drain in a colander for about 1 hour. Put in a saucepan with the water and kelp and bring to a boil over high heat. Reduce to medium heat and simmer for about 15 minutes, until the rice is cooked and the water has been absorbed. Turn off the heat. Remove the lid and cover the top of the pan with a towel to absorb any condensation. Put back the lid and

---

leave the covered saucepan to one side for 20 minutes.

While the rice is cooking, mix the dressing ingredients in a small bowl, stirring until the sugar has dissolved, then set aside. Put the cooked rice in a wide wooden tub or plastic bowl. Stir gently in a circular motion with a rice paddle or wooden spoon, sprinkling in the dressing little by little, until it has been absorbed. Ideally, the rice mixture should be fanned to help cool it while the dressing is being stirred in.

Cover the bowl containing the vinegared rice with a damp cloth until it is needed for sushi. Keep at room temperature, not in the refrigerator, and use within 12 hours.

Gari
Pickled Ginger

- 8 oz (250 g) young ginger
- 6 tablespoons rice vinegar
- 2 tablespoons *mirin*
- 2 tablespoons *sake*
- 5 teaspoons sugar

Brush the ginger under running water, then blanch in boiling water for 1 minute. Drain.

Put the vinegar, *mirin*, *sake*, and sugar in a small saucepan and bring to a boil, stirring until the sugar dissolves. Allow to cool.

Put the ginger into a sterilized jar and pour over the cooled vinegar. Cover and keep 3 to 4 days before using. This will keep refrigerated for up to 1 month.

Ponzu Sauce
Citrus Sauce

- 3 x 2$\frac{1}{2}$ in (8 x 6 cm) dried kelp (*konbu*)
- 1$\frac{3}{4}$ cups (450 ml) musk lime (*ponzu* or kalamansi) juice, or lemon juice
- 1$\frac{3}{4}$ cups (450 ml) dark soy sauce
- $\frac{1}{3}$ cup (90 ml) *mirin*
- $\frac{1}{4}$ cup (70 ml) *tamari* soy sauce
- 4 cups (40 g) dried bonito flakes

Heat the dried kelp over a gas flame or under a broiler (grill), then put into a bowl with all other ingredients. Refrigerate for 3 days, then strain. Can be stored for up to 1 year. (Bottled *ponzu* can be purchased in Japanese stores.)

An old Korean saying reads: "A man can live without a wife but not without *kimchi*."

KOREA

A rugged land of mountains, forests, and jagged coastline has produced an equally robust, and delicious, cuisine.

Left: A stall operator in a Korean market prepares for a busy day.

Right: Chinese cabbage on sale at an auction market.

Many factors have contributed to the evolution of Korean cooking over the centuries, and the most important of these are the geography and climate, the importance of medicinal vegetables and herbs, and the various influences that have presented themselves throughout the history of this Land of Morning Calm.

Mountains, Forests, and Seas

The Korean peninsula juts out like a spur from the Asian mainland, just below Manchuria in north-eastern China, and eastern Siberia. To the west lies the Yellow Sea and China; to the east the East Sea and Japan. Scattered off the jagged coastline are some 3,000 islands. But apart from the encircling sea, Korea is a land of mountains. Only 20 percent of the country consists of arable land, and of this a large proportion is represented by the rice-growing Honam plain in southwest Korea.

Korea is also rich in forests with mountain parks full of juniper, bamboo, willow, red maples, and flowering fruit and nut trees such as apricot,

pear, peach, plum, cherry, persimmon, chestnut, walnut, ginkgo, and pine nut. Korea has four distinct seasons: spring and autumn are temperate, winter and summer verge on the extremes. Winter is particularly cold, with temperatures dropping to 24°F (-15°C) or less, and it often lasts from November until late March. This climate, in combination with the mountainous interior, has given Koreans an appetite for hearty, stimulating food, which helps to keep out the cold and produce energy—meat, soup, chilies, garlic, ginseng, and many medicinal vegetables, berries, and nuts. At the same time, the four seasons have guaranteed the Koreans a steady flow of seasonal produce. The lowland fields provide excellent grains and vegetables, while the uplands grow wild and cultivated mushrooms, roots, and greens.

The surrounding seas produce a host of fish, seafood, seaweed, and crustaceans. However, it is the sense of food as medicine and long-term protection that has governed the evolution of the Korean diet. Even raw fish sashimi is given extra vitality by being seasoned with red chili. Most meals are served with a gruel or a soup, as well as the ubiquitous, fortifying *kimchi* and a range of vegetarian side dishes collectively known as *namul*, which are delicately seasoned with soy, seasame, and garlic.

Medicinal Approach

Koreans often look to herbal remedies for illnesses, the result of their grounding in Chinese medical belief about the yin-yang balance of the body and the warming-cooling properties of certain foods. The most common medicinal foods used in cooking are dried persimmon, jujube (red dates), pine seeds, chestnut, ginkgo, tangerine, and ginseng. The sapodin in garlic, which Koreans often eat raw wrapped in a lettuce leaf round barbecued meat, is said to cleanse the blood and aid digestion. Chicken and pork are considered the first steps to obesity, so are largely avoided. Nuts are supposed to be good for pregnancy as well as the skin; jujube and bellflower root for coughs and colds; raw potato juice for an upset stomach; while dried pollack with bean sprouts and tofu is said to be good for hangovers.

In the past, close to the forests and mountain streams, Buddhist monks studied the scriptures; they also developed a "mountain cuisine" that has become the foundation of Korean cooking today. For example, meat, which is forbidden to the Buddhist monk, and anything that is strong smelling, such as garlic and scallion, did not feature in temple cuisine. While modern Korean Buddhism is not so rigid about garlic, this cuisine has retained its traditional dependence on roots, grasses, and herbs. Other stalwarts of the Korean table originate from the mountains, too, such as vegetable pancakes or *jeon*, which are usually filled with lentils or leeks and are sometimes fashioned in the shape of a flower.

Kimchee, Spices, and Ginseng

Even today it is virtually impossible to find a Korean house, apartment, or monastery without rows of big, black enameled *kimchi* pots on the porch or balcony, or, in the snowy months, beneath the earth. *Kimchi* can be preserved for a long time. Its hot and spicy taste stimulates the appetite, and it is nutritious, providing vitamins, lactic acid, and minerals otherwise lacking in the winter diet. The introduction of chili into the pickling process of vegetables in the 17th century, a process that dates back a thousand years or more, was an important innovation in Korean food culture. Using chilies in combination with vegetables and fish resulted in a unique method of food preservation and led to the adoption of *kimchi* as a Korean staple. Red chili and garlic are the mainstays of the basic *kimchi* formula, which calls for heads of fresh cabbage to be cut open, salted, placed in brine with lots of red chili and garlic and set to ferment. In summer, when fermentation is rapid, *kimchi* is made fresh every day. In winter, the big *kimchi* pots are packed in straw and buried in the earth to prevent freezing, then left to ferment for months. There are literally hundreds of *kimchi* types.

Wrapped kimchee (*bossam kimchi*), comprising seafood such as octopus, shrimp, and oyster; white cabbage kimchee (*baek kimchi*), mainly made in the south and containing pickled fish, and sometimes eaten with noodles in winter; stuffed cucumber kimchee (*oisobaegi*), made with cucumbers stuffed with seasonings; hot radish kimchee (*kkaktugi*), made with Korean white radishes cut into small cubes, seasoned and fermented; "bachelor" radish kimchee (*chonggak kimchi*), made with small salted white radishes and anchovies; and sliced radish and cabbage kimchee (*nabak kimchi*), with small pieces of white radish or cabbage pickled in seasoned brine, mixed with whole green or red chilies, and served chilled.

There are also many fermented pastes and sauces for dipping,

called *chang*. Every restaurant and home has its own formula for making *chang*. Based on a fermented mash of soy beans, the three most common varieties are *kan chang* (dark and liquid), *daen chang* (thick and pungent), and *gochu chang* (fiery and hot).

Ginseng (*insam*) is also a staple of the Korean diet; it is also one of Korea's most universally recognized symbols. The roots are grown in long, neat rows protected from the elements by thatched shelters. After harvesting, they are washed, peeled, and dried, then sorted according to age and quality into white ginseng types. Red ginseng, which is regarded by Koreans as the very best, is steamed before being dried in the sun, which is believed to increase its medicinal powers. Koreans consume an enormous amount of ginseng—as root, pills, capsules, candies, chewing gum, cigarettes, tonics, and beauty products. Ginseng tea (*insam-cha*) is a national drink, and is available in tea shops everywhere. Perhaps the most famous ginseng dish is ginseng chicken soup (*samgyetang*). The chicken is stuffed with ginseng, jujube, sticky rice, and garlic, then stewed. The result is a sweet, tender, flavorsome dish that is sublimely cooling on hot summer days.

Table Settings and Etiquette

Korean table settings are classified into 3-*cheop*, 5-*cheop*, 7-*cheop*, 9-*cheop*, and 12-*cheop*, according to the number of side dishes served at a meal. For an everyday Korean meal, the average family takes about four side dishes, along with rice—traditionally the center of all table arrangements—soup, and *kimchi*. The main meals include breakfast, which is the most fortifying meal of the day, a lighter lunch (called *jeomsin*, which means "to lighten the heart"), and a not-too-heavy dinner.

The basic *bansang* setting includes seven side dishes with boiled rice, soup, three seasoning sauces—such as red chili paste, *kimchi*, and hot radish *kimchi*—and two heavier soups, such as hot pollack or rib stew. These soups are considered an accompaniment to the meal and not a starter. Except for the individual bowl of rice and soup, the dishes are shared. Rice, soup, and stews are eaten with spoons, and the rather dry side dishes are eaten with metal chopsticks, but spoon and chopsticks are not used at the same time. Bowls and plates are also not raised from the table.

The Korean barbecue is well-known throughout the world and in Korea it is a popular way of cooking beef in restaurants and in street stalls. At home, families usually use a table-top grill on which to cook *bulgogi* and *galbi* ribs.

The ceremonial aspect of Korean dining has been greatly influenced by Confucianism and the royal court. There are abundant archives of royal dishes in Korea, and some of them can still be experienced in their entirety. For example, *gujeolpan* (nine-sectioned royal platter) is served in an octagonal lacquered platter with nine compartments. Delicate pancakes are placed in the center, surrounded by eight other treasures to be carefully interwoven into the pancakes. Another royal delicacy is *shinseolo*, which comes in a brass pot with a chimney.

Many families also own a special pot used in steamboat or fire-kettle meals. This unusual vessel has a central chimney surrounded by a moat which is filled with morsels of food and kept in the fridge until ready to eat. An hour or more before mealtime, coals are lit in an outside barbecue so that when the vessel is removed from the fridge and placed at the dining area, the glowing red coals can be inserted into the chimney. A hot broth is poured into the moat and is kept hot by the chimney. Diners are then able to select food items from the hot broth—this is a delicious and very social way of dining!

SUGGESTED MENUS

Family meals

Enjoy a Korean-style family meal at home with rice and:
• Whole Cabbage Kimchi (page 112);
• Beancurd with Spicy Sauce (page 112);
• Noodle Soup with Vegetables (page 114).

Dinner parties

For a smart dinner party with Korean dishes, serve rice and:
• Crab and Vegetable Hotpot (page 113);
• Whole Cabbage Kimchi (page 112);
• Chicken Stuffed with Rice and Ginseng (page 113);
• Barbecued Seasoned Beef (page 114).

Finger food

For fun snacks and appetizers that can be eaten with the fingers, try:
• Scallion, Shellfish, and Egg Pancakes (page 112);
• Grilled Beef Ribs (page 114);
• and serve some refreshing Persimmon Tea (page 115).

A melting pot menu

For an interesting tasting menu that takes in many special Asian dishes, serve your guests:
• Miso Soup with Mushrooms (page 96) from Japan;
• Barbecued Seasoned Beef (page 114) from Korea with plain rice;
• Spicy Pomelo Salad (page 162) from Thailand;
• White Fungus with Melon Balls (page 46) from China or seasonal fresh fruits as dessert.

THE ESSENTIAL FLAVORS OF KOREAN COOKING

Ingredients common to the Koeran pantry include Korean chili in its many guises: **fresh red chili** is used in the preparation of *kimchi*, **chili flakes**, **chili powder**, and **chili threads** are all made from dried red chilies and are used as garnishing items and to add heat to a dish. **Chili paste** is available from Korean stores. Korean **medium grain rice** would be ideal but Japanese rice is an acceptable substitute (do not use long or short grain rice.) If you are not making your own *kimchi,* then keep a steady supply on hand for every meal.

Whole Cabbage Kimchi

Korea's regional foods offer tastes and culinary experiences as colorful as its temple-filled valleys and rocky bays. This selection of dishes offers a mouth-watering cross section of Korean cuisine, from time-honored *kimchi* recipes to spicy soups and healthful rice and soup dishes.

Pa Jeon
Scallion, Shellfish, and Egg Pancake

If desired, the oysters can be omitted and the amount of scallions doubled to make a Scallion Pancake.

 1/3 cup (40 g) glutinous rice flour or cornflour
 1/3 cup (40 g) rice flour
 1/3 cup (40 g) all-purpose (plain) flour
 1 egg, lightly beaten
 1 teaspoon salt
 Liberal sprinkling white pepper
 3/4 cup (185 ml) water
 3–4 scallions (spring onions), cut in 1 1/4-in (3-cm) lengths (some green stems left whole)
 1/2 cup (100 g) fresh oysters, rinsed and drained
 Generous pinch of dried chili strips, or 1 red chili, finely julienned
 1/4 cup (60 ml) vegetable oil
 1 portion Soy and Vinegar Dip (see below)

Combine the flours, egg, salt, and pepper, stirring in water to make a smooth, reasonably thin batter. Stir in the scallions, oysters, and chili, and set aside.

Heat 2 tablespoons of the oil in a skillet and, when moderately hot, add a small ladleful of batter, spreading to make a thin pancake about 4 in (10 cm) across. Cook until golden brown underneath and starting to set on top, about 2 minutes, then turn over and cook until light brown on the other side. Repeat until all the mixture is used up.

Serve hot with the Soy and Vinegar Dip.

Soy and Vinegar Dip

Make this dip as an accompaniment for Scallion, Shellfish, and Egg Pancake (*Pa Jeon*).

 3 tablespoons light soy sauce
 1 tablespoons rice vinegar
 1 teaspoon very finely chopped garlic
 1 teaspoon sesame oil
 1 teaspoon sesame seeds, toasted and coarsely crushed while warm
 1/4 teaspoon freshly ground black pepper

Combine all the ingredients in a bowl and set aside.

Scallion, Shellfish, and Egg Pancake

Kimchi
Whole Cabbage Kimchi

Never use a reactive metal container to store *kimchi*; use porcelain or stainless steel. Plastic will be permanently stained by chili. Store *kimchi* in a cool, dark place—a fridge is best.

 1 long white napa (Chinese) cabbage, about 1 lb 3 oz (600 g)
 1/2 cup (125 g) coarse or pickling salt
 4 cups (1 liter) water
 1 small long white radish, about 5 oz (160 g), cut in 1 1/2-in (4-cm) julienne strips
 1 scallion (spring onion), cut in 1 1/2 -in (4-cm) julienne strips
 1 small leek, white part only, cut in 1 1/2-in (4-cm) julienne strips
 2 teaspoons very finely chopped garlic
 1 teaspoon finely grated ginger
 1 1/2–2 tablespoons chili powder
 1 teaspoon sugar
 1/6 oz (5 g) pickled shrimp
 2/3 oz (20 g) salted anchovies

Trim off the root end of the cabbage but do not cut or separate the leaves. Put all but 1 1/2 tablespoons of the salt in a large bowl and add 4 cups (1 liter) water. Stir to dissolve, then add cabbage, bending the end if necessary to fit the cabbage in tightly. Add more water if needed to cover. Put a weighted plate on top to keep the cabbage under the salted water, and keep at room temperature for 12 hours or longer if needed until the cabbage has softened. Drain the cabbage, rinse well under running water, and squeeze dry.

Combine all other ingredients in a bowl, tossing to mix well. Stand the cabbage upright in a bowl and separate the leaves, one by one, pushing in some of the radish mixture by hand to fill. Pack the cabbage, pushing it down firmly into a covered jar just large enough to hold it. Press down to remove any pockets of air, then cover the jar.

Refrigerate 2 hours, then transfer jar to a warm place, around 78°F (25°C), for about 24 hours to ferment. Transfer to a fridge and chill. Chop before serving.

Yangnyeumjang Sundubu
Beancurd with Spicy Sauce

A delicious and spicy way of serving beancurd.

 10 oz (300 g) soft beancurd, chilled and cut in 4 pieces or left whole

Sauce

4 teaspoons light soy sauce
1 teaspoon sesame seeds,
    toasted and lightly crushed
    while warm
1 teaspoon sesame oil
1 clove garlic, smashed and very
    finely chopped
1 teaspoon chili powder
1 teaspoon water
1 teaspoon very finely chopped
    scallion (spring onion)
1 fresh chili, finely chopped
    (optional)
A generous pinch of dried red chili
    strips, for garnishing

Put a piece of beancurd on each of 4 small bowls (or the whole beancurd on one serving bowl).

Combine all sauce ingredients, stirring to mix well, then drizzle the sauce over the top of each serving of beancurd. Garnish with finely chopped fresh chili and a generous pinch of dried red chili strips, if desired.

Serve as a side dish with rice and other dishes.

Yukgaejang
Spicy Beef Soup

Whether you serve this in the middle of winter or summer, you'll find it a robust soup ideal with rice.

4 cups (500 g) all-purpose (plain)
    flour
1/2 teaspoon baking powder
1 teaspoon salt
1/2 cup (125 ml) milk
1 tablespoon sugar
1 egg
4 tablespoons oil
1 teaspoon nigella seeds

Put beef in a saucepan with the water and salt. Bring to a boil, cover, lower heat, and simmer until the beef is tender. Remove beef and shred very finely.

Return beef to the stock and add bean sprouts and scallions. Bring to a boil and simmer 5 minutes. Add soy sauce, garlic, chili powder, chili paste, and sesame oil, and simmer for a few seconds. Just before serving, stir in the eggs gently.

Kimchi Jjigae
Kimchi Stew

The beef in this spicy recipe can be substituted with pork. Some cooks like to substitute about 1 cup (250 ml) of the beef stock with juice drained from the *kimchi* jar.

1 tablespoon vegetable oil
4 oz (120 g) beef sirloin, finely
    shredded
1–2 teaspoons smashed and very
    finely chopped garlic
2 1/4 cups firmly packed (480 g)
    sliced *kimchi*
6 cups (1 1/2 liters) Beef Stock
    (page 114)
4 oz (120 g) beancurd, sliced into
    rectangles about 1 1/4 by 1 in
    (3 by 2 cm)
1–2 teaspoons chili powder
2 scallions (spring onions), thinly
    sliced
1 small red or green chili, sliced

Heat the oil in a cast iron pot and stir-fry the beef until it changes color. Add the garlic and kimchi and stir-fry for a couple of minutes, then add the beef stock. Bring to a boil and simmer 1 minute. Add the beancurd and chili powder, return to a boil, and simmer 2 minutes. Sprinkle with scallions and sliced chilies, and serve hot.

Kkotgetang
Crab and Vegetable Hotpot

A delicious, warming seafood dish, ideal for cold winter evenings.

2 lb (1 kg) raw blue swimmer crab
4 clams, scrubbed with a brush
5 tablespoons Korean chili paste
    (*gochujang*)
8 cups (2 liters) water
1 1/2 teaspoons salt
6 cloves garlic, smashed and
    chopped
1 small leek, white part only thinly
    sliced
1/2 red bell pepper (capsicum),
    julienned
1/2 green bell pepper (capsicum),
    julienned
2 scallions (spring onions), sliced
1–2 teaspoons chili powder
2 tablespoons chopped fresh
    cilantro (coriander) leaves
Fresh crown daisy, for garnishing

Chicken Stuffed with Rice and Ginseng

Remove the back from the crab and wash, discarding any spongey matter. Cut the crab into 4 pieces, cracking the legs with a cleaver. Set aside. Simmer the clams in water until they just begin to open, set aside.

Put the chili paste, water, and salt in a large saucepan and bring to a boil. Cover, lower heat, and simmer 10 minutes. Add the crab and clams and simmer with the pan uncovered for 5 minutes. Add the garlic, leek, bell pepper, scallion, and chili powder. Simmer until crab is cooked, about 5 minutes.

Scatter with fresh cilantro or crown daisy and serve with rice and other dishes or such as pan-fried green chili.

Samgyetang
Chicken Stuffed with Rice and Ginseng

Ginseng, one of Korea's most famous products, gives a special flavor as well as medicinal value to the filling of glutinous rice, jujubes (dried red dates), and chestnuts.

2 spring chickens (Cornish hens),
    about 1 lb (500 g) each, or
    1 chicken, about 2 lb (1 kg)
1/2 cup (100 g) glutinous
    rice, soaked in warm water
    30 minutes, drained
2 pieces dried ginseng, each
    about 2 in (5 cm) long
6 dried jujubes (dried red dates)
2 dried chestnuts, soaked in
    water 30 minutes, coarsely
    chopped (optional)
1 1/2 teaspoons salt
Liberal sprinkling white pepper
2 thin slices fresh ginger
2 cloves garlic, halved lengthways
1 scallion (spring onion), finely
    sliced

Wash and dry the chickens and clean inside. Combine rice, ginseng, 4 jujubes, chestnuts and 1/2 teaspoon of the salt in a bowl, stirring to mix. If using spring chickens, divide the mixture between the two, ensuring each chicken has 1 piece of ginseng and 2 jujubes. If using one larger chicken, put all the rice mixture inside. Do not pack the chickens too tightly with the mixture, as it will swell during cooking. Close the cavity of the chicken by threading a skewer in and out of the flap several times.

Place the spring chickens or chicken in a saucepan just large enough to hold them, then add water to just cover. Add the 1 teaspoon salt, pepper, 2 jujubes, ginger, garlic, and scallion and bring to a boil. Cover, lower the heat, and simmer gently for 30 minutes. Turn and cook until very tender and the flesh is almost falling off the bone, 20 to 30 minutes for spring chickens and 30 to 40 minutes for the whole chicken.

To serve, halve the spring chickens or cut larger chicken in quarters. Return the chicken and filling to the soup and serve. If preferred, the chicken and rice can be served together, with the soup in separate small bowls. Serve with the dip, made by combining salt and pepper and, if liked, small bowls of *kimchi*.

Bulgogi
Barbecued Seasoned Beef

Traditionally, *bulgogi* is made by cooking slices of marinated beef over a wood fire, but these days, it is usually cooked on a table-top gas grill or on a metal convex broiler.

- 1¹/₂ lb (750 g) sirloin or rib eye beef, thinly sliced, cut in pieces about 2 x 4¹/₂ in (5 x 12 cm), excess fat removed
- 1 tablespoon vegetable oil
- 1 green bell pepper (capsicum), thinly sliced, or 1 large green chili, thinly sliced
- 1 medium onion, thinly sliced
- 6¹/₂ oz (200 g) button or fresh *shiitake* mushrooms, sliced (optional)

Marinade
- 1 tablespoon rice wine
- ¹/₂–1 Asian pear (*nashi*), grated to yield 1 tablespoon pear juice (optional)
- ¹/₄ cup (60 ml) light soy sauce
- 2 tablespoons sesame oil
- 1 tablespoon soft brown sugar
- 1 tablespoon very finely chopped garlic
- 2 scallions (spring onions), finely chopped
- ¹/₂ cup (125 ml) Beef Stock (see below, optional)

In a large bowl, mix the beef slices, rice wine, and pear juice thoroughly, massaging well with the hand for about 1 minute. Then, add all the other marinade ingredients. Cover and leave to marinate for 3 to 4 hours.

Heat a large skillet, drain the beef slices, and sear in the pan, without any oil, for 1 minute on each side, and set it aside. Next, heat the oil in the skillet and stir-fry the bell pepper, onion, and mushrooms over medium heat until cooked but still slightly firm, about 3 minutes.

Add the meat and mix well. Serve with the salad, Korean chili paste (*gochujang*), and rice.

Helpful hints: An alternative way of preparing this dish is to heat a barbecue or grill and cook the beef slices over high heat for about 1 minute on each side; prepare the vegetables as above, and mix in the meat when ready.

Koreans enjoy serving their grills with lettuce leaves, sesame leaves, sliced raw garlic, and sliced green chili on the side. Arrange these ingredients and the meat on a leaf, then wrap and dip the package in a spicy sauce before eating.

Galbi Gui
Grilled Beef Ribs

- 1¹/₂–2 lb (³/₄–1 kg) beef short ribs, cut in 1¹/₂-in (4-cm) lengths

Marinade
- ¹/₄ cup (60 ml) light soy sauce
- ¹/₄ cup (40 g) soft brown sugar
- 1¹/₂ tablespoons sesame oil
- 1¹/₂ tablespoons very finely chopped garlic
- 1¹/₂ tablespoons rice wine
- ¹/₄ teaspoon freshly ground black pepper
- 1 scallion (spring onion), finely chopped
- ¹/₂ cup (125 ml) Beef Stock (see below)

Put beef ribs in a bowl. Mix all marinade ingredients in a small bowl, then pour over the beef; massage with the hand for about 1 minute. Cover and leave to marinate for at least 4 hours.

Heat a grill or broiler and cook the ribs, turning to brown on both sides. Serve on a plate.

Beef Stock

- 2 lb (1 kg) shin beef, in one piece
- 8 cups (2 liters) water

Put beef in a pan with water and bring to a boil. Simmer 10 minutes, then skim off all the material that has risen to the top of the liquid. Cover the pan, lower the heat and simmer very gently for 1¹/₂ hours. Strain stock and use beef for another recipe, if desired.

Barbecued Seasoned Beef

Noodle Soup with Vegetables

Kalguksu
Noodle Soup with Vegetables

This easy-to-prepare dish makes for a satisfying meal.

- 6 cups (1¹/₂ liters) Beef Stock (see above)
- 1 small potato, about 5 oz (150 g), peeled and diced
- 1 small piece zucchini (courgette), about 5 oz (150 g), peeled and julienned
- 12 to 20 small clams
- Salt to taste
- 13 oz (400 g) fresh wheat noodles, or 250 g dried buckwheat noodles
- Dried crushed chili to serve (optional)

Sauce
- 1 tablespoon soy sauce
- 1 tablespoon beef stock
- 1 teaspoon minced ginger
- 1 teaspoon chopped scallion (spring onion)
- 1 teaspoon sesame oil
- 1 teaspoon fried sesame seeds

Prepare the sauce by combining all the sauce ingredients. Transfer to a sauce dish and set aside.

Heat the stock and add potato. Simmer until potatoes are almost tender, then add zucchini and clams. Simmer until done, taste and add salt if desired. Keep warm. If using fresh noodles, plunge into boiling water and cook 1 to 2 minutes, until done; dried noodles require about 4 minutes.

Drain noodles and divide between 4 large noodle bowls. Add the soup and vegetables to the bowls containing the noodles and serve hot with crushed chili for adding to taste, together with the sauce.

Dolsot Bibimbap
Pot Rice with Fried Beef and Vegetables

Dolsot Bibimbap is a popular dish of steamed rice with vegetables and beef in a pot. Sometimes the *bibimbap* is served without any side dishes.

- 3–4 tablespoons vegetable oil
- 4 dried black *shiitake* mushrooms, soaked in hot water to soften, and sliced; stems discarded
- 1 teaspoon salt
- 1 small zucchini (courgette), julienned
- 6¹/₂ oz (200 g) bracken, sliced and soaked 10 hours
- 2 teaspoons soy sauce
- Small bundle soy bean sprouts, about 6¹/₂ oz (200 g) tails cut off, or mung bean sprouts
- 6¹/₂ oz (200 g) minced beef
- 6¹/₂ oz (200 g) spinach, coarsely chopped
- 4 cups (600 g) hot cooked rice
- 4 tablespoons Korean chili paste (*gochujang*)
- 4 tablespoons shredded dried laver
- 1 tablespoon sesame seeds, toasted and coarsely crushed while still warm
- 2 teaspoons sesame oil

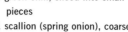

Heat 2 teaspoons oil in a wok and add the mushrooms. Stir-fry over medium heat until cooked, 3 to 4 minutes. Season with a pinch of salt, remove and drain on paper towel.

Add another 2 teaspoons of oil to the wok and stir-fry the zucchini, seasoning with a pinch of salt and 1 teaspoon soy sauce. Add 1 to 2 tablespoons water while stir-frying, and cook until the zucchini is tender and almost dry. Put on a dish and keep warm.

Add 2 teaspoons oil to the wok and stir-fry the soy bean sprouts over medium heat until cooked, 3 minutes. Season with a little salt and transfer to the dish with the other cooked vegetables.

Add 2 teaspoons oil to the wok and stir-fry the beef until cooked, seasoning with a pinch of salt and the remaining 1 teaspoon of soy sauce. Add to the plate and keep warm.

Add 1 teaspoon oil to the wok and stir-fry the spinach until cooked, 2 to 3 minutes, then season with a pinch of salt.

Divide hot rice between 4 bowls. Add 1/2 to 1 teaspoon chili paste to each, and scatter each with laver, sesame seeds, and sesame oil. If preferred, add some of the mushrooms, zucchini, bean sprouts, beef, and spinach to each, or put the accompaniments on a plate in the center of the table. Serve with the chili paste (*gochujang*) and, if desired, add a fried egg to the top of each portion of rice. If clay or other individual heat-proof casseroles are available, grease the inside of each lightly with oil, add rice and put over medium heat for 3 to 4 minutes. Garnish with the beef and vegetables.

Kimchi Bokeumbap
Stir-fried Rice with Kimchi and Beef

This is a handy way of using left-over cooked rice, which can be kept refrigerated in a covered container. (In fact, it's preferable for all fried rice dishes that the rice is kept overnight, so that it is completely dry.) The rice is stir-fried with shredded beef, spicy *kimchi*, onion, scallion, and garlic, and seasoned with soy sauce and sesame oil for a quick and very tasty dish ideal for lunch or a light supper.

- 6 1/2 oz (200 g) beef sirloin, finely shredded
- 1 tablespoon sesame oil
- 1 1/2 tablespoons soy sauce
- 1–2 teaspoons very finely chopped garlic
- 2 tablespoons vegetable oil
- 1 small onion, finely chopped
- 1 green chili, sliced into small pieces
- 1 scallion (spring onion), coarsely chopped
- 1 1/2 cups firmly packed (300 g) chopped *kimchi*
- 3 cups (450 g) cold cooked rice
- Black sesame seeds to garnish

Put beef in a bowl and sprinkle with 1 tablespoon of the sesame oil. Add the soy sauce and garlic, mix well and leave beef to season for 5 minutes.

Heat 1/2 tablespoon of the oil in a wok then add beef and stir-fry over very high heat until cooked, about 1 minute. Remove from wok and set aside.

Reduce heat to medium, add 1 tablespoon of the remaining vegetable oil to the wok and when hot, add onion, chili, and scallion. Stir-fry until onion softens, 1 to 2 minutes, then add *kimchi* and stir-fry 1 minute. Remove from wok and set aside.

Increase heat to maximum and add 1 tablespoon vegetable oil. When hot, add rice and stir-fry over high heat for 1 minute. Return beef and *kimchi* mixture to the wok and continue stir-frying until heated through. Transfer to a serving bowl and sprinkle with tablespoon of sesame oil. Garnish with sesame seeds.

Pot Rice with Fried Beef and Vegetables

Insam-Cha
Ginseng Tea

Ginseng is Korea's most famous product, a medicinal root whose amazing properties have been known for around 5000 years.

- 1 2/3 oz (50 g) dried ginseng root
- 4 jujubes (dried red dates)
- 8 cups (2 liters) water
- 1/3 cup (85 g) sugar, or more to taste
- 1 tablespoon pine nuts

Put ginseng, jujubes, and water in a large saucepan. Bring to a boil, cover, reduce heat to minimum and cook very gently for 4 hours. Add sugar and stir to dissolve. Pour through a strainer into glasses or porcelain tea bowls, and serve with a few pine nuts floating on the top.

Note: Although top quality, whole aged Korean ginseng root is very expensive, packets of younger creamy white dried rootlets (available in Chinese medicine shops and most Asian stores) are moderately priced and ideal for this recipe.

Sujeonggwa
Persimmon Tea

- 2 4-in (10-cm) cinnamon sticks
- 1 1/2 in (4 cm) fresh ginger, thinly sliced
- 4 black peppercorns
- 4 jujubes (dried red dates)
- 6 cups (1 1/2 liters) water
- 3 tablespoons sugar, or more to taste
- 12 pine nuts
- 4 dried persimmons, soaked in water
- 30 minutes, drained (chopped if desired)

Put cinnamon sticks, ginger, peppercorns, jujubes, and water into a large saucepan and bring to a boil. Cover, lower heat and simmer for 1 hour. Add sugar to taste and stir until dissolved. Pour the mixture through a sieve into a bowl and add the dried persimmons. Allow to cool, then refrigerate until chilled. When serving, divide the liquid between 4 bowls or glasses and add some pine nuts and a whole dried persimmon (or chopped persimmon) to each serving.

"Malaysians and Singaporeans of all ethnic backgrounds view eating as a communal activity—as a quick visit to any hawker stall will show you."

MALAYSIA & SINGAPORE

Culinary exchange between the Chinese, the Indians, and the Malays has made the peninsula a true melting pot.

Left: Malay food can now be found on many a smart restaurant's menu but the flavors remain true to the *kampung* (village).

Right: Rice is the staple food in both countries and comes in many varieties.

It is not possible to live cheek by jowl with people of another ethnic community without picking up ideas on food. Over the centuries, the Malay peninsula saw sailing ships arriving from the west from Arabia, India and, much later on, from Europe. From the east came Chinese junks, Siamese vessels, and the inter-island sailing craft of the Buginese and Javanese people of the Indonesian archipelago. This has resulted in a melting pot culture, where the delicacy of Chinese cooking, the exuberance of Indian spices and the fragrance of Malay herbs co-exist.

The original people of the peninsula—known collectively as *orang asli*—consist of about twenty different tribes belonging to two distinct linguistic groups. Later arrivals to the area, who spread south from Yunnan in southern China and began settling in Malaysia around 4000 years ago, are the ancestors of today's dominant ethnic group, the Malays.

The ethnic and social structures of the Muslim Malaccan sultanate were to change irrevocably from the 16th century. Since then it has witnessed the settlement of the Portuguese, the Dutch and, in the 19th century, the British. With the British came large numbers of Chinese and Indian workers, which changed the face of the country forever.

In 1963, the Federation of Malaysia was formed, consisting of the states of the peninsula; Singapore, the island at the tip of the peninsula, and the former British colonies of Sabah and Sarawak. Singapore broke away in 1965, and has since come into its own as an important entrepôt. Today Singapore is one of Asia's most dynamic and modern cities.

The Land and its People

Their location near the equator means that Malaysia and Singapore are humid and steamy all year-round. Tropical rains frequently bring freshness during the afternoons, and in contrast with

During the Feast of the Hungry Ghosts, offerings of food and incense are made to the spirits.

the usually hot days, nights are balmy and the early mornings fresh and cool.

The postcard-pretty tropical landscape—rice paddies, beaches fringed by groves of coconut palms—exists along the coasts, and much of the lush alluvial plains of the peninsula's west coast is planted with palm oil and rubber. Orchards proliferate here and luscious tropical fruits such as the highly prized durian, furry rambutan, mangosteen, starfruit, and *langsat* can be found. To the far north of the peninsula, the climate is often dry and the landscape of endless paddy fields relieved by abrupt limestone hills.

The temperate climate on the main mountain range that runs north-south along the peninsula, the Banjaran Titiwangsa, makes getaways such as Cameron Highlands perfect not only for holiday makers but for the tea plantations and market gardens that provide much of the fresh produce for the peninsula's markets.

The generally muddy coastal waters of the Malacca Straits on the west coast are ideal for crabs and shellfish. The small *kampungs* (villages) along the east coast are ideal fishing grounds and make their livelihood from the South China Sea.

Over on the Borneo peninsula, Sabah has a mountain range that culminates in Southeast Asia's tallest peak, Mount Kinabalu (13,455 feet). Much of the terrain of Sarawak is low-lying.

Singapore is for the most part low-lying, and urban development has accelerated swamp reclamation and deforestation. Dense equatorial rain forests and a few low hills which once shaped the landscape have given way to a dense cover of high-rise office blocks, shopping complexes, condominiums, and public housing. Singapore has grown almost none of its food for decades; much of its scarce land is devoted to industry and housing its population.

Located as they are in the middle of the world, and with produce coming in from all over, few foods are ever out of season in Singapore and Malaysia.

The Making of a Cuisine

Perhaps the contemporary food of Malaysia and Singapore is best represented by the open-air eating stalls. Here, you might start dinner with some *popiah* (spring roll), move on to a fish-head curry and spicy *kangkung* with rice, and take home a packet of *hokkien mee* for supper. Almost any self-respecting Malaysian or Singaporean cook can whip up a tasty Malay-style chicken or fish curry, *roti canai* or *murtabak*, or a very fine Chinese stir-fry.

When Chinese merchants sailed their junks across the South China Sea, they set in train a process that was to have a profound influence on the region. A few of these Chinese traders stayed on in the Malay peninsula, often marrying local women and forming the beginnings of Nonya or Straits-Chinese culture. The British encouraged Chinese migration to supply labor for the tin mines. Thousands of Chinese workers poured in to Singapore and the Malay peninsula. Others headed straight for the gold mines and coal fields of Sarawak to try their luck, or moved to British North Borneo (now Sabah) to work on the land.

The Chinese brought with them the cooking styles of their homeland, mostly the southern provinces of Guangdong and Fukien, and introduced to the indigenous people of the Malay peninsula and northern Borneo a range of ingredients now used by every ethnic group in Malaysia and Singapore today: noodles, beansprouts, beancurd, and soy sauce. In turn, the Chinese developed a penchant for spices and chilies.

Like their Chinese counterparts, Indian traders have been recorded in the region for more than a thousand years, but it was in the 19th century that they came to Malaya in large numbers as contract laborers.

Malay cuisine is the link between Indonesia to the west and south, and Thailand to the north. Although the results are rather different, there is overlap, especially with the food of nearby Sumatra and, in the northern states of Malaysia, with Thailand. Although Malay food is not as prominent in Singapore as Chinese, familiar favorites such as the *korma*, *rendang*, chicken curry, and various *sambals* are very much part of a mainstream diet.

While the Malays, Chinese and Indians continue to create their traditional foods, cross-cultural borrowing in the kitchen has led to a number of uniquely "Malaysian" and "Singaporean" dishes, such as *mee goreng* and *rojak*.

The Food of the People

Despite regional differences, Malay food can be described as spicy and flavorful, although this does not necessarily mean chili-hot. But you can rest assured that even if the main dishes are not hot, there'll be a chili-based *sambal* on hand.

Over the centuries, traditional Southeast Asian spices have been joined by Indian, Middle Eastern, and Chinese spices, so the partnership of coriander and cumin (the basis of many Malay "curries") is enhanced by pepper, cardamom, star anise, and fenugreek.

The Malaysian northern states of Kedah, Perlis, and Kelantan, all of which border Thailand and Trengganu, show distinct Thai influences. (So, too, does Penang.) Fiery hot chilies, so much a part of Thai food, are popular in the northern states. In addition to Malaysian herbs such as lemongrass, pandan leaf, the fragrant leaf of the kaffir lime, and the pungent *polygonum* or *daun kesum*, *daun kemangia*, a basil popular in Thailand, leaves of a number of rhizomes such as turmeric and zedoary (known locally as *cekur*), and the wonderfully fragrant wild ginger bud are used. Tamarind, sour carambola, and limes give food a tangy and fragrant sourness.

Food without seasoning is unthinkable—even a piece of fish is rubbed with turmeric powder and salt before cooking. Many of the seasonings that enhance Malay food are not dried spices but rhizomes such as fresh turmeric and *lengkuas* (galangal), and other "wet" ingredients such as chilies, onions, and garlic. Fresh seasonings and dried spices are pounded to a fine paste and cooked gently in oil before liquid—either creamy coconut milk or a sour broth—is added, together with the vegetables, meat or fish.

Produce from the sea is an important part of the Malay diet. Tiny dried anchovies (*ikan bilis*) and dried shrimp are popular flavorings, and dried shrimp paste (*belacan*) is used to give an inimitable finish to many dishes.

The *kenduri* or feast is one time when Malay cuisine comes into its own. All the women of the family or village take out their giant cooking pots and work through the night, scraping and squeezing coconuts for milk, pounding shallots, garlic, chilies, and spices, cutting and chopping, simmering and stirring, until they have created an impressive array of fish curries, *gulai* (curries) of vegetables bathed in coconut milk and seasoned perhaps with fresh shrimp; coconut-rich *rendang* of beef or chicken, tingling hot shrimp *sambals*, and a colorful array of desserts. With their innate courtesy and hospitality, the Malays consider it an honor to be able to invite any fortunate passer-by to join in the *kenduri*.

Nonya—the Food of Love

The so-called Straits-born Chinese, descendants of early settlers in Penang and Malacca, combine elements of both Chinese and Malay culture, quite unlike the mass of Chinese migrants who arrived around the turn of this century and up until the 1930s. These pioneering Chinese traders took Malay wives, although as time went on, children of these early mixed marriages generally married pure

A selection of pickles to be served with the main meal.

were all transformed in the kitchen, added to and blended with aromatics such as the kaffir lime leaf, polygonum or *laksa* leaf, zedoary, fresh turmeric leaves, and pandan.

One of the most popular Nonya dishes among Malaysians of any background is *laksa*, a rice-noodle soup that marries Malay seasonings with Chinese noodles. Nonya cakes are renowned for their richness and variety. Most are based on Malay recipes, using freshly grated tapioca root, sweet potato, agar-agar, glutinous rice, palm sugar, and coconut milk

The Kitchen and Table

Whatever the ethnic community in Malaysia and Singapore, eating is a communal activity, whether at home or in a restaurant. The assortment of dishes appear all at once, diners get individual servings of rice and then help themselves to the dishes using a serving spoon. One exception to this is the Chinese banquet, a formal eight or ten-course dinner, where the dishes appear sequentially.

"Don't use your fingers" is not an admonishment you will hear often in Malaysia and Singapore. Indians, Malays, and Straits Chinese will tell you that curry and rice taste best when you can literally feel the food with your fingers. Eating with your hand has its own etiquette too. Only the right hand is used, and just the tips of the fingers; the palm is kept perfectly clean. Washing the hands before eating is not only polite but more hygienic. In the finer Indian and Malay restaurants, a waiter will bring a bowl of warm water before and after a meal. In the more pedestrian curry shops or "banana leaf" restaurants, there will be a row of wash basins and soap for customers to clean up. Even with clean hands, diners should touch only the food on their plate, never that in the communal dishes, and the left hand is used to hold the serving spoon to keep it clean.

Chinese food is more likely to be eaten with chopsticks, although at some Chinese food stalls and in many Chinese homes, forks, spoons, and plates are used. However, at a ten-course Chinese meal, chopsticks are *de rigueur*. Sucking or licking the tips of the chopsticks is impolite and contact between mouth and the tips is kept to a minimum. Spoons are set out for larger mouthfuls. Often before and always at the end of the meal, hot towels are handed round for cleaning the face and hands.

Although Chinese tea is the traditional drink with Chinese food, there is nothing quite like beer to take the heat off your tongue and to cool you down when you eat spicy food on a steamy evening.

Most urban kitchens in Malaysia and Singapore these days are a curious blend of old and new: the microwave next to the mortar and pestle; the food processor next to a well-seasoned wok.

Above: A spread of Nonya food, which is often time consuming to prepare but well worth the effort. *Below right:* The owner of a hawker stall in Singapore entices customers with his fresh produce.

Chinese or the children of other Straits Chinese. The women, known as *Nonyas*, and the men, *Babas*, generally spoke a mixture of Malay and Chinese, dressed in modified Malay style, and combined the best of both cuisines in the kitchen.

Typical Chinese ingredients (such as beancurd, soy sauce, preserved soybeans, black shrimp paste, sesame seeds, dried mushrooms, and dried lily buds) were blended with Malay herbs, spices, and fragrant roots. Being non-Muslim, the Straits Chinese cooked pork dishes in the Malay style, and added distinctive local ingredients (coconut milk, spices, and sour tamarind juice) to basic Chinese recipes.

Distinct differences evolved between the cuisine of the Penang Nonyas and that of Malacca. In Penang, which is geographically much closer to Thailand, the Nonyas developed a passion for sour food (using lots of lime and tamarind juice), fiery hot chilies, fragrant herbs, and pungent black shrimp paste. Malacca Nonyas prepare food that is generally rich in coconut milk and Malay spices (such as coriander and cumin), and usually use more sugar than their northern counterparts.

Many fruits and vegetables were prepared in imaginative ways by the Nonyas. Unripe jackfruit, the heart of the banana bud, sweet potato leaves, and tiny sour carambola

SUGGESTED MENUS

A family meal

For a family dinner, serve the following with rice:
• Chicken with Lime Leaf (page 132), a little bit of Shrimp Sambal (page 131) and Snake Gourd (page 133);
• Sago with Honeydew (page 134) is a popular sweet treat with both the young and old.

Snacks

Curry Puffs (page 122) are great as a mid-morning or afternoon snack, as are the Stuffed Deep-Fried Yam Dumplings (page 122). The Nonya Pancakes (page 134) and Mango Jellies (page 134) would normally be eaten in-between meals as fillers in Malaysia and Singapore.

A light lunch

The recipes in this chapter are particularly well suited to smorgasbords. For a light lunch:
• Popiah (page 122) make a delighful start;
• Shrimp Noodle Soup (page 125) or Indian Fried Noodles (page 127);
• finish with some sliced fresh fruit.
Other great lunch dishes include Claypot Rice or Chicken Rice (page 128).

A dinner party

For a formal dinner, impress your guests with these dishes:
• Oyster Omelets (page 123), cooked in individual servings, and small portions of Tea-Smoked Seabass (page 132);
• Duck in Fragrant Soy Sauce (page 128) or the Chili Crab (page 131), which is a sure-fire hit;
• Cooling Almond Jelly (page 134) is a good way to round off the meal.

A melting pot menu

You could start your Asia-wide menu with
• Noodles in Spicy Coconut-Milk (page 126);
• Pork Cutlets on Rice (page 101) from Japan are an interesting blend of East and West, serve with Vietnamese Pan-Fried Water Convolvulus with Yellow Bean Sauce (page 181);
• finish with the wonderful Mixed Ice from Indonesia (page 84).

THE ESSENTIAL FLAVORS OF MALAYSIAN AND SINGAPOREAN COOKING

The aromatic curry pastes need **chilies**, **garlic**, **ginger**, **limes**, **lemongrass**, and **shallots**, but these ingredients are also used by themselves. **Coconut milk** and **palm sugar** are frequently added to soften the heat of curries and, in desserts, the fragrant **pandan leaf** is used. **Rice** and **soy sauce** are must-haves.

Popiah

The recipes given in this section are not usually eaten as appetizers as such during a meal, but as snacks or in-between meals. However, they make excellent nibbles to be served with drinks at the start of a meal.

Popiah

This Nonya version of a popular Chinese snack is ideal for lunch. *Popiah* wrappers are similar to the fresh wrappers used for Filipino *lumpia*. If neither are available, use egg roll wrappers.

- 6 *popiah* wrappers
- 1 red chili, sliced, or 4 red chilies pounded to a paste with a little salt
- 2 shallots, finely chopped
- 1 teaspoon pounded garlic
- 1 tablespoon sweet black sauce (*tim cheong*)

Filling
- 1 tablespoon oil
- 1 jicama, peeled and shredded
- 4 shallots, sliced
- Pinch of five-spice powder
- 1/2 teaspoon salt
- 6 lettuce leaves
- 2/3 cup (60 g) beansprouts
- 1/2 cup (60 g) crabmeat

- 12 medium-sized cooked shrimp, peeled and halved lengthwise
- 1 hard-boiled egg, halved length wise then sliced across
- 1 Chinese sausage (*lap cheong*), sliced and blanched in hot water

Prepare the filling by sautéing the jicama and shallots in oil for about 5 minutes, until soft. Seson with five-spice powder and salt and leave to cool. To stuff the popiah, lay a skin flat on a plate or board. Smear with a little of the black sauce and pounded garlic, then smear with chili paste or sprinkle with sliced chilies and shallots. Lay a lettuce leaf on top and add one-sixth of the bean sprouts, crabmeat, shrimp, egg, Chinese sausage, and cooked jicama. Tuck in the sides and roll up the popiah firmly. Repeat for remaining 5 popiah. Cut each popiah across in 4 to 5 pieces before serving. Serve immediately.

Curry Puffs

A perennial favorite originally created by Indian cooks.

Filling
- 5 tablespoons oil
- 1 medium-sized red or brown onion, finely chopped
- 1 1/2 teaspoons *kurma* powder or chicken curry powder
- 2 teaspoons meat or chicken curry powder

- 1 teaspoon chili powder
- 1/2 teaspoon turmeric powder
- 2 cups (200 g) finely diced, cooked chicken
- 2 large potatoes, boiled and finely diced
- 1 1/2 teaspoons sugar
- 1/2 teaspoon black pepper
- 1/2 teaspoon salt

Pastry
- 4 cups (500 g) all-purpose (plain) flour
- 10 tablespoons butter or margarine
- Just over 3/4 cup (200 g) water
- 1/2 teaspoon salt

Make the filling first. Heat oil and fry the onion gently until golden brown. Add the curry powders, chili, and turmeric and fry gently. Add the chicken, potatoes, sugar, pepper, and salt and cook for 5 minutes. Mix well and leave aside to cool.

To make pastry, mix flour with butter or margarine, water, and salt and knead well. Let it rest for 1/2 hour. Cut the dough into circles 3 in (8cm) in diameter. Take a tablespoon of filling and place it in the center. Fold pastry over to make a half circle and crimp at edges. Deep-fry in hot oil until golden.

Note: Not all margarines are suitable for pastry, owing to their high moisture content. The Malaysian brand, Planta, is recommended; Crisco is a suitable substitute. If meat or chicken curry powder is not available, substitute plain curry powder.

Curry Puffs

Pork Ribs Fried in Pandan Leaves

6 in (15 cm) of the leaf protruding at one end. Fry in very hot oil for 3 to 5 minutes until cooked. Serve hot still in the pandan leaf, allowing each diner to unwrap his or her own portions.

If you cannot obtain pandan leaves, use parchment paper cut in squares. Fold up the pork ribs envelope style and fasten with a staple before frying.

Pork Ribs Fried in Pandan Leaves

The fragrance of pandan (screw-pine) leaves enriches a number of savory rice, meat, and chicken dishes of Malay or Nonya origin. The use of pandan leaves to wrap food before deep-frying is a Thai influence. This Singapore adaptation uses pork ribs.

2 lb (1 kg) pork ribs, cut in 1 $^1/_2$-in
  (4-cm) pieces
8 cloves garlic
8 shallots
6 tablespoons honey
2 tablespoons red sweet sauce
1 tablespoon five-spice powder
3 tablespoons Lea & Perrins sauce
1 tablespoon HP sauce
2 tablespoons sour plum sauce
4 tablespoons oil
1 teaspoon sesame oil
24 pandan leaves
Oil for deep-frying

Choose meaty pork ribs and have them cut to the correct length. Pound or blend together the garlic and shallots, then mix with all other ingredients, except pandan leaves and oil for deep frying. Leave to marinate for about 2 hours.

Wrap each of the pork ribs with pandan leaves, tying a simple knot and leaving about

Wu Kok
Stuffed Deep-fried Yam Dumplings

A Teochew delicacy filled with red-roasted pork (*char siew*). *Char siew* is readily available from Chinese barbecue stores.

1 yam, about 1$^1/_4$ lb (600 g)
9 tablespoons tapioca starch
$^1/_2$ cup (125 ml) pork oil or
  vegetable shortening (Crisco)
1 tablespoon five-spice powder
1 teaspoon sesame oil
1 tablespoon sugar
$^1/_2$ teaspoon ground white pepper
Oil for deep-frying
1 teaspoon salt

Filling
8 oz (200 g) red roasted pork
  (*char siew*), diced (page 135)
$^1/_3$ cup (50 g)green peas
1 small onion, finely diced
1 small carrot, diced
$^1/_2$ cup (125 ml) oyster sauce
$^1/_2$ teaspoon five-spice powder
$^1/_2$ teaspoon sesame oil
$^1/_2$ teaspoon sugar
2 tablespoons light soy sauce
1 tablespoon cornstarch

Put all filling ingredients in a bowl and mix well. Set aside to chill in the refrigerator.

Peel yam and cut in pieces. Steam for about 30 minutes over boiling water until it is soft. Mash the yam and set aside. Mix the tapioca starch with enough boiling water and knead to form a dough. Knead well. Add the pork oil, five-spice powder, sesame oil, salt, sugar, and pepper and the mashed yam. Mix and divide into 10 to 12 portions. Flatten each portion into a round shape.

Divide the filling into 10 to 12 portions. Put a portion in the middle of each piece of dough. Squeeze together to enclose the filling and make into a dumpling. Heat oil in a wok or deep-fryer and deep-fry the yam dumplings until golden brown. Serve hot.

Pork oil or lard is made by chopping hard (back) pork fat into fine dice and cooking over low heat with about 2 tablespoons water until the water evaporates and all the oil runs out. Tapioca starch or "flour" is available in 1-lb (500-g) packages in Asian food stores. If you cannot find any, substitute instant tapioca that has been ground to a fine powder in a blender or grinder.

Oyster Omelet

Fresh oysters are cooked in a light omelet flavored with soy sauce and Chinese wine.

8–10 large fresh oysters
2 tablespoons tapioca starch
1 tablespoon rice flour
8 tablespoons water
1 tablespoon oil
2 cloves garlic, finely chopped
3 whole eggs, beaten
1 tablespoon light soy sauce
1 tablespoon Chinese wine
Ground white pepper
Sprigs of fresh cilantro (coriander)
  leaves as garnish

Wash the oysters and drain well. Mix both tapioca starch and rice flour together with the water to make a very thin batter. Heat a large heavy skillet until very hot and add oil. Pour in the batter and cook for about 15 seconds before adding the beaten eggs.

When the eggs are almost set, make a hole in the center, pour in a little oil and fry the garlic for a few seconds. Mix, then season with soy sauce, Chinese wine and pepper. Add oysters and cook just long enough to heat through. Serve sprinkled with fresh coriander and accompanied by Chili Sauce (page 135).

HELPFUL HINT
Oyster omelets make elegant dinner-party entrées. The omelets can be made in two-oyster lots for individual servings.

Stuffed Deep-fried Yam Dumplings

The Chinese principle of the "restorative" dish meets the hot and spicy in the selection of soups here. Once again, one-bowl or one-plate noodle dishes proliferate—a testament to their popularity in Malaysia and Singapore.

Bak Kut Teh
Spiced Pork Bone Soup

A popular hawker stall snack, eaten as a late-night or early morning pick-me-up. The Chinese herbs should be available from any Chinese medicine shop. They can be omitted, although the flavor will be less rich and the soup presumably less of a restorative.

1 lb (500 g) pork ribs, cleaned and cut into 2-in (5-cm) lengths
8 oz (250 g) lean pork, in one piece
12 cups (3 liters) water
Salt and ground white pepper to taste

Seasoning
4 *gan cao*
1 *luo han guo*
2 1/2 oz (50 g) *dang xin*
1 oz (25 g) *chuan kong*
1 oz (25 g) *dang guei*
1/2 oz (15 g) *sheng di*
5 whole star anise
1 cinnamon stick, about 3 in (8 cm) long
10 cloves
1 piece dried Mandarin orange peel
1/2 cup (125 ml) light soy sauce
1/4 cup (60 ml) black soy sauce
2 tablespoons sugar

Put the pork ribs, meat and water in a large pan. Wrap all the seasoning ingredients except soy sauces and sugar in a piece of clean cheesecloth and add to the pan. Add both types of soy sauce and sugar and bring to the boil. Simmer gently, uncovered, for 1 1/2 to 2 hours, until the meat is almost falling off the bones. Season to taste with salt (if needed) and ground white pepper.

When serving, cut the lean pork meat into small pieces. Put in a bowl together with the pork ribs and top with the stock.

Superior Wonton Soup

Stuffed ravioli-like dumplings or *wonton* in soup are found in Chinese restaurants throughout the world, usually served with thin egg noodles for a quick meal. This is a luxurious version.

15 *wonton* skins
6 cups (1 1/2 liters) basic stock (see below)
1 1/2 cups snow peas, blanched
6 dried black mushroom, soaked, boiled until soft, thinly sliced
Salt and pepper

Basic Stock
3 dried scallops
10 oz (300 g) boneless chicken
1/2 cup very fine dried Chinese anchovies
12 cups (3 liters) water
2 cloves garlic, smashed
1/2 in (1 cm) ginger, sliced
1/2 teaspoon white peppercorns
3 carrots
7 ribs celery

Filling
8 oz (200 g) shrimp, peeled and deveined
4 oz (100 g) boneless chicken or pork
4 oz (100 g) water chestnuts, peeled
1 1/2 oz (30 g) dried black fungus or 2 dried mushrooms, soaked
1 tablespoon oyster sauce
1/2 teaspoon salt
A dash of sesame oil
2 tablespoons sugar
A dash of Chinese wine

1 egg, beaten
2 tablespoons cornstarch
1 tablespoon light soy sauce

Prepare the stock first by putting all the ingredients in a pot and bringing to the boil. Remove the scum from the surface, lower heat and simmer, covered, for 2 hours. Strain thoroughly before using.

Superior Wonton Soup

To make the filling, chop the shrimp, chicken, water chestnuts, and fungus together with a cleaver until fine. Mix in all other filling ingredients.

Put 1 small spoonful of the filling in the center of a *wonton* wrapper and squeeze the edges together in the center. Repeat until all the filling is used.

Bring the cooked stock to a boil, add the *wonton* and simmer for 3–5 minutes or until they rise to the top. Add the snow peas, mushrooms, salt, and pepper and serve immediately. If you are unable to find dried scallops (which are very expensive), 1 lb (500 g) of pork bones can substituted to make the stock.

HELPFUL HINT

Don't bother making small batches of *wontons*: they freeze well and are very handy for deep-fried pre-dinner nibbles or to be added to noodle soups, so make heaps!

Spiced Pork Bone Soup

Yen's Brown Noodles

This version of a Cantonese-style dish is named after the chef who created it. Packets of *yee mien* noodles should be available from any Chinese provision shop. The distinctive flavor of this type of noodle makes this simple dish well worth sampling.

| 5 oz (150 g) dry brown noodles (*yee mien*)
| 5 oz (150 g) mustard greens or spinach
| Oil for frying
| 1 clove garlic, finely chopped
| 150 g (5 oz) peeled shrimp
| 150 g (5 oz) chicken or pork, shredded
| 3 cups (750) ml water
| 2 tablespoons oyster sauce
| 2 tablespoons light soy sauce
| 1/2 teaspoon black soy sauce
| 1/2 teaspoon sesame oil
| 1/2 teaspoon white pepper
| 1 heaped tablespoon cornflour, blended with 3 tablespoons water
| 2 eggs, lightly beaten

Put the noodles in a colander, sprinkle with a little cold water and leave aside to soften.

Discard hard ends of the greens and cut into 1 1/2 in (4 cm) lengths. Heat about 2 in (5 cm) oil in a wok and fry the noodles, a handful at a time, turning over until crisp and golden (about 1 minute). Drain and set aside. Repeat with remaining noodles. Arrange noodles in a large wide bowl or deep serving platter.

Leave about 1 tablespoon of oil in the wok and fry the garlic for a few seconds, then add prawns and chicken or pork. Stir-fry until they are cooked, then add water and seasoning. Bring to a boil, add vegetables and simmer for a minute. Add the cornflour mixture and stir until the sauce thickens. Stir in the egg and pour over the noodles. Serve immediately.

The noodles should have a firm texture, although not crisp and crunchy, after cooking.

Hae Mee
Shrimp Noodle Soup

The flavor of this relatively simple noodle dish depends on the stock, so take the care (and time!) and you will be amply rewarded.

| 8–12 large shrimp
| 3 1/2 oz (100 g) hard back pork fat or salt pork, cut in 1/4-in (1/2-cm) dice (optional)
| 5 oz (150 g) fresh egg noodles
| 1/2 cup (50 g) beansprouts, blanched, or a few blanched leafy greens
| 1 scallion (spring onion), finely sliced
| Ground white pepper
|
| **Stock**
| 1 tablespoon oil
| 3 1/2 oz (100 g) small fresh shrimp
| 3 tablespoons dried prawns
| 1 dried chili (optional)
| 5 shallots, very finely chopped
| 5 cloves garlic, very finely chopped
| 5 whole white peppercorns, coarsely ground and gently fried until fragrant
| 8 oz (200 g) pork or chicken bones
| 8 cups (2 liters) water
| 1 tablespoon sugar

Peel the 8 to 12 large shrimp, saving the head and shells for the stock but leaving the tails on. Put the shrimp in the refrigerator.

To make the stock, heat the oil and fry the reserved shrimp heads and shells together with the fresh small shrimp, dried prawns and dried chili.

Shrimp Noodle Soup

Cook over low heat, stirring, for about 5 minutes. Crush firmly with the back of a wooden spoon against the side of the pan, then add all other stock ingredients, except the sugar. Simmer gently, uncovered, until the liquid is reduced by half.

Heat the sugar in a small pan with an equal amount of water and cook until it turns a dark caramel color. Add to the stock. Strain the stock, pressing firmly with the back of a spoon to extract all the liquid, then season to taste with salt. Keep hot if using immediately.

While the stock is cooking, put the pork dice in a pan and cook gently until the oil runs out and the pork turns golden and crisp. Drain and set aside.

To finish the dish, plunge the noodles in boiling water for about 1 minute to heat through, then divide among 4 bowls. Add bean sprouts or leafy greens, top with hot stock, then add 2 to 3 shrimp to each bowl. Sprinkle with the fried pork, scallions and a liberal dash of white pepper. Serve immediately with sliced red chili in a bowl of light soy sauce, or with the *sambal* of your choice.

Yen's Brown Noodles

Laksa Lemak
Noodles in Spicy Coconut Milk

This Nonya version of *laksa* comes from Malacca. The sauce can be prepared in advance, and the garnishing ingredients readied although not sliced to ensure maximum freshness.

1/2 cup (125 ml) oil
6 sprigs polygonum (*daun kesum*)
2 wild ginger buds, finely sliced
6 cups (1 1/2 liters) water
1 1/2 cups (375 ml) thick coconut milk
1 heaped tablespoon sugar
Salt to taste
1 lb (500 g) thin fresh yellow noodles, or dried noodles, cooked and drained
1 chicken breast, steamed and shredded
1 1/2 cups (150 g) beansprouts, blanched
4 oz (125 g) peeled shrimp, steamed (about 10 large)

Spice Paste
8 red chilies
10 shallots
1 stalk lemongrass
3/4 in (2 cm) galangal
1/4 in (1/2 cm) fresh turmeric (or 1/2 teaspoon powder)
1/2 teaspoon dried shrimp paste (*belacan*)

Garnish
3 sprigs polygonum (*daun kesum*), sliced
1 wild ginger bud, finely sliced

Sour Penang Noodle Soup

Noodles in Spicy Coconut Milk

1 cucumber, in matchstick shreds
3 eggs, beaten, made into thin omelets and shredded
2 red chilies, sliced
2 scallions (spring onions), sliced
6 tablespoons *Sambal Belacan* (page 135)
6 small limes, cut in wedges

Chop and blend all the spice paste ingredients finely, adding a little of the oil if necessary to keep the blades turning. Heat remaining oil and gently fry the blended ingredients for 10 minutes, stirring from time to time. Add the polygonum, ginger buds, and water and bring to a boil.

Add thick coconut milk, sugar and salt. Reduce heat and simmer very gently, uncovered, for 10–15 minutes.

To serve, plunge noodles in boiling water for a few seconds, to heat through. Divide the noodles, chicken, beansprouts, and shrimp among 6 individual noodle bowls and top with the sliced polygonum and ginger bud. Pour sauce on top and add a little cucumber, omelet, chilies, and scallion. Serve with side dishes of *sambal belacan* and cut limes.

> **HELPFUL HINT**
> Dried rice vermicelli (*meehoon*) or any dried Chinese wheat-flour noodles can also be used for this dish.

Asam Laksa Penang
Sour Penang Noodle Soup

This is the Penang version of *laksa*, which is more sour and boasts the addition of fish.

1 1/4 lb (600 g) small Chubb mackerel (*ikan kembong*)
6 cups (1 1/2 liters) water
5 tablespoons tamarind pulp, soaked and squeezed for juice
2 wild ginger buds, sliced
3 sprigs polygonum (*daun kesum*), sliced
1/2–1 tablespoon sugar, to taste

1 1/4 lb (600 g) fresh coarse rice noodles (*laksa*)

Spice Paste
5 shallots
2 stalks lemongrass
1 in (1 1/2 cm) fresh turmeric (or 2 teaspoons powder)
3 dried red chilies, soaked in warm water
6 fresh red chilies
1 teaspoon dried shrimp paste (*belacan*)

Garnish
1 cucumber, peeled and shredded
6 sprigs polygonum (*daun kesum*), sliced
Few sprigs mint, torn
3 large red onions, sliced
3 red chilies, sliced
1/2 fresh pineapple, cut in shreds
Small bowl of black prawn paste (*hae ko*), diluted in a little warm water

Simmer the cleaned whole fish in water until cooked. Remove fish, cool, and remove the flesh from the bones. Break up the flesh. Strain the stock carefully and return to a large pan with the fish, tamarind juice, ginger buds, polygonum, and sugar.

Blend the spice paste ingredients finely and add to the fish stock. Simmer for 20–30 minutes.

Prepare all garnish ingredients. Blanch the noodles in boiling water, drain and divide among 6 bowls. Pour over the fish stock and garnish the top of each bowl.

Indian Mutton Soup

Allow diners to add the black prawn paste themselves, as the taste is rather pungent.

If Chubb mackerel is not available, choose another well-flavored fish to ensure the soup has its characteristic fishy taste.

Indian Mee Goreng
Indian Fried Noodles

Although noodles were brought to Malaysia by the Chinese, all other ethnic groups have adapted them to suit their tastes.

- 10 dried chilies, soaked in hot water
- 1/2 cup (125 ml) oil
- 1 teaspoon dried shrimp paste
- 3 cloves garlic, finely chopped
- 6 oz (200 g) large shrimp, peeled and deveined
- 6 oz (200 g) boneless chicken, shredded
- 12 oz (400 g) fresh yellow noodles
- 2 cups mustard greens
- 1 cup (100 g) beansprouts
- 2 hard beancurd cakes, deep fried and sliced
- 3 tablespoons light soy sauce
- 1 teaspoon salt
- 1 red chili, sliced
- 1 green chili, sliced
- Sprig of cilantro (coriander) leaves, roughly chopped
- Sprig of Chinese celery leaves, roughly chopped
- 2 scallion (spring onions), sliced
- 2 tablespoons fried shallots (page135)
- 6 small fresh limes, halved

Blend softened chilies to a paste, adding a little oil if necessary. Keep aside 2 tablespoons of oil and heat the remainder over medium heat, add dried shrimp paste and fry for 1 minute. Add chili paste, reduce heat to low and cook, stirring from time to time, for 30 minutes. Remove from pan.

Heat the 2 tablespoons of oil in a wok. Add garlic, cooked chili paste, shrimp and chicken and fry for 3 minutes. Add noodles and fry over medium heat for 3 minutes. Add mustard greens and bean sprouts. Fry for 2 minutes, then add bean curd and stir fry for 3 minutes. Lastly, add soy sauce and salt mixed together. Stir fry for 1 minute.

Garnish with fresh chilies, cilantro, celery leaf, scallions, fried shallots and fresh lime and serve immediately.

HELPFUL HINT
Cabbage or spinach can be used instead of mustard greens, if preferred.

Sop Kambing
Indian Mutton Soup

Also known as *Sop Tulang* or Bone Soup, this robust dish is one of the more popular stall foods in Singapore. It makes a great late-night supper or luncheon, especially if served with crusty French bread.

- 2 in (5 cm) ginger
- 6 cloves garlic
- 1 lb (500 g) meaty mutton or lamb ribs
- 1 heaped tablespoon ground coriander
- 1 teaspoon ground fennel
- 1/2 teaspoon ground cumin
- 1 teaspoon salt
- 8–12 cups (2–3 liters) water
- 2 tablespoons oil
- 2 leeks, sliced (white part only)
- 1 cinnamon stick, 3 in (8 cm) long
- 4 whole star anise
- 5 cardamom pods, bruised
- Fried shallots to garnish (page 135)
- 1 tomato, quartered
- Chopped Chinese celery or cilantro (coriander leaves) to garnish

Pound or blend the ginger and garlic together, then put in a pot with the mutton or lamb ribs, coriander, fennel, cumin and salt. Add 12 cups (3 liters) of water if using mutton, but only 8 cups (2 liters) if using lamb, which will cook more quickly. Simmer, uncovered, until the meat is soft.

Heat the oil in a small pan and sauté the leeks, shallots, cinnamon, star anise, and cardamom until the leeks are tender. Add to the mutton soup and simmer for another couple of minutes. Add tomato, taste and add more salt if desired. Serve sprinkled with fried shallots and Chinese celery leaves, and accompany with crusty French bread.

Indian Fried Noodles

Chicken Rice

Nasi Ayam
Chicken Rice

This is another popular coffee-shop and hawker staple in Malaysia and Singapore.

Roast Chicken
1/2 fresh chicken
3 cloves garlic
4 shallots
2 in (5 cm) ginger
3 tablespoons oyster sauce
1 tablespoon black soy sauce
2 tablespoons light soy sauce
1 tablespoon tomato sauce
1 tablespoon chili sauce
1 teaspoon chili powder
1 teaspoon salt

Rice
2 cups (400 g) uncooked rice, washed thoroughly
1 in (2 1/2 cm) ginger
3 cloves garlic
4 tablespoons butter
2 pandan leaves
Pinch salt
3 tablespoons fried shallots (page 135)

Chili Sauce
5 red chilies
4 cloves garlic
1 in (2 1/2 cm) ginger
3 tablespoons lime juice
1 teaspoon sesame oil
Salt and sugar to taste

Garnish
1 cucumber, sliced

Prepare the chicken well in advance. Prick the chicken with a fork to allow seasonings to penetrate. Blend or pound garlic, shallots, and ginger, then mix with all other ingredients and rub into chicken. Marinate 4 hours or overnight, if possible. Roast chicken in a 450°F (230°C, gas mark 8) oven for about 20 minutes. Cut into serving pieces and put on a platter garnished with sliced cucumber.

Wash the rice, drain and put in a saucepan or rice cooker. Pound the ginger and garlic together and add to rice together with butter, pandan leaves, salt, and sufficient water to cook the rice. When the rice is cooked, fluff up with a fork, put in a serving bowl and decorate with fried shallots.

Blend all the chili sauce ingredients together until fine.

Serve the rice with the chicken, cucumber, and chili sauce, with a bowl of clear chicken soup to accompany it if desired.

Claypot Rice

This Cantonese one-pot dish is very popular in the food stalls of Singapore and Malaysia. The Chinese believe that a claypot is essential to ensure the correct flavor and fragrance of this dish, though any other type of covered earthenware container could be used.

2 cups (400 g) uncooked long-grain rice, washed
3 cups (750 ml) chicken stock
1/2 fresh chicken, about 1 1/2 lb (750 g), cut into small cubes
1 Chinese sausage, sliced
6 dried black mushrooms, soaked, simmered until cooked and quartered
1 1/2 in (4 cm) ginger, thinly sliced
1 scallion (spring onion), thinly sliced

Marinade
2 tablespoons oil
3 tablespoons oyster sauce
1 tablespoon soy sauce
1 tablespoon Chinese wine
1/2 teaspoon sesame oil
1 teaspoon black soy sauce
1 teaspoon sugar
1/2 teaspoon ground white pepper
1 tablespoon cornstarch

Put the rice in a claypot with chicken stock, cover and cook over low heat for about 20 minutes.

While the rice is cooking, mix the marinade ingredients together and pour over the chicken, mixing well. When the rice has cooked for 20 minutes, spread the marinated chicken, Chinese sausage, mushrooms and sliced ginger on top. Cover and cook for another 10 minutes. Sprinkle with scallion and serve.

> **HELPFUL HINT**
>
> Claypot Rice. If you do not have a clay or earthenware pot, a saucepan with a heavy base or rice cooker will do at a pinch.

Duck in Fragrant Soy Sauce

A Teochew favorite sometimes made with goose, this is a simple, tasty way of simmering duck in soy sauce flavored with cinnamon, star anise, and cloves. The addition of fresh turmeric and lemongrass, which are Southeast Asian rather than Chinese seasonings, is a Singaporean touch. *Jin kok* is a dried Chinese root, available from Chinese medicine or provision shops.

1 fresh duck, about 4 lb (2 kg)
1 tablespoon five-spice powder
7 cinnamon sticks about 3 in (8 cm) long
15 star anise
20 cloves
10 shallots, lightly bruised
10 cloves garlic, lightly bruised
3 tablespoons *jin kok* (optional)
4 cups (1 liter) light soy sauce
3 tablespoons black soy sauce
2 tablespoons sugar
1 stalk lemongrass, bruised
1/2 in (1 cm) fresh turmeric, bruised, or 2 teaspoons turmeric powder
24 cups (6 liters) water

Clean the duck and rub inside with the five-spice powder. Leave in the refrigerator overnight.

Rinse the duck inside and out with water and put in a large wide pan with all the seasonings and water. Bring to a boil and simmer gently, uncovered, until the duck is very tender. Serve with white rice.

Devil Chicken Curry

Devil by name... this is quite a hot dish, tempered with lemongrass and galangal, so serve with lots of steamed rice.

1/4 cup (60 ml) oil
2 onions, quartered
2 in (5 cm) ginger, shredded
5 cloves garlic, sliced
2 red chilies, halved lengthwise
1 teaspoon salt
1 teaspoon light soy sauce
4 tablespoons sugar
4 potatoes, peeled and quartered
1/2 chicken, cut into serving
    pieces
1/2 cup (125 ml) distilled white
    vinegar
3–4 cups (3/4–1 liter) water

Spice Paste
30 shallots
30 dried chilies, soaked and
    deseeded
1 1/4 inches fresh turmeric
    (or 2 1/2 teaspoons powder)
1 in (2 1/2 cm) galangal
2 stalks lemongrass
1 teaspoon brown mustard seeds,
    soaked in water for 5 minutes

Chop spice paste ingredients and blend with a little of the oil until fine. Set aside.

Heat remaining oil and fry the onions, ginger, garlic, and chilies for 2 minutes. Drain off the oil and set mixture aside.

Rich Coconut Beef

Fry the blended ingredients with 4 tablespoons oil for 10 minutes, adding the salt and soy sauce. Add sugar, stir well, then put in the potatoes, chicken, vinegar and water. Simmer, uncovered, until chicken is cooked. Taste and adjust seasonings, adding a little more vinegar for a sourer taste, if desired. Add the reserved fried ingredients, stir well and serve with rice.

Note: Cut the chilies into pieces before soaking, and discard the seeds—which will fall to the bottom of the bowl—to help reduce the heat.

Rendang Daging
Rich Coconut Beef

1/2 cup (125 ml) oil
1 1/4 in (3 cm) cinnamon stick
2 cloves
4 star anise
2 cardamom pods
1 lb (500 g) top round beef,
    cubed
1 cup (250 ml) thick coconut milk
1 slice *asam gelugor*, or
    2 teaspoons dried tamarind pulp
    soaked in warm water for juice
2 fragrant lime leaves, very finely
    sliced
1 turmeric leaf, very finely sliced
2 tablespoons *kerisik* (see below)
1 1/2 teaspoons sugar
Salt to taste

Spice Paste
2 shallots
3/4 in (2 cm) galangal
3 stalks lemongrass
2 cloves garlic
3/4 in (2 cm) ginger
10 dried chilies, soaked in hot water

To prepare the *kerisik*, roast 10 oz (300 g) grated fresh coconut in a slow oven until brown. Alternatively, cook in a dry wok, stirring constantly. Cool, then grind finely until the oil comes out. Chop the spice paste ingredients, then purée in a blender until fine. Heat the oil, add the spice paste, cinnamon, cloves, star anise, and cardamom and fry for 5 minutes.

Add the beef, coconut milk, and *asam gelugor* or tamarind juice. Simmer uncovered, stirring frequently, until the meat is almost cooked. Add the lime and turmeric leaves, *kerisik*, sugar and salt. Lower the heat and simmer until the meat is really tender and the gravy has dried up. Approximate cooking time is 1 to 1 1/2 hours.

Buntut Asam Pedas
Sour Hot Oxtail Stew

1 whole oxtail, about 4 lb (2 kg),
    cut in 1 1/2-in (4-cm) pieces
10 shallots

8 cloves garlic
25 red chilies, de-seeded
10 bird's-eye chilies
1 in (2 1/2 cm) turmeric, or
    1 teaspoon turmeric powder
3 tablespoons tomato paste
2/3 cup (200 g) tamarind pulp,
    soaked in 2 cups (500 ml) of
    water, squeezed and strained
    for juice
2 tablespoons sugar
5 kaffir lime leaves (*daun limau
    purut*)
2 stalks lemongrass, bruised
1 1/2 in (4 cm) galangal, sliced
12 cups (3 liters) water
Salt and pepper to taste
Fried shallots (page 135)
    to garnish

Trim all fat off the oxtail and discard. Chop, then pound or blend the shallots, garlic, chiles and turmeric, adding a little water if necessary to keep the blades turning. Combine the blended mixture with all other ingredients except water and garnish. Mix well with the oxtail. Leave to marinate for 2 hours.

Bring the water to a boil in a large pot and add the marinated oxtail. Simmer, uncovered, over low heat until the oxtail is tender and liquid is reduced by about half. Season to taste with salt and pepper, garnish with fried shallots and serve with white rice.

Devil Chicken Curry

Indian Mutton Curry

Kambing Korma

Indian Mutton Curry

A mixture of dried ground spices, whole spices and the usual trinity of shallots, garlic, and ginger provide the basic flavorings for this rich mutton curry. The Singapore touch is evident in the use of candlenuts (not found in India) to enrich and thicken the gravy.

- 2 lb (1 kg) mutton or lamb, cubed
- 10 shallots
- 10 cloves garlic
- 2 in (5 cm) ginger
- 10 green chilies
- 3 tablespoons oil
- 1 large onion, sliced
- 6 cardamom pods, bruised
- 5 whole star anise
- 2 sticks cinnamon about 3 in (8 cm) long
- 4 tablespoons meat curry powder
- 20 curry leaves
- 3 potatoes, quartered
- 1 cup (250 ml) plain yogurt
- 1 teaspoon salt
- 10 candlenuts, pounded or blended
- 2 slices *asam gelugur* or 1 tablespoon tamarind pulp, soaked in 4 tablespoons water, squeezed and strained for juice
- 4–6 green chilies, halved lengthwise
- 6 tomatoes, quartered

Put the mutton in a pan with 8 cups (2 liters) water. Chop, then blend the shallots, garlic, ginger, and 10 green chilies with a little water. Add to the mutton and bring to the boil. Simmer, uncovered, until the meat is just tender.

Heat oil and gently sauté the onion, cardamom, star anise, cinnamon, curry powder and curry leaves. When it smells fragrant, add to the meat together with the potatoes, yogurt, salt, candlenuts, and tamarind. Continue simmering until the meat is soft. Add the green chilies and tomatoes just before serving.

Borneo Marinated Fish

This no-cook dish is a favorite among Sarawak's Melanau people, who call their version *umai*. Sabah's Kadazans call it *hinava*. Use only the very freshest fish for this recipe, as it is "cooked" only with lime juice.

- 1 lb (500 g) very fresh white fish (Spanish mackerel preferred)
- 1/3 cup (85 g) freshly squeezed lime or lemon juice
- 2–3 red chilies
- 1 teaspoon salt
- 6–8 shallots, thinly sliced
- 2 in (5 cm) ginger, very finely shredded

- 2 sprigs fresh cilantro (coriander) leaves, roughly chopped
- 2 sprigs Chinese celery, roughly chopped

Remove all skin and bones from the fish and cut it in thin slices. Keep aside 2 tablespoons of lime juice, then soak the fish in the remaining juice for at least 30 minutes, stirring once or twice, until the fish turns white. Drain and discard lime juice.

While the fish is marinating, pound the chilies with salt until fine. When fish is ready, mix it with the chilies, shallots, ginger, fresh herbs, and reserved lime juice. Taste and add more salt if desired. Serve immediately as part of a rice-based meal.

Ikan Asam Pedas

Hot and Sour Fish Curry

This fragrant and spicy curry is enriched by a touch of coconut milk.

- 1/3 cup (85 ml) oil
- 1/2 in (1 cm) galangal, smashed
- 2 slices *asam gelugur*, or 1 heaped tablespoon tamarind pulp, soaked in water for juice
- 2 1/2 cups (625 ml) water
- 6 thick fish fillets or cutlets
- 4 sprigs polygonum (*daun kesum*), chopped
- Salt to taste
- 1 teaspoon sugar
- 3 tablespoons thick coconut milk

Spice Paste
- 15 dried chilies, soaked in hot water
- 2 candlenuts
- 4 cloves garlic
- 10 shallots
- 1/2 teaspoon turmeric powder
- 1 cup (250 ml) water

Chop and blend spice paste ingredients finely. Heat oil in a saucepan, then fry the galangal and blended ingredients for 5 minutes. Add the *asam gelugur* or tamarind pulp. Add 1/2 cup of the water and cook for another 5 minutes. Add the rest of the water and bring to a boil. Add the fish, polygonum, salt, sugar, and coconut milk and simmer, uncovered, for another 5 minutes.

Teochew Steamed Fish

A very delicious dish that demands the freshest of fish to shine. Salted plums are available in jars from Asian food stores.

- 1 whole pomfret, about 2 lb (1 kg)
- 1/4 cup (50 g) packed salted Chinese cabbage (*kiam chye*), chopped
- 1 tomato, cut in wedges
- 3 in (8 cm) ginger, finely sliced
- 2 red chilies, sliced
- 6 salted plums (obtainable in jars)
- 1 scallion (spring onion), cut in 2-in (5-cm) lengths
- 3 dried black mushrooms, softened then sliced
- 2 oz (60 g) shredded pork (optional)

Teochew Steamed Fish (left) and Oyster Omelet (right, recipe on page 123)

Butter Shrimp

A relatively recent Malaysian creation, this combines traditional Malay, Chinese, Indian, and Western ingredients.

1 1/4 lb (600 g) large shrimp
Oil for deep-frying
2–3 tablespoons butter
15 bird's-eye chilies, roughly chopped
10–15 sprigs curry leaves
2 cloves garlic, finely chopped
1/2 teaspoon salt
2 tablespoons sugar
1/2 teaspoon light soy sauce
1/2 teaspoon Chinese wine
1/2 grated coconut, dry fried until golden

Remove heads from shrimp but leave shells. Slit down the back to remove intestinal tract, trim feelers and legs and dry shrimp thoroughly. Heat the oil and deep-fry. Drain and reserve.

Melt the butter, add chilies, curry leaves, garlic, and salt and fry for 2 minutes. Add shrimp, sugar, soy sauce, wine, and grated coconut. Cook over high heat for 1–2 minutes, stirring frequently. Serve immediately.

Chili Crab

1 tablespoon light soy sauce
1 teaspoon sesame oil
1 cup (250 ml) chicken stock
1 tablespoon cornstarch, mixed with 3 tablespoons water
1 egg, lightly beaten
Salt and pepper to taste
1 scallion (spring onion), sliced

Deep-fry the crabs in hot oil just until bright red. Remove and set aside. Pour out the oil and put 1/4 cup (60 ml) fresh oil into the wok. Heat and add garlic, ginger and chilies. Stir until fragrant, then add chili sauce, tomato sauce, sugar, soy sauce, and sesame oil. Simmer for 1 minute, then season with salt and pepper. Add the fried crab and stir to coat well with sauce. Add chicken stock and cook over high heat for 3 minutes. Stir thoroughly and thicken with cornstarch and egg. Season to taste with salt and pepper and sprinkle with scallions.

Seasoning
4 tablespoons garlic oil (page 135)
4 tablespoons oyster sauce
1 teaspoon sesame oil
2 tablespoons light soy sauce
1 tablespoon sugar
2 tablespoons Chinese wine
1/2 cup (125 ml) chicken stock

Clean and dry the fish thoroughly. Combine all other ingredients except seasonings in a bowl.

Combine all seasoning ingredients and mix well. Stir into the bowl with the other items and mix. Lay the fish on a plate which

will fit into a steamer or on a tray inside a wok and spread the mixture on top of the fish. Cover and steam over rapidly boiling water for 15 to 20 minutes until fish is cooked. Do not overcook or the texture will be spoiled.

Sambal Udang
Shrimp Sambal

1/2 cup (125 ml) oil
2 tablespoons brown sugar
1 teaspoon salt
3 tablespoons thick coconut milk
4 tablespoons lime juice
1 pound medium-sized shrimp, peeled and deveined

Spice Paste
10 red chilies
3 medium-sized red onions
1 in (2 1/2 cm) galangal
10 cloves garlic
3 candlenuts

Chop all the spice paste ingredients, then blend until fine, adding a little of the oil if necessary to keep the blades turning. Heat oil in a saucepan and fry the blended ingredients for about 10 minutes until fragrant. Add brown sugar, salt and coconut milk and bring to a boil. Add lime juice and shrimp and simmer for 5 minutes or until the shrimp are cooked.

Chili Crab

This is virtually Singapore's national dish. Provide finger bowls of warm water (in Asia they use tea) for diners to use—this dish is more delicious eaten with the fingers!

2 lb (1 kg) fresh crabs, cleaned and halved
Oil for deep-frying
4 cloves garlic, finely chopped
2 in (5 cm) young ginger, roughly chopped
3 red chilies, finely chopped
1/4 cup (60 ml) chili sauce
1/4 cup (60 ml) tomato sauce
1 tablespoon sugar

Shrimp Sambal

Ayam Limau Purut

Chicken with Lime Leaf

The charm of this Nonya curry comes from its aromatic fresh herbs and seasonings.

- 1/2 cup (125 ml) oil
- 1/2 chicken, cut in serving pieces
- 1 slice *asam gelugur* or lime juice to taste
- 1/2 cup (125 ml) water
- 1 cup (250 ml) thick coconut milk
- 4 kaffir (*daun limau purut*) lime leaves
- Salt to taste

Spice Paste
- 2 medium-sized red or brown onions
- 8 red chilies
- 3 cloves garlic
- 1 stalk lemongrass
- 1 1/4 in (3 cm) galangal
- 1 teaspoon turmeric powder

Chop and blend the spice paste ingredients, adding a little of the oil if necessary to keep the blades turning. Heat oil and fry the blended ingredients for about 5 minutes, until fragrant.

Add the chicken, *asam gelugur*, and water and simmer until the chicken is half cooked. Add the coconut milk and lime leaves and simmer, uncovered, until the chicken is tender. Add salt and, if using, lime juice to taste.

Salted Fish and Pineapple Curry

Salted Fish and Pineapple Curry

Salted fish is popular in Malaysia, and not just as a standby for times when fresh fish may be unavailable owing to monsoon storms. This Eurasian curry uses good quality dried fish.

- 1 just-ripe pineapple
- 4 oz (125 g) salted fish, cut in large cubes
- 1/4 cup (65 ml) oil
- 1/2 cup (125 ml) water
- 1 1/2 cups (375 ml) thick coconut milk
- Salt to taste

Spice Paste
- 6 shallots
- 3 red chilies
- 1 in (1/2 cm) fresh turmeric (or 2 teaspoons powder)
- 1 in (1/2 cm) galangal
- 2 stalks lemongrass
- 1/2 teaspoon dried shrimp paste (*belacan*)
- 1/2 teaspoon salt

Peel the pineapple, clean and quarter, remove cores, wash and cut into triangular pieces. Blend half the pineapple with about 1/4 cup (60 ml) water to make a purée and set aside.

Soak the fish in water for about 10 minutes, then drain and dry well.

Chop spice paste ingredients, then blend until fine. Heat the oil in a saucepan, add the blended spice paste and stir fry gently for 5 minutes. Add pineapple cubes and stir fry until well coated

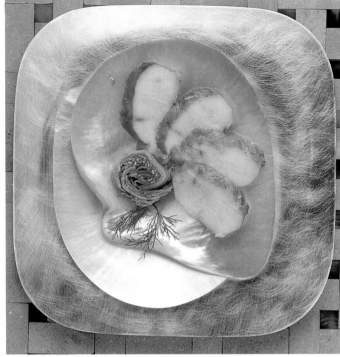

Tea-smoked Seabass

with spices. Add the salted fish, the pineapple purée, water and coconut milk. Reduce heat and simmer gently for about 10–15 minutes, until pineapple is tender. Add salt to taste.

Tea-smoked Seabass

Smoking food over a mixture of tea leaves is a popular method of preparing food in Yunnan and Sichuan provinces in China.

Make sure the exhaust fan is turned on and the room well ventilated (windows open) before you start smoking, or you'll be smoked out.

- 1 whole seabass fillet, about 1–1 1/4 lb (500–600 g), or other firm white fish fillet such as snapper or garoupa
- 5 tablespoons Chinese black tea leaves
- 5 star anise
- 3 cinnamon sticks, about 3 in (8 cm) long
- 20 cloves
- 5 tablespoons uncooked rice
- 5 cloves garlic, crushed

Marinade
- 2 cups (500 ml) iced water
- 5 tablespoons soy sauce
- 1 tablespoon sugar
- 1/2 cup (125 ml) ginger juice (page 135)
- 1 tablespoon salt

Mix the marinade, put in the fish and leave for about 3 hours. Remove the seabass from the marinade, drain, dry with paper towels and set aside.

Heat a wok over a low heat and put in the remaining ingredients. Put the fish on wire grill or round bamboo rack inside the wok at least 2 in (5 cm) above the smoking ingredients. Cover the wok and smoke over a low heat for 10 to 15 minutes, until the fish has turned brown and is cooked through. Slice and serve either hot or cold.

Spicy Kangkung

You will need lots of water convolvulus (*kangkung*) for this dish, as this popular Southeast Asian vegetable cooks down to virtually nothing.

- 2 lb (1 kg) water convolvulus (*kangkung*)
- 3 tablespoons dried shrimp, soaked to soften
- 6 cloves garlic
- 6 shallots
- 5 red chilies
- 1 in (2 1/2 cm) ginger
- 2 teaspoons dried shrimp paste (*belacan*)
- 3–4 tablespoons oil
- 2 tablespoons sugar
- 1 teaspoon sesame oil
- 1 tablespoon light soy sauce
- Salt and pepper to taste
- 1 red chili, finely sliced

Chicken with Lime Leaf (left) and Vegetables in Coconut Milk (right)

Use tender tips and leaves of the *kangkung*, discarding tough stems. Pound or blend the dried shrimp until fine. Set aside. Blend garlic, shallots, chilies, and ginger until fine, using a little of the oil if necessary to keep the blades turning. Add the shrimp paste and blend for another few seconds.

Heat the remaining oil in the wok or heavy pan and add the blended mixture together with the dried shrimp. Cook over low heat, stirring frequently, for about 5 minutes, until fragrant. Add sugar, sesame oil, and soy sauce, stirring until well mixed, then add *kangkung* and stir well. Cook with the lid on until the *kangkung* is tender. Season to taste with salt and pepper and sprinkle with sliced chili.

Sayur Lemak
Vegetables in Coconut Milk

A Nonya adaptation of Malay-style vegetables simmered in coconut milk.

- 3 tablespoons oil
- 1¹/2 cups (375 ml) water
- 1¹/2 cups (375 ml) thick coconut milk
- 1 carrot, cut in 1¹/2-in (4-cm) matchsticks
- 1 small eggplant, cut in 1¹/2-in (4-cm) matchsticks
- 3 long beans, cut in 1¹/2-in (4-cm) lengths

- ¹/4 cabbage, coarsely shredded
- 1 hard beancurd cake, deep-fried and quartered
- Salt to taste

Spice Paste
- 2 red chilies
- 3 candlenuts
- 5 shallots
- ¹/2 teaspoon turmeric powder
- ¹/2 teaspoon dried shrimp paste (*belacan*)
- 1 teaspoon dried prawns, soaked 5 minutes in warm water

To make the spice paste, blend all ingredients finely, adding a little oil if necessary to keep the blades turning. Heat the oil and fry the paste for 5 minutes, then add water and coconut milk. Bring slowly to a boil.

Add the vegetables, beancurd and salt and simmer, uncovered, until the vegetables are just cooked.

Spicy Pumpkin

Gourds are very popular among Malaysians of Southern Indian origin, especially sweet-tasting pumpkin, which goes well with spices.

- 1¹/2 lb (750 g) pumpkin, peeled and cut in 1-in (¹/2-cm) pieces
- 3 tablespoons oil

- 1 large onion, finely chopped
- 1 tablespoon brown mustard seeds
- 2 sprigs curry leaves
- 1 tablespoon fish or chicken curry powder
- 2–3 teaspoons chili powder
- ¹/2 teaspoon turmeric powder
- 2 cups (500 ml) water
- 1 teaspoon salt
- Sugar to taste

Prepare the pumpkin and set aside. Heat the oil and fry the onion until golden, then add mustard seed and curry leaves and fry until mustard seeds pop. Add the spice powders and fry for 30 seconds, then put in pumpkin and stir for a minute or two, until well coated with spices. Slowly add the water, stirring, then add salt and sugar to taste. Simmer, uncovered, until tender and dry.

Snake Gourd

Colors and textures contrast beautifully in this southern Indian dish.

- 1 cup yellow lentils
- ¹/2 teaspoon turmeric powder
- 2 cups (500 ml) water
- 1 snake gourd
- 4 shallots, sliced
- 1 clove garlic, sliced
- 2 tablespoons oil
- 1 tablespoon brown mustard seed
- 1 teaspoon salt
- 1 sprig curry leaves
- 2 red chilies, seeds removed, sliced

Wash lentils thoroughly, combine with turmeric and water and simmer until soft.

While the lentils are cooking, prepare the gourd. For a more decorative appearance, scrape the skin deeply lengthwise with a fork and cut in half lengthwise. Remove the pulpy center and cut across in ¹/2-in (1-cm) slices. Alternatively, peel the gourd, remove the center and cut in circles ¹/2 in (1 cm) thick.

Fry the shallots and garlic in oil until soft, then add mustard seeds and cook until they begin to pop. Add cooked lentils, gourd and salt, and cook until tender. Just before removing from heat, add curry leaves and chili. Toss and serve.

HELPFUL HINT

If snake gourd is not available, substitute 1 lb (500 g) long beans or sliced marrow or summer squash.

Snake Gourd (left) and Spicy Pumpkin (right)

Mango Jellies

In Malaysian and Singaporean homes, desserts are not commonly served at the end of a meal, although elaborate restaurant meals often finish with some of the dishes featured here.

Mango Jellies

- 4 cups (1 liter) water
- 1 cup (250 g) sugar
- 2 tablespoons unflavored gelatin, softened in warm water
- 1 cup (250 ml) coconut milk
- 1/2 cup (125 ml) evaporated milk
- 2 eggs, beaten
- 1 medium-sized mango (1 1/2 cups chopped), puréed
- 1 large mango, very finely diced

Combine the water and sugar in a pan and stir over low heat until sugar is dissolved. Add softened gelatin and continue heating until thoroughly dissolved. Remove from heat and add all ingredients, except the diced mango. Mix until well blended, then add the diced mango.

Pour into individual molds and refrigerate until set. Garnish when serving with fresh fruit and a little mango purée.

Almond Jelly

A classic Chinese restaurant dish, this is very simple to make and can be prepared well in advance.

- 4 cups (1 liter) water
- 3 teaspoons agar-agar powder
- 1/2 cup (125 g) sugar, or more to taste
- 1 teaspoon almond extract
- 1 can (15 oz/480 g) longans or lychees
- Ice cubes (optional)

Put water in a saucepan and sprinkle with agar-agar powder. Bring gently to the boil, stirring, then add the sugar and almond essence. Simmer for a minute, then pour into a dish about 6 in (15 cm) square. Leave to set, then refrigerate until required. Make sure the fruit is also placed in the refrigerator.

Just before serving, drain the chilled longans or lychees in a large bowl. Cut the almond jelly into squares and add to the fruit. Add a few ice cubes if desired and serve immediately.

Sago with Honeydew

- 3/4 cup pearl sago
- 7 cups (1 3/4 litres) water
- 1 cup (250 ml) coconut milk
- 1 cup (220 ml) sugar
- 1/2 cup (125 ml) water
- 1/2 honeydew melon

Soak sago in 2 cups (500 ml) water for 30 minutes. Drain. Bring the remaining 5 cups (1 1/4 litres) water to the boil and add sago. Cook until transparent. Drain in a sieve and wash under cold running water. Leave sago aside until cool.

Boil sugar and 1/2 cup (125 ml) water together to make a syrup.

Peel the melon, cut in half and discard seeds. Blend half the honeydew to make juice and cut the other half into small cubes, or make small balls with a melon baller. Mix the sago, coconut milk, honeydew juice, honeydew cubes, and sugar syrup to taste. Serve chilled.

Nonya Pancake

A Nonya version of the Malay stuffed pancake, *kuih dadar*, is served with a coconut sauce as a tea-time treat or snack, rather than a dessert, in Malaysia.

Batter
- 10 pandan leaves
- 1 cup (250 ml) water
- 1 cup plus 3 tablespoons (150 g) all-purpose (plain) flour
- 1 egg
- Scant 1/3 cup (80 ml) fresh milk
- 1/4 teaspoon salt
- 2 teaspoons melted butter

Filling
- 2 cups (200 g) grated coconut
- 1 1/2 cups (375 ml) water
- 3 pandan leaves
- 1/4 teaspoon salt
- 3/4 cup (125 ml) palm sugar, chopped

Coconut Sauce
- 1/2 cup (125 ml) thick coconut milk
- 1/2 cup (150 g) water
- 3 pandan leaves
- 1 teaspoon sugar
- 1 teaspoon cornstarch
- Pinch of salt

Prepare the batter by blending the pandan leaves with water and straining to obtain the juice. Sift the flour into a bowl and add egg, milk, salt, and pandan juice. Stir until smooth, adding more water if necessary to obtain a thin consistency. Set aside while preparing the filling and sauce.

Combine all filling ingredients in a saucepan and simmer over very low heat, stirring occasionally, for about 45 minutes, until thick and dry. Set aside to cool.

Combine all the coconut sauce ingredients in a saucepan and stir continuously over low heat until the sauce thickens and clears. Sieve and serve warm or at room temperature.

Cook the pancakes. Grease a nonstick pan with a little butter and pour in enough batter to make a pancake about 6–8 in (15–20 cm) in diameter. Cook gently on both sides and reserve. Repeat until all the batter is used.

To serve, put 2–3 tablespoons of the filling in the center of a pancake. Tuck in the edges and roll up cigar fashion. Serve the pancakes, preferably still warm or at room temperature, with the coconut sauce.

Sago with Honeydew

Fried Shallots and Garlic Oil

24 shallots or 10–15 cloves garlic
1 cup (250 ml) oil

Peel and slice the shallots or garlic finely, and dry well with a paper towel. Heat the oil and deep-fry the shallots or garlic until golden brown and crisp. Take care not to let them burn or the flavor will be bitter. Drain and cool completely before storing. Keep shallot or garlic oil and use for frying or seasoning other dishes.

Ginger Juice

Use young ginger if possible—they are much juicier.

1 cup (125 g) sliced fresh ginger (young ginger if possible)
5 tablespoons water

Scrape the skin off the ginger, chop coarsely and put in a blender with water. Process until very fine. Strain through a sieve, pushing down with the back of a spoon to extract all the juice, to provide about 1/2 cup (125 ml) ginger juice, which can be stored in a refrigerator for up to 1 week.

Char Siew
Red Roasted Pork

This is often used with Chinese noodle dishes, in fried rice and as a stuffing in steamed buns (*pau*).

1 1/4 lb (600 g) pork belly (part meat, part fat), or pork fillet, if less fat is preferred
1/2 cup (125 g) sugar
4 tablespoons light soy sauce
2 tablespoons black soy sauce
1 tablespoon red food coloring
1 teaspoon five-spice powder
1 teaspoon sesame oil
1 teaspoon Chinese wine

Marinate the pork with remaining ingredients, first mixed well in a bowl, for about 1 hour. Roast on a wire rack in a 400°F (200°C, gas mark 6) oven for about 30 minutes. Leave to cool and slice only when needed. Can be refrigerated for several days.

Chicken Stock

2 large chickens, quartered
5 quarts (5 liters) water
3 in (8 cm) ginger, crushed
2 leeks, sliced
1 large onion, halved
1 carrot, diced
5 stalks Chinese celery (with leaves)

Wash chickens well, then blanch in the boiling water to cover for 3 minutes. Remove chickens and discard water. Bring 5 quarts (5 liters) fresh water to a boil with the chicken and vegetables. Simmer, uncovered, over low heat for 2 to 3 hours. This makes 3 to 4 quarts (4 liters) of stock, which can be divided into smaller portions and stored in the freezer.

Chili Sauce

5 red chilies, roughly chopped
10 tablespoons water
3 tablespoons sugar
10 tablespoons distilled white vinegar
1 teaspoon salt

Blend chilies with water. Add the remaining ingredients and bring to the boil. Remove from heat and allow to cool.

Popiah Wrappers

1 cup plus 2 tablespoons (185 g) rice flour
3 tablespoons all-purpose (plain) flour
1/2 teaspoon salt
4 eggs
1 teaspoon oil
2 cups (500 ml) water
1/2 teaspoon salt

Sift both types of flour and salt into a bowl. Mix eggs, oil and water together and stir into the dried ingredients, mixing until smooth. Leave in the refrigerator for a minimum of 1 hour. Cook in a non-stick pan, greasing it with the minimum amount of oil to stop the batter from sticking. Pour in just a little batter, swirl the pan to make a very thin pancake and cook on one side only over moderate heat until set. Put on a plate and repeat until the batter is used up. This makes about 20 to 25 *popiah* skins.

Chili Peanuts with Anchovies

4 red chilies
1 shallot
1 tablespoon oil
1/2 teaspoon salt
1 tablespoon sugar
3/4 cup (100 g) roasted peanuts with skin
1 oz (30 g) dried anchovies (*ikan bilis*), heads and intestinal tract removed and fried till crisp

Blend the chilies and shallot together. Heat the oil and gently fry the blended mixture with the salt and sugar for 1 minute. Add the peanuts and anchovies. Stir fry for 3 minutes and remove from heat. Keep in a bottle in the refrigerator up to 3 weeks.

Sambal Belacan
Shrimp Paste Sambal

12 large red chilies, roughly chopped
2 tablespoons dried shrimp paste, (*belacan*) roasted
2/3 cup (150 ml) water
4 tablespoons lime juice

Blend the chilies and shrimp paste with the water. Season to taste with lime juice.

Dried Cucumber Acar

2 cucumbers, halved lengthwise, seeds removed
1 large carrot, peeled

Dressing
3/4 cup (150 ml) distilled white vinegar
3 tablespoons sugar
1/2 teaspoon salt
Pinch of turmeric powder
2 shallots, sliced
1/2 in (1 cm) ginger, julienned
1 clove garlic, peeled and shredded
2 tablespoons raisins

Cut the carrot and cucumbers into matchstick pieces 1 1/2 in (3 cm) long. Dry the cucumbers and carrot in the sun for 2 hours.

Chili Sauce

Combine the vinegar, sugar, salt, and turmeric and bring to a boil. Remove from the heat and cool. Add the shallots, ginger, garlic, and raisins and mix with the cucumbers and carrot. Store in the refrigerator up to 1 month.

Chili Ginger Sauce

6 red chilies, roughly chopped
1 1/4 in (3 cm) ginger, chopped
4 cloves garlic
10 tablespoons water
2 teaspoons salt
5 tablespoons sugar
5 tablespoons lime juice
1 teaspoon sesame oil

Blend the chilies, ginger, garlic, and water. Season to taste with the salt, sugar, lime juice, and sesame oil.

In this land of over 7000 islands, regoinal diversity can not only be seen but tasted.

PHILIPPINES

Compared to her neighbors' fiery fare, Philippine cuisine is more reserved: a gentle cuisine accented by strong-flavored condiments.

Left: Bananas, gourds and tomatoes are not only for eating. Local produce is used to decorate the houses in Lucban during the fiesta of San Isidro Labrador.

Right: Emerald green rice terraces are part of the spectacular scenery in the cordillera of Northern Philippines.

The land and the waters gave the Filipinos their food. Over 7000 islands are surrounded by seas, threaded by rivers and brooks, edged by swamps, and dotted with lakes, canals, ponds, and lagoons, providing a multitude of fish and aquatic life that make up the basic food of Filipinos. This variegated land of mountains and plains, shores and forests, fields and hills is inhabited by land, water, and air creatures that generously transform into regional dishes.

Culinary Adaptation

Foreign influences made a deep impact on native island culture. Chinese traders had been coming to the islands since the 11th century and many stayed on. Their foodways also stayed. Perhaps they cooked the noodles of home; certainly they used local condiments; surely they taught their Filipino wives their dishes, and thus Filipino-Chinese food came to be. The names identify them: *pansit* (Hokkien for something quickly cooked) are noodles; *lumpia* are vegetables rolled in edible wrappers; *siopao* are steamed, filled buns; *siomai* are dumplings. All, of course, came to be indigenized—Filipinized by the ingredients and by local tastes. Today, for example, *pansit Malabon* has oysters and squid, since Malabon is a fishing center; and *pansit Marilao* is sprinkled with rice crisps, because the town is within the Luzon rice bowl. When restaurants were established in the 19th century, Chinese food became a staple of the *pansiterias*, with the food given Spanish names for the ease of the clientele: thus *comida China* (Chinese food) includes *arroz caldo* (rice and chicken gruel); and *morisqueta tostada* (fried rice).

In the 16th century, the Spanish colonizers imported Christianity, and the culture related to colonization lasted three centuries. The food influences the Spaniards brought with them were from both Spain and Mexico, as it was through the vice-royalty of Mexico that the Philippines were governed. This meant the production of food for an elite, non-food-producing class, and a food for which many ingredients were not locally available.

Fil-Hispanic food had new flavors and ingredients—olive oil, paprika, saffron, ham, cheese, cured sausages—and new names. *Paella*, the dish cooked in the fields by Spanish workers, came to be a festive dish combining pork, chicken, seafood, ham, sausages, and vegetables, a luxurious mix of the local and the foreign. *Relleno*, the process of stuffing festive capons and turkeys for Christmas, was applied to chickens, and even to *bangus*, the silvery milkfish. Christmas, a new feast for Filipinos that coincided with the rice harvest, came to feature not only the myriad native rice cakes, but also *ensaymadas* (*brioche*-like cakes buttered, sugared and cheese-sprinkled) to dip in hot thick chocolate, and the apples, oranges, chestnuts, and walnuts of European Christmases. Even the Mexican corn *tamal* turned Filipino, becoming rice-based *tamales* wrapped in banana leaves.

After the Revolution of 1889, the Battle of Manila Bay, and the pact of exchange between the US and Spain, the Philippines became an American colony. The Americans introduced to Philippine cuisine the ways of convenience: pressure-cooking, freezing, pre-cooking; sandwiches, and salads; hamburgers, fried chicken, and steaks.

National and Regional Dishes

Several dishes comprise the "national" cuisine: *bistek* (beef and onion rings braised in soy sauce); *lumpia* (spring rolls); and the popular *adobo*—chicken and pork stewed in vinegar and soy sauce, garlic, peppercorns, and bay leaf. Every province boasts of having the best version of *adobo*. Manila's is soupy with soy sauce and garlic. Cavite cooks mash pork liver into the sauce. Batangas adds the orange hue of annatto; Laguna likes hers yellowish and piquant with turmeric. Zamboanga's adobo is thick with coconut cream.

Three other items represent mainstream tastes and might be called "national" dishes. *Sinigang*, the lightly boiled, slightly sour soup, has a broth as tart as the heart (or taste buds) desires. An array of souring agents—unripe guavas; tamarind leaves and flowers; belimbi; tomatoes—help make a home-cooked *sinigang* of seafood or meat and vegetables as varied as the 7107 islands. There is the stew known as *dinuguan*—basically pig blood and innards simmered with vinegar and hot peppers. Most regions do the *dinuguan* stew in their own versions. Finally there's *lechon*, the whole roast pig or piglet, star of many fiesta occasions. *Lechon* is slowly roasted over live coals, basted regularly—and made crisp and luscious. The tasty sauce is concocted from the pig's liver, simmered with vinegar, sugar, and herbs.

The Philippine archipelago has conjured a people with a stubborn sense of regional identity. The scattered island geography sustains multiple cultures—and many distinctly different cuisines, all alive and well. Regionalism can be sensed—rather, tasted—on Philippine islanders' taste buds. While Filipino food comprises essentially a simple, tropical cuisine, diverse styles have evolved among seven major regions of the 7107 islands.

The northwest coast of Luzon is the Ilocos region, a strip of land between the mountains and the sea, where five provinces share the same language, food, and tough challenges of nature. Ilocanos eat meat sparingly, preferring vegetables and rice as the bulk of their diet. *Pinakbet* is a popular vegetable medley identified with the Ilocanos, a combination of tomatoes, eggplant, and bitter melon, lima beans, okra, and squash—all bound together with *bagoong*, a salty sauce made from fermented fish or shrimp.

Two cuisines in the rice-and-sugar lands of Central Luzon—Pampanga and Bulacan—claim superiority over the other. Many exotic dishes are attributed to land-locked Pampanga: fried catfish with *buro*, a fermented rice sauce; fermented crabs; frogs or milkfish in a sour soup; fried mole crickets, and cured pork slices called *tosino*. From here comes *bringhe* (a fiesta rice made with coconut milk);

ensaymada, a buttery bun; *leche flan*, a crème brûlée made with water buffalo milk; and a great array of sticky rice cakes. In Bulacan cooking, river fish are boiled with citrus or in palm wine, then flamed. Eels are simmered in coconut cream; saltwater fish, in vinegar and ginger. Mudfish are fermented or packed in banana stalks and buried in live coals; crabs sautéed with guava; shellfish flavored in a gingery broth. Bulakeños specialize in meat dishes: a chicken "sits" in a claypot lined with salt and is slowly roasted. Typically, Bulakan cooks claim the best *relleno* and *galantina* (stuffed chicken rolls); *estofado* (pork leg) and *asado* (pot roast); as well as *kare-kare* (oxtail stewed in peanut sauce).

The Bicol Region—six provinces along the southeastern peninsula of Luzon—is synonymous with *gata* or coconut cream. Chili and *gata* come together deliciously, especially in the famous Bicol dish called *pinangat*. Little bundles of *gabi* (taro) leaves are filled with shredded taro leaves and bits of tasty meat; the bundles are simmered in *gata*, and laced with a fistful of chilies.

The Visayas are the big island group in the center of the archipelago, where several cuisines reflect the influence of the Chinese community and the taste of the seas. Iloilo City is famous for its delicious noodle soups. *Pancit molo* is a hearty soup designed around shrimp-and-chicken-and-pork dumplings. From Iloilo also, the delectable *lumpiang ubod*: heart of palm in soft crêpes. Bacolod and Iloilo share credit for *binakol*, a chicken soup based not on chicken stock but on *buko*, the sweet water of the young coconut.

In Mindanao, the frontier land of the far south, everyday cuisine is more Malay in influence and distinctly exotic in taste. Spices are used liberally: turmeric, ginger, garlic, chilies, and roasted coconut. Seafood eaten raw, broiled, or fried; or put in soups with lemongrass, ginger, and green papayas; or coconut cream and turmeric. Chicken is served in curry; or combined with taro in a stinging soup. Glutinous rice is often mixed with shrimp, spices, or coconut milk; or cooked with turmeric and pimento. Finally is Zamboanga, a Catholic town with a distinct Spanish accent. *Cocido*, the traditional Sunday platter, is prepared like its Iberian prototype, with sausage, salted pork, pork ribs, sweet potatoes, corn, and cooking bananas.

The Filipino Table

Whether at home or out in a restaurant, Filipinos love to eat communal-style, all together in an informal social gathering called a *salu-salo*. The components of a typical Filipino meal—fresh fish or other seafood; chicken, pork or beef; vegetables; hearty soups mixed with coconut and noodles—are arrayed around a large container of steamed white rice. Eating is done frequently. On an ordinary day, there are generally five small but tasty meals to munch through—breakfast; morning *merienda* (10 am snack); lunch; afternoon *merienda* (4 pm snack), and dinner. Filipinos eat rice from morning until night, supported by rice cakes, nuts, and sugary snacks in between. Plus there's happy hour and the traditional *pulutan* or finger-foods, the sometimes exotic "appetite-ticklers" that accompany the pre-dinner beer.

What's most unique to the Filipino eating tradition is the *saw-sawan*—the mixing and matching of cooked foods with salty, sour or savory dipping sauces, called *sawsawan*. These myriad table sauces in tiny plates turn the bland white rice and the simply roasted seafood and meats into a meal that's sour, salty, sweet-salty or even bitter-sour—as one chooses. The most common condiments are: *patis* (fish sauce), *toyo* (dark soy sauce), *suka* (native vinegar), and *bagoong* (fermented shrimp paste). These conspire tastily with garlic, ginger, red chilies, peppercorns, onions, tomatoes, *wansoy* (cilantro), belimbi (a sour fruit), and *kalamansi* (the small, sweet native lime).

SUGGESTED MENUS

Family meals

For an easy family meal at home, serve rice and:
• Chicken Rice Soup with Ginger (page 141);
• Beef Stew with Tamarind (page 142);
• Bitter Melon Salad (page 140);
• Sour Shrimp Stew (page 141).

Dinner parties

For a fun Filipino party, serve rice with:
• Philippine Fried Egg Rolls (page 140);
• Fresh Coconut Noodles (page 141);
• Chicken and Pork Adobo (page 142);
• Stuffed Crab (page 142).

Finger food

Pulutan, or finger food to accompany alcoholic drinks, are very popular, so crack open a beer and nibble on:
• Pork Crackling (page 140) with Vinegar Dipping Sauce;
• Philippine Fried Egg Rolls (page 140) with Sweet and Sour Sauce (page 140).
• Pork Crackling (page 140)

Sweet snacks are often eaten throughout the day:
• Brown Rice Cakes (page 142)
• Rice Patties with Sesame and Coconut (page 143)
• Cassava Patties with Coconut (page 143)

A melting pot menu

For a sampling of various Asian flavors, serve:
• Beef Soup with Chilies and Tamarind (page 76) from Indonesia;
• Chicken and Pork Adobo (page 142) from the Philippines and Shrimp Sambal (page 131) from Malaysia with plain rice or with Indian Unleavened Bread (page 54);
• Indian Ice Cream (page 63) for dessert.

THE ESSENTIAL FLAVORS OF FILIPINO COOKING

Flavorings essential to Filipino cooking include **bagoong** (salty, fermented fish paste), **patis** (fish sauce), **toyo** (soy sauce), and **suka** (native vinegar; substitute with white vinegar). Other common ingredients include fresh **red chilies** and small **bird's-eye chilies**, **coconut milk**, **kamias** (belimbi; substitute with citrus juice or tamarind), fresh **cilantro** (coriander), **kalamansi** limes, Spanish **chorizo** sausage, and **tamarind** pulp (and sometimes leaves if available). **Lumpia** (spring roll) wrappers are a must too and are readily avialable.

Pork Cracking and Philippine Fried Egg Rolls

Filipino food is a tantalizing concoction of textures, flavors, and colors. It is among the most exciting and diverse cuisines in Asia, as this delicious selection of recipes illustrates.

Chicharon
Pork Crackling

A favorite *pulutan* (finger food to accompany alcoholic drinks), especially when it is just cooked and dipped in vinegar sauce.

- 2 lb (1 kg) pork rind, cut into 1-in (2¹/₂-cm) squares
- 3 cups (750 ml) water
- 1 tablespoon salt
- 1 cup (250 ml) vegetable or corn oil

Boil cut pork rind in water and salt for 30 minutes. On a baking pan, spread out the cooked pork rind and bake at 300°F (150°C, gas mark 2) for 3 hours. Set aside and let cool.

Deep-fry the rinds in a skillet in hot oil over high heat until they puff up. Serve with Vinegar Dipping Sauce.

Sawsawang Suka
Vinegar Dipping Sauce

- ¹/₄ cup (60 ml) soy sauce
- ¹/₃ cup (80 ml) white vinegar
- 3 garlic cloves, peeled and crushed
- Salt and freshly ground pepper to taste
- ¹/₈ teaspoon ground cayenne

Combine all ingredients in a bowl. Mix well.

Lumpiang Shanghai
Philippine Fried Egg Rolls

A popular Filipinized version of the Chinese egg roll, usually stuffed with meat, shellfish or vegetables.

- ¹/₂ lb (250 g) ground pork
- ¹/₂ lb (250 g) shrimp, finely chopped
- ¹/₂ cup chopped water chestnuts
- ¹/₂ cup finely chopped scallions (spring onions)
- 1 egg, beaten
- 1 tablespoon soy sauce
- 1 teaspoon salt
- 1 teaspoon ground black pepper
- 1 package egg roll wrappers (sold in Asian food stores)
- Oil for deep-frying

Mix pork, shrimp, water chestnuts, scallions, egg, and soy sauce together. Season with salt and pepper.

Place a level tablespoon of filling on each egg roll wrapper, roll tightly and seal with a few drops of water. Continue until filling is all used. Deep-fry in hot oil and drain on paper towels. Serve with Sweet and Sour Sauce.

Agre Dulce
Sweet and Sour Sauce

- 3 cups (750 ml) water
- ¹/₂ cup (125 ml) ketchup
- ¹/₃ cup (80 g) sugar
- 1 teaspoon salt
- 1 teaspoon red-hot (Tabasco) sauce (optional)
- 2 tablespoons cornstarch dissolved in 4 tablespoons of water

Mix all ingredients together. Bring to a boil and simmer for 5 minutes or until sauce thickens. Makes about 3 cups (750 ml).

Ensaladang Ampalaya
Bitter Melon Salad

- 2 cups seeded and julienned bitter melon
- 5 shallots, sliced
- 3 tablespoons shrimp paste (*bagoong*)
- 4 small, ripe plum tomatoes, sliced

Sprinkle the bitter melon with salt and let stand in a colander for 30 minutes. Rinse off the salt.

In a large mixing bowl, mix the bitter melon with the remaining ingredients. Let stand for 10 minutes so the flavors develop, then serve.

Manggang Hilaw
Green Mango Salad

- 2 cups shredded green mango
- 1 cup sliced ripe plum tomato
- 2 salted eggs, peeled and chopped (see below)
- 3 shallots, chopped

Mix all the ingredients together and serve. Serves 2.

To make salted eggs, pour ³/₄ cup salt into a saucepan. Add a dozen eggs in the shell and water to cover. Boil for 2 minutes, then transfer the eggs to sterilized jars and add salted water. Cover and leave for 1 ¹/₂ months. Hard cook the eggs before using.

Arroz a La Cubana
Cuban-style Rice

A favorite one-pot meal. This "comfort food" is especially good during the rainy season.

- 3 tablespoons vegetable or corn oil
- 1 tablespoon minced garlic
- ¹/₄ cup minced shallots
- ¹/₂ cup diced tomatoes
- ¹/₂ lb (250 g) ground beef
- ¹/₂ lb (250 g) ground pork
- 3 tablespoons soy sauce
- ¹/₄ cup raisins
- ¹/₂ teaspoon salt
- ¹/₄ teaspoon ground black pepper
- ¹/₂ cup peas
- 5 tablespoons peanut oil
- 3 ripe plantains, peeled and sliced
- 6 eggs
- 5 cups (750 g) freshly cooked rice, kept warm

Bitter Melon Salad and
Green Mango Salad

In a large stockpot, heat the oil and sauté the garlic until light brown. Add the shallots and cook until transparent.

Add the tomatoes and cook for 5 minutes. Stir in the beef, pork, and soy sauce. Cook until the meat is brown. Add the raisins, salt, and pepper and stir constantly. Add the peas and simmer for another 5 minutes.

In a separate skillet, heat 3 tablespoons of the peanut oil and fry the plantain slices. Remove from the heat and set aside. Put 2 more tablespoons peanut oil in the pan and fry the eggs sunny-side up. Set aside.

On a large serving platter, arrange the cooked rice with the meat in the center. Top with the fried eggs and surround the sides of the platter with the fried plantains. Serve hot.

Pancit Buko
Fresh Coconut Noodles

Fresh coconut is used instead of noodles in this reinterpretation of the traditional *pancit*.

1 teaspoon cooking oil
1 teaspoon finely minced garlic
1/2 cup finely minced onion
1/2 cup sliced chicken
1/2 cup sliced pork belly
1/2 cup shrimp, shelled and deveined
1/2 cup sliced green beans
1/2 cup sliced carrots
1 tablespoon fish sauce (*patis*)
1/4 teaspoon ground black pepper
1 tablespoon annatto oil (see note)
1/2 cup (125 ml) chicken broth
1 1/2 cups shredded fresh coconut
2 stalks fresh Chinese cabbage
1 cup shredded green cabbage

Heat the oil in a saucepan and sauté the garlic until brown and onion until transparent. Add the chicken and pork and fry until slightly brown.

Add the shrimp, beans, and carrots. Stir and season with fish sauce and pepper. Stir in the annatto oil.

Pour in the broth and bring to a boil. Add the coconut and both kinds of cabbage and cook until the vegetables are done but still crisp. Serve hot. Serves 4.

Note: To make annatto oil, fry 1 tablespoon annatto or achiote seeds in 2 tablespoons oil for several minutes. When cool, crush the seeds and leave in the oil for 15 minutes, then strain and discard seeds.

Sinigang Na Sugpo
Sour Shrimp Stew

8 cups (2 liters) rice water (mix 8 cups of water with 4 cups of rice thoroughly, then drain, reserving rice water)
1/2 cup (125 ml) lemon or kalamansi juice, or one 1 1/2-oz (50-g) package of tamarind ready-mix powder (available in Asian food stores)
2 tablespoons oil
1 tablespoon finely minced garlic
1 cup chopped onion
2 cups diced ripe tomatoes
2 cups radishes, left whole
2 lb (1 kg) jumbo shrimp
3 fresh, long hot green peppers
1 1/2 lb (750 g) watercress or spinach
Fish sauce (*patis*) to taste
Ground black pepper to taste

In a saucepan, bring rice water and tamarind ready-mix or lemon juice to a boil. Simmer for 15 minutes. In a skillet, heat the oil and sauté the garlic, onion, and tomatoes, then add this to the rice water. Add radishes and shrimp and bring to a boil. Simmer until the radishes are tender yet crisp. Add the hot peppers and watercress or spinach. Add the fish sauce and pepper to taste.

Arroz Caldo Con Pollo
Chicken Rice Soup with Ginger

5 tablespoons vegetable or corn oil
4 tablespoons minced garlic
2 in (5 cm) ginger, cut crosswise into 1/2-in (1-cm) slices
1 large onion, peeled and diced
1 1/2 cups (300 g) uncooked rice
10 cups (2 1/2 liters) water
1 chicken, about 2–3 lb (1–1 1/2 kg), cut into bite-size pieces
1 1/2 teaspoons fish sauce (*patis*)
1/4 teaspoon ground black pepper
1/4 cup finely chopped scallion (spring onion)

In a stockpot, heat 3 tablespoons oil and sauté 2 tablespoons of garlic, the ginger, and the onion. The garlic is done when light brown and the onion when transparent.

Chicken Rice Soup with Ginger

Add rice and sauté for 5 minutes. Add water. Bring mixture to a boil, stirring occasionally. Reduce the heat to a simmer, add chicken, and continue cooking for another 30 minutes or until rice is done.

While waiting for the rice to cook, heat the remaining 2 tablespoons of oil in a skillet and fry the 2 remaining tablespoons of garlic until golden brown. Set aside.

When the rice is finally cooked, add fish sauce and continue cooking over low heat for another 3–5 minutes. Serve in a soup tureen or soup bowls. Sprinkle the fried garlic, pepper, and chopped scallion, on top.

The flavor of the soup is improved if it is made the day before serving and left overnight in the refrigerator.

Sotanghon
Chicken Vermicelli

Noodles signify long life and Filipinos consume an abundance of them. This popular Chinese-influenced dish, uses cellophane noodles as the main ingredient.

1/2 cup dried Chinese mushrooms (soak in 2 cups/500 ml warm water, strain and reserve liquid for stock)
3 tablespoons cooking oil
1 tablespoon finely minced garlic
1/2 cup minced onion
1/2 cup annatto water (see note)
1/2 cup julienned carrots
1/2 cup julienned leeks
1/4 cup julienned celery leaves
1/2 lb (250 g) cellophane noodles (*sotanghon*), soaked in water and when soft, cut into 6-in (15-cm) lengths
Fish sauce (*patis*) to taste
Ground black pepper to taste
1 cup finely minced scallion (spring onion)

Chicken stock
1 chicken, about 2–3 lb (1–1 1/2 kg)
2 bay leaves
1 teaspoon peppercorns
1 cup minced onion
Reserved mushroom water

Soak the mushrooms and obtain mushroom water for the stock. To make the stock, boil the chicken bay leaves, peppercorns, water from mushrooms, and 1 cup minced onion in a stockpot until chicken is tender. Set aside and let cool. Strain the stock through a sieve. Set aside. Remove all flesh from the boiled chicken. Discard skin and cut chicken meat into thin strips.

In a wok or frying pan, heat the oil and sauté garlic and 1/2 cup onion until transparent. Stir in the chicken. Add the annatto water and 3 cups of chicken broth and bring to a boil over high heat. Stir in the carrots, leeks, and celery leaves and cook for 3 minutes. Add the cellophane noodles. Add the fish sauce and pepper to taste. Garnish with scallions.

Note: To make annatto water, place 1 tablespoon annatto seeds in 4 tablespoons water and crush using fingers to get red color. Leave 30 minutes then strain to get water.

Beef Stew with Tamarind

Rellenong Alimango
Stuffed Crab

Rellenado is a culinary technique inherited from Spain. This dish highlights the delicacy and richness of the shellfish.

- 4 to 5 *alimasag* (native crabs) (blue or rock crabs may be substituted)
- 2 onions, finely minced
- 8 garlic cloves, finely minced
- 1 lb (500 g) ground pork
- 4 eggs
- Salt and ground black pepper to taste
- Oil for frying

Steam the crabs. Remove shells and flake the meat. Do not remove the claws and legs.

In a mixing bowl, combine the crabmeat, onion, garlic, pork, 1 egg, salt, and pepper. Return the mixture to the shells.

Beat the other eggs and dip the crab shells into the beaten egg. Fry in small amount of oil until golden brown.

Apritadang Manok
Chicken Simmered In Tomatoes

A classic dish with Spanish influences.

- 2 tablespoons vegetable oil
- 2 garlic cloves, peeled and crushed
- 1 cup chopped onions
- 1 chicken, about 2–3 lb (1–1 1/2 kg), cut into 8 pieces
- 1 6-oz (185 g) can puréed tomatoes
- 2 bay leaves
- 3 tablespoons ground black pepper
- 4 teaspoons salt
- 1 cup (250 ml) water
- 5 medium-size potatoes, peeled and cut in cubes
- 6 4-oz (125-g) cans pimentos

Chicken Adobo with Turmeric

In a large saucepan, heat the oil and sauté the garlic and onion. Add the chicken, puréed tomatoes, bay leaves, pepper, salt, and water. Let simmer for 20 minutes over low heat.

Add the potatoes and pimentos. Continue to cook until the potatoes are tender. Serve hot.

Adobong Manok At Baboy
Chicken and Pork Adobo

This recipe is for just one of the many versions of the ever-popular *adobo*.

- 1/2 lb (250 g) pork, cut into 1-in (2 1/2-cm) cubes
- 1/4 cup (60 ml) white vinegar
- 1/2 cup (125 ml) soy sauce
- 1 whole bulb garlic, peeled and crushed
- 1 cup finely minced onions
- 1 teaspoon ground black pepper
- 2 bay leaves
- 2 cups (500 ml) water
- 1/2 lb (250 g) chicken, cut into cubes

Combine the pork, vinegar, soy sauce, garlic, onions, pepper, bay leaves, and water and bring to a boil. Simmer until the pork is medium cooked. Add the chicken and simmer for 20 minutes. Serve hot.

Beef Sinigang
Beef Stew with Tamarind

Sinigang, the quintessential Filipino dish, is any fish, meat or crustacean soured-stew with vegetables.

- 10 pieces fresh tamarind or one 1 1/2-oz package tamarind ready-mix powder (sold at Asian food stores)
- 2 lb (1 kg) beef ribs, cut into pieces
- 5 cups (1 1/4 liters) water
- 4 tomatoes, sliced
- 1 onion, sliced
- 3 taros, peeled and halved
- 1 lb (500 g) green beans, cut into 2-in (5-cm) lengths
- 1 lb (500 g) water spinach, leaves and stalks separated, stalks cut into 2-in (5-cm) lengths
- Fish sauce (*patis*) to taste
- Black pepper to taste

Cook the fresh tamarind in 1 1/2 cups (375 ml) water until tender. Mash, then strain to get the juice and set aside. You should have approximately 1 cup (250 ml) of tamarind liquid.

In a saucepan, boil the beef in 5 cups water. Add the tomatoes, onion, and tamarind juice. If using tamarind liquid, add this to the saucepan.

Add the taro pieces, and when the taro is slightly tender, add the green beans and water spinach stalks. Season to taste with fish sauce and pepper. Add the water convolvulus leaves and cook for another 3 minutes.

Kutsinta
Brown Rice Cakes

A favorite snack, especially when served with freshly grated coconut.

- 2 cups (125 g) rice flour
- 2 cups (500 g) brown sugar
- 3 cups (750 ml) water
- 1 teaspoon lye water (potassium carbonate solution sold in Asian food stores)
- Freshly grated coconut

In a mixing bowl, combine all the ingredients and mix well. Pour into muffin pans, until halfway full.

Steam in a large pan with a cover; the water should be 2 in (5 cm) deep. Cook for 30 minutes or until a toothpick inserted comes out clean. Add more water if needed until cooking is done. Remove from the muffin pans and serve with freshly grated coconut.

Palitao
Rice Patties with Sesame and Coconut

- 1 cup (125 g) sweet rice flour (sold in Asian food stores under the brand name "Mochiko")
- 3 cups (750 ml) water
- 3 cups (300 g) grated fresh coconut
- 2 cups toasted sesame seeds
- 2 cups (500 g) sugar

In a mixing bowl, combine the sweet rice flour and water to make a smooth dough.

With floured hands shape the dough into small patties, 3 in (8 cm) in diameter and ¹/₂ in (1 cm) thick.

Bring water in a saucepan to a boil and drop in the patties. When they float to the top, scoop them out and coat with grated coconut. Sprinkle with sesame seeds and sugar and serve immediately.

Pichi-Pichi
Cassava Patties with Coconut

- 1 cup grated cassava (frozen cassava is available in Asian food stores)
- 1 cup pandan water (boil pandan leaves with water or use McCormick pandan extract)
- 1 cup sugar
- 2 teaspoons lye water (available in Asian food stores)
- 3 cups grated fresh coconut

Squeeze the juice from the cassava and discard. In a bowl, combine cassava, pandan water, sugar, and lye water. Mix well and pour into small muffin pans. Steam until soft and transparent, approximately 5 minutes. Remove from pans and roll in grated coconut.

Halo Halo Supreme
Exotic Fruit Mix

Known as the "Queen of Desserts"—this is the country's most popular dessert. Similar to Malaysia's *ais kachang*, it features the exotic fruits and vegetables that Filipinos enjoy.

Base
- 1 teaspoon sweetened red mung beans
- 1 teaspoon sweetened white beans
- 1 tablespoon sweetened plantains
- 1 tablespoon violet yam (*ube*)
- 1 tablespoon coconut sport (*maca puno balls*)
- 1 tablespoon coconut gelatin (*nata de coco*)
- 1 teaspoon palm nut (*kaong*)
- 1 tablespoon creamed corn
- Ice

Topping 1
- 2 tablespoons pandan syrup
- ¹/₃ cup (85 ml) water buffalo milk or evaporated milk

Topping 2
- 1 tablespoon crème caramel
- 1 tablespoon *pinipig* (rice crispies, available at Asian food stores)
- 2 scoops *mantecado* ice cream or French vanilla ice cream

Fill the bottom half of a coupe glass with the base ingredients. Add enough ice to reach the top.

Pour the pandan syrup and the milk onto the ice. Top with Crème Caramel, *pinipig* and a scoop of *mantecado* ice cream.

Rice patties with Sesame and Coconut (left), Brown Rice Cakes (middle), and Cassava Patties with Coconut (right)

Exotic Fruit Mix

Sri Lankan cuisine is a cuisine expressed in spices—cinnamon, cloves, nutmeg, coriander, mace, pepper, cardamom, red chilies, mustard seeds, cumin, fenugreek, and turmeric are all used to flavor curries, while some add flavor to desserts and cakes.

SRI LANKA

Coursing through the cuisine of Sri Lanka is a great observance to details and tradition. It truly is like tasting history.

Left: Stilt fishermen wedge wooden poles into rock crevices to use as a perch while fishing.

Right: (Clockwise from top left) cinnamon, cloves, nutmeg, coriander, mace, pepper, cardamom, dried red chilies, mustard seeds, cumin, fenugreek, fennel, and turmeric.

Sri Lanka, the fabled island of sapphires, rubies, and other precious stones, is home to one of Asia's least known cuisines. Rarely found in restaurants outside the island itself, Sri Lankan fare is often mistaken for yet another Indian regional cuisine. To the culinary explorer, however, Sri Lankan food is as intriguing and unique as the many other customs of this island paradise.

Multiethnic Influences

Sri Lanka, formerly known as Ceylon, is located off India's southeast coast. The rugged terrain of the central highlands—characterized by high mountains and plateaus, steep river gorges, and swathes of tea plantations—dominates much of the island. This falls away to sandy lowlands, rice paddies, and long stretches of palm-fringed beaches. Sri Lankan cuisine, which is based upon rice with vegetable, fish, or meat curries, and a variety of side dishes and condiments, reflects the geographical and ethnic differences of the land.

The multiethnic mix of people living on this small island comprises Sinhalese, Tamils, Moors (Muslims), Burghers and Eurasians, Malays, and Veddhas. Over the centuries, the cooking of the Sinhalese has evolved into two slightly different styles: coastal or "low country" Sinhalese, and Kandy or "upcountry" Sinhalese. Regardless of where they live, the staple food for Sinhalese (and indeed, for all Sri Lankans) is rice. This is usually accompanied by a range of spiced vegetables, fish, poultry, meat, or game dishes.

In coastal Sinhalese cuisine, fish, and other seafood feature far more widely than poultry or meat, and coconut milk is the preferred base for curries. One Sinhalese specialty from the coast is *ambulthiyal*, or sour claypot fish. At its best in the Southern town of Ambalangoda, *ambulthiyal* is a dish of *balaya* (bonito) which uses *goraka* (gamboge) as both a flavoring and a preservative. Crab curries and numerous shrimp dishes are also popular. An ingredient known as Maldive fish is widely used as a seasoning throughout Sri Lanka, but especially in coastal regions. It is made from a type of bonito (also known as skipjack) which is boiled, smoked, and sun-dried until it is rock hard.

Kandy, the heart of upcountry Sri Lanka, remained an independent Sinhalese kingdom until the British finally took over in 1815, thus it largely escaped the social and culinary influences of the Portuguese and Dutch. Many Kandian curries are made with unusual ingredients such as young jackfruit, jackfruit seeds, cashews, breadfruit, and green papaya, while various edible flowers such as turmeric, hibiscus, and sesbania may end up in an omelet or curry. Game, including deer and wild birds, was also an upcountry favorite.

The first Tamils are believed to have arrived at about the same time as the Indo-Ayrans, around 2,000 years ago. Successive waves of Tamils from southern India established themselves in Sri Lanka, mostly in the north, on the Jaffna peninsula. Popular Tamil dishes found in Sri Lanka include *rasam*, a spicy sour soup that is an aid to digestion; *kool*, a thick seafood soup originating from Jaffna fisherfolk; *vadai*, or deep-fried savories made with black gram flour; and many types of vegetable *pachadi*, where cooked vegetables are tossed with curd or yoghurt, and freshly grated coconut. *Thosai*, slightly sour pancakes made with black gram and rice flours, constitute another delicious Tamil contribution to the culinary scene.

Malays, who were brought by the Dutch, have intermarried with the Muslim community and brought with them several dishes which have since become part of the Sri Lankan kitchen. *Sathe* is the Sri Lankan equivalent of satay, or cubes of meat threaded on skewers and served with a peanut and chili sauce. Other Malay dishes include *gula melaka* (sago pudding with jaggery), *nasi kuning* (turmeric rice), *barbuth* (honeycomb tripe curry), *seenakku* and *parsong* (two types of rice flour cakes.)

Colonial Tastes

The wave of Western expansionism, which began at the end of the fifteenth century, was also to have a significant impact on Sri Lanka. Colonialism affected not only the agriculture, social structure, and religions of the country, but also the cuisine. The first Portuguese ships chanced upon Sri Lanka in the early sixteenth century and set about trading in cinnamon and other spices. There followed four hundred years of Western presence in the form of Portuguese, Dutch, and finally the British before Sri Lanka regained her independence in 1948. The Portuguese introduced a number of plants they had discovered in the Americas, the most important being chili, as well as corn, tomatoes, and guavas. It is hard to imagine Sri Lankan cuisine without chili, but prior to the introduction of this taste-tingling plant, all Asians had to rely on pepper for heat. The Portuguese impact on the cuisine of Sri Lanka has lasted until today, but almost exclusively in the area of rich cakes: *bolo de coco* (a coconut cake), *foguete* (deep-fried pastry tubes with a sweet filling), and *bolo folhadao* (a layered cake). The Dutch left a number of cakes to become part of the culinary legacy of Sri Lanka, and particularly of the Burgher community, including *breudher*, a rich cake made with yeast. Dutch meatballs, or *frikadel*, appear as part of a cross-cultural dish served on special occasions in many Sri Lankan homes. *Lampries* (a corruption of the Dutch *lomprijst*) combines these meatballs with a typically Sinhalese curry made with four types of meat and a tangy *sambol*, all wrapped up in a piece of banana leaf and steamed. Another Dutch recipe is *smore*, or sliced braised beef.

Spice and Other Things Nice

Spices, so important to the Sri Lankan kitchen, actually helped shape the history of the island. The Portuguese arrived at the beginning of the sixteenth century, and it was Sri Lanka's famous cinnamon which became the prime source of revenue for the Europeans. Sri Lanka's cinnamon trees, which grew wild on the southern and western coasts of the island, were said to produce the finest cinnamon in the world. Cinnamon was still the most important source of revenue by the time the Dutch seized control of the island. They introduced penalties to protect it, making it a capital offence to damage a plant, and to sell or to export the quills or their oil. The Dutch did eventually succeed in cultivating cinnamon, but still relied largely on the wild supply. By the nineteenth century, however, the supremacy of cinnamon was challenged by the cheaper cassia bark grown elsewhere in Asia. Cardamom, indigenous to both Sri Lanka and southern India, was another valuable spice which flourished in the wetter regions of the country. All of Sri Lanka's spices are used to flavor savory dishes such as curries; some also add their fragrance and flavor to desserts and cakes. Spices such as cinnamon therefore command a very important position in Sri Lankan culture, not only as culinary flavorings but also by virtue of their having played such a major role in the country's history.

The Sri Lankan Table

Breakfast in Sri Lanka is often a batter of rice flour cooked in special hemispherical pans to make *appa* or hoppers. These are small, bowl-shaped pancakes with a soft, bready center and crisp brown edges that goes well with treacle and buffalo-milk yoghurt. Crack an egg into the middle of a hopper before turning the pan results in an egg hopper; these go best with thick, highly spiced *sambol*. Another rice-batter dish, called the "string hopper," is quite different. These are tangled little circles of steamed noodles usually served with a *hodhi* or thin curry sauce.

Sri Lankans lunch between noon and two, often with a plate of "short eats." These divide equally between crisply baked filo-dough biscuits and *frikadels* or deep-fried rolls or balls. The interiors are filled with meat, fish, or vegetables. Short eats are joined by *vadai*, or deep-fried donuts of lentils, spices, and flour. Another common snack is *roti*, a square or triangular wrap of dough stuffed with fresh chilies, onions, vegetables, and cooked egg, meat, or fish, which is fried on a searing sheet-metal griddle over a propane burner. Many prefer a rice-and-curry lunch packet. Inside a banana leaf or thin plastic wrap is a cup or two of boiled rice, a piece of curried chicken, fish, or beef for non-vegetarians, or simply some curried vegetables.

A proper rice-and-curry dinner involves three or more accompaniments, at least two of them vegetables. When choosing which curries to serve with the rice, Sri Lankan cooks ensure that there is a variety of textures as well as flavors, with at least one fairly liquid, or soupy, curry to help moisten the rice, and usually a relatively dry curry with a thick gravy. One of the curries will most likely be a spiced lentil dish, and there is sure to be at least one pungent side dish or condiment known as a *sambol*. These *sambol*, also know as "rice pullers," are guaranteed to whet the appetite with their basic ingredient—anything from onion to bitter gourd, dried shrimp to salted lime—heightened by the flavors of chili, onion, salt, and Maldive fish. One of the most popular *sambol*, *pol sambol*, is made with freshly grated coconut.

There are few native desserts but many *rasokavili* or sweets. *Kaum* is a battercake made of flour and treacle deep-fried in coconut oil. *Aluvas* are thin, flat, diamond-shaped halvas, or wedges of rice flour, treacle, and sugar cane. Coconut milk laboriously boiled down with jaggery and cashew nuts yields *kalu dodol*. *Kiribath*, a festive dish of rice cooked in milk, is the first solid food fed to babies. *Kiri peni* or "curd and honey" is buffalo-milk yoghurt and treacle.

SUGGESTED MENUS

Family meals

For a simple family meal, serve plain basmati rice and Coconut Sambol (page 148) with:
• Eggplant Pickle (page149);
• Sour Claypot Fish (page 150) or Seer Fish Lemon Stew (page 150)
• Spicy Lamb Curry (page 151);
• Fresh fruits for dessert.

Dinner parties

For a dinner party with a Sri Lankan seafood theme, serve plain basmati rice and Bird's-eye Chili Sambol (page 149) with:
• Jaffna Seafood Soup (page 149);
• Tempered Eggplant (page 149);
• Crab curry (151);
• Seer Fish Lemon Stew (page 150);
• Mixed Spice Coconut Slices (page 151) for dessert.

Finger food

The following snacks and appetizers may be eaten throughout the day, even as breakfast:
• Hoppers (page 148) with or without an egg;
• String Hoppers (page 148).

Serve both with Coconut Sambol (page 148), Bird's-eye Chili Sambol (page 149), and Coconut Milk Gravy (page 148).

A melting pot menu

For a fun pan-Asian menu, serve:
• Hoppers (page 148) from Sri Lanka as a starter;
• Green Chicken Curry (page 165) from Thailand with plain rice;
• Creamy Shrimp Curry (page 60) from India;
• Grilled Eggplant Salad (page 26) from Burma;
• Rich Rice Pudding (page 62) from India for dessert.

THE ESSENTIAL FLAVORS OF SRI LANKAN COOKING

Ingredients common to the Sri Lankan pantry include dried spices such as **cardamom**, **cinnamon**, **cloves**, **coriander**, **cumin**, **fennel**, **fennugreek**, **mustard seeds**, and **turmeric**. A good supply of **basmati rice** is a must. Fresh or dried **curry leaves**, fresh **cilantro**, **coconut milk**, and **tamarind** are also easy to come by and will prove indespensible. **Fresh green chilies** are used in curries and *sambols*, **dried red chilies**, **chili flakes**, and **chili powder** are common too. If **Maldive fish** is unavailable, substitute with small dried shrimps.

Sri Lanka, famous for its pristine beaches and stunning land-scapes, also boasts one of the most intriguing cuisines in Asia. The fruits of land and sea are plentiful, and sitting down to a Sri Lankan meal is a truly fantastic epicurean adventure.

Roasted Curry Powder

This is used as an ingredient in curries or can be sprinkled on vegetables before serving.

- 1/2 teaspoon fennel seeds
- 1/2 teaspoon cumin seeds
- 1/2 teaspoon fenugreek seeds
- 3/4 oz (20 g) cinnamon sticks
- 6 cardamoms
- 3 1/2 oz (100 g) coriander seeds
- 6 cloves

Dry-roast all the ingredients in a skillet until the mix becomes a deep golden color. Grind them to a fine powder in an electric blender. Store in an air-tight container.

Appa
Hoppers

Hoppers are small bowl-shaped rice flour pancakes which are eaten with curries and sambols (it is usual to serve each person one hopper with an egg baked in its center and the rest plain). Although the traditional method of preparing them requires placing a hopper pan on hot coals (with more coals on its lid), hoppers may be prepared on regular stoves. Hopper pans are readily available from Indian and Sri Lankan foodstores.

- 3 cups (500 g) rice flour
- 1/4 cup (60 ml) kitul palm toddy (1/3 oz or 10 g fresh yeast or 1 teaspoon dried yeast may be substituted)
- 2 teaspoons sugar
- 3/4 cup (200 ml) thin coconut
- Salt to taste
- 2 cups (500 ml) thick coconut milk

Combine the rice flour, toddy (or yeast), sugar, and thin coconut milk in a mixing bowl. Stir to form a thick batter. Cover with a damp tea towel and leave to stand overnight, or 6 to 8 hours, by which time the batter should have doubled in volume. When the batter has risen, soften it by working in the salt and thick coconut milk to form a thinner batter.

Heat a greased hopper pan (or any high-sided, small hemi-spherical pan with two handles) over low heat. Pour a large spoonful of batter into the pan and, being mindful to use oven gloves or pot holders, pick up the pan by both handles and swirl the pan so the batter rides up the sides almost to the rim. Replace the pan over the heat, cover with any saucepan lid, and cook until the surface of the hopper at the bottom is almost firm and the sides are crispy and brown, about 5 minutes.

Remove the hopper with a metal spatula (a curved instrument would be ideal) and serve hot. Grease pan again and repeat with remaining batter. Makes about 20 hoppers.

Idappam
String Hoppers

- 3 cups (500 g) rice flour
- 1 1/2 teaspoons salt
- 220 ml (1 cup less 2 tablespoons) boiling water, or as needed

Warm the flour in a low oven, then sieve into a bowl. Add the salt, then slowly add the hot water and work into a soft dough. Place the dough in a string hopper or vermicelli press, and press the plunger to squeeze small, flat noodle patties onto hopper mats.

Place the mats in a steamer, or a large pot with a trivet at the bottom and sufficient water to just reach the trivet's rungs. Steam until strings are fully cooked and springy in texture, about 10 minutes.

Remove string hoppers from the steamer and serve hot with Pol Sambol and Kiri Hodi.

String Hoppers (left) and Egg Hopper (right)

Pol Sambol
Coconut Sambol

- 1 teaspoon finely chopped dried chili
- 1 tablespoon finely chopped onion
- 1 teaspoon pepper
- 1 teaspoon Maldive fish, ground (optional)
- 2 cups (200 g) freshly grated coconut
- 3 tablespoons lime juice
- Salt to taste

Grind together the chili, onion, pepper, and Maldive fish. Add grated coconut and season with lime juice. Mix well by hand to ensure all the coconut is coated. Best served freshly made.

Kiri Hodi
Coconut Milk Gravy

- 1 tablespoon fenugreek seeds
- 2 cups (500 ml) chicken stock
- 1 Bombay or large red onion, finely chopped
- 2 sprigs curry leaves
- 2 pieces pandanus leaf (*rampe*)
- 3 cloves garlic, finely chopped
- 1 in (2 1/2 cm) stick cinnamon
- 4 pods cardamom, crushed
- 2 green chilies, deseeded and finely sliced
- 1 teaspoon turmeric powder
- 2 teaspoons powdered Maldive fish
- 2 cups (500 ml) coconut milk
- Salt and lemon juice to taste

Wash the fenugreek seeds and soak them in the chicken stock in a saucepan for 30 minutes. Add all the remaining ingredients except the coconut milk, salt, and lemon juice. Bring to a boil and simmer on very low heat until the onions are tender.

Add the coconut milk and heat the entire mix to boiling point, then reduce the heat and simmer for about 5 minutes. Remove from heat and cool slightly. Add lemon juice and salt to taste

Jaffna Seafood Soup

Kochchi Sambol
Bird's-eye Chili Sambol

1/2 cup (100 g) bird's-eye chilies
1/4 cup (50 g) finely chopped
   red onion
1 teaspoon pepper
3 tablespoons lime juice
Salt to taste

Combine chilies and onions and grind finely. Add pepper, lime juice, and salt. Best when served freshly made. Store in covered container in a cool place and use as desired.

Jaffna Kool
Jaffna Seafood Soup

Jaffna, in the north of Sri Lanka, is famous for its *kool*, or rich seafood soup. Originating from the Tamil fishing communities of the north, this soup is traditionally made with whatever leftover seafood is available.

6 cups (1 1/2 liters) fish or shrimp
   stock, or water
1/4 cup (50 g) red (or other) rice
3 1/2 oz (100 g) long beans, cut
   lengthwise
1 1/2 oz (50 g) tapioca (or potato),
   cut into 1/2-in (1-cm) cubes
1 1/2 oz (50 g) jackfruit seeds
3 1/2 oz (100 g) jackfruit, cubed
1 teaspoon turmeric
1/2 teaspoon palmyra root flour
   (substitute with potato flour,
   or other strong flour)
Salt to taste

3/4 oz (20 g) dried chilies, broken
   into pieces
1/2 tablespoon tamarind juice
1 fish head (about 1 lb/500 g)
   of grouper, cod, or other mild-
   flavored fish
7 oz (200 g) flesh of the same
   fish, cubed
3 1/2 oz (100 g) medium shrimp,
   peeled, with tails intact

In a large pan, bring the stock, rice, long beans, tapioca, jack-fruit seeds, and jackfruit pieces to a boil, reduce heat and simmer for 5 minutes.

Add the turmeric, flour, salt, chiles, and tamarind juice, and simmer for a further 2 minutes. Add the fish and fish head, and simmer 10 minutes then add the shrimp and cook until shrimp are cooked, about 5 minutes. Serve hot.

Thibattu Beduma
Tempered Eggplant

Thibattu are tiny round eggplants (aubergines) which may be substituted with pea eggplants.

500 g (1 lb) *thibattu*, substitute
   with pea eggplants (pea
   aubergines)
1 cup (250 ml) oil
5 oz (150 g) red onions, sliced
2 in (5 cm) pandanus leaf (*rampe*)
1 sprig curry leaves
1 in (2 1/2 cm) cinnamon stick
1/2 teaspoon sliced green chilies
1/2 teaspoon ground Maldive fish
4 tablespoons coconut milk or water

1/2 teaspoon red chili flakes
Salt to taste
3 tablespoons lime juice

Wash the *thibattu* eggplants then crush with a spoon. Fry in the hot oil until they lose their firmness.

In another pan, heat 2 table-spoons of oil, add the onion, pandanus leaf, curry leaves, cinnamon, and green chilies, and sauté until the onions are golden brown. Add the Maldive fish, coconut milk or water, chile flakes, and salt, and cook over medium heat for 5 minutes. Add the fried *thibbattu* eggplants and lime juice, and season to taste. Serve hot as an accompaniment to other dishes.

Brinjal Pahie
Eggplant Pickle

2 tablespoons oil
500 g (1 lb) eggplant (aubergine),
   thinly sliced
1 1/2 oz (40 g) onions, cut into rings
2 teaspoons mustard seeds,
   ground
1 teaspoon sugar
1/2 teaspoon turmeric powder
3 tablespoons vinegar
5–8 green chilies, halved lengthwise
2 tablespoons Maldive fish, ground
Salt and pepper to taste

Heat oil and fry eggplant slices until golden brown. Remove

with a slotted spoon and set aside to cool.

In the same pan, add onions and sauté until soft. Add remaining ingredients and the fried eggplant slices. Cook for 10 to 15 minutes. Serve at room temperature. Serve as an accompaniment to other dishes.

Amba Maluwa
Mango Curry

This classical Sinhalese dish can be traced back to the fifth century, when it was served at the court of King Kasyapa of Sigiriya.

1 tablespoon oil
3 1/2 oz (100 g) onion, chopped
1 1/2 oz (40 g) garlic, chopped
1/2 oz (10 g) ginger, chopped
2 sprigs curry leaves
2 red chilies, sliced
4 teaspoons Roasted Curry Powder
   (page 148)
1 in (2 1/2 cm) cinnamon stick
1 teaspoon salt
1 lb (500 g) green mangoes, peeled
   and cut into long, thick pieces
1/3 cup (100 ml) thin coconut milk
4 teaspoons mustard seeds
3 tablespoons vinegar
3/4 cup (200 ml) thick coconut milk
1 tablespoon sugar

Heat the oil in a pan and sauté the onion, garlic, ginger, curry leaves, and red chilies until onion is soft.

Add the curry powder, cin-namon, salt, mango, and thin coconut milk. Bring to a boil and simmer until the mango is just tender, about 10 minutes.

Eggplant Pickle (above) and
Tempered Eggplant (below)

Meanwhile, grind the mustard with a little vinegar to a paste. Stir the mustard paste into the thick coconut milk and, when the mango is tender, add the mustard and thick coconut milk, and the sugar, to the curry.

Bring to a boil, reduce the heat, and simmer for about 5 minutes. Adjust the seasoning. The gravy should be thick enough to thoroughly coat the mango.

Beef Smore

A dish of Dutch origin, beef smore appears in various guises throughout the region, wherever the Dutch maintained a presence. In Sri Lanka, beef smore is a real treat—a whole beef filet or loin which is slowly simmered in a spicy coconut milk gravy and then sliced and served in its own gravy. Eat with rice or breads of your choice.

  - 1 lb (500 g) whole beef filet or loin
  - 2 tablespoons distilled vinegar
  - Salt and pepper to taste
  - 2 tablespoons ghee or vegetable oil for sautéing
  - 2 sprigs curry leaves
  - 2 in (5 cm) pandanus leaf (*rampe*), sliced
  - 1 in (2¹/₂ cm) lemongrass, finely sliced
  - 1 shallot or Bombay onion, sliced
  - 3 green chilies, deseeded and finely sliced
  - ¹/₂ teaspoon chili powder
  - 1 cup (250 ml) coconut milk

Pierce the beef all over with a fork or skewer and marinate in vinegar, salt and pepper for 2 to 4 hours.

Heat the ghee or oil very hot and sear the beef until lightly brown on all sides. This seals the meat and helps to retain the juices. Remove the meat from the pan and set aside.

To the same pan add the curry leaves, pandanus leaf, lemongrass, Bombay onions, and green chilies. Fry until half cooked, about 3 minutes. Add the chili powder and mix well. Return the beef to the pan and add the coconut milk. Stir well and simmer until the coconut milk reduces into a thick gravy and the meat is done to your liking, about 25–35 minutes.

Remove from the heat, slice the meat into the desired thickness, and pour the gravy over the slices.

Thora Malu Istuwa

Seer Fish Lemon Stew

Seer, or Spanish mackerel, is arguably Sri Lanka's tastiest fish. Certainly it is one of the most popular with visitors, many of whom are accustomed to seeing it listed on the menu as pan-fried. There are, however, many other ways to bring out its delicious flavors, such as in this delicate stew recipe.

  - 1 lb (500 g) Spanish mackerel (*seer*) filets (substitute with kingfish or cod)

Beef Smore

  - Salt and pepper to taste
  - 1 teaspoon ground white pepper
  - 5 tablespoons vegetable oil
  - 3 Bombay or large red onions, 1 chopped and 2 sliced into rings
  - 2 in (6 cm) pandanus leaf (*rampe*), sliced
  - 2 sprigs curry leaves
  - 4 cloves garlic, finely chopped
  - 2 green chilies, finely sliced
  - 4 pods cardamom, crushed
  - ¹/₂ teaspoon fenugreek seeds
  - 1 in (2¹/₂ cm) lemongrass, finely sliced
  - 2 teaspoons coriander powder
  - 1 teaspoon cumin powder
  - ¹/₂ teaspoon turmeric powder
  - 1 cup (250 ml) coconut milk
  - Juice of 1 lemon

Season the fish filets with salt and pepper. Heat the oil until hot in a large sauté pan and sear the filets to firm the flesh, then set aside.

Reheat the oil and add the chopped onion (not the onion rings), pandanus leaf, curry leaves, garlic, green chilies, cardamom pods, fenugreek, and lemongrass. Sauté over medium heat until fragrant.

Add the coriander, cumin, and turmeric, and sauté until the oils are released and their aroma is strong. Add the coconut milk and bring to a boil. Lower the heat and add the onion rings and the fish filets. Simmer until the onion rings and fish filets are tender, about 15 minutes. Remove from heat. Cool slightly and add lemon juice to taste.

Seer Fish Lemon Stew

Balaya Ambulthiyal

Sour Claypot Fish

The southwestern coastal town of Ambalangoda first made this dish famous. A classic example of claypot cookery, the tamarind both imparts its characteristic sharp taste and also acts as a preservative. Even in Sri Lanka's heat and humidity, an *ambulthiyal* can keep for up to a week. Serve with plain rice.

  - 1 tablespoon tamarind pulp soaked in 4 tablespoons water
  - 1 lb (500 g) tuna or other firm fish
  - Juice of 1 lime
  - 4 teaspoons chili powder
  - 1 teaspoon ground pepper
  - Salt to taste
  - ¹/₂ cup (125 ml) water
  - 6 cloves
  - 1 slice of ginger
  - 5 cloves of garlic
  - 1 sprig curry leaves

Soak the tamarind pulp in 4 tablespoons water, stir and strain, discarding any solids.

Cut the fish into eight pieces, wash them well with the lime juice and arrange the pieces in a single layer in a pan.

Blend the tamarind water, chili powder, pepper, salt, and a little water to a paste. Mix this paste with the fish in the pan, coating each piece thoroughly. Add the cloves, ginger, garlic, curry leaves, and the water, and bring to a boil. Simmer until all the gravy has reduced and the fish pieces are quite dry, about 15 minutes.

Elumas Curry
Spicy Lamb Curry

- 2 tablespoons oil
- 3 1/2 oz (100 g) onion, chopped
- 5 cloves garlic, chopped
- 1 oz (25 g) chopped ginger
- 2 green chilies, chopped
- 4 in (10 cm) lemongrass
- 1 in (2 1/2 cm) cinnamon stick
- 2–3 cardamom pods, crushed
- 1 lb (500 g) lamb, cubed
- 6 teaspoons Roasted Curry Powder (page 148)
- 3 teaspoons chili powder
- 2 teaspoons turmeric powder
- 2 teaspoons ground pepper
- 2 large tomatoes, chopped
- 3/4 cup (200 ml) thick coconut milk
- Salt to taste

Sauté the onions, garlic, ginger, green chilies, lemongrass, cinnamon, and cardamoms in oil until the onions are golden brown.

Add the lamb and stir well to coat, then add the curry, chili, and tumeric powders, the pepper, and the tomatoes. Cook on medium heat until the meat becomes tender, about 40 minutes. Add the thick coconut milk, bring to a boil and simmer a few minutes longer, adjust the seasoning, and serve.

Urumas Curry
Pork Curry

- 2 tablespoons oil
- 3 1/2 oz (100 g) onion, chopped
- 1 oz (25 g) garlic, chopped
- 1 oz (25 g) ginger, chopped
- 1/3 oz (10 g) lemongrass, chopped
- 1 lb (500 g) pork, cubed
- 2 teaspoons tamarind pulp soaked in 2 tablespoons water, stirred and strained
- 1 3/4 cups (400 ml) water
- 2 sprigs curry leaves
- 4 teaspoons Roasted Curry Powder (page 148)

- 2 teaspoons crushed black pepper
- 2–3 cloves
- 1 in (2 1/2 cm) cinnamon stick

Heat the oil in a pan and sauté the onions, garlic, ginger, and lemongrass until the onions are golden brown.
Add all the remaining ingredients, and bring to a boil. Reduce the heat and simmer in an uncovered pot until the gravy is thick and the pork tender, about 25 minutes.

Crab Curry

Sri Lankan crab is famous throughout the region and rightly so. Fresh crabs, so plentiful in the seas here, are simmered to perfection in a spiced coconut curry gravy. Delicious!

- 4 large crabs
- 3 1/2 oz (100 g) red onion, sliced
- 2 green chilies, chopped
- 3 1/2 tablespoons Roasted Curry Powder (page 148)
- 2 teaspoons turmeric powder
- 1/2 teaspoon chili powder
- 1 teaspoon fenugreek
- 2 teaspoons tamarind pulp soaked in 2 tablespoons water, stirred and strained
- 1 sprig curry leaves
- 2 cups (500 ml) water
- 4 cups (1 liter) thick coconut milk
- 1/2 teaspoon mustard powder
- Juice of 1 lime
- Salt and pepper to taste

Clean the crabs, divide each into 4 portions, and place in a large pan. Add all the other ingredients except the coconut milk, mustard powder, lime juice, and salt.

Bring to a boil then add the coconut milk, return the mixture to simmering point, and simmer gently for 20 minutes. Add the lime juice, mustard powder, and salt, and stir for a few minutes until flavors are married. Remove from the heat and serve hot.

Spicy Lamb Curry (above) and Pork Curry (below)

Bibikkan
Mixed Spice Coconut Slices

This dessert hails from the kitchens of the Portuguese colonial era.

- 2 lb (1 kg) grated fresh coconut
- 1 1/2 cups (375 ml) coconut milk
- 2 lb (1 kg) jaggery or dark brown sugar
- 1 lb (500 g) caster sugar
- 3 1/2 oz (100 g) all-purpose (plain) flour
- 7 oz (200 g) cashew nuts, chopped
- 2 teaspoons mixed cloves, cardamom, and cinnamon powder
- 1/2 teaspoon salt
- 2 teaspoons grated lemon rind

Preheat oven to 325°F (160°C, gas mark 3). Dissolve the jaggery (or brown sugar) and caster sugar in the coconut milk. Place this liquid into a pan, add the salt and bring to a boil. Add the coconut pulp and cook until mixture is sticky but not burnt.

Remove from the heat and slowly stir in the flour, mixing well. Stir in the cashews and mixed spices. Add the lemon rind and pour into a 9 in x 12 in (22 1/2 cm x 30 cm) pan. Bake until done, about 30 minutes. The cake will be done when a toothpick pushed into the center has no batter sticking to it as it is withdrawn. Cool and cut into slices.

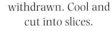

Crab Curry

THAILAND

From the Kingdom of Sukhothai comes a cuisine that
balances the sweet and the sour with the hot and the salty.

Left: Floating markets, where everything you might need is piled onto a boat and paddled along rivers and canals.

Right: A woman winnowing wheat.

The Thais have a saying, *gan gin gan yu*—as you eat, so you are, which perfectly encapsulates their approach to food. Whether Thai cuisine comes about because of the fresh ingredients used, or the meticulous act of preparation, or the seasoning or garnishing is immaterial; Thai food has an elegance and refinement that is all its own. The only country in Southeast Asia to remain independent during the era of colonization, Thailand's blends of hot and sweet, sour and salty are different from the dishes of its neighbors, even though they may use some of the same ingredients: chili, garlic, lemongrass, fish sauce, palm sugar, and lime.

It is easy to see an analogy between the various aspects of Thai culture, including its cuisine. One of the most notable characteristics of Thai decorative art, for instance, is its passion for intricate detail, particularly apparent in complex mosaics of colored glass and porcelain that adorn so many religious buildings. From afar, these suggest a solid, seamless pattern; only on closer inspection are the separate components revealed, and the skillful way they have been put together. So, too, in Thai cuisine, a wide variety of elements has been brought together and artfully composed into something that is intrinsically quite special.

The Land and its People

A stone tablet credited to King Ramkhamhaeng of Sukhothai, the first independent Thai kingdom founded in the early 13th century, bears the couplet: "In the water there are fish, in the fields there is rice." This testifies to a natural abundance that was to sustain a series of capital cities along the length of the fertile Chao Phraya River valley and, more specifically, to the two mainstays of the Thai diet then and now. Rice culture came with the earliest settlers, long before the Thais themselves arrived on the scene, and led to a vast complex of paddy fields watered by an intricate system of canals, rivers and reservoirs. Fish were plentiful, not only in the waterways, but also in the seas.

Other ingredients were gradually added over the centuries from a wide variety of cultures: from China and India, from Persia (modern-day Iran) and Portugal. Even such a seemingly essential element as the pungent chili was, in fact, from South America. However these ingredients came, though, they were subtly modified and refined into a cuisine that is today distinctively Thai.

Like its cuisine, Thailand encompasses a wide range of topography that covers some 198,500 square miles over some 73 provinces (*changwat*). To the north is a complex system of forested mountain ranges divided by the fertile Ping, Yom, Wang, and Nan river valleys. The northeast consists of a sparsely vegetated, semi-arid plateau that stretches to the Mekong River. The flat central plains, watered by the Chao Phraya River, form one of the richest rice-growing regions on earth. The colorful checkerboard of paddy fields, orchards and vegetable gardens that makes up these plains sustains the greater part of the country's agricultural and industrial growth. The mountainous southern isthmus, extending down to the border with Malaysia, is bordered on one side by the Gulf of Thailand and on the other by the Indian Ocean.

The Thais are an agricultural people. Even today, despite the growth of urban areas, the great majority of the population can be found in villages; most villagers still derive their living from agriculture. The tropical climate allows year-round cultivation of rice, fruits and

Chilies pinned out in the sun to dry.

vegetables. There are three distinguishable seasons: wet (June to October), cool (November to February), and hot (March to May).

Evidence of settlers dates back to the Paleolithic age some 500,000 years ago. The most extensive prehistoric remains come from the northeast, where a remarkable culture flourished from around 4000 BC. to just after the start of the Christian era. Indian traders later established ports along the southern peninsula, bringing not only Buddhism but numerous cultural and culinary influences. Mon settlers arrived around the same time in the Chao Phraya valley and founded the Dvaravati kingdom, to be replaced eventually by the Khmers.

Between the 7th and 11th centuries, the ethnic Thais, originating as a minority group from the northern parts of Burma and southern China, gradually migrated southward in search of greater independence and fertile land. By the 13th century, the Thais had established themselves in such numbers that they were eventually able to overthrow their Khmer overlords and establish a kingdom of their own.

This kingdom was called Sukhothai (Sanskrit for "Dawn of Happiness"), and though its power lasted less than two centuries, its influence proved far more enduring. Under King Ramkhamhaeng, the Thai alphabet was devised, works of Buddhist art were created and a truly indigenous Thai culture emerged.

Ayuthia, the next capital, began in 1350 as a small city-state on the Chao Phraya River and over the next 400 years became one of the most cosmopolitan cities in Southeast Asia. In this period, first contact was made with Europe and an active trade established with other Asian countries. Ayuthia fell to an invading Burmese army in 1767. King Rama I founded the present Chakri Dynasty in 1782 and moved the capital across the Chao Phraya to what is now Bangkok.

Bangkok prospered and the Chinese immigrants and Western traders who were drawn in large numbers to it helped bring diversity to the new city. By the end of the 19th century, Bangkok was well on its way to becoming a modern, Western-style city—at least in appearance.

The Making of a Cuisine

Little is known about the cooking of Sukhothai, but rice and fish were no doubt major ingredients. Fruits were plentiful, as were mushrooms that grew wild in the forests and a variety of vegetables. One item not present, however, was the chili, which was either brought directly by the Portuguese, who opened relations in 1511, or came via Malacca or India. Simon de la Loubere, who came with a French diplomatic mission in 1687, was struck by the fact that the people ate sparingly. Good salt was rare, and despite its abundance, fresh fish was seldom eaten. Jesuit missionary Nicolas Gervaise noted that *kapi*, the popular fermented shrimp paste, "has such a pungent smell that it nauseates anyone not accustomed to it," and gives perhaps the first general recipe for a typical Thai condiment based on it: "salt, pepper, ginger, cinnamon, cloves, garlic, white onions, nutmeg, and several strongly flavored herbs . . . mixed in considerable quantities with this shrimp paste."

The complex seasonings that we now regard as typical of Thai cuisine, including chilies, were certainly well established by the Rattanakosin, or Bangkok, period. Sir John Bowring regarded the essential sauce *nam prik* as "one of the most appetite-exciting condiments."

Alongside the development of this individual cuisine was a more refined one that prevailed in royal and aristocratic households, "Palace cooking," which focused on subtlety and visual appeal.

The Food of the People

Thai food today may be plain or fancy: a dish can be prepared in a few minutes over a charcoal brazier or require hours of chopping, grinding and carving. It may vary considerably from region to region. Always, though, it remains a singular creation, not quite like any of the influences that have shaped it over the centuries.

In the mountainous north, where borders are shared with Burma and Laos, the cuisine is as distinctive as the handicrafts for which the region is noted. Here, the earliest Thais settled on their migration southward from China, forming first a group of small city-states and then a loose federation known as Lanna, with Chiang Mai as the principal city.

The north has retained much of its native culture: its language, crafts, customs, and food. Instead of the soft-boiled rice of the central region, northerners prefer a steamed glutinous variety, rolled into small balls and dipped into liquid dishes. Curries of the region tend to be thinner, without the coconut milk widely used in central and southern cooking. There is also a distinctive local version of *nam prik ong*, a basic dipping sauce served with raw vegetables and crispy pork skin, as well as a pork sausage called *naem*, eaten plain with rice or mixed into various dishes. When it is in season, the favorite local fruit is the succulent longan, which grows in almost every compound.

The influence of neighboring Burma and Laos is apparent in many northern dishes. The former for the popular khao soi, a curry broth with egg noodles and chicken, pork or beef, and *gaeng hang lay*, a pork curry seasoned with ginger, tamarind, and turmeric; the latter for *nam prik noom*, a sauce with a strong chili-lime flavor, and *ook gai*, a red chicken curry with lemongrass.

Northeastern Thailand was long regarded as remote from the cosmopolitan world of Bangkok—not so much because of geography as a perceptible social prejudice on the part of city dwellers. Isan, as Thais call the northeast, was the poorest of the country's four main regions; its infertile soil and devastating droughts frequently drove farmers to the capital in search of work. The people of Isan have a definite skill for transforming food in ways that show both imagination and ingenuity. Barbecued chicken (*gai yang*) is grilled with lashings of peppery sauce and garlic, while catfish is the base of a delectable curry and *laab* dip is made with raw meat and ground roasted rice. Some of the region's delicacies are unique: grubworms, grasshoppers, ant eggs, snail curry, and fermented fish of exceptional pungency. Increasingly, the less challenging dishes typical of the region have won widespread admiration, and some diners are known to look upon a properly prepared *som tam* (spicy green papaya salad) or *laab* (even spicier minced pork or chicken) as being the true marks of a superior Thai cook. Perhaps because chilies add such character to the most mundane dish, northeasterners tend to use them with greater abandon than Thais of other areas.

Much northeastern cooking reflects the influence of Laos just across the Mekong River—not surprising, since many residents are ethnically Lao. Dill (*pak chee Lao* or "Laotian coriander") is widely used as a garnish, and glutinous rice is preferred. Also of Lao origin and popular on festive occasions is *khanom buang*, a crispy crêpe stuffed with dried shrimp, bean sprouts and other ingredients.

Southern Thailand, by contrast, is nurtured by rain that falls for eight months of the year. Cultivated areas tend to be vast rubber and coconut plantations rather than the rice fields and fruit orchards of the central plains. Coconuts growing plentifully everywhere provide milk for thickening soups and curries, oil for frying and grated flesh as a condiment for many

dishes. Thousands of boats fish the surrounding waters from villages along the coastlines on the Gulf of Thailand and the Indian Ocean, bringing back seafood for local consumption and profitable export.

The south is home to most of Thailand's two million Muslims, its largest religious minority. In other southern places like Songkhla and the island of Phuket, the Chinese predominate. Southern food reflects the cross-pollination. Seafood may be prepared simply, grilled or steamed; or baked in a claypot with thin noodles and garlic; or included as the main component of *tom yam*, the ubiquitous Thai soup laced with lemongrass and chilies. In general, southerners like their food chili-hot, and are fond of the bitter taste of a flat, native bean called *sataw*, which other Thais tend to find less appealing. Small, juicy pineapples are a popular end to a meal.

Contributions from other cultures include *gaeng mussaman*, an Indian-style curry of chicken or beef perfumed with cardamom, cloves and cinnamon; Malay fish curries; and Indonesian satay.

The central plains is the Thai heartland. Here, you'll find the best jasmine rice, pearly white and fragrant, and mangoes, durians, mangosteens, rambutans, guavas, papayas and pomelos, even grapes. Vegetables such as cabbage, mushrooms, water convolvulus (water spinach), cucumber, tomatoes, and pumpkins, as well as more recent introductions like asparagus and baby corn, are grown in vast quantities.

Food in the villages amid the fields tends to be plain: rice with stir-fried vegetables, fish from a nearby canal or river, perhaps some minced chicken with garlic, chilies, and basil and a salad of salted eggs, chilies, and scallion with a squeeze of lime.

In Bangkok, everything is available, even the most exotic regional delicacies, if you know where to look. The city streets are punctuated with the many fast foods based on Chinese noodles, prepared at a moment's notice at any sidewalk café or by vendors who push their carts along residential streets. Tasty, nourishing, occasionally even distinguished, these quick meals epitomize the busy life of Bangkok and also the Thai capacity for making something special out of simple ingredients. Such is its popularity that Thai street food has evolved into a distinctive culinary category all its own, generally characterized by speed of preparation and easy portability of equipment.

Palace Cooking

Dr Malcolm Smith, who served as physician to some members of the Thai royal family in the early years of this century, describes the innermost part of Bangkok's mile-square Grand Palace known as the "Inside," where the women of the court lived, thus: "A town complete in itself, a congested network of houses and narrow streets, with gardens, lawns, artificial lakes, and shops. It had its own government, its own institutions, its own laws and law-courts. It was a town of women, controlled by women."

At its peak, during the reign of King Rama V (Chulalongkorn), the "Inside" had a population estimated at nearly 3000, a select few of them bearing the exalted rank of Queen but the great majority ladies-in-waiting and lower attendants. The inner palace can be viewed as a kind of ultra-exclusive finishing school where the most refined aristocratic skills were perfected and passed on.

The royal women learned how to prepare various foods that were not merely more subtle in flavor than their outside versions, but highly memorable in visual appeal. The most visible of palace skills was the art of fruit and vegetable carving, garnishes and delicacies that sometimes required as long to prepare as the dishes that they adorned.

The hallmarks of so-called "palace food"—which was, in fact, to be found in most aristocratic homes as well—were painstaking hours of preparation and a highly refined style of presentation. *Foi thong*, for instance, is a blend of egg yolks and sugar transformed into a nest of silky golden threads, while *look choop* are tiny imitation fruits shaped by hand from a mixture of sweet bean paste and coconut milk, tinted to exactly match their real-life models.

When royal polygamy ended under King Rama VI, the ladies of the "Inside" and their numerous attendants gradually left their protected existence. Fortunately, palace cooking did not vanish with the hidden world but survived through the descendants of the royal women. In recent years, it has been discovered by a wider public through several restaurants that take pride in their re-creations of this unique cuisine.

The Thai Kitchen and Table

The hospitality and generosity of the shared Thai table is easily achieved in the home. In this section you will find recipes for popular Thai salads, curries, soups, steamed, deep-fried and stir-fried dishes, grilled dishes, desserts, relishes, and accompaniments. When cooking, try to use only the freshest ingredients. Taste as you go along, and aim to balance the flavors and textures within the dish and between the compilation of dishes to be served.

Rice is the mainstay of Thai meals, mostly steamed long-grain jasmine rice, a nod to the traditions and ritual of its cultivation. All other dishes—salads, curries, soups—are called *gap kao*, to be served with rice; they are mere condiments. There is no set progression of dishes; all main course dishes are served at once. When cooking for a gathering of four, rather than increase the quantity of a single dish, do as the Thais do and increase the variety of dishes: perhaps a soup, a curry, a salad, a steamed dish, and a selection of relishes. Diners are free to help themselves, in any order they want, mixing dishes at will and seasoning them with a wide variety of condiments to achieve the desired taste.

The ideal Thai meal is a harmonious blend of the spicy, sweet, hot, wet, mild, crisp, sour, and soft, and is meant to be satisfying to the eye, nose, and palate. Complex dishes are accompanied by simpler ones: the richness of this dish may be cut by the piquancy of that, the saltiness of this recipe is a perfect foil for another. As a result the palate is not overwhelmed; there is give and take. The Thais call this harmonious layering of flavor upon flavor *rot chart*—the heart and soul of true Thai cuisine.

Many Thai desserts are based on glutinous rice, coconut milk, palm sugar, pandan leaf, and agar-agar, but the most common dessert is one or more of the abundant fresh fruits, usually brought out after the other dishes have been removed. On special occasions, more elaborate desserts such as *foi thong* (golden threads) or banana-leaf cups of *takaw*, a confection of tapioca starch, sugar and coconut that comes in a wide variety of forms, may be served.

Snacks are so popular in Thailand they deserve special mention. They may consist of nothing more than freshly sliced fruit sprinkled with salt, sugar, dried chilies or a combination of these seasonings. Or they may be a selection of traditional sweets. Some vendors offer noodle creations. To produce the universally popular *kwayteow*, a bowl of freshly cooked rice noodles is given a few ladles of meat stock, topped with cooked pork or chicken, and sprinkled with sugar, crushed peanuts, and dried chili flakes. For *pad thai*, noodles are quickly stir-fried with garlic, scallions, salted dried shrimp, and a variety of spices. Whether eaten in a restaurant, on a city sidewalk, on the open verandah of a farm house, even in the middle of a rice field at harvest time, a Thai meal is nearly always a social affair.

Kantoke, a meal taken while seated at a low round table, is a traditional way of dining in the north of Thailand.

SUGGESTED MENUS

Family meals

For a simple family meal, try serving steamed jasmine rice with:
• Spicy Shrimp Soup with Lemongrass (page 160);
•Dry Beef Curry (page165) and Kale with Crispy Pork (page164);
• finish with Bananas in Coconut Milk (page 168);

or

• Green Papaya Salad (page 162);
• Red Chicken Curry with Bamboo Shoots (page 165) served with rice;
• fresh fruit like jackfruit, mango, or rambutan.

A dinner party

For a stylish dinner party, serve:
• Patty Shells with Minced Chicken (page 158) for a stunning canapé;
• Spicy Pomelo Salad (page 162), the elegant River Fish with Chili Sauce (page 166) and Roast Duck Curry (page 165);
• glittering Red Rubies (page 168) as a palate cleanser.

Finger food

The appetizers in this section make particularly good finger food—try the following at your next party or picnic:
• Pork and Shrimp Rolls (page 158);
• Chicken Fried in Pandan Leaves (page 158);
• Steamed Seafood Cakes (page 159).

A melting pot menu

For a refined but simple Asian tasting menu:
• Shrimp Mousse on Sugar Cane (page 177) from Vietnam as a starter;
• Indonesian Pork in Sweet Soy Sauce (page 79) with Stir-fried Mixed Vegetables (page 40) from China combine well for a main course that is not too heavy;
• Red Bean Pancakes (page 46), also from China, are a delicious dessert with which to finish.

THE ESSENTIAL FLAVORS OF THAI COOKING

Thai cuisine uses the redolent **fish sauce** in almost everything besides desserts. The curries are built on subtle blends of **cilantro**, **lemongrass**, **galangal**, **chilies**, and **kaffir lime leaf** and **rind**. Other typically Thai flavors include **Thai sweet basil** (*horapa*), **ginger**, **shrimp paste,** and **tamarind**. **Coconut milk** and **palm sugar** are added to curries and sweets. Staples you will need include **jasmine** and **glutinous rice**.

Thai people love good food, and the emphasis on quality applies to both palace cuisine and street food. An array of sweetmeats and treats is available —Thais seem to find it more satisfactory to eat a little of this and a little of that— along the *klongs* and sidewalks, and outside offices and shopping centres. The ready-to-eat delicacies may include barbecued or grilled food on or off skewers, salads, noodle soups, wrapped in dough or edible leaves, or be a sweet. Here are a few dishes that would work well as finger food.

Filling

2 tablespoons peanut or corn oil
4 tablespoons finely diced onion
2 cups (200 g) cooked chicken or pork, finely chopped
1/4 cup (60 ml) corn kernels (sweetcorn)
2 tablespoons finely diced carrot
2 tablespoons sugar
1/4 teaspoon black soy sauce
1/2 teaspoon salt
1/2 teaspoon white pepper
Cilantro (coriander) leaves for garnish
1 red chili, finely sliced

Pork and Shrimp Rolls (left) and Patty Shells with Minced Chicken (right)

Krathong Thong
Patty Shells with Minced Chicken

The delicate crisp shells used for this snack are made using a special brass mould. Thin short-crust pastry shells or even *vol-au-vent* cases can be used instead. The recipe makes 20–25 cups.

Patty Shells

1/2 cup (80 g) rice flour
6 tablespoons all-purpose (plain) flour
4 tablespoons thin coconut milk
2 tablespoons tapioca flour
1 egg yolk
1/4 teaspoon sugar
1/4 teaspoon salt
1/4 teaspoon baking soda (bicarbonate of soda)
4 cups (1 liter) peanut or corn oil

Make the patty shells first by mixing all ingredients, except oil, together in a bowl. Heat the oil, then dip the *krathong* mold in the oil to heat up. Dip the mold into the batter and plunge back into oil. Fry for about 5 minutes until light brown, then shake to remove the cup from the mold. Place on paper towels to drain. Repeat to make 20 to 25 cups.

Now make the filling. Put the oil in a hot wok and stir fry onion and pork or chicken for 2 minutes. Add the rest of the ingredients and fry for about 3 minutes until the vegetables are fairly soft. Leave them to cool, then divide the filling among the patty shells. Garnish with cilantro leaves and slices of fresh red chili.

Tong Geon Yong
Pork and Shrimp Rolls

The Chinese influence is evident in the use of dried beancurd skin. The filling can be made in advance and the rolls assembled just before frying.

4 oz (125 g) shrimp, finely chopped
4 oz (125 g) pork, finely chopped
1 tablespoon light soy sauce
1 teaspoon each of cilantro (coriander) root, garlic and peppercorn, pounded together
Squares of dried beancurd skin (available in Asian food markets)
4 cups (1 liter) corn oil
1 scallion (spring onion), separated, tying (optinal)

Mix shrimp and pork together with soy sauce and the pounded ingredients. Wipe sheets of dried beancurd skin with a moist cloth to soften. Cut circles about 4 1/2 in (11 cm) in diameter and place a little filling in the center. Squeeze in the sides to make a bundle and tie with a strip of scallion.

Alternatively, cut beancurd skin into 4 x 6 in (10 x 15 cm) squares. Put a spoonful of the filling in the middle and roll up like a cigar, tucking in the ends.

Deep-fry the rolls in hot oil over medium heat until golden brown. Serve with soy sauce or plum sauce.

Gai Hor Bai Toey
Chicken Fried in Pandan Leaves

If the pandan leaves are unavailable the chicken can be stir-fried and served with steamed rice.

2 lb (1 kg) chicken thighs
20 pandan leaves
Oil for deep-frying

Marinade

2 tablespoons light soy sauce
2 tablespoons oyster sauce
1 teaspoon sugar
2 teaspoons sesame oil
1 teaspoon each garlic and cilantro (coriander) root, pounded together to a paste

Sauce

1 cup (250 ml) distilled white vinegar
1/2 cup (100 g) sugar
2 tablespoons black soy sauce
1 teaspoon white sesame seeds, fried
1/4 teaspoon salt

Debone chicken and cut thighs into 4 pieces. Mix marinade and marinate the chicken meat for 3 hours. Mix sauce ingredients together and set aside.

Wrap two or three pieces of chicken with pandan leaves to form a bundle (see photo). Deep-fry until fragrant. Serve with dipping sauce and steamed rice.

Chicken Fried in Pandan Leaves

Haw Mok Thalay
Steamed Seafood Cakes

This fragrant mixture of seafood, coconut milk, and seasonings is steamed in small cups made of banana leaf. It is possible to use small ramekins or any other small heat-proof dishes as a substitute.

3/4 cup (180 ml) coconut cream
1 teaspoon rice flour
4 oz (100 g) filleted fish, cut into thin slices
4 oz (100 g) shrimp, peeled and cleaned
4 oz (100 g) squid, cleaned and cut into 2-in (5-cm) pieces
2 eggs, beaten
2 tablespoons fish sauce
1 1/4 cups (300 ml) thin coconut milk
1/2 cup (20 g) finely chopped basil leaves (*horapa*)
2 tablespoons shredded kaffir lime leaves
Cilantro (coriander) leaves to garnish
1 finely sliced red chili
Banana leaf cups 2 in (5 cm) square, or individual ramekins

Spice Paste
5 dried chilies, soaked in water and deseeded
3 cloves garlic
2 tablespoons finely sliced galangal
1 teaspoon grated kaffir lime rind
2 teaspoons finely sliced cilantro (coriander) root
5 black peppercorns
1/2 teaspoon salt
1 teaspoon shrimp paste
1 teaspoon finely sliced *krachai*, optional

Pound the spice paste ingredients well in a mortar or process in a blender.

Mix coconut cream with the rice flour and bring to a boil, stirring until thickened. Remove from the heat, cool and set aside for topping.

Mix the spice paste with the fish, shrimp, squid, egg, fish sauce, and then add the remaining coconut milk, a little at a time. Add half the basil and kaffir lime leaves and mix in.

Place one of the remaining basil leaves in the bottom of each cup, top with the fish mixture, cover and steam for 15 minutes. Remove the cups from steamer, and top each one with a little of the boiled coconut cream, cilantro leaf, kaffir lime leaf, and sliced chili. Return to the steamer, cook for 1 more minute, then remove from the steamer.

Sakuna Chomsuan
Shrimps with Sweet and Sour Sauce

A simple but always popular appetizer. The shrimp can be prepared in advance and deep-fried just before serving. Use your favorite sweet and sour sauce for dipping or the one on page 187.

1 lb (500 g) large shrimp
2 eggs, lightly beaten
4 cups (300 g) fine breadcrumbs
Cooking oil for deep-frying

Peel the shrimp, discard the heads but leave on the tail sections. Slit down the back of each shrimp, remove the intestinal tract and flatten the shrimp into a butterfly shape by pressing gently with the hand. Dip the shrimp in the egg and breadcrumbs. Deep-fry until golden and serve with sweet and sour sauce.

Chor Ladda
Dumplings with Minced Pork and Shrimp

The surprising but brilliant color of these delicate dumplings is obtained by soaking a blue flower (*anchun*), although commercial food coloring can be substituted.

Filling
1/2 cup (80 g) roasted unsalted peanuts, chopped
1/2 teaspoon salt
2 tablespoons sugar
1/2 cup (80 g) minced pork
3/4 cup (100 g) minced shrimp
1 cup (100 g) chopped salted radish
2 tablespoons cooking oil

Dumplings
1/4 cup (30 g) tapioca flour
About 2 tablespoons dried *anchun* flowers or 1/2 teaspoon blue food coloring
2 cups (250 g) rice flour
1/4 cup (60 ml) coconut milk
2 tablespoons cooking oil
1/4 cup (60 ml) water
1/2 cup (125 ml) coconut cream
Banana leaf or aluminum foil

Stir-fry all the filling ingredients together in oil until cooked and let cool.

Make the dumplings by mixing all ingredients together. Cook over low heat, stirring constantly, until the mixture turns into an elastic dough. Cover with plastic wrap while making the individual dumplings to prevent the dough from drying out.

Pinch off a small ball of dough and flatten into a circle about 2 1/2 in (6 cm) in diameter. Place a teaspoonful of stuffing in the center of the dough and pinch edges together to enclose. Use special tongs or pinch to give the dumplings a flower shape. Place on an oiled banana leaf or aluminum foil and put about 1 teaspoon of coconut cream over the top of each dumpling to prevent it from drying out.

Steam dumplings for 8 minutes until cooked. Serve warm on a bed of crisp-fried golden garlic and top with coconut cream.

HELPFUL HINT

In Thailand, a pair of miniature tongs with serrations on the inside is used to pinch the dough to create the "petals." Failing such an esoteric utensil, use your fingers to pinch the dough into a decorative shape.

Shrimps with Sweet and Sour Sauce

Thai soups are usually light, accentuated with fresh aromatics, and have the four main flavors—hot, sour, sweet, and salty. They are drunk throughout a meal, but make a perfectly acceptable first course to a dinner party with an Asian theme.

Gaeng Som
Sour Soup with Vegetables and Shrimps

Sour but fragrant tamarind juice adds a special touch to this relatively mild soup, which is full of vegetables and flavored with pounded shrimps or fish. As with other types of *gaeng*, this has very little liquid.

- $3/4$ lb (400 g) shrimp or fish fillets
- 3 cups (750 ml) water
- $1/4$ lb (125 g) straw mushrooms
- 1 large white radish, sliced
- $1/2$ cup (80 g) sliced green papaya
- $1/2$ cup (60 g) green beans, cut in 1-in ($2^1/2$-cm) pieces
- $2/3$ cup (60 g) cauliflower, broken into florets
- 1 cup (60 g) Chinese white cabbage, cut into 1-in ($2^1/2$ cm) pieces
- 4 tablespoons tamarind juice
- 2 tablespoons lime juice (optional)
- 1 tablespoon chopped palm sugar
- 1 teaspoon salt

Spice Paste

- 3 dried chilies, soaked until soft
- 2 teaspoons finely chopped *krachai* (optional)
- 2 teaspoons finely chopped garlic
- 2 teaspoons finely chopped shallots

Simmer the shrimp or fish fillets in 3 cups of water until cooked. Allow to cool in the stock, then peel the shrimp or remove any bones from the fish. Keep all the remaining stock and set aside.

Pound or process the fish or shrimp until well mashed and set aside. Pound or blend the spice paste ingredients, then put in a pan with the reserved stock, shrimp or fish, and vegetables. Bring to a boil and simmer until just cooked. Add the tamarind juice, lime juice, sugar, and salt to taste.

Any combination of vegetables can be used; suggested alternatives include chayote (christophene), any other summer squash or zucchini (courgette), eggplant (aubergine), green cabbage, and button mushrooms.

Tom Yam Goong
Spicy Shrimp Soup with Lemongrass

- 4 cups (1 liter) chicken stock (page 169)
- 3 kaffir lime leaves
- 2 in (5 cm) galangal, sliced
- 3 stems lemongrass
- 6–8 medium to large shrimp
- 5 oz (150 g) straw mushrooms
- 5 green and red bird's-eye chilies
- 3 tablespoons lime juice, or to taste
- $1/2$ tablespoon fish sauce, or to taste
- 3 bunches cilantro (coriander) leaves
- 3–4 cilantro (coriander) roots, washed (optional)

Bring the stock to a boil, add galangal, kaffir lime leaves, cilantro roots, and lemon grass. Simmer for 15 minutes. Add the shrimps, mushrooms, and chilies, and simmer for 3 minutes. Add the lime juice and fish sauce to taste. The soup should be spicy-sour and a little salty. Serve garnished with fresh cilantro.

Gaeng Jued Woon Sen
Clear Soup with Glass Noodles

- 10 oz (300 g) ground pork
- $1/2$ teaspoon light soy sauce

Sour Soup with Vegetables and Shrimps

- $1/4$ teaspoon white pepper powder
- 4 cups (1 liter) chicken stock (page 169)
- 3 white peppercorns, crushed
- 5 cloves garlic, crushed
- 4 oz (100 g) cellophane (glass) noodles, soaked in warm for 5 minutes
- 1 teaspoon fish sauce
- 6 dried mushrooms, soaked in water to soften, roughly chopped
- $1/4$ teaspoon sugar
- 3 scallions (spring onions), cut into $1/2$ -in (1-cm) pieces
- 2 tablespoons chopped cilantro (coriander)

Mix the pork, soy sauce, and white pepper together. Form into roughly shaped, small meatballs.

Heat the chicken stock, add crushed peppercorns and garlic, and bring to a boil. Place the meatballs in the boiling stock and add the noodles, fish sauce, mushrooms, and sugar. Simmer until meatballs are cooked. Add scallion and cilantro and remove from heat immediately. Serve with rice.

Clear Soup with Glass Noodles (left) and Mixed Vegetable Soup (right)

Gaeng Noppakao
Mixed Vegetable Soup

This is less a soup in the Western sense than vegetables, with a little pork, chicken, and shrimp, simmered in seasoned stock.

5 cups mixed vegetables, such as summer squash or zucchini (courgette), pumpkin, straw mushrooms, baby corn, green beans, cut into bite-sized pieces
5 oz (150 g) lean pork, thinly sliced
5 oz (150 g) chicken, very thinly sliced
5 oz (150 g) shrimp, peeled but with tails left intact
4 cups (1 liter) chicken stock (page 169)
2 tablespoons fish sauce
1 cup (40 g) lemon basil (*manglak*) leaves

Seasoning
10 black peppercorns
1/2 tablespoon shrimp paste
10 shallots
1/4 cup (40 g) dried shrimps

Place seasoning ingredients in a mortar or blender and pound or blend until fine. Add to chicken stock and bring to a boil, stirring to prevent sticking. Add the vegetables, pork, chicken and shrimp and simmer until just cooked. Season to taste with fish sauce or salt, then remove from heat. Add basil and serve.

Tom Kha Gai
Spicy Chicken Soup with Coconut Milk

A delightful soup, creamy with coconut milk and redolent with the flavor of galangal, kaffir lime, and lemongrass. Vary the amount of chilies according to taste. Cook gently to prevent the coconut milk from separating.

1 cup (250 ml) chicken stock (page 169)
2 stems lemongrass
2 in (5 cm) galangal
3 kaffir lime leaves, torn into small pieces
3/4 lb (400 g) chicken, cut into 1/2 -in (1-cm) strips
4 oz (100 g) straw mushrooms
1 teaspoon salt
4 tablespoons lime juice
3 tablespoons fish sauce
1/2 teaspoon sugar
3 cups (750 ml) coconut milk
6 red bird's-eye chilies, bruised

Place the stock in a pot, add the lemongrass, galangal, and kaffir lime leaves. Bring to a boil over medium heat. Add the chicken, mushrooms, salt, lime juice, fish sauce, and sugar. Cook slowly, uncovered, for 10 minutes, then add coconut milk and chilies. Bring almost to a boil, stirring frequently, then remove from heat and serve.

Rice Noodles with Fish Curry Sauce

Kanom Jeen Nam Yaa
Rice Noodles with Fish Curry Sauce

Because of their length, *kanom jeen* noodles are commonly served at family ceremonies; they are never broken until served and signify long life.

Sauce
7 shallots, coarsely chopped
2 cloves garlic
2 slices galangal
2 tablespoons sliced lemongrass
1 cup (150 g) minced *krachai* (optional)
3 dried chilies, seeds removed
1 teaspoon salt
1 teaspoon shrimp paste
1 cup (250 ml) water

Stock
1 small, well-flavored fish, about 1/2 lb (250 g)
4 1/2 cups (1 1/8 liters) coconut milk
1/2 cup (250 ml) coconut cream
2–3 tablespoons fish sauce

Accompaniments
2 lb (1 kg) fresh rice noodles (*kanom jeen*) or fresh angel-hair pasta
2 hard-boiled eggs, peeled and quartered
1/2 cup (75 g) sliced cabbage
1/2 cup (90 g) sliced cucumber
1/2 cup (50 g) blanched beansprouts

1 small bunch lemon basil (*manglak*)
1 tablespoon ground dried chilies

Place all sauce ingredients in a pot and simmer over low heat until soft. Remove from heat, cool, place in mortar or blender and pound or blend until fine.

Prepare the stock next. Wash and clean the fish, removing head, and simmer in just enough water to cover until soft. Drain and save the water in which the fish was boiled. Remove the meat from the fish, add to the sauce in the mortar or blender and pound or blend to mix thoroughly.

Put the sauce into a pot and add the coconut milk. Bring to a boil, then add the fish broth and fish sauce. Simmer, stirring regularly to prevent sticking, until the sauce has thickened and the surface glistens bright red. Add the coconut cream and remove from heat.

Arrange a portion of the rice noodles and a little of each of the accompaniments in individual bowls. Spoon the sauce over just before serving.

Spicy Chicken Soup with Coconut Milk

Most Thai salads are hot and sour, and like most of Thai cooking, call for the use of copious amounts of fresh herbs and greens. You can vary the combination of greens and spices, or perhaps combine aspects of several recipes to provide a modern twist. It is important to balance the flavors of the dressing.

Khao Yam Pak Tai
Southern-style Rice Salad

This is a popular way of using left-over rice and makes an ideal light lunch. The seasonings added to the rice can be varied according to taste and availability.

- 2 cups (320 g) cold cooked rice
- 2 cups (180 g) grated coconut, browned in an oven for 5–8 minutes
- 1 small pomelo or grapefruit, sectioned
- 1 small green mango, shredded (optional)
- 1/2 cup (80 g) dried shrimp, chopped
- 1/2 cup (50 g) beansprouts
- 1/2 cup (80 g) finely sliced lemongrass
- 1/4 cup (25 g) sliced green beans
- 1 egg, beaten, cooked into an omelet and shredded
- 2 dried red chilies, pounded
- 1 tablespoon very finely shredded kaffir lime leaf
- 1 tablespoon chopped fresh cilantro (coriander)

- 4 oz (100 g) cooked shrimps as garnish (optional)
- Lime wedges

Sauce
- 1 cup (250 ml) water
- 2 tablespoons chopped anchovies in brine
- 1 tablespoon chopped palm sugar
- 2 kaffir lime leaves, torn into small pieces
- 1/2 in (1 cm) lemongrass, very finely sliced

Put all the sauce ingredients in pan, bring to a boil and simmer for 5 minutes. Remove from heat, strain and set aside.

Place the rice in small bowls, each holding about half a cup. Press down then invert onto a large serving platter. Arrange the rest of raw ingredients around the edge of rice in separate piles.

To eat, spoon some rice onto individual plates and take a little of each ingredient to mix with the rice according to taste. Spoon the sauce over the top.

HELPFUL HINT

Canned anchovies packed in Europe make an acceptable substitute for the preserved Thai variety. If the very fine dried shrimps used in Thailand are not available, substitute with packaged fish floss.

Southern-style Rice Salad

Som Tam Thai
Green Papaya Salad

Originally an Isan dish from the northeast, this salad is now prepared by roadside hawkers all over the country. *Som tam* captures the essential flavors of Thailand: chili hot, redolent with garlic and fish sauce, and sour with lime juice. Prepare the salad just before eating.

- 7 green bird's-eye chilies
- 10 oz (300 g) unripe green papaya, peeled and cut in very fine matchsticks
- 5 cloves garlic
- 1/2 cup (50 g) long beans, cut in 1/2-in (1-cm) pieces
- 2 tablespoons unsalted roasted peanuts
- 1 tablespoon dried shrimp, soaked in warm then chopped
- 6 cherry tomatoes, quartered, or 1 large tomato, in wedges
- 3 tablespoons lime juice
- 1 tablespoon chopped palm sugar
- 1 tablespoon fish sauce

Take a little of the chilies, papaya, and garlic and pound roughly in a mortar and pestle or process briefly in a blender. Set aside in a bowl and repeat until the chilies, papaya, and garlic are used.

Stir in the beans, peanuts, dried shrimp, and tomato, mix well and add the seasonings.

Serve accompanied by raw vegetables such as cabbage, water convolvulus, and sprigs of basil; for a complete meal, add glutinous rice and roasted chicken.

Yam Som-O
Spicy Pomelo Salad

- 1 pomelo or 2 grapefruits
- 2 tablespoons lime juice
- 1 tablespoon fish sauce
- 1 tablespoon sugar
- 1/3 lb (150 g) cooked shrimp
- 2 cups (200 g) cooked chicken breast, shredded
- 2 tablespoons grated fresh or dried coconut
- 1/2 cup (125 ml) coconut cream
- 1 tablespoon dried shrimp, finely chopped

Peel the pomelo and shred the flesh (if using grapefruit, peel and section). Place the lime juice, fish sauce, and sugar in a bowl and stir to mix. Then add the shrimp, chicken, grated coconut, and coconut cream and continue stirring until blended. Add the pomelo and toss to coat thoroughly.

Transfer to serving plate, sprinkle with dried shrimp and serve.

Fried Mixed Vegetables

Pla Nuea Makreua Orn
Beef Salad with Eggplant

This salad also works with left-over roast or grilled beef.

- 3 small round (or 1 long thin) green eggplants (aubergines)
- 3 tablespoons oil
- 10 oz (300 g) uncooked or cooked beef fillet, sliced
- 1 tablespoon sliced shallots
- 5 green bird's-eye chilies, coarsely chopped
- 2 tablespoons lime juice
- 1 tablespoon fish sauce
- 1/4 teaspoon sugar

Cut the eggplant into 1/2-in (1-cm) slices and fry until cooked. Put into a bowl.

If using uncooked beef, sauté in a skillet in a little oil over high heat until done. Combine the beef with the eggplant and the remaining ingredients and mix well. Serve at room temperature with white rice.

Pad Pak Ruam Mit
Fried Mixed Vegetables

This method of cooking vegetables can be used for individual vegetables such as kale or broccoli, or a combination, depending on availability and your preference.

- 1/2 cup (50 g) snow peas
- 2 cups (400 g) chopped young kale
- 3/4 cup (120 g) chopped cabbage
- 3/4 cup (150 g) chopped broccoli
- 1/2 cup (100 g) chopped cauliflower
- 3/4 cup (50 g) sliced mushrooms
- 1/2 cup (50 g) baby sweet corn
- 1/4 cup (60 ml) peanut or corn oil
- 3 tablespoons finely chopped garlic
- 1/2 cup (125 ml) chicken stock (page 169)
- 4 tablespoons oyster sauce
- 1 tablespoon light soy sauce
- 1/4 teaspoon black soy sauce
- 1/2 teaspoon ground white pepper

Cut or slice the vegetables into bite-sized pieces and mix together in a bowl. Plunge them into boiling water for a few seconds to blanch, then drain and set aside.

Heat a wok until lightly smoking and add the oil. When hot, add the garlic and stir well. Add the vegetables and chicken stock all at once and stir fry for about 3 to 4 minutes until just cooked; the vegetables should still be slightly crisp. Add the oyster sauce and soy sauces, then sprinkle with pepper. Mix well and cook for 1 minute. Serve accompanied by rice.

> **HELPFUL HINT**
> Use maximum heat to stir-fry the vegetables to ensure the right texture and flavor.

Savory Stuffed Omelets

Kai Yad Sai
Savory Stuffed Omelets

Frequently found on the menu of simple restaurants as well as at roadside stalls, this is often eaten at lunch time. The omelets can be served individually as entrées.

- 1/4 cup (60 ml) oil
- 4 oz (100 g) ground pork
- 3 tablespoons diced tomatoes
- 3 tablespoons cooked green peas
- 2 tablespoons finely diced onion
- 1/2 tablespoon sugar
- 1 tablespoon fish sauce
- 1/4 teaspoon ground white pepper
- 1/4 teaspoon black soy sauce
- 3 eggs, beaten
- 3 tablespoons chopped cilantro (coriander) leaves
- 1 red chili, sliced

Heat half of the oil in a wok over high heat and stir fry the pork for 2 minutes. Add all the remaining ingredients except for the eggs, cilantro, chili, and remaining oil. Fry until cooked then set aside.

Heat an omelet pan of 6 to 8 in (12 to 20 cm) in diameter, add a drop of the remaining oil. Pour in enough egg to thinly cover the base. Brown the omelet lightly on both sides, flipping over halfway through cooking. Repeat until all the egg is used up.

To stuff the omelets, place a spoonful of pork mixture in the center, fold two opposite sides toward the center and then fold in the remaining sides so that it resembles a square. Put onto a serving plate and repeat until all the egg and pork mixture is used up.

Garnish with cilantro leaves and finely sliced red chili. Serve accompanied by rice.

Taud Man Goong
Deep-fried Shrimp Cakes

Hawkers in coastal towns, especially around Songkhla, Surat Thani and Phuket, offer a similar but highly seasoned snack made with fish (*Taud Man Pla*). This more delicate version is served with a savory accompaniment of pickled vegetables.

- 11/4 lb (600 g) large shrimp
- 5 oz (150 g) lard (hard pork fat)
- 1 teaspoon salt
- 1/2 teaspoon sugar
- 2 cups (500 ml) fresh breadcrumbs
- 4 cups (1 liter) oil

Accompaniment
- 1 cup (250 ml) distilled white vinegar
- 1/2 cup (100 g) sugar
- 5 bird's-eye chilies
- 2 shallots, sliced
- 1 tablespoon finely sliced cauliflower
- 1 tablespoon finely sliced baby corn
- 1 tablespoon sliced small cucumber

To prepare the accompaniment, bring the vinegar and sugar to a boil, then leave to cool. Add all vegetables, mix and set aside.

Chop shrimp and lard together or process in a blender until fine. Add salt, sugar, and breadcrumbs, then shape into patties. Deep-fry in the oil until golden brown and fragrant.

Serve hot with the accompaniment.

> **HELPFUL HINT**
> The accompaniment and shrimp cakes can be prepared in advance. Fry the shrimp cakes just before serving.

Red Pork Curry

In Thailand main cours-es are usually served with rice. The dishes are served at once, and stay on the table throughout the meal. The recipes here serve four as part of a shared meal.

Kana Moo Grob
Kale with Crispy Pork

When making family meals vegetables are frequently cooked with a little meat, poultry or seafood to add flavor and a con-trasting texture. Kale, known in Thailand by its Chinese name, *kai lan*, is enjoyed for its firm stems. If kale is not available, try using broccoli stems.

- 2 lb (1 kg) kale or 1 lb (500 g) broccoli stems
- 3 tablespoons oil
- 1 tablespoon finely chopped garlic
- 10 oz (300 g) crispy pork, diced
- 4 tablespoons oyster sauce
- 1/4 teaspoon salt
- 1/4 teaspoon ground white pepper
- 1 teaspoon sugar
- 1 cup (250 ml) chicken stock (page 169)

Discard the leaves and tough bottom part of the kale stems. Peel the skin off the tender stems and discard. Cut stems in 2 to 3-in (5 to 8-cm) lengths.

Heat the oil in a wok. When it is very hot, fry the garlic until fragrant, then add the kale and crispy pork. Stir to mix well, and then add all the seasonings and stock. Mix well, heat through and then serve immediately.

Roasted pork with a layer of meat, a thin layer of fat and crisp, golden-brown skin, contrasts beautifully in taste and texture with the vegetable. Although unconventional, thick slices of crisp fried bacon make an excel-lent substitute.

Gaeng Ped Moo
Red Pork Curry

Pork is the most popular meat in Thailand. This is a very simple, quickly prepared curry.

- 1/2 cup (125 ml) coconut cream
- 1 tablespoon red curry paste (page 169)
- 12 oz (400 g) pork tender fillet, cut in 1/2-in (1-cm) slices
- 1/3 cup (90 ml) pea-sized eggplants (optional)
- 1 1/2 cups (375 ml) coconut milk
- 1 1/2 tablespoons fish sauce
- 1 1/2 teaspoons sugar
- 5 kaffir lime leaves, halved
- 1 fresh red chili, finely sliced lengthwise
- 1/2 cup (20 g) basil leaves (*horapa*)

Bring the coconut cream to a boil, stirring constantly. Put in the red curry paste, pork, and eggplant, stir well, and cook until done (about 5 minutes).

Add the fish sauce, sugar, kaffir lime leaves, and chili. Stir and heat through, then remove from heat and garnish with basil.

Gaeng Mussaman
Mussaman Beef Curry

Spices such as cardamom and cin-namon were brought to Thailand by Indian Muslim traders. This curry uses the basic Mussaman curry paste and other spices.

Mussaman Beef Curry

- 3 tablespoons Mussaman curry paste (page 169)
- 1/2 cup (125 ml) coconut cream
- 1 lb (500 g) beef sirloin or stewing beef
- 2 cups (500 ml) thin coconut milk
- 5 cardamom seeds, roasted until fragrant
- 1 cinnamon stick about 3 in (8 cm) in length
- 2 medium-sized (200 g) potatoes, peeled and cut into large chunks
- 1 heaped tablespoon unsalted peanuts, chopped
- 10 shallots
- 3 bay leaves
- 3 tablespoons chopped palm sugar
- 2 tablespoons fish sauce
- 3 tablespoons tamarind juice

Cook the curry paste and coconut cream together for 5 minutes, then add the beef and fry for 8 to 10 minutes. Add the rest of the coconut milk, bring to a boil and simmer gently for 10 minutes.

Add all the remaining ingre-dients and cook until the potatoes and meat are tender.

Serve accompanied by sliced pickled ginger, pickled vegetables and rice.

Red Chicken Curry with Bamboo Shoots

Gaeng Kheow Wan Gai
Green Chicken Curry

A fragrant, creamy curry that is sure to wake up your tastebuds. Remove the skin from the chicken if you wish to reduce the oiliness. This dish can be prepared in advance—just add the basil and chilies when reheating the dish before serving.

- 1/2 cup (125 ml) coconut cream
- 3 tablespoons green curry paste (page 169)
- 12 oz (400 g) chicken breast, sliced
- 1 1/2 cups (375 ml) coconut milk
- 2 kaffir lime leaves
- 1 1/2 tablespoons fish sauce
- 1 teaspoon sugar
- 1 1/3 cups (150 g) eggplant (aubergine), cut into bite-sized pieces
- 1/4 cup (10 g) basil leaves (*horapa*)
- 2–3 red chilies, cut in strips lengthwise

Heat coconut cream until it begins to have an oily sheen, then add the curry paste and stir well. Add the chicken and cook until it changes color.

Add coconut milk, lime leaves, fish sauce, and sugar. Bring to a boil, then add the eggplant. Simmer until the chicken is cooked, then add the basil and chilies. Serve.

Panaeng Nuea
Dry Beef Curry

- 1 tablespoon coriander seeds, ground
- 2 teaspoons cumin seeds, ground
- 3 tablespoons Mussaman curry paste (page 169)
- 1/2 cup (125 ml) coconut cream
- 12 oz (400 g) beef, cut into thin strips
- 1 1/2 cups (375 ml) coconut milk
- 1/2 cup (90 g) ground roasted peanuts
- 1 1/2–2 tablespoons fish sauce
- 3 tablespoons chopped palm sugar
- 6 kaffir lime leaves, torn in half
- 1 red chili, thinly sliced

Mix the ground coriander and cumin with the Mussaman curry paste.

Heat coconut cream until some of the oil surfaces, then add the curry paste and lowly bring to a boil, stirring constantly.

Put in beef strips and cook for 5 minutes, add remaining coconut milk and the rest of ingredients, except for the kaffir lime leaves and chili. Stir well and simmer until the meat is tender, and the oil has come out of the coconut milk.

Add the kaffir lime leaves and chili, remove from the heat and serve with white rice.

Gaeng Ped Gai Naw Mai
Red Chicken Curry with Bamboo Shoots

- 1/2 cup (125 ml) coconut cream
- 1 tablespoon red curry paste (page 169)
- 12 oz (400 g) boneless chicken, diced
- 1 1/2 cups (375 ml) coconut milk
- 10 oz (300 g) bamboo shoots, sliced lengthwise (see Note)
- 2 tablespoons fish sauce
- 1/4 teaspoon salt
- 1 1/2 teaspoons sugar
- 5 kaffir lime leaves, halved
- 1 fresh red chili, finely sliced lengthwise
- 1/2 cup (20 g) basil leaves (*horapa*)

In a pot, bring the coconut cream to a boil. Simmer, stirring constantly, until the surface takes on an oily sheen. Put in the red curry paste and chicken, stir well, and add coconut milk and bamboo shoots.

Cook until the chicken is tender, then add fish sauce, salt, sugar, kaffir lime leaves, and chili. Remove from heat and garnish with basil.

Note: If using canned bamboo shoots, drain and boil in fresh water for about 5 minutes to get rid of any metallic taste. Fresh bamboo shoots should be sliced and simmered until just tender before being added to the curry.

Gaeng Ped
Roast Duck Curry

Buy a red-roasted duck from an Asian barbecue shop or restaurant for this curry. Pea aubergines or snake beans, added at the last moment, add a slightly crunchy texture to the smooth curry and provide a nice foil to the richness of the roasted duck.

- 1 roasted duck
- 1/2 cup (125 ml) coconut cream
- 3 tablespoons red curry paste (page 169)
- 1 1/2 cups (375 ml) thin coconut milk
- 2–3 large tomatoes, in wedges
- 1 cup (150 g) pea-sized eggplants (aubergines), or 1 small eggplant cut into 1/2 -in (1-cm) slices
- 4 kaffir lime leaves
- 2 tablespoons fish sauce
- 1 teaspoon sugar
- 1/2 teaspoon salt
- 10 basil leaves (*horapa*)
- 4 red or green chilies, cut into fine lengthwise strips

Remove all bones from the duck and cut the meat into bite-sized pieces.

Heat the coconut cream over medium heat and add the red curry paste, stirring well. Add the duck and stir well, then add the remaining coconut milk, tomatoes, eggplant, kaffir lime leaves, fish sauce, sugar, and salt. Bring to a boil, then remove from heat.

Sprinkle with the basil leaves and red or green chilies. Serve with plain rice.

Roast Duck Curry

Kha Kob Phad Ped
Frogs' Legs with Chili and Basil

Frogs, found in the *klongs* or canals and rice paddies of Thailand, are sometimes euphemistically called "paddy chicken." Their flavor is delicate and similar to chicken.

- 1/3 cup (90 ml) oil
- 8 pairs of frogs' legs
- 1 tablespoon green peppercorns
- 3 red chilies, sliced lengthwise
- 3 in (8 cm) galangal, cut into fine matchsticks
- 2 teaspoons fish sauce
- 1/2 teaspoon chopped palm sugar
- Large handful basil leaves (*horapa*)

Heat the oil in a wok until very hot. Add frogs' legs and peppercorns and stir fry over high heat for a couple of minutes. Add chilies, galangal, fish sauce, and sugar. Mix well and cook for another minute. Stir in the basil, take off the heat and serve.

Pla Nuea Orn
River Fish with Chili Sauce

Although freshwater fish are preferred for this dish in Thailand, any good white-fleshed sea fish can be used. A stunning dish that is also very easy to make.

- 1 whole freshwater fish weighing about 2 lb (1 kg), or 2 smaller fish
- 5 oz (150 g) dried red chilies, soaked in the water and deseeded
- 1/2 cup (100 g) garlic, peeled
- 1/2 cup (100 g) shallots, peeled
- 1/2 tablespoon shrimp paste
- 4 cups (1 liter) oil

- Fish sauce to taste
- 1 teaspoon sugar
- 10 kaffir lime leaves, very finely shredded

Scale and clean the fish thoroughly, leaving on the head if liked. Make cuts about 1/2 in (1 cm) deep along the back of each fish to give them a decorative appearance.

Finely chop the chilies, garlic, and shallot, then mix with the shrimp paste. Fry in 3 tablespoons of oil until fragrant, then add fish sauce and sugar.

Dry the fish thoroughly, then deep-fry until cooked. Put on a serving plate topped with the sauce. Sprinkle with kaffir lime leaves and serve immediately.

Pla Muk Tod
Fried Squid with Garlic and Black Pepper

This is a quick and delicious way of cooking squid. Be sure to use fresh and not frozen squid, as the latter exudes water when cooked, causing the squid to stew rather than fry.

Casseroled Crabs with Glass Noodles

- 1 1/4 lb (600 g) fresh squid
- 2 tablespoons oil
- 1/2 cup (100 g) chopped garlic
- 1 teaspoon black peppercorns, crushed
- 2 tablespoons oyster sauce
- 1 tablespoon light soy sauce
- 1 teaspoon sugar
- Cilantro (coriander) leaves to garnish

Remove the tentacles from the squid and cut out the hard beaky portion. Remove the skin from the body of the squid, clean inside and cut into bite-sized pieces. Dry thoroughly and set aside.

Put the oil in a wok over medium heat. Fry the garlic until golden-brown, then add the squid and its tentacles, together with the seasonings. Cook for a couple of minutes until the squid turns white. Serve hot sprinkled with cilantro leaves.

Poo Jaa
Deep-fried Stuffed Crab Shell

- 4 whole crabs
- 3 eggs, well beaten
- 5 cups (1 1/4 liters) oil
- 1 tablespoon cilantro (coriander) leaves
- 2 red chilies, cut into lengthwise strips

Stuffing
- 1/2 cup (175 g) ground pork
- 1/3 cup (75 g) minced shrimp
- 1/2 cup (60 g) fresh crabmeat
- 2 tablespoons finely chopped onion
- 1 tablespoon finely sliced scallion (spring onion)
- 1 teaspoon ground white pepper
- 1 teaspoon sugar
- 1/4 teaspoon light soy sauce
- 1/4 teaspoon salt

If using cooked crabs, remove the backs carefully and discard any spongy matter. Wash backs and set aside. Remove crabmeat from body, legs and claws and measure out 1/2 cup (60 g), keeping the rest aside for another dish.

If using raw crabs, steam first, then prepare as directed above.

Mix all the stuffing ingredients together and fill the crab shells.

Heat the oil in a pan, dip the stuffed crabs in the beaten egg to coat them well all over and then deep-fry for about 10 to 15 minutes until cooked. Remove and drain well on paper towels. Sprinkle with cilantro and chilies before serving.

Charcoal-grilled Prawns with Sweet Sauce

Poo Ob Woon Sen
*Casseroled Crabs with
Glass Noodles*

Use either crab claws or whole
crabs cut into serving pieces for
this recipe. Although slices of pork
fat are usually used in Thailand,
bacon improves the flavor.

- 2 slices lean bacon, cut into 1-in
  (2^1/2-cm) pieces
- 2 whole crabs, shelled, or 1 lb
  (500 g) crab claws
- 2 cilantro (coriander) roots, halved
- 2 in (5 cm) ginger, pounded or
  chopped finely
- 3–4 cloves garlic, chopped
- 1 tablespoon white peppercorns,
  crushed
- 8 oz (250 g) cellophane (glass)
  noodles (*woon sen*) soaked in
  cold water for 5 minutes
- 1 teaspoon butter
- 3 tablespoons black soy sauce
- ^{1}/4 cup (10 g) chopped cilantro
  (coriander) leaves and stems
- 2 scallions (spring onions), cut in
  1^1/2-in (4-cm) lengths

Stock
- 2 cups (500 ml) chicken stock
  (page 169)
- 2 tablespoons oyster sauce
- 2 tablespoons black soy sauce
- ^{1}/2 tablespoon sesame oil
- 1 teaspoon brandy or whisky
- ^{1}/2 teaspoon sugar

Place all the stock ingredients in
a pan, bring to a boil and simmer
for 5 minutes. Leave to cool.

Take a heat-proof casserole
dish and place the bacon over
the base. Put in the crab, cilantro

root, ginger, garlic, and peppercorns. Place the noodles over
the top, then add the butter,
soy sauce, and soup stock.

Cover and bring to a boil.
Simmer for 5 minutes. Mix well
with tongs and add the cilantro
and scallion. Cover and simmer
for about 5 minutes more, until
the crabs are cooked. Remove
excess liquid before serving.

Goong Pow
*Charcoal-grilled Prawns with
Sweet Sauce*

The fragrance of seafood grilling
over charcoal is irresistible. In
Thailand, this dish is made with
large freshwater prawns.

- 3 large fresh-water prawns or
  small crayfish
- Foil or banana leaf

Sauce
- ^{1}/3 cup (90 ml) water
- 1 tablespoon sugar
- ^{1}/2 teaspoon salt
- 1^1/2 tablespoons chopped garlic
- ^{1}/2 tablespoon chopped chilies
- 1 teaspoon chopped fresh cilantro
  (coriander)
- 2 tablespoons lime juice

Prepare the sauce first. Heat the
water and sugar in a pan over
low heat, stirring until the sugar
has dissolved. Turn off the heat,

Fried Clams in Roasted Chili Paste (below) and Steamed Mussels (above)

add the salt and stir well. Remove
from heat and allow to cool, then
add the remaining ingredients
and mix thoroughly.

Clean the crayfish or prawns
and wrap each securely in
foil or banana leaf. Grill over a
hot charcoal fire for about
12 minutes. Serve with sauce.

Hoi Ma-laeng Poo Ob
Steamed Mussels

This simple dish lives and dies
on the strength of its ingredients,
so use the best mussels you can
afford and add lots of fresh,
sweet-smelling basil.

- 4^1/2 lb (2 kg) mussels, cleaned
  well
- Large handful basil leaves
  (*horapa*)

Sauce
- ^{1}/2 cup (125 ml) lime juice
- 2 tablespoons fish sauce
- 1 teaspoon sugar
- 2 cilantro (coriander) roots,
  chopped
- 2 cloves garlic, crushed
- ^{1}/2 cup (125 ml) water

Place the mussels in a steamer
over boiling water and sprinkle
with the basil leaves. Steam for
10 minutes. Remove from the
heat and wait for 2 minutes
before opening the steamer.

Meanwhile, mix the sauce
ingredients together, bring to a
boil, then leave to cool.

Serve the mussels accompanied by the sauce, used for dipping.

Hoy Lai Ped
*Fried Clams in Roasted
Chili Paste*

- ^{1}/3 cup (90 ml) oil
- 1^1/4 lb (600 g) clams in their
  shells, cleaned well
- 1^1/2 tablespoons chopped garlic
- 5 fresh red chilies, sliced length
  wise
- 2 tablespoons roasted chili paste
  (page 169)
- 2 teaspoons light soy sauce
- ^{1}/2 cup (125 ml) chicken stock
  (page 169)
- Large handful basil leaves
  (*horapa*)

Heat the oil in wok, add the
clams and garlic and cook until
the clams open slightly. Add the
fresh chilies, chili paste, and
soy sauce, mix well, then add
chicken stock. Stir in the basil
and serve immediately,
accompanied by rice.

HELPFUL HINT
Soak the clams in several
changes of water for an hour or
so before cooking to ensure
they are thoroughly clean.

Fresh fruit is the mainstay of Thai desserts—what Westerners may called desserts are usually eaten between meals as fillers. Rice and tapioca flours, sticky rice, coconut milk, a twist of pandan leaf, and palm sugar are indispensable ingredients.

Tab Tim Grob
Red Rubies

This rather poetic name is given to tiny diced water chestnuts colored bright red and served in sweetened coconut milk. Although troublesome to peel, fresh water chestnuts have a delicate sweetness and excellent texture. If these are unavailable, jicama (yam beans) can be used.

- 1 cup (200 g) finely diced water chestnuts or jicama
- Red food coloring
- 1/2 cup (60 g) tapioca flour
- 1/2 cup (100 g) sugar
- 3/4 cup (180 ml) water
- 3/4 cup (180 ml) thick coconut milk
- Crushed ice

Sprinkle the water chestnuts with red food coloring and stir until bright red. Put the tapioca starch in a plastic bag and add the water chestnuts and shake so the pieces become well coated.

Red Rubies (top), Bananas in Coconut Milk (right) and Rice Balls in Coconut Milk

Put in a colander or sieve and shake to allow excess flour to fall away.

Bring 5 cups water to a boil, add the water chestnuts and simmer for 3 minutes. Drain and plunge in cold water. Drain again and set aside on a cloth.

Boil the sugar and the water to make syrup, allow to cool, then add the coconut milk. To serve, put a little of the water chestnut into dessert dishes and add some of the syrup and ice.

Kloey Buad Chee
Bananas in Coconut Milk

There are more than a dozen different types of bananas in Thailand. This recipe uses the tiny sweet variety sometimes known as finger bananas or lady finger bananas. If using large bananas, cut on the diagonal into 3 in (8 cm) lengths.

- 2 cups (500 ml) thin coconut milk
- 1/2 cup (100 g) sugar
- 1/4 teaspoon salt
- 3 small bananas, cut diagonally in half

Pour coconut milk into a pot, add sugar and salt. Bring to a boil, stirring constantly to prevent the coconut milk from separating. Add the bananas and cook gently for 5 minutes then remove from the heat. Serve hot or cold.

Sangkaya Fak Thong
Pumpkin Custard

A simple sweet that goes straight from the stove to the table, this rich coconut cream custard is a favourite in Thailand.

- 5 eggs (2 of them duck eggs if possible)
- 1 cup (250 ml) coconut cream
- 1 cup (150 g) chopped palm sugar or 1/2–3/4 cup (100–150 g) white sugar
- 1 whole small pumpkin, about 8 in (20 cm) in diameter

Pumpkin Custard

Beat the eggs with coconut cream and sugar until the mixture is frothy.

Cut the top off the pumpkin and carefully scoop out the seeds and any fibers. Pour in the coconut cream mixture, cover with the top of the pumpkin and place in a steamer. Cover the steamer and place over boiling water. Cook for about 30 minutes or until the mixture has set.

Leave to cool (preferably refrigerate) and cut in thick slices to serve.

Note: The duck eggs add richness and a firmer texture to the custard. If using palm sugar, strain the custard through a sieve before pouring into the pumpkin.

Bua Loi
Rice Balls in Coconut Milk

- 3 cups (450 g) glutinous rice flour
- 4 cups (1 liter) coconut cream
- 2 cups (420 g) sugar
- 1 teaspoon salt

Mix the rice flour with enough water to make a stiff paste. Knead well and then form into pea-sized balls. Bring a large pot of water to a boil, toss in the balls and remove when they float to the surface. Drain.

Bring half the coconut cream to a boil, stirring constantly to prevent it from separating, then add the flour balls. When the mixture returns to a boil, remove from the heat and stir in the remaining coconut cream. Serve as dessert in small bowls.

Add canned sweet corn kernels for a more colorful dessert.

Khao Mao Tod
Deep-fried Bananas

Bananas are rolled in a mixture of rice flakes, grated coconut and palm sugar before being dipped in batter and deep-fried.

- 1 1/4 lb (600 g) freshly grated coconut
- 1 cup (150 g) palm sugar, chopped
- 12 oz (400 g) rice flakes (*khoa mao*)
- 10 small finger bananas

Batter
- 3 cups (450 g) glutinous rice flour
- 1 cup (250 ml) thin coconut milk
- 1 cup (250 ml) water
- 1 egg, lightly beaten
- 1 tablespoon sesame seeds

Combine the coconut, palm sugar, and rice flakes and sauté in a non-stick pan, stirring frequently, for 1/2 hour. Set aside. Mix the batter ingredients and let it stand for 3 hours.

Just before serving, roll each banana in the sautéed mixture, then dip in the batter and fry in the hot oil until golden brown. Serve hot.

HELPFUL HINT
Flattened rice grains or rice flakes are found under a variety of names in most Asian countries, and are often known by the Filipino name, *pinipig*. Any type of rice flake or even wheat flake can be substituted.

Chicken Stock

Homemade chicken stock greatly improves the flavor of recipes in which it is used. The stock can be put in 4-cups (1-litre) containers and deep-frozen for up to 3 months.

- 5–6 1/2 lb (2 1/2–3 kg) chicken bones
- 6 quarts (6 liters) water
- 1 1/2 cups (250 g) chopped onion
- 1 cup (125 g) chopped celery
- 1 tablespoon coriander seeds
- 1 teaspoon black peppercorns

Wash bones in cold water then put in a stockpot and cover with cold water. Bring rapidly to the boil, then drain and discard water. Cover bones with 6 quarts water and add all other ingredients. Simmer for 4 hours, removing the scum as it accumulates. Strain through a cloth.

Nam Prik Gaeng Ped

Red Curry Paste

Basic curry pastes can be stored in a covered glass jar in a refrigerator for 1 month, or in the freezer for 3–4 months.

- 1 tablespoon coriander seeds
- 1 teaspoon cumin seed
- 13 dried bird's-eye chilies, cut, soaked in hot water for 15 minutes and deseeded
- 3 tablespoons finely chopped shallots
- 4 tablespoons finely chopped garlic
- 1 tablespoon finely chopped galangal
- 2 tablespoons finely sliced lemon grass
- 2 teaspoons finely chopped kaffir lime rind
- 1 tablespoon finely chopped cilantro (coriander) root
- 20 black peppercorns
- 1 teaspoon shrimp paste

Dry-fry the coriander and cumin seeds in a wok over low heat for about 5 minutes, then grind to a powder. Add the remaining ingredients, except the shrimp paste, and blend well. Add the ground spice mixture and shrimp paste and blend again to obtain about 3/4 cup (180 ml) of fine-textured paste.

Nam Prik Gaeng Kheow Wan

Green Curry Paste

- 1 tablespoon coriander seeds
- 1 teaspoon cumin seeds
- 15 green bird's-eye chilies
- 3 tablespoons finely chopped shallots
- 1 tablespoon finely chopped garlic
- 1 teaspoon finely chopped galangal
- 1 tablespoon finely sliced lemon grass
- 1/2 teaspoon finely chopped kaffir lime rind
- 1 teaspoon finely chopped cilantro (coriander) root
- 5 black peppercorns
- 1 teaspoon salt
- 1 teaspoon shrimp paste

Dry-fry the coriander and cumin seeds in a wok over low heat for about 5 minutes, then grind into a powder. Put the rest of the ingredients except the shrimp paste into a blender and blend to mix well. Add the spice seed mixture and shrimp paste and blend to obtain 1/2 cup (125 ml) of fine-textured paste.

Nam Prik Gaeng Mussaman

Mussaman Curry Paste

- 3 tablespoons finely chopped shallots
- 1 tablespoon finely chopped garlic
- 1 teaspoon finely chopped galangal
- 1 heaped tablespoon finely sliced lemongrass
- 2 cloves
- 1 tablespoon coriander seeds
- 1 teaspoon cumin seeds
- 5 black peppercorns
- 3 dried chilies, cut, soaked in hot water for 15 minutes and deseeded
- 1 teaspoon salt
- 1 teaspoon shrimp paste

Dry-fry the shallots, garlic, galangal, lemongrass, cloves, coriander and cumin seeds in a wok over low heat for about 5 minutes, then grind into a powder. Add the rest of the ingredients, except the shrimp paste, and blend to mix well. Combine the blended mixture and the shrimp paste and blend again to obtain 1/2 cup (125 ml) of fine-textured paste.

Nam Thai Orn

Green Peppercorn Dip

- 2 tablespoons fresh or bottled green peppercorns
- 3 cloves garlic
- 1 teaspoon sugar
- 1/2 tablespoon dried shrimps
- 2–3 tablespoons lime juice
- 6 sour fruits such as green mango or green apple, sliced

If using bottled or canned green peppercorns, be sure to wash off brine thoroughly first. Pound in a mortar or blend the garlic and 1 tablespoon of peppercorns, then add sugar, dried shrimps, and lime juice. Mix well and add the remaining tablespoon of peppercorns. Stir until well mixed. Serve with sour fruit, vegetables, and fried or grilled fish.

Nam Prik Pow

Roasted Chili Paste

- 2 cups (500 ml) vegetable oil
- 8 shallots, sliced
- 6 cloves garlic, sliced
- 1 cup (160 g) dried shrimps
- 1/2 cup (50 g) small dried chilies
- 1 tablespoon palm sugar
- 3 tablespoons fish sauce
- 1 1/2 tablespoons tamarind juice
- 1/3 teaspoon salt

Heat the oil in a wok and fry the shallots and garlic until golden brown; remove from oil and drain. Add the dried shrimps and chilies and fry until golden brown; remove from oil and drain.

In a food processor or blender, process the prawns, garlic, chilies, shallots, and sugar until the mixture is well blended. Add the fish sauce, tamarind juice, salt, and cooled oil from the wok and blend to obtain a finely textured paste.

Kapi Kua

Shrimp Paste and Coconut Milk Dip

- 2 dried chilies, cut and soaked
- 5 shallots
- 5 stems lemongrass, finely sliced
- 3 slices galangal
- 3 tablespoons minced *krachai*
- 3 tablespoons shrimp paste, roasted

- 1 cup (150 g) coarsely chopped smoked fish
- 4 cups (1 liter) coconut milk
- 1 tablespoon palm sugar
- 2 tablespoons fish sauce
- 5 red chilies

Pound dried chilies, shallots, lemon grass, galangal, *krachai* and shrimp paste with half the smoked fish until well mixed. Heat coconut milk and simmer until oil comes to the surface and the quantity has reduced.

Add the paste and continue cooking until fragrant. Add sugar, the rest of the fish, fish sauce and chilies and simmer until thick. Serve with grilled shrimp or fluffy crisp fish flakes in a pan and cook over low heat, stirring frequently, until the sauce has thickened and reduced. Cool to room temperature and garnish with cilantro leaves when serving.

Nam Prik Pla Yaang

Dip with Grilled Fish

- 3–4 red bird's-eye chilies
- 1 dried chili, cut and soaked
- 3 cloves garlic, grilled in skin until blackened
- 2 shallots, grilled in skin until blackened
- 1 cup (150 g) flaked fish
- 1/2 teaspoon shrimp paste, roasted
- 2 tablespoons lime juice
- 1 tablespoon fish sauce
- 1 teaspoon sugar
- 1 teaspoon kaffir lime juice

Pound bird's-eye chilies, then add dried chili, peeled garlic, and shallots and continue pounding until ground into a fine paste. Add lime juice, fish sauce, and sugar. Mix well and add kaffir lime juice. Serve with vegetables and grilled or fried fish.

HELPFUL HINT
Serve dips with a selection of raw baby vegetables, salted duck egg and crisp pork skin.

"The land of the Perfume River has been blessed with an astonishing variety of foods from the earth and from the water."

VIETNAM

Not only is Vietnam the site of an economic revival but a great culinary tradition is re-emerging too.

Left: The quiet journey home from market.

Right: Fresh carrots being readied for market in the central highlands. Vietnamese food is characterized by its lavish use of fresh vegetables and herbs.

With lengths of unspoiled dramatic coastline, sheltered harbors, well-irrigated lowlands and vast forests, Vietnam is a remarkably beautiful and fertile land, rich in agricultural resources.

It is also a country in the process of change; with the start of a new millenium, a great sense of optimism hangs in the air. The effects of *doi moi*, the economic reform policy allowing small-scale private enterprise, introduced by the communist government in 1986, are becoming more and more evident. The accumulation of personal wealth is now encouraged.

The food markets are a hive of activity: these days produce is trucked in from nearby villages, coastal waters, and the central highlands. Throughout the day, crowds of people fill their baskets from the rows of fresh vegetables and tropical fruits, live fish and game, pickled meats and vegetables, candied fruit, dried and packaged goods, rice, and bottles of pungent *nuoc mam* fish sauce.

The Land and its People

Vietnam is fortunate in being able to grow a diverse variety of vegetables and fruits throughout the country and little food is imported. Rice and seafood are in abundant supply, due in part to its location on the eastern coast of the southeast Asian Indochinese peninsula and a 1600-mile coastline. It boasts countless dykes, canals, and waterways, which include the Red River, the Perfume River, and the Mekong River, one of the longest rivers in Southeast Asia.

Vietnam shares its border with China, Laos, and Cambodia. In the cooler northern region, where undulating limestone hills recall southwest China and where many of Vietnam's ethnic groups have their homes, the cuisine shares distinct similarities with Chinese food.

The center of the country is less agriculturally rich, and in the temperate south, the cuisine more closely resembles that of neighboring Southeast Asian countries, such as Thailand and Malaysia.

The food of the south is more varied and rich than that of Hué or Hanoi, and generously spiced.

The Red River Delta in the north and the Mekong Delta in the south are the two main rice-growing areas, although lush green rice paddies dotted with water buffalo and rows of women with their distinctive conical hats can be seen throughout the country. Sixty percent of arable land in Vietnam is given over to rice production, leaving little pasture for cattle farming. Hence beef, in particular, is a luxury for most Vietnamese, and the famous series of dishes, *bo bay mon* (literally, beef done seven ways), is highly regarded.

In spite of urbanization and increasingly populated cities, roughly 80 percent of the population relies on rice for its livelihood. Rice is used in a diverse range of dishes and in the production of wine and vinegar. The grains are also converted into flour and used to make rice noodles and transformed into rice paper sheets for *goi cuon*, the Vietnamese fresh spring rolls. Glutinous rice cooked overnight, then wrapped into attractive banana leaf parcels, becomes breakfast-time *xoi* or the traditional *banh tay* and *banh chung* eaten during Tet, the Vietnamese Lunar New Year holiday.

The Making of a Cuisine

The Vietnamese people have a history of foreign influences, from neighbors, sojourners and settlers, all of whom have left their mark: Malay, Chinese, Indian, Thai, French, and American. The Chinese offered their use of beancurd, soy beans, and spices such as the star anise. The use of dill in *cha ca*, Hanoi's famous fish dish served at the popular Cha Ca La Vong restaurant, and also in fish congee, could have been a French influence. The Indians left their ground rice pancakes.

At the heart of Vietnamese cuisine is the salty, pale brown fermented fish sauce known as *nuoc mam*. The cuisines of Cambodia, Thailand and Burma use a similar sauce, however, the Vietnamese variety seems to have a particularly pungent flavor. *Nuoc mam* is made by layering fresh anchovies with salt in huge wooden barrels, a process that takes about six months and involves pouring the liquid which drips from the barrel back over the anchovies. Arguably, the best *nuoc mam* comes from the island of Phu Quoc near the Cambodian border.

Nuoc mam cham, the ubiquitous dip made of *nuoc mam* diluted with lime juice, vinegar, water, crushed garlic, and fresh red chilies is used as a dipping sauce at the table, served with dishes like *cha gio* (spring rolls) and *chao tom* (sugar cane shrimp), or simply as a dip for pieces of fish or meat.

What sets Vietnamese cuisine apart from that of other Southeast Asian countries is the pervasive use of fresh leaves and herbs, mak-ing it lighter and more refreshing than, say, Thai food. Its use of crisp, uncooked vegetables, subtle seasonings, raw herbs and unique flavor combinations—sharp, sweet and fresh and fragrant at the same time—is unforgettable.

While Vietnamese restaurants in other regions of the world rarely manage to offer more than one kind of mint, basil or cilantro, markets throughout Vietnam sell a remarkable array of such herbs, as well as leaves such as the deep-red, spicy perilla leaf, *tia to*, and the pungent saw-leaf herb (long coriander).

Fresh herbs turn up in all sorts of dishes. Soup kitchens serving the glorious noodle soup *pho* also offer a huge plate of raw herbs to be stirred into the steaming soup. The herbs are also served with *ban xeo*, a kind of crêpe enclosing shrimp, pork, mung beans, and bean sprouts, and with spring rolls or grilled meats, and in salads.

Other factors that contribute to the subtlety and uniqueness of Vietnamese food are the refined cooking techniques, the often unusual serving of varying dishes and the combination of flavors.

A simple but refined meal in Hué, once the political centre and today still an important culinary city.

Imperial Cuisine

Hué, situated on the banks of the tranquil Perfume River, was once an important seat of learning and culture, as well as the imperial seat for nearly 150 years.

To satisfy jaded imperial palates, but lacking in the agricultural diversity of either the north or the south, the imperial kitchens at Hué had to show an enormous amount of ingenuity by refining ordinary dishes until they became something truly special, so that eating could be viewed as art, ritual and sensory pleasure at the same time.

A typical imperial banquet today would include up to a dozen dishes, such as a beautifully fragrant, peppery chicken soup with lotus seeds (*sup ga*), crisp, golden brown spring rolls (*nem ran*), delicate rice flour patties stuffed with minced shrimp (*banh* Hué), grilled pork in rice paper (*thit nuong*) served with a tasty peanut sauce, delicious crab claws stuffed with pork (*cua phich bot*), and the famous minced shrimp wrapped around sugar cane (*cha tom lui mia* or *chao tom*). Main dishes might include fish grilled in banana leaf (*ca nuong la chuoi*), pungent beef in wild betel leaves (*bo la lot*), rice with vegetables (*com* Hué), gently sautéed shrimp with mushrooms (*tom xao hanh nam*), and finally the glutinous rice dessert husband-and-wife cake (*phu the*), which comes in a perfectly formed little box made from pandan leaf.

These dishes are actually variations of those served in other parts of Vietnam, and the ingredients may be vegetables, eggs or fish, rather than exotic sea delicacies or the best cuts of meat. What sets these dishes apart is the sophisticated cooking techniques and the careful presentation.

For example, the favorite *chao tom lui mia* seems so simple—if only! Tiny shrimp are carefully shelled, then marinated in *nuoc mam*. They are then pounded until they form a thick paste, and egg white, onion, garlic, sugar, and pepper added. The mixture is pounded again with a touch of pork fat, and finally wrapped around sugar cane sticks and grilled.

The presentation of food was—and is—very important, not only in the use of color and the arrangement of food on the plate, but also in the manner of serving. Rice, for example, might be draped with an omelet coat, or cooked inside a lotus leaf and further enhanced with the addition of delicate lotus seeds.

Portions are delicate, since perhaps dozens of dishes are served in the course of a meal. All these naturally increased the length of preparation time, with the result that the number of cooks and kitchen staff reached unprecedented heights—a luxury which perfectly befitted the privileged life of an emperor.

The most talented proponents of imperial cuisine today are virtually all women, each of them descended by some route or other from imperial households. Due to its size and relatively small population, Hué today is not a culinary mecca compared with Ho Chi Minh City or Hanoi. There is, however, a renewed interest in the cuisine of Hué, and a number of modern Vietnamese chefs have made it their mission to turn the simple art of cooking into something extraordinary.

The Food of the People

Through the more than four troubled decades of constant struggle and fighting in Vietnam, there was barely enough rice to go around, let alone interest in what to buy at the market and how to perfect a particular recipe. But since the mid-1980s, a combination of economic upturn and the return of many overseas Vietnamese (encouraged by the government to start new businesses) has resulted in, among other things, the rebirth of a thriving restaurant scene.

Culinary skills are being relearned, courses for the training of professional chefs are being launched and the Vietnamese are once again discovering the joys of cooking. Top-quality, fresh ingredients are widely available.

All over Ho Chi Minh City and, to a slightly lesser extent, in Hanoi, restaurants are built around courtyards in French colonial buildings or designed to resemble old Vietnamese family homes. French restaurants are once again establishing themselves and fashionable Italian restaurants are making an appearance.

Vietnamese cuisine is based on rice, fish, and fresh vegetables. Little oil is used in cooking, except for deep-frying, and salads are lightly dressed. Healthy, invigorating soups such as the tasty *canh chua thom ca loc* are featured on menus, fresh fruit and delicious home-made yogurts are often served for dessert, and drinks like freshly squeezed sugar cane juice are widely available.

Modern Vietnamese cuisine is a marriage of the old and the new. Recipes from past generations are coupled with new dishes created for the increasingly sophisticated and well-traveled local consumer. A good example is *thit kho to*, pork cooked slowly in a claypot, a dish of peasant origins that now appears on restaurant menus alongside *cua rang me*, a fried crab dish richly perfumed with tamarind.

Baguettes at a food stall are a reminder of Vietnam's colonial past.

The sometimes lengthy preparation times and cooking processes required by Vietnamese cuisine can render it something of a luxury for people with busy lives, so many chefs and teachers within Vietnam have begun experimenting with new and innovative methods that preserve the spirit of the cuisine, but allow it to be prepared quickly and simply at home.

As this move towards quicker cooking has been evolving, there has also been a resurgence of interest in the traditional dishes of the Hué court. While more attention is being paid to the presentation of food, very few changes, if any, are made to cater to the tourist trade. What changes are occurring in the recipes are subtle and often imperceptible: *ga bop*, a chicken salad flavored with onion, *rau ram* (*laksa* leaf or polygonum) and a simple seasoning of salt, pepper, and lime juice, has traditionally been made with chicken skin and bones, but new restaurants are preparing it with lean chicken meat.

The Vietnamese Table and Kitchen

Eating in Vietnam is a shared experience, an informal ritual. On the small table that the family has gathered around is a large bowl of steaming rice, a cauldron of aromatic soup, a meat dish, a vegetable dish, and a generous plate of leaves for each diner to wrap around a delicious hand roll and dip into the *nuoc mam cham*. Tea is drunk throughout the meal.

The adage "the fresher the ingredients, the better the food," is especially true of Vietnamese cooking. The various herbs and lettuces are almost always served raw, and salads are never over-dressed, so that the full flavors are present. Vegetables and fish in particular, which make up a large part of the Vietnamese diet, are gently cooked and lightly seasoned, allowing the true flavors of the food to come through.

The home and its kitchen are central to Vietnamese culture. A week before Tet, the god of the hearth (Tao Quan) must be supplicated with a ceremony performed in the kitchen, where offerings of fruit, paper models of luxury consumer goods and a ceremonial costume are placed on the altar.

Traditional Vietnamese cooks generally squat, feet tucked beneath them, preparing much of their food on the floor around the stove on a wet, tiled area, where all utensils, pots, pans, and food items are cleaned before use. Even as incomes gradually increase and some of the modern conveniences (refrigerators, plumbed sinks, built-in work surfaces, and electric rice cookers) are making their way into a number of Vietnamese kitchens, much of the preparation and cooking is still done in the traditional manner.

Most of the cooking is done over an open hearth (ovens are not used), with one member of the family on duty to fan the flames. A wok is still the most versatile implement in any Vietnamese kitchen, usually set over a wood fire. Grilling is another common cooking method. A large pot is standard for soups and stocks, and since rice is the staple, a simple rice cooker with its lid is usually steaming away on a low fire.

As in other countries, food stalls are a popular haunt, both for local gossip and a quick meal, and usually appear on the sidewalks in front of old shophouses. Clusters of tiny chairs and tables surround a steaming hot cauldron of soup set on an open flame, with people huddled over their morning bowl of restorative *pho*. At another streetside restaurant, a team of busy female chefs is busy making open-faced omelets in blackened pans over small charcoal grills. Or it may be vendors with carts filled with baguettes, cheese, sliced pâté, and sausages making sandwiches. It's all in a day's work.

The result of time-consuming preparation is a memorable dining experience.

SUGGESTED MENUS

Family meals

- Stuffed Steamed Rice Wrapper Rolls (page 176);
- Stuffed Squid (page 182), Stir-Fried Vegetables with Fish Sauce (page 180) and Pork Stew with Coconut Juice (page 184) served with rice;
- Husband and Wife Cakes (page 186).

Or, lead off with the
- Preserved Salted Fish Stew (page 181); followed by
- Shrimp and Green Mango Salad (page 179), Fried Beancurd with Lemongrass (page 185) and Grilled Beef in Wild Betel Leaves (page 185) served with rice;
- Banana Cake (page 186) is a popular way to finish.

A dinner party

Most of the recipes in the appetizers section lend themselves readily to dinner-party nibbles, so try serving
- a selection of fried and steamed rice paper rolls (pages 176–77) with a few dipping sauces;
- Banana Blossom Salad with Duck and Ginger (page 179), served either from a platter in the middle or in individual portions;
- Braised Mushrooms with Soy Sauce (page 180), Spicy River Shrimp (page 182) and a Spicy Beef Stew (page 185) served with rice;
- Pineapple Tartlets (page 186) and vanilla ice cream.

One-pot meals

The noodle soups of Vietnam deserve honorable mention, so for breakfast, lunch or dinner, do as the locals do and try one of the following:
- Hanoi Chicken Soup (page 178);
- Beef Noodle Soup (page 178);
- Grilled Pork with Rice Noodles (page 185). Very satisfying!

A melting pot menu

- Simmered Winter Squash (page 101) from Japan;
- Squid with Bamboo Shoots from China (page 44) and from Vietnam, Fried Grouper with Ginger Sauce (page 183), served with rice and a simple salad or stir-fried vegetables;
- freshly sliced seasonal fruits, such as mangoes or pineapple.

THE ESSENTIAL FLAVORS OF VIETNAMESE COOKING

The key to Vietnamese cuisine is freshness, so choose the best of available herbs and leaves for the table salad: **laksa leaf** (*daun kesum*), **lettuces**, **beansprouts**, **basil,** and **cilantro**. These also accompany rice paper rolls. **Chilies** are sliced into **nuoc mam** for dipping sauces. Flavorings widely used include **garlic**, **lemongrass**, **shallots,** and **scallions**. **Rice** is a must.

The freshness and exuberance of Vietnamese food is no more evident than in the range of hand rolls they make, which make use fragrant, crispy leaves and a little meat or seafood. The rolls are filling and substantial without heaviness.

Goi Cuon
Shrimp Rolls

1/2 cup (125 ml) water
2 tablespoons white vinegar
1 tablespoon rice wine
1/2 teaspoon salt
1 lb (500 g) shrimp, with shells on
2 tablespoons vegetable oil
8 oz (200 g) pork loin
20 pieces dried rice paper
1 medium head butter lettuce
1 cup (40 g) fresh basil leaves
1 cup (40 g) fresh mint leaves
2 small red chilies, thinly sliced
1 cup (80 g) beansprouts
1 bunch chives, cut in 3 to 4-in (8 to 10-cm) lengths

In a skillet, combine water, vinegar, rice wine, and salt. Bring to a boil. Add shrimp, simmer until just done. Cool and peel. Heat oil in a separate pan, sear pork in pan for about 2 minutes or until lightly browned all over. Add liquid from cooking shrimp to the pan, simmer pork for 15 minutes or until tender. Remove from heat, drain and cut into

thin slices. Follow the same steps as for wrapping the pork roll using lettuce, basil, mint, chilies, beansprouts, and chives. Serve with Peanut Sauce (page 187).

HELPFUL HINT

If you find that the dried wrappers do not soften sufficiently when you wipe them, soak them in tepid water until flexible. Place on a tea towel to soak up any excess moisture and proceed with the recipe. Work in small batches.

Banh Cuon
Stuffed Steamed Rice Wrapper Rolls

This is a variation on the spring rolls that use freshly steamed wrappers. The steaming of the fresh rice flour wrappers is actually quite easy and fun once you get the hang of it.

Stuffing
1/2 cup (15 g) dried wood ear mushrooms
Water to cover
2 tablespoons vegetable oil
8 shallots, chopped
1 clove garlic, crushed
1 cup (150 g) finely diced pre served white radish
10 oz (300 g) minced pork or shrimp

Fresh Rice Flour Wrappers
1 cup (160 g) rice flour
3 cups (750 ml) water
Salt

Garnish
1/4 cup (10 g) cilantro (coriander) leaves
1/2 cup (50 g) fried shallots
1 red chili, shredded

Sauce
1 tablespoon sugar
1/4 cup (60 ml) water
2 tablespoons fish sauce
1 tablespoon rice wine vinegar
1 tablespoon fresh lime juice
1 medium red chili, shredded
2 cloves garlic, finely chopped

To make the stuffing, soak the wood ear mushrooms in water for 1 hour, drain and dice. Heat oil in a wok and sauté the shallots, garlic, radish, pork, and mushrooms until tender. Set aside.

To prepare wrappers, mix flour, water, and salt to form the batter. Fill steamer two-thirds full of water, double and stretch a piece of cheesecloth tightly over the top and secure it with string. When water begins boiling, brush the surface of the cheesecloth with oil, pour on a small ladle of rice flour batter and spread it

Shrimp Mousse on Sugar Cane

around in a circular motion. If possible, cover with an inverted bowl or lid, and leave for a few moments. Remove the steamed rice flour wrapper with a spatula, carefully lifting up at the corners. Repeat until all the batter is used. Set wrapper on a smooth surface.

To make the sauce, dissolve sugar in water, add fish sauce, vinegar, and lime juice. Add finely chopped chili and garlic before serving.

Place roughly 1 tablespoon of filling on the wrapper. Roll up gently. Garnish with cilantro, shallots, and chili and serve with the sauce.

Banh Uot Thit Nuong
Grilled Beef Roll

1 stem lemongrass, finely chopped
1 tablespoon soft brown sugar
1/4 cup (60 ml) fish sauce
12 oz (400 g) beef, thinly sliced
5 fresh steamed rice flour wrappers (see previous recipe)
1/2 cup (20 g) fresh mint leaves
1/2 cup (20 g) fresh basil leaves
1/2 head butter lettuce
1 tablespoon sesame seeds, toasted
1/2 cup (20 g) fresh cilantro (coriander) leaves

Dipping Sauce
1 cup (250 ml) Yellow Bean Sauce (see page 187)

Grilled Beef Roll with fish sauce dip (left) and Hué Spring Roll with shrimp paste dip (right)

4 tablespoons sweet chili sauce

1 tablespoon finely chopped roasted peanuts

Combine lemongrass, sugar, and fish sauce. Marinate beef in sauce mixture for 30 minutes, then briefly grill over a medium heat until lightly browned, but still rare inside. Remove from grill and cut into small pieces. To make the dipping sauce, combine yellow bean sauce, chili sauce, and peanuts. Mix well. Place some of the beef, a little of the mint, basil, and lettuce leaves on a rice flour wrapper, then sprinkle with sesame seeds and add a cilantro leaf. Fold to the inside, leaving the top end open with the cilantro leaf extended.

Cuon Hué
Hué Spring Roll

5 fresh steamed rice flour wrappers (see page 176)

1 large rice paper, sprinkled with water

8 sprigs water convolvulus (*kangkung*)

1/2 cup (20 g) fresh fragrant leaves (mixture of basil, mint, and cilantro/coriander)

1 medium sweet potato, peeled, cooked and thinly sliced

1/4 cup (20 g) steamed rice vermicelli noodles

4 oz (100 g) lean pork, boiled and thinly sliced

4 oz (100 g) preserved sour shrimp

Shrimp Paste Dip

2 cloves garlic, finely chopped

2 tablespoons vegetable oil

1 tablespoon shrimp paste

1 sweet potato, boiled and mashed

1 tablespoon sugar

To make the dip, sauté garlic in oil until fragrant. Add shrimp paste, potato, and sugar. Stir well, cook for a few minutes.

Spread steamed rice flour wrappers over softened rice paper (which makes it easier to roll but is discarded). Place water spinach, fragrant leaves, sweet potato, and rice noodles in a line along the paper. Roll tightly. Cut into 1-in (2 1/2 -cm) segments and display them on a plate, topping each segment with a slice of pork and a shrimp. Serve with shrimp paste dip.

Cha Gio
Vietnamese Spring Rolls

These are the classic, deep-fried Vietnamese spring rolls, also referred to as Imperial Rolls. The leaves and the lettuce are wrapped around the rolls and then dipped into the sauce. This is a fun recipe to experiment with. Try using different ingredients, such as chicken or duck.

Stuffing

1 lb (500 g) lean, ground pork

8 oz (200 g) shrimp, minced

4 oz (100 g) crabmeat

5 shallots, finely chopped

2 cloves garlic, crushed

2 or 3 wood ear mushrooms, soaked in water

1 1/2 oz (45 g) cellophane noodles, soaked in water

1/2 medium carrot, cut in julienne

1 egg white (optional)

Pinch pepper

1 teaspoon sugar

Pinch salt

1 tablespoon fish sauce

Wrapping

25 pieces dried rice paper

Water

Vegetable oil for deep-frying

Garnish

1 cup (40 g) fragrant leaves (basil, cilantro/coriander, and mint)

1 small head iceberg lettuce

1/4 cup (20 g) beansprouts

2 tablespoons fish sauce dip (see page 187)

2 tablespoons Carrot and Radish Pickles (see page 187)

1/2 cup (50 g) rice noodles, softened

In a large bowl, combine the stuffing ingredients; mix thoroughly.

Cover rice paper with banana leaf or sprinkle with water until flexible. Put a heaped teaspoon of stuffing on the rice paper. Start folding the left and right side of the rice paper into the center, then roll up from the bottom edge away to the far end. Do not roll too tight, as this will cause the rolls to split. Deep-fry over medium heat until golden brown.

Serve with fragrant leaves, lettuce, beansprouts, fish sauce dip, carrot and radish pickles, and fine rice noodles.

Chao Tom
Shrimp Mousse on Sugar Cane

This dish from the imperial city of Hué uses fresh sticks of sugar cane as skewers. The heated cane releases a burst of sweet cane juice when bitten into.

1 1/4 cups (300 g) shrimp, minced

1/2 teaspoon salt

1 teaspoon sugar

Pinch of pepper

2 tablespoons vegetable oil

8 sugar cane pieces, 4 in (10 cm) long

1 red chili, seeded and sliced

1 cup (250 ml) sweet and sour sauce (see page 187)

1/2 cup (20 g) cilantro (coriander) leaves

Grind or pound shrimp with salt, sugar and pepper. Using the oil, form the shrimp paste around the sugar cane until tight. Grill over medium charcoal heat until crisp and slightly browned.

Serve with chili, sweet and sour sauce and cilantro leaves.

HELPFUL HINT
Although the pounding is normally done in a mortar, you can use a blender or a food processor. Crab is a good substitute for shrimp. If grilling is not possible, oven bake at 375°F (190°C, gas mark 5) for about 20 minutes.

Nem Nuong
Minced Pork Balls on a Skewer

1 lb (500 g) ground lean pork neck

1/2 teaspoon salt

8 oz (200 g) pork fatback

2 tablespoons sugar

2 cloves garlic, diced

2 red chilies, finely chopped

Salt to taste

1 tablespoon pepper

2 tablespoons ground roasted peanuts

1/4 cup (60 ml) fish sauce dip (see page 187)

Garnish

1 cup (80 g) beansprouts

2 medium starfruit, peeled and sliced

2 medium unripe bananas, thinly sliced

1 medium cucumber, peeled and sliced

1 head butter lettuce

1 cup (40 g) mint leaves

20 pieces rice paper

Mix the ground pork meat with 1/2 teaspoon of salt and set aside. Fry the pork fatback for 10 minutes, then cut into very small strips. Marinate with sugar, garlic, chili, salt, and pepper for 5 minutes.

Combine the pork meats and shape into small balls. Place them on a bamboo skewer (3 or 4 to a skewer) and cook evenly over the charcoal grill. Sprinkle with peanuts, fish sauce dip, and garnishes.

Vietnamese Spring Rolls

Thin but flavorsome, soups are drunk throughout a meal in Vietnam rather than at the beginning as in the West. The soups can be served in individual bowls or, as is often the case, set in one large bowl from which everyone helps themselves.

Bun Thang
Hanoi Chicken Soup

This is one of the many warming winter soups that is now commonplace throughout the country.

1 medium chicken
1/2 cup (80 g) dried shrimp
12 oz (400 g) pork spareribs, cut into large pieces
12 cups (3 liters) lightly salted water
Pepper
Sugar
1/4 cup (60 ml) fish sauce
1/2 cup (60 g) diced shallots
4 baby leek stalks or scallions (spring onions), finely cut
1 medium onion, sliced
4 cups (400 g) fine rice noodles, blanched
1 egg, beaten, fried and cut into strips
10 oz (300 g) Vietnamese sausage, cut into thin strips
2 baby leek or scallion (spring onion) greens, chopped
3 tablespoons finely chopped cilantro (coriander) leaves
1/4 cup (20 g) fried shallots
Fresh ground pepper
1 lime, cut into wedges
2 small red chilies, sliced
1 cup (80 g) beansprouts
1 medium head butter lettuce
1 cup (140 g) shaved banana blossom
2 tablespoons shrimp paste

Boil chicken, dried shrimp, and pork ribs in lightly salted water for about 20 minutes. Skim fat and season with pepper, sugar, and fish sauce. Simmer for another 45 minutes, until the chicken is cooked. Remove both the chicken and shrimp. Let cool, then shred the chicken. Set aside. Add shallots, baby leeks, and onion to the stock. Simmer for 20 minutes, season to taste.

Place a handful of the blanched rice noodles in a soup bowl and cover with a portion of the egg, chicken, spareribs, sausage, baby leek greens, cilantro, and some of the fried shallots; add boiling stock to cover.

Sprinkle with freshly ground pepper, remaining fried shallots and lime juice. Serve with chilies, beansprouts, lettuce, banana blossom, and shrimp paste.

HELPFUL HINT
Vietnamese soups can be served in individual bowls or, set in one large bowl from which everyone helps themselves.

Pho Bo
Beef Noodle Soup

This is the classic breakfast meal, but it is just as delicious served any time of day or night.

1 medium piece of fresh ginger
1 large onion
10 cups (2 1/2 liters) water
2 lb (1 kg) beef bones
12 oz (400 g) beef brisket
Pinch of salt
3 pieces star anise
1 cinnamon stick
Salt
Pepper
1 cup (80 g) beansprouts
8 oz (250 g) rice noodles
8 oz (250 g) raw beef sirloin, thinly sliced
1 medium onion, sliced
1/4 cup (35 g) finely cut baby leeks or scallions (spring onions)

Beef Noodle Soup

1/2 cup (20 g) chopped *ngo gai* (saw-leaf herb) leaves
1/2 cup (20 g) chopped cilantro (coriander) leaves

Garnish
1 tablespoon chili sauce
3 tablespoons yellow bean sauce (see page 187)
2 small red chilies, sliced
2 limes, cut into wedges
Mint leaves
Ngo gai leaves
Cilantro (coriander) leaves

Grill ginger and onion until the skins are burnt. In a deep pan, combine water, bones, and beef brisket. Bring to a boil, skimming frequently, to remove residue. Add salt, grilled ginger, and onion, star anise and cinnamon. Cook for 1 hour or until tender, then remove the cooked beef and slice it very thinly. Strain the soup into a separate container, adding salt and pepper to taste.

Wash and drain beansprouts. Quickly blanch rice noodles and bean sprouts in boiling water, to soften, but do not overcook. Arrange in a soup bowl. Top with sliced beef brisket, raw beef sirloin, sliced onion, chopped baby leeks, *ngo gai*, and cilantro leaves. Pour the boiling soup into the bowl and sprinkle with freshly ground pepper. By that time the raw beef should be medium-cooked.

Serve with chili and yellow bean sauces, sliced chilies, lime wedges, mint, *ngo gai*, and cilantro leaves.

HELPFUL HINT
Grill the ginger and onion over an open flame or in a pan. Chicken is a delicious alternative to beef, and most Vietnamese restaurants offer both versions.

Clam Soup

Pungent with fish sauce, Vietnamese salads are a little like the Thai—the bite of chili is soothed by crunchy leaves, tempered with sweet palm sugar and finished with little crispy bits of shallots and peanuts . . . the explosion of flavors in the mouth is quite a sensation! Most salads are quickly and easily assembled once the preparation is done, often requiring nothing more than a light toss with a small amount of dressing just before serving.

In a large bowl combine lotus stems, *rau ram*, salt, sugar, and lime juice. Toss gently. Place on a serving plate.

Cut shrimps in half lengthwise and arrange on the salad. Garnish with peanuts, cilantro and shallots. Serve with fish sauce dip and prawn crackers.

Lotus Stem Salad with Shrimps

Goi Ngo Sen
Lotus Stem Salad with Shrimps

The lotus flower is the symbol of purity. The stems have a crisp, crunchy texture similar to celery, which can be used as a substitute.

- 250 g (8 oz) cleaned lotus stems, cut into 5 cm (2 in) lengths
- 1 tablespoon *rau ram* (polygonum) leaves, finely chopped
- 1 teaspoon salt
- 1 1/2 tablespoons sugar
- 1 tablespoon lime juice
- 6 medium shrimps, cooked, peeled and deveined
- 1 tablespoon peanuts, coarsely ground
- 3 tablespoons cilantro (coriander) leaves
- 2 tablespoons fried shallots (page 187)
- 80 ml (1/3 cup) fish sauce dip (see page 187)
- 6 prawn crackers

Squid Salad

Goi Muc
Squid Salad

Piquant, sweet, and hot, the flavors of this salad really get the tastebuds working. Squid is easy to work with but becomes rubbery if overcooked, so barely cook the squid and quickly plunge it into iced water to keep its texture.

- 1 lb (500 g) cleaned squid
- 4 cups (1 liter) water
- 2 tablespoons lime juice
- 1/4 cup (60 ml) rice wine
- 3 cloves garlic, crushed
- 1 teaspoon sesame oil
- 1 teaspoon sugar
- 1 teaspoon cracked black pepper
- 1/2 cup (80 g) thinly sliced baby celery
- 1/2 cup (20 g) cilantro (coriander) leaves
- 1 small red chili, finely chopped
- 1/3 cup (50 g) pickled baby leeks or shallots (optional)
- 2 tablespoons crushed peanuts
- 1/4 cup (60 ml) fish sauce dip see page 187)
- Rice crackers, to garnish

Cut squid crosswise, in narrow sections, about 2 in (5 cm) long. Bring large pan of water to a boil and blanch squid quickly (1 to 2 minutes). Cool down in ice water, to preserve soft texture. Combine remaining ingredients with the squid. Mix well in a large bowl. Arrange on a platter. Serve with rice crackers.

Goi Xoai Xanh Tom Hap
Shrimp and Green Mango Salad

This is essentially a variation on the traditional Vietnamese shrimp salad, using tart, unripe mango instead of lotus root. Green papaya may also be used.

- 12 medium shrimp
- 1 cup (150 g) finely sliced green mango
- 1 tablespoon chopped *rau ram* (polygonum) leaves
- 1/4 cup (60 ml) fish sauce dip (see page 187)

Garnish
- 1 small red chili, finely sliced
- 2 tablespoons fried shallots
- 2 tablespoons chives

Peel and devein the shrimp. Quickly steam in a pan with very little water until bright pink and tender. Remove from pan and cool. In a large bowl, combine the shrimp, mango, *rau ram*, and fish sauce dip. Toss well. Arrange on a platter. Top with chili, shallots and chives.

Goi Vit Bap Chuoi
Banana Blossom Salad with Duck and Ginger

The richness of duck is combined with ginger in this unusual salad.

- 1 young banana blossom, finely cut
- 2 cups (500 ml) iced water
- 1 tablespoon lemon juice
- 2 duck breasts
- 1/2 cup (125 ml) fish sauce dip (see page 187)
- 1 teaspoon finely cut *rau ram* (polygonum leaves)
- 1 tablespoon finely chopped ginger
- 1 tablespoon coarsely ground peanuts
- 1 tablespoon fried shallots
- 1/4 cup (10 g) cilantro (coriander) leaves

Place the sliced banana blossom in cold water with lemon juice, and let soak for 1 hour. Boil (or steam) the duck in a shallow saucepan with a little water until tender. Let cool, remove skin and cut into thin slices. Drain the banana blossom, then toss in a large bowl with fish sauce dip, *rau ram*, ginger, peanuts, and the sliced duck. Arrange on a platter and sprinkle with fried shallots. Garnish with cilantro leaves.

These dishes are meant to be served as part of a shared meal with steamed jasmine rice. Seafood and fish are very popular in Vietnam, and cooked in many styles.

Nam Xao Nuoc Tuong
Braised Mushrooms with Soy Sauce

The sweet, soy sauce gravy really lifts the bland flavor of the mushrooms. Any variety of large mushrooms will do and different types can be mixed together for variety.

8 oz (200 g) straw mushrooms
2 cloves garlic, crushed
1 tablespoon vegetable oil
Pinch of pepper
Pinch of salt
1 teaspoon sugar
2 tablespoons soy sauce
1/4 cup (60 ml) water
Freshly cracked pepper
Cilantro (coriander) leaves

Rinse the mushrooms, pat dry on absorbent paper towels. Sauté garlic in oil until lightly browned and fragrant, add mushrooms, stirring quickly, then season with pepper, salt, sugar, and soy sauce. Add water and simmer for three minutes. Spoon onto a serving dish and sprinkle with fresh cracked pepper and cilantro leaves.

Canh Bi Ro Ham Dua
Braised Pumpkin with Coconut Milk

This is a traditional Buddhist vegetarian dish finished with raw peanuts.

2 cups (230 g) peeled 3/4-in (2-cm) pumpkin cubes
2 cups (300 g) 3/4-in (2-cm) sweet potato or taro root cubes
1/2 cup (15 g) dried wood ear mushrooms, soaked in water for 10 minutes, chopped
2 cups (500 ml) thin coconut milk
1/4 cup (60 ml) thick coconut cream
1/2 cup (80 g) raw peanuts, soaked in warm water
1/2 cup (80 g) thinly sliced loofah (or green zucchini/courgette)

Stir-fried Vegetables with Fish Sauce

Salt
1 teaspoon sugar
Cilantro (coriander) leaves
2 tablespoon sliced *rau ram* (polygonum) leaves

Place pumpkin, sweet potatoes, mushrooms, and thin coconut milk in a deep sauté pan. Bring to a boil and simmer until nearly done. Add the thick coconut milk, peanuts, and loofah and bring to a boil again. Remove from heat. Season to taste with salt and sugar.

Serve in a bowl and sprinkle with fresh cilantro and *rau ram* leaves.

Ca Tim Nuong
Grilled Eggplant with Crab

This recipe is common to southern Vietnam and makes surprising use of eggplant, one of the many vegetables grown in central Vietnam.

6 long (Japanese) eggplants (aubergine)
1/4 cup (60 ml) cooking oil
1 1/2 cups (180 g) cooked crabmeat
2 tablespoons fried shallots

1 tablespoon scallions (spring onions), finely sliced
Cilantro (coriander) leaves

Sauce
1 medium red chili, minced
1 1/2 tablespoons crushed peanuts
1/4 cup (60 ml) fish sauce
1/2 teaspoon sugar or honey
3 tablespoons water

Cut eggplants in half and brush with some of the oil. Grill over an open flame or under a broiler, turning regularly, until the skin turns a darkish brown and the flesh is soft. Peel off the skin and discard. Fry the shallots in the remaining oil until light gold in color. Remove and drain on paper towel. Combine the ingredients for the sauce and pour over the eggplant. Serve garnished with the fried shallots, scallion, and cilantro leaves.

Rau Xao
Stir-fried Vegetables with Fish Sauce

12 cups (3 liters) salted water
1 cup (110 g) sliced carrots
1 cup (200 g) cauliflower pieces

1 cup (120 g) baby corn
1 cup (75 g) black mushrooms
1 cup (200 g) tender kale or broccoli stems
2 tablespoons vegetable oil
1 tablespoon rice wine
2 tablespoons fish sauce
2 cloves garlic, crushed
Salt
Pepper

Blanch the vegetables in lightly salted boiling water, remove and place in a large bowl of cold water. Using a wok or large sauté pan, heat the oil, then stir-fry the drained vegetables, adding the rice wine. Finish the stir-fry with fish sauce and garlic. Season with salt and pepper to taste. Serve with steamed rice.

HELPFUL HINT
When blanching vegetables, they should remain in the water just long enough to slightly soften. Place them in cold (or iced) water immediately after cooking to ensure a crisp texture.

Preserved Salted Fish Stew

done. Mix with steamed rice and stir well. If egg is used, add to the fried mixture at the same time as the rice. Remove from heat and place on lotus leaf. Sprinkle with chopped baby leek. Fold into a neat package.

Note: As a substitute for lotus leaf, use either a large grape, fig, or banana leaf.

Mam Kho
Preserved Salted Fish Stew

This hearty stew calls for *mam sac* (salted fish), considered a delicacy in Vietnam. Substitute halibut, mackerel, or cod for the snake-head mullet.

2 tablespoons vegetable oil
3 cloves garlic, finely chopped
1/2 cup (60 g) finely chopped shallots
1/4 cup (25 g) sliced fresh pork belly
11/2 cups cubed eggplant (aubergine)
1/3 cup (30 g) finely chopped lemongrass
1/2 teaspoon cracked black pepper
21/2 cups (625 ml) water
10 oz (300 g) salted fish (*mam sac*)
10 oz (300 g) snake-head mullet
2 small red chilies, seeded and sliced
2 teaspoons sugar
1/2 cup (80 g) shrimp, peeled and washed
1 tablespoon finely sliced scallions (spring onions)
1 tablespoon fried garlic (optional)

Heat oil in a large pan, add garlic, shallots, pork belly eggplant, lemongrass, and pepper. Sauté 5 minutes.

In a large saucepan, add water and both types of fish; bring to a boil. Simmer for 10 minutes. Remove the fish, debone and set aside. Strain the stock, then boil again, adding the sliced chili, sugar, and the pork/eggplant mixture. Simmer for 5 minutes or until reduced by one-third. Add shrimp and cook for another 3 minutes. Set a portion of the fish in individual bowls. Add stock. Serve garnished with scallions and fried garlic.

There are many different grades of *mam sac*, however, any dried or salted fish will work with this recipe—salted cod is a good choice. Rinse and clean the salted fish thoroughly. Soak for 10 to 15 minutes and brush clean.

Rau Muong Xao Tuong
Pan-fried Water Convolvulus with Yellow Bean Sauce

Water convolvulus, which is available in many specialist Asian grocery shops, has hollow, crunchy stems. The best substitute is mature spinach.

Grilled Eggplant with Crab

1 lb (500 g) water convolvulus, (*kangkung*), washed
2 cloves garlic, crushed
2 baby leeks or scallions (spring onions), finely sliced (white part only)
2 tablespoons vegetable oil
2 tablespoons yellow bean sauce (see page 187)
Salt
Pepper

Blanch spinach in boiling water and drain well. Fry garlic and leeks in oil until soft, then add the vegetable and yellow bean sauce. Fry over high heat. Season with salt and pepper.

Com Hoang Bao
Imperial Rice

The dried lotus leaf used to wrap the rice imparts a slight smokiness to this dish.

4 shallots, chopped
2 tablespoons cooking oil
1 cup (100 g) pork (or chicken), diced
1 cup (100 g) small shrimp
4 oz (100 g) dried lotus seeds, boiled and drained
1/4 teaspoon salt
1 pinch pepper
1 bowl steamed rice
1 egg, fried and chopped (optional)
1 large lotus leaf
2 baby leeks or scallions (spring onions), chopped

Quickly sauté shallots in oil. Add pork, shrimp, lotus seeds, salt, and pepper. Cook until

Muc Nhoi Thit
Stuffed Squid

Use squid tentacles in the stuffing mixture and save the sacs for stuffing.

10 medium washed and cleaned squid (use the tentacles in the stuffing mixture and save the sacs for stuffing)

Stuffing
1 tablespoon peanut oil
3 tablespoons finely sliced shallots
1 clove garlic, finely sliced
1 lb (500 g) lean, ground pork
1/4 cup (15 g) cellophane noodles
6 wood ear mushrooms, soaked in water for 10 minutes, then finely chopped
1 teaspoon five-spice powder
1 tablespoon soy sauce
10 sets of squid tentacles, finely chopped

Seasoning
Pinch salt
Pinch pepper
1 teaspoon sugar

Sauce and Garnish
1/4 cup (30 g) diced shallots
3 cloves garlic, crushed
1/4 cup butter or oil
3 large tomatoes, peeled, seeded and chopped
Salt and pepper
Cilantro (coriander) leaves
Freshly ground pepper

For the stuffing, heat oil in pan, add shallots and garlic, cook, stirring until soft. Combine shallot mixture with the other stuffing ingredients in a bowl and mix Stuff well. Add seasoning. the squid sacs with the mixture and secure with a small toothpick.

To prepare the sauce, sauté shallots and garlic in butter until soft. Add stuffed squid and sauté on both sides for about 10 minutes or until slightly browned and cooked through. Remove from pan, set aside and keep warm. Add tomatoes, and salt and pepper to taste to the pan, and simmer until the tomatoes have been reduced to a thick sauce. Place squid on a large platter and remove toothpicks. Pour the tomato sauce over the squid. Garnish with cilantro and fresh ground pepper. For a variation on the cooking technique, try grilling the squid.

Muc Nuong
Grilled Squid

Grilled meats and seafood are very popular in Vietnam and many recipes, like this, rely upon the specific flavors imparted from the open wood-burning grill.

1 lb (500 g) cleaned squid
1 tablespoon salt
1/2 cup (20 g) cilantro (coriander) leaves

Marinade
Pinch of pepper
2 cloves garlic, crushed
2 tablespoons peanut oil
1 teaspoon five-spice powder
1 teaspoon curry powder

Crab with Tamarind Sauce

1 tablespoon finely chopped lemongrass
1 tablespoon thick soy sauce
1 teaspoon sesame oil
1 tablespoon lime juice
1 teaspoon sugar

Rub the squid with salt and rinse. Slit and flatten the squid sac and make diagonal cuts on the inside surface. Cut into bite-sized pieces. Combine marinade ingredients, then marinate squid for 1 hour.

Grill squid over a charcoal grill, until just tender (about 2 minutes each side). Arrange on a serving platter and garnish with cilantro. Serve with fish sauce dip (see page 187).

> **HELPFUL HINT**
> This is a versatile marinade, suitable for other types of fish or poultry.

Tom Cang Kho
Spicy River Shrimp

This is a southern recipe that calls for giant, freshwater shrimp, which are often as big as lobsters.

3 cloves garlic, finely diced
1 small red chili, finely chopped
2 tablespoons cooking oil
1 teaspoon cracked black peppercorns
2 tablespoons sugar
1/4 cup (60 ml) fish sauce
1/2 cup (125 ml) water
6 giant shrimp, unpeeled
1/2 cup (20 g) cilantro (coriander) leaves

In a deep pan, sauté garlic and chili in oil until soft. Add peppercorns, sugar, fish sauce, water, and shrimp. Cook uncovered for 10 minutes, or until the shrimp turn bright pink. Remove shrimp and arrange on a platter. Reduce the stock until slightly sticky. Pour over the shrimp and garnish with cilantro.

Cua Rang Voi Sot Me
Crab with Tamarind Sauce

4 whole medium crabs
Peanut oil for deep-frying
1 tablespoon tamarind pulp

Fried Grouper with Ginger Sauce

1/4 cup (60 ml) rice wine
4 cloves garlic, chopped
2 tablespoons vegetable oil
1/4 cup (60 ml) chopped baby leeks or scallions (spring onions), white part only, cut in 1-in (21/2-cm) pieces
3 tablespoons fish sauce
1 teaspoon crushed white pepper

Clean the crabs, take off the tops, rinse thoroughly, cut in half and break the claws. Heat peanut oil in wok until very hot, deep-fry crabs for 30 seconds, or until color changes. Set on paper towels to absorb excess oil.

Dissolve tamarind pulp in rice wine. In a large pan or wok, sauté garlic in vegetable oil until soft, add crab and continue cooking for 2 to 3 minutes on a high heat. Add tamarind mixture, fish sauce, and pepper. Reduce for another 2 minutes, then add baby leeks. Remove from heat. Place crabs on a platter and pour tamarind sauce over. Serve with steamed rice.

Note: Although this dish is traditionally prepared in a wok, the use of a deep-fryer might make the cooking easier. You can also substitute freshly ground black pepper, although white pepper is often the preferred ingredient of Vietnamese cooks.

1 tablespoon diced garlic
2 tablespoons diced shallots
2 tablespoons finely chopped
    lemongrass
1 tablespoon finely chopped red
    chili
3 tablespoons finely chopped wood
    ear mushrooms
2 tablespoons vegetable oil
1 tablespoon five-spice powder
1 tablespoon Vietnamese curry
    powder
3/4 lb (400 g) baby eel, finely
    chopped
2 tablespoons coarsely chopped
    peanuts
1/2 cup (20 g) cilantro (coriander)
    leaves
1 red chili, thinly sliced
Sesame seed rice crackers

Sauté garlic, shallots, lemongrass, chili, and mushrooms in the oil. Add five-spice powder, curry and eel. Sauté for 5 minutes, or until eel is cooked. Place on a platter and garnish with peanuts, cilantro, and chili. Serve with crackers.

HELPFUL HINT
Wood ear mushrooms are used primarily for texture. However, any fresh mushroom that adds texture and flavor is a good substitute. Some dried varieties will also work.

Mu Chien Voi Gung
Fried Grouper with Ginger Sauce

Vietnam boasts an abundance of ocean and freshwater fish. Ginger and galangal, both members of the ginger family, have been used to impart their unique flavors to this dish.

1 whole grouper or sea bass, about
    2 lb (1 kg), slit along both sides
1 teaspoon salt
1 teaspoon ground white pepper
2 tablespoons oil
2 tablespoons finely chopped
    scallions (spring onions)

Sauce
1 tablespoon oil
3 fresh *shiitake* mushrooms,
    julienned
2 tablespoons julienned ginger
1 tablespoon finely sliced lemon
    grass
2 red chilies, julienned
1 teaspoon soy sauce
1/4 cup (60 ml) fish sauce
1/2 cup (125 ml) water (or chicken
    or fish stock)

Combine the sauce ingredients, simmer on low heat for 5 minutes and set aside. Salt and pepper the fish, brush with oil and broil slowly on both sides until the fish is cooked. Place fish on a large platter, pour the sauce over the fish and garnish with scallions.

Cua Hap Bia
Crab in Beer Broth

This innovative dish, which uses beer in its broth, is said to have been developed by a French colonial administrator.

4 whole large crabs, about 3 1/2 lb
    (1 1/2 kg), rinsed, cleaned, and
    cut in half
2 tablespoons vegetable oil
1/2 teaspoon salt
1/2 teaspoon pepper
1 teaspoon sesame oil
1 tablespoon oyster sauce
1 clove garlic, crushed
1 large onion, cut into wedges
1 large tomato, cut into wedges
1 red chili, sliced
3/4 cup (180 ml) beer
1 cup (60 g) watercress
1 tablespoon fried garlic (optional)

Fry crabs in vegetable oil with salt, pepper, sesame oil, oyster sauce, and garlic over a very high heat for 5 minutes. Add onion, tomato, and chili. Stir fry quickly and add beer. Cover and simmer for 10 minutes or until crabs are cooked. Serve garnished with watercress and fried garlic.

Ca Chep Kho Rieng
*Braised Carp with
Galangal Sauce*

Use this recipe with a variety of whole fish, steaks or fillets.

6 carp or halibut steaks, each
    4 oz (100 g)
3 tablespoons vegetable oil
2 tablespoons julienned galangal
3 tablespoons fish sauce
1/2 tablespoon caramel syrup
    (see page 187)
1/2 cup (125 ml) water

Sauté fish in oil with galangal. Add fish sauce, caramel syrup, and water. Braise slowly on both sides until fish is done. Arrange on a platter. Serve with steamed rice.

Luon Xao Lan Xuc Banh Trang Me
*Minced Eel with Sesame Seed
Rice Crackers*

This recipe must have been created to make use of sesame rice crackers—the mixture is perfect for dipping into.

Crab in Beer Broth

Pork Stew with Coconut Juice

Pour the marinade over the chicken. Place in oven at 375°F (190°C, gas mark 5).

Baste the chicken with the remaining marinade 1 every 10 to 15 minutes. Bake until skin is a golden brown and chicken is well cooked.

Cut up the chicken and assemble on a serving platter. Serve with deep-fried sweet buns or steamed sticky rice. Helpful hint: Basting is the secret to this recipe.

Thit Heo Kho Nuoc Dua
Pork Stew with Coconut Juice

2 lb (1 kg) pork leg, cut into 3-oz (100-g) pieces
3 tablespoons vegetable oil
4 cups (1 liter) young coconut juice
5 eggs, hard-boiled and peeled

Marinade
4 cloves garlic, finely chopped
Salt to taste
1 tablespoon palm sugar
4 tablespoons fish sauce

Combine marinade ingredients and marinate pork for 1 hour.

In either a wok or a frying pan, sear pork in heated oil. Add coconut juice. Skim the top, reduce heat and simmer until tender (30 to 45 minutes). Add the eggs and simmer another 15 minutes.

Serve with preserved bean sprouts, pickled or preserved mustard greens and steamed rice.

Cha Lua
Pork Sausage

1 lb (500 g) pork loin
8 oz (200 g) meat from small pig's head, or increase Pork loin
2 cups (500 ml) salted water
1/4 cup (60 ml) cooking oil
5 shallots, diced
2 cloves garlic, crushed
1/2 cup (15 g) wood ear mushrooms, finely chopped
2 tablespoons cracked black pepper
1/4 cup (35 g) sesame seeds, toasted
2 eggs, beaten
1 large banana leaf
3 tablespoons fish sauce
2 limes, cut into wedges

Boil pork and pig's head in salted water for 20 minutes, drain and debone; cut into small cubes. Heat oil in a large skillet, cook shallots and garlic until soft. Add pork, mushrooms, and peppercorns. Cook, stirring until mushrooms are soft; finish with sesame seeds. Remove from heat, stir eggs through pork mixture.

Place mixture on the banana leaf, wrap and tie with a string. Steam for 2 hours (above boiling water). Unwrap and slice thinly. Serve with fish sauce and lime wedges.

Ca Nau Ngot
River Fish with Dill and Tomato

6 cups (1 1/2 liters) light chicken stock
1 1/4 lb (600 g) freshwater fish fil lets, cut into large chunks
2 medium tomatoes, cut into wedges
Salt
Pepper
1 tablespoon chopped dill
Fresh dill

Bring stock to a boil, add fish and simmer for 5 minutes. Skim the top, add the tomatoes and season with salt, pepper, and dill. Cook another few minutes. Garnish with fresh dill before serving.

Marinade 2
3 tablespoons honey
2 tablespoons sweet soy sauce
1 tablespoon lime juice
1 tablespoon annatto seed oil (see page 187)
1 teaspoon sesame oil

Combine all the marinade 1 ingredients. Use half of the marinade to rub onto the outside and inside of the chicken, reserve the remaining marinade. Sew chicken with a needle or a bamboo stick. Marinate for 1 hour.

Set chicken in a baking pan. Combine marinade 2 ingredients.

Ga Quay Mat Ong
Honey-roasted Chicken

This recipe works well with any type of fowl or game. Since considerable time is involved with the marinades and cooking, it is probably best suited for a large bird and special occasion.

1 large, whole chicken

Marinade 1
2 teaspoons pepper
2 teaspoons salt
2 tablespoons sugar
2 teaspoons sesame oil

Minced Pork Balls on a Skewer (left), recipe on page 177, and Grilled Pork with Rice Noodles (right)

Spicy Beef Stew

Dau Hu Chien Sa
Fried Beancurd with Lemongrass

- 1 cup (250 ml) peanut oil
- 1¼ lb (600 g) beancurd, cut into 1 x 2-in (2 x 4-cm) pieces
- 3 tablespoons finely chopped lemongrass
- 1 red chili, finely chopped
- 2 cloves garlic, chopped
- 1 tablespoon vegetable oil
- 1 teaspoon five-spice powder
- Salt
- Pepper

Heat peanut oil in deep pan, fry beancurd in hot oil, drain on absorbent paper towels, set aside. In a separate sauté pan or wok, sauté the lemongrass, chili, and garlic in hot vegetable oil until soft. Add the beancurd and mix well. Season with five-spice powder, salt, and pepper. Set on a serving platter.

Bun Thit Nuong
Grilled Pork with Rice Noodles

- 1 lb (500 g) pork loin, cut into medium cubes

Marinade
- 1 teaspoon finely chopped garlic
- ⅓ cup (50 g) sliced baby leeks or scallions (spring onions)
- 3 tablespoons fish sauce
- Pepper
- Sugar

Garnish
- 12 oz (400 g) rice noodles blanched
- 2 cups (500 ml) carrot and radish pickles (see page 187)
- 1 cup (80 g) beansprouts
- 2 medium cucumbers, finely sliced
- ½ cup (20 g) basil leaves
- ⅓ cup (50 g) chopped baby leeks or scallions (spring onions)
- ¼ cup (60 ml) peanut sauce (see page 187)

Combine the marinade ingredients and marinate pork for 20 minutes.

Skewer the pork and grill over charcoal. Turn frequently so that the pork is evenly cooked, and continue basting with the marinade. Serve with garnish.

Bo La Lot
Grilled Beef in Wild Betel Leaves

The Vietnamese are famous for their hand rolls and almost every dinner features two or three versions at the start of the meal.

- 1¼ lb (600 g) ground beef
- 10 oz (300 g) pork fatback
- Salt
- Sugar
- 21 wild betel leaves
- 7 wooden skewers
- Vegetable oil

Marinade
- 1 tablespoon five-spice powder
- 1 tablespoon curry powder
- 1 teaspoon turmeric powder
- 1 tablespoon sugar
- 1 tablespoon soy sauce
- 1 tablespoon finely chopped lemongrass
- 2 cloves garlic, finely chopped
- 1 teaspoon pepper

Garnish
- 2 starfruit, thinly sliced
- 3 unripe bananas, thinly sliced
- 1 cucumber, peeled and thinly sliced
- 1 cup (250 ml) fish sauce dip (see page 187)
- Lettuce leaves for wrapping

Combine the marinade ingredients and marinate the beef for 30 minutes. Fry pork fatback, allow to cool and then cut into fine slices (vermicelli size). Marinate with salt and sugar and set aside for 15 minutes. Soak wild betel leaves and drain.

Combine beef and pork fat, mix thoroughly, then wrap portions in wild betel leaf, with the shiny side of the leaf outermost. The rolls should be roughly 2 in (5 cm) long. Place 3 rolls on each skewer. Brush with oil and grill on both sides for 5 minutes, until the leaves are slightly charred. Serve with garnish and fish sauce dip.

> **HELPFUL HINT**
> You can also try adding fresh rice noodles into the wrap. Grape leaves may be substituted for the betel leaves.

Grilled Beef in Wild Betel Leaves

Bo Kho
Spicy Beef Stew

- 6 tablespoons cooking oil
- 2 tablespoons annatto seeds
- 2 lb (1 kg) top round (top-side) beef, cut into large cubes
- 1 large onion, finely chopped
- 5 cloves garlic, finely chopped
- 1 tablespoon salt
- 2 tablespoons sugar
- 1 tablespoon curry powder
- 1 cup (250 ml) beer
- 1 stalk lemongrass, bruised
- 3 pieces star anise
- 1 cinnamon stick
- 1 cup (130 g) thickly chopped carrots

Garnish
- 1 cup (40 g) mint leaves
- 2 red chilies, sliced
- Salt, pepper, and lime mix (see page 187)

Heat half of the oil with the annatto seeds and stir quickly until the oil takes on the reddish-brown color of the seeds. Set aside, strain and remove the seeds.

Marinate the beef cubes mixture. Heat the remaining annatto seed oil and cook the remaining garlic until soft. Add curry powder, beer, and marinade. Braise the beef, adding a little water, lemongrass, star anise, and cinnamon. Before the meat is tender, add carrots. Simmer 3 to 5 minutes or until done. Serve with garnish.

As in other countries, these "desserts" are not eaten at the end of a meal as a sweet but rather, throughout the day as fillers or snacks. In any case they make good finales, and despite the strangeness of some of the ingredients, all are delicious!

Banh Goi
Wrapped Rice Cakes

- 1³/4 cups (300 g) rice flour
- 1¹/3 cups (350 g) sugar
- 2¹/2 cups (625 ml) pandan leaf juice, or 2¹/2 cups (625 ml) water and 1 teaspoon pandan essence
- 5 oz (150 g) yellow mung beans, soaked in water for 5 hours or overnight
- 1 tablespoons vanilla extract
- 1¹/2 cups (375 ml) coconut milk
- 3 tablespoons sugar, pinch of salt
- ¹/2 tablespoon cornstarch
- 2 tablespoons cooking oil
- 6 blanched banana leaf squares, 8 x 8 in (20 x 20 cm)
- 2 tablespoons sesame seeds, toasted

Mix rice flour with ²/3 cup (175 g) sugar and 2 cups (500 ml) pandan leaf juice. Cook over a low heat, stirring constantly, until mixture thickens to a paste-like consistency. In a separate pot, cook mung beans with remaining sugar and vanilla extract to a similar consistency. Cool down and roll into small balls.

Brush cooking oil on banana leaves, then place a spoonful of the rice flour paste in the middle of each. Top with mung bean "ball" and cover with more rice flour paste. Wrap into small, rectangular packages and steam for 10 minutes.

To make the sauce, simmer coconut milk, add sugar, salt, remaining pandan leaf juice, and cornstarch. Serve with sauce and toasted sesame seeds.

Banh Phu The
Husband and Wife Cakes

The name of this traditional dessert comes from the two parts that are traditionally tied together with a string of coconut and encased in a delicate box made of pandan leaves.

- 4 cups (1 liter) water
- 1 lb (500 g) tapioca flour
- 1¹/3 cups (350 g) sugar
- ¹/2 cup (45 g) shredded coconut
- 5 oz (150 g) yellow mung beans, soaked overnight
- ²/3 cup (150 g) sugar syrup
- 1 tablespoon cooking oil
- 1 tablespoon pomelo blossom essence, or ¹/2 tablespoon pomelo blossom essence and ¹/2 tablespoon orange juice
- 20 pandan leaves (optional)

To make the dough, mix the water, flour, sugar, and shredded coconut. Stir constantly on low heat for 10 minutes.

For the stuffing, steam mung beans for 15 minutes or until tender. Mash to a paste. Stir in sugar syrup and cooking oil. Cook over low heat until thick, then add the pomelo blossom essence and remove from heat

Put a thin layer of dough in individual cupcake tins or small molds, add a portion of the stuffing and top with another layer of dough. Place tins in a steamer and cook for 20 minutes. When the dough is transparent, they are ready.

Banh Chuoi Nuong
Banana Cake

This cake is also delicious served with a scoop of vanilla ice-cream.

- 1¹/4 lb (600 g) ripe bananas
- 1 cup (220 g) sugar
- 1 cup (250 ml) coconut milk
- ¹/2 teaspoon vanilla extract
- 2 tablespoons melted butter
- 7 slices of sandwich bread

Slice the banana diagonally and sprinkle with half the sugar. Cook the remaining sugar in coconut milk until dissolved, then add the vanilla. Remove crusts from the bread. Soak the bread in the sweetened coconut milk.

Butter a 12-in (30-cm) non-stick pan. Arrange a layer of banana on the bottom of the pan. Cover with a layer of bread, then another layer of bananas, another bread layer, and then finish with a layer of bananas. Do not add the remaining coconut milk. Drizzle the remaining butter over the top, then cover with foil and bake in a preheated oven at 350°F (180°C, gas mark 4) for 1 hour. Rest for 12 hours before cutting.

Serve with a scoop of vanilla ice cream, if desired.

Banana Cake (left) and Pineapple Tartlets (right)

Banh Nuong Nhan Thom
Pineapple Tartlets

Dough
- 1 cup (225 g) soft butter
- ¹/4 cup (50 g) sugar
- ¹/2 cup (125 ml) milk
- 4 cups (450 g) flour

Filling
- 1 pineapple, peeled, cored and chopped
- ¹/2 cup (100 g) sugar
- 1 drop vanilla extract
- 1 egg, beaten

To prepare the dough, in a mixing bowl, blend butter, sugar and milk with a whisk. Add flour and continue whisking until the texture is smooth. Place the dough on a lightly floured surface and roll it out to a thickness of ¹/8 in (¹/4 cm) with a rolling pin. Press dough into a small mold to make shells. Cut remaining dough into small strips.

To make the filling, place pineapple and sugar in a saucepan over a low heat and stir continuously until pineapple mixture thickens. Add vanilla extract. Fill shells with mixture, then lay dough strips in a crisscross over the tops of the tartlets. Brush the top with egg. Bake in oven, at 300°F (150°C, gas mark 2), until golden brown.

Wrapped Rice Cakes (left) and Husband and Wife Cakes (right)

Ca Rot
Carrot and Radish Pickles

1 cup (110 g) julienned carrot
1 cup (160 g) julienned daikon
  (giant white radish)
1 tablespoon salt
2 tablespoons sugar
$^1/_4$ cup (60 ml) white vinegar

Sprinkle carrot and radish with salt, allow to stand for 10 minutes. Press vegetables gently with a dry towel to remove excess moisture. Rinse and drain. In a mixing bowl, combine sugar and vinegar with vegetables, then marinate for at least 2 hours before serving. Best when served chilled.

Nuoc Mam Cham
Fish Sauce Dip

$^1/_4$ cup (60 ml) water or fresh
  coconut juice
1 teaspoon rice vinegar
1 teaspoon sugar
1 red chili, seeded, finely
  chopped
2 cloves garlic, crushed
1 tablespoon lime juice
2 tablespoons fish sauce

Boil water or coconut juice with vinegar and sugar; allow to cool. Combine chili, garlic, and lime juice, and add to the coconut mixture. Stir in the fish sauce.

    Try adding shredded radish and carrot pickles as a variation on *nuoc mam cham*.

Mam Nem
Fermented Anchovy Dip

2 tablespoons fermented anchovy
  sauce or paste
$^1/_2$ cup (125 ml) water
2 teaspoons vinegar
2 tablespoons crushed pineapple
$^1/_4$ stalk lemongrass, finely
  chopped
1 red chili, finely chopped
1 clove garlic, crushed
1 teaspoon sugar
Pinch of pepper

Combine all the ingredients and stir well. Season to taste with pepper and sugar.

Nuoc Tuong
Yellow Bean Sauce

1 cup (120 g) yellow beans, boiled
  and drained
2 tablespoons coconut milk
2 tablespoons ground peanuts
2 teaspoons sugar
3 cloves garlic
1 medium red chili
1 stalk lemongrass
2 tablespoons vegetable oil

Combine all ingredients, except oil, in a food processor. Blend until finely chopped and well combined. Heat oil in pan, stir-fry all ingredients and simmer for 2 minutes. Cool before serving.

Sot Dau Phong
Peanut Sauce

1 clove garlic, finely sliced
2 teaspoons vegetable oil
4 oz (100 g) pork or chicken liver
1 tablespoon finely chopped red
  chili
$^1/_2$ cup (125 ml) yellow bean
  sauce (see above)
1 stem lemongrass, finely
  chopped
$^1/_4$ cup (60 ml) coconut milk
1 teaspoon sugar
1 teaspoon salt

Sauté garlic in oil until soft, add liver, chili, yellow bean sauce, lemongrass, half the coconut milk, sugar, salt, tamarind juice, and peanuts. Bring to a boil. Remove from heat. Blend in a food processor and add remaining coconut milk.

Nuoc Mau
Caramel Syrup

1 cup (250 ml) water
1 cup (160 g) brown sugar

Bring water and sugar to a boil. Stir and reduce until dark brown in color. Remove from heat, add a few tablespoons of water and stir. Pour into a heatproof container. Cover with a lid.

Muoi Tieu Chanh
Salt, Pepper, and Lime Mix

1 teaspoon salt
1 teaspoon pepper
$^1/_2$ lime

Combine salt and pepper, squeeze lime juice into the mixture and stir well.

Sot Chua Ngot
Sweet and Sour Sauce

3 cloves garlic, finely chopped
1 tablespoon oil
2 tablespoons sliced shallots
2 pickled shallots, sliced
1 small carrot, diced
1 small green bell pepper
  (capsicum), diced
1 medium red chili, diced
1 tablespoon sugar
  salt and pepper
1 teaspoon tomato sauce
2 tablespoons vinegar
1 tablespoon cornflour mixed
  with 1 teaspoon water

Sauté garlic in oil until slightly colored. Add sliced shallots, pickled shallots, carrot, green bell pepper, chili, sugar, and salt and pepper to taste. Keep frying, add tomato sauce and vinegar. Bring combination to a boil, add cornstarch mixture. Reduce heat, stir and simmer for 1 minute.

Peanut Sauce (top) and fish sauce
with garlic and chilies (bottom)

Nuoc Leo Ga
Chicken Stock

3 quarts (3 liters) water
3 lb (1$^1/_2$ kg) chicken
1 tablespoon whole white pepper
  corns
1 cup (160 g) sliced onions
1 medium carrot, chopped
1 stalk celery, chopped
Pinch of salt
Pinch of pepper

Combine the ingredients in a large stock pot; bring to a boil. Simmer for 2 to 3 hours, until stock is reduced by half, strain and set aside. Once cool, remove solid fat residue layer off the top.

    Note: Use cooked chicken for other recipes.

Nuoc Leo Bo
Beef Stock

4 quarts (4 liters) water
4$^1/_2$ lb (2 kg) beef bones
2 tablespoons sliced ginger
2 pieces star anise
Pinch of salt and pepper

Combine all ingredients, bring to a boil and simmer for 3 hours. Strain and set aside. Once cool, remove solid fat residue off the top.

HELPFUL HINT
Place stock in sealed containers and refrigerate or freeze if storing for a longer time. Refrigerated stock ast for a week.

MEASUREMENTS AND CONVERSION TABLES

Measurements in this book are given in volume as far as possible. Teaspoon, tablespoon and cup measurements should be level, not heaped, unless otherwise indicated. Australian readers please note that the standard Australian measuring spoon is larger than the UK or American spoon by 5 ml, so use only ³/4 tablespoon when following the recipes.

LIQUID CONVERSIONS

Imperial	Metric	US cups
¹/2 fl oz	15 ml	1 tablespoon
1 fl oz	30 ml	¹/8 cup
2 fl oz	60 ml	¹/4 cup
4 fl oz	125 ml	¹/2 cup
5 fl oz (¹/4 pint)	150 ml	²/3 cup
6 fl oz	175 ml	³/4 cup
8 fl oz	250 ml	1 cup
12 fl oz	375 ml	1¹/2 cups
16 fl oz	500 ml	2 cups

Note:
1 UK pint = 20 fl oz
1 US pint = 16 fl oz

SOLID WEIGHT CONVERSIONS

Imperial	Metric
¹/2 oz	15 g
1 oz	30g
1¹/2 oz	50 g
2 oz	60 g
3 oz	90 g
3¹/2 oz	100 g
4 oz (¹/4 lb)	125 g
5 oz	150 g
6 oz	185 g
7 oz	200 g
8 oz (¹/2 lb)	250 g
9 oz	280 g
10 oz	300 g
16 oz (1 lb)	500 g (0.5 kg)
32 oz (2 lb)	1 kg

OVEN TEMPERATURES

Heat	Fahrenheit	Centigrade/Celsius	British Gas Mark
Very cool	225	110	1/4
Cool or slow	275–300	135–150	1–2
Moderate	350	175	4
Hot	425	220	7
Very hot	450	230	8